MATHEMATICS IN
COMMUNICATION THEORY

MATHEMATICS AND ITS APPLICATIONS

Series Editor: G. M. BELL, Professor of Mathematics,
King's College London, University of London

STATISTICS, OPERATIONAL RESEARCH
AND COMPUTATIONAL MATHEMATICS

Editor: B. W. CONOLLY, Emeritus Professor of Mathematics (Operational
Research), Queen Mary College, University of London

Mathematics and its applications are now awe-inspiring in their scope, variety and depth. Not only is there rapid growth in pure mathematics and its applications to the traditional fields of the physical sciences, engineering and statistics, but new fields of application are emerging in biology, ecology and social organization. The user of mathematics must assimilate subtle new techniques and also learn to handle the great power of the computer efficiently and economically.

The need for clear, concise and authoritative texts is thus greater than ever and our series endeavours to supply this need. It aims to be comprehensive and yet flexible. Works surveying recent research will introduce new areas and up-to-date mathematical methods. Undergraduate texts on established topics will stimulate student interest by including applications relevant at the present day. The series will also include selected volumes of lecture notes which will enable certain important topics to be presented earlier than would otherwise be possible.

In all these ways it is hoped to render a valuable service to those who learn, teach, develop and use mathematics.

Mathematics and its Applications

Series Editor: G. M. BELL, Professor of Mathematics, King's College London,
University of London

Anderson, I.	**Combinatorial Designs**
Artmann, B.	**Concept of Number: From Quaternions to Monads and Topological Fields**
Arczewski, K. & Pietrucha, J.	**Mathematical Modelling in Discrete Mechanical Systems**
Arczewski, K. and Pietrucha, J.	**Mathematical Modelling in Continuous Mechanical Systems**
Bainov, D.D. & Konstantinov, M.	**The Averaging Method and its Applications**
Baker, A.C. & Porteous, H.L.	**Linear Algebra and Differential Equations**
Balcerzyk, S. & Jösefiak, T.	**Commutative Rings**
Balcerzyk, S. & Jösefiak, T.	**Commutative Noetherian and Krull Rings**
Baldock, G.R. & Bridgeman, T.	**Mathematical Theory of Wave Motion**
Ball, M.A.	**Mathematics in the Social and Life Sciences: Theories, Models and Methods**
de Barra, G.	**Measure Theory and Integration**
Bartak, J., Herrmann, L., Lovicar, V. & Vejvoda, D.	**Partial Differential Equations of Evolution**
Bell, G.M. and Lavis, D.A.	**Statistical Mechanics of Lattice Models, Vols. 1 & 2**
Berry, J.S., Burghes, D.N., Huntley, I.D., James, D.J.G. & Moscardini, A.O.	**Mathematical Modelling Courses**
Berry, J.S., Burghes, D.N., Huntley, I.D., James, D.J.G. & Moscardini, A.O.	**Mathematical Modelling Methodology, Models and Micros**
Berry, J.S., Burghes, D.N., Huntley, I.D., James, D.J.G. & Moscardini, A.O.	**Teaching and Applying Mathematical Modelling**
Blum, W.	**Applications and Modelling in Learning and Teaching Mathematics**
Brown, R.	**Topology: A Geometric Account of General Topology, Homotopy Types and the Fundamental Groupoid**
Burghes, D.N. & Borrie, M.	**Modelling with Differential Equations**
Burghes, D.N. & Downs, A.M.	**Modern Introduction to Classical Mechanics and Control**
Burghes, D.N. & Graham, A.	**Introduction to Control Theory, including Optimal Control**
Burghes, D.N., Huntley, I. & McDonald, J.	**Applying Mathematics**
Burghes, D.N. & Wood, A.D.	**Mathematical Models in the Social, Management and Life Sciences**
Butkovskiy, A.G.	**Green's Functions and Transfer Functions Handbook**
Cartwright, M.	**Fourier Methods: Applications in Mathematics, Engineering and Science**
Cerny, I.	**Complex Domain Analysis**
Chorlton, F.	**Textbook of Dynamics, 2nd Edition**
Chorlton, F.	**Vector and Tensor Methods**
Cohen, D.E.	**Computability and Logic**
Cordier, J.-M. & Porter, T.	**Shape Theory: Categorical Methods of Approximation**
Crapper, G.D.	**Introduction to Water Waves**
Cross, M. & Moscardini, A.O.	**Learning the Art of Mathematical Modelling**
Cullen, M.R.	**Linear Models in Biology**
Dunning-Davies, J.	**Mathematical Methods for Mathematicians, Physical Scientists and Engineers**
Eason, G., Coles, C.W. & Gettinby, G.	**Mathematics and Statistics for the Biosciences**
El Jai, A. & Pritchard, A.J.	**Sensors and Controls in the Analysis of Distributed Systems**
Exton, H.	**Multiple Hypergeometric Functions and Applications**
Exton, H.	**Handbook of Hypergeometric Integrals**
Exton, H.	**q-Hypergeometric Functions and Applications**
Faux, I.D. & Pratt, M.J.	**Computational Geometry for Design and Manufacture**
Firby, P.A. & Gardiner, C.F.	**Surface Topology**
Gardiner, C.F.	**Modern Algebra**

Series continued at back of book

MATHEMATICS IN COMMUNICATION THEORY

R. H. JONES B.Sc., FIMA
Mathematics Department
Coventry Polytechnic

N. C. STEELE B.Sc., M.Sc., FIMA, MRAeS
Mathematics Department
Coventry Polytechnic

ELLIS HORWOOD LIMITED
Publishers · Chichester

Halsted Press: a division of
JOHN WILEY & SONS
New York · Chichester · Brisbane · Toronto

First published in 1989 by
ELLIS HORWOOD LIMITED
Market Cross House, Cooper Street,
Chichester, West Sussex, PO19 1EB, England
The publisher's colophon is reproduced from James Gillison's drawing of the ancient Market Cross, Chichester.

Distributors:

Australia and New Zealand:
JACARANDA WILEY LIMITED
GPO Box 859, Brisbane, Queensland 4001, Australia

Canada:
JOHN WILEY & SONS CANADA LIMITED
22 Worcester Road, Rexdale, Ontario, Canada

Europe and Africa:
JOHN WILEY & SONS LIMITED
Baffins Lane, Chichester, West Sussex, England

North and South America and the rest of the world:
Halsted Press: a division of
JOHN WILEY & SONS
605 Third Avenue, New York, NY 10158, USA

South-East Asia
JOHN WILEY & SONS (SEA) PTE LIMITED
37 Jalan Pemimpin # 05–04
Block B, Union Industrial Building, Singapore 2057

Indian Subcontinent
WILEY EASTERN LIMITED
4835/24 Ansari Road
Daryaganj, New Delhi 110002, India

© 1989 R.H. Jones and N.C. Steele/Ellis Horwood Limited

British Library Cataloguing in Publication Data
Jones, R. H.
Mathematics in communication theory.
1. Electronic communication systems. Mathematics. Optimisation
I. Title II. Steele, N. C.   III. Series
621.38'0413

Library of Congress Card No. 89–27722

ISBN 0–7458–0304–0 (Ellis Horwood Limited — Library Edn.)
ISBN 0–7458–0779–8 (Ellis Horwood Limited — Student Edn.)
ISBN 0–470–21246–2 (Halsted Press)

Typeset in Times by Ellis Horwood Limited
Printed in Great Britain by Hartnolls, Bodmin

D
621. 382
JON

M.F.E.

Table of contents

Preface 11

Part I — Graphs in communications

Chapter 1   Graphs and algorithms
    1.1   Introduction 19
    1.2   Undirected graphs 20
    1.3   Directed graphs. 22
    1.4   Computer representation of graphs 25
    1.5   Algorithms 26
    Further reading 28
    Exercises 28

Chapter 2   Trees
    2.1   Introduction and basic definitions 30
    2.2   Minimum spanning tree algorithms 31
    2.3   Associated problems 35
    2.4   Networks immune to isolated failures. 36
    References 48
    Exercises 48

Chapter 3   Some network design algorithms
    3.1   Multipoint connections in centralized networks 51
    3.2   Heuristic algorithms. 55
    3.3   Terminal connections and concentrator sites in centralized networks. .58
    References 63
    Exercises 64

Chapter 4   Routing
    4.1   Introduction 66
    4.2   Networks with all arc (or edge) weights positive 66
    4.3   Networks with positive and negative arc weights. 73
    Appendix A: Warshall's algorithm 79

    Appendix B. 82
    References 83
    Exercises 83

Chapter 5   Flows in networks
    5.1   Introduction. 88
    5.2   The Ford–Fulkerson algorithm for maximum flow 91
    5.3   Associated problems 94
    5.4   Applications. 100
    5.5   Multicommodity flow 102
    References 105
    Exercises 106

Chapter 6   An introduction to line capacity assignment
    6.1   Basic assumptions 109
    6.2   Capacity assignment in centralized networks 111
    6.3   Capacity assignment in distributed networks 117
    6.4   Some generalizations 119
    Appendix 119
    References 123
    Exercises 123

Answers to selected exercises 125

Part II — Signals, systems and the filtering process

Chapter 7   Signals and linear system fundamentals
    7.1   Introduction. 131
    7.2   Signals and systems 131
    7.3 L–C–R circuits 133
    7.4   Linear systems 139
    7.5   Block diagrams. 144
    7.6   The Laplace transformation. 146
    7.7   A summary of properties of the transform. 148
    7.8   Application to linear time invariant systems 151
    7.9   Transfer functions 157
    References 165
    Exercises 165

Chapter 8   System responses
    8.1   Introduction. 168
    8.2   Stability of linear time invariant systems. 168
    8.3   Introduction to generalized functions. 172
    8.4   The impulse response 178
    8.5   The step response 186

8.6   Signal decomposition and convolution 189
8.7   Frequency response 201
References 207
Exercises 207

Chapter 9   Fourier methods
9.1   Introduction 210
9.2   Fourier series 210
9.3   The Fourier transform 217
9.4   The Fourier spectrum 223
9.5   Properties of the Fourier transform 225
9.6   Signal energy and power 234
9.7   A generalization of the Fourier transform 237
9.8   The convolution theorems 243
9.9   Sampling of time signals and its implications 245
References 251
Exercises 251

Chapter 10   Analogue filters
10.1   Introduction 255
10.2   Analogue filter types 255
10.3   A class of low-pass filters 256
10.4   Butterworth filters — the general case 265
10.5   Filter transformations 283
10.6   Other filter designs 292
References 300
Exercises 300

Chapter 11   Discrete-time signals and systems
11.1   Introduction 302
11.2   Sequences 302
11.3   The Z-transform 305
11.4   Properties of the Z-transform 310
11.5   Discrete-time systems and difference equations 314
11.6   The Z-transfer function 328
11.7   Time domain signal decomposition and convolution 334
11.8   The frequency response of a discrete-time system 340
11.9   A frequency domain representation of discrete-time signals 345
11.10 The discrete Fourier transform 348
11.11 The fast Fourier transform 356
11.12 Estimating Fourier transforms 369
Appendix 379
References 381
Exercises 382

Chapter 12   The design of digital filters
12.1   Introduction 384

8 **Table of contents**

12.2 An 'indirect' design method — the impulse invariant approach 384
12.3 The step invariant method 390
12.4 The bilinear transform method 393
12.5 A direct design method — the Fourier series approach 399
12.6 Windows 403
References 406
Exercises 407

Index 408

To Jan, Richard and Alison — not forgetting Ming

Also to Corinne and Emily

Preface

Communication is the process by which information is imparted or exchanged between human beings, between machines, or between human beings and machines. Communication theory is the theory of this transmission process, and the language of this theory is mathematics. This book sets out to explain some of the mathematical concepts and techniques which form the elements and syntax of that language and thus to enable the reader to appreciate some of the results from the theory.

In some ways the degree of evolution of a nation or state may be measured by the sophistication of its communication processes, particularly those based on electronic means. Within the lifetime of the authors, the telephone has become an everyday means of communication, and television has moved from being a rarely seen novelty to being the means of mass entertainment. Instantaneous communication over long distances, across continents or oceans, by voice or text has become an everyday requirement in many walks of life. More recently, advantage has been taken of the ability of digital computers to communicate information at very high speeds, perhaps to provide almost instantaneous access to vast databases for a large number of remote 'satellites'. These forms of communication are conducted by the transmission of electronic signals using an appropriate method. Often such signals will pass through networks consisting of nodes which are information sources or receivers or which simply form an essential part of the information distribution network itself. The network nodes are linked by appropriate pathways or transmission lines, which may take a variety of physical forms.

An examination of some methods for the design and operation of such networks is the major task of the first part of this book. The second part concentrates on the description of signals and systems which may be used to process signals. Such processing is for the purpose of enabling the transmission of information by, and the extraction of information from, signals.

Computer communication networks have grown in importance over the last few decades to such an extent that some level of understanding of them should now be part of the body of knowledge of all applied mathematicians and systems/electronic engineers.

There are many excellent books dealing with the design and analysis of such networks, but, as they are usually written by engineers for engineers, the mathematical aspects of the subject often appear swamped in a mass of engineering detail. In this book an attempt has been made to fill a gap by presenting relevant network results and algorithms within a simpler framework.

Over the last few years, the unifying concepts of signals and linear systems have come to be recognized as a particularly convenient way of formulating and discussing those branches of applied mathematics concerned with the design and control of 'processes'. The process under discussion may be mechanical, electrical, biological, economic or sociological. In this text we consider only a restricted subset of such processes — those related to communication by electronic means. There are several first-class treatments of the general field of signals and linear systems and, indeed, some specifically related to communication theory. However, in many cases the haste to discuss the engineering applications of the material means that the mathematical development takes second place. Such a treatment may not appeal to, or even be readily accessible to, those whose first subject or interest is mathematics and who thus may not be able to supply the necessary engineering insight to follow the discussion easily. This book is aimed in part at such readers who may wish to gain some understanding of this fascinating application area of mathematics.

We are also aware from our teaching experience that many of our engineering students (possibly more than is commonly acknowledged!) also appreciate such a development to complement and support their engineering studies. The book is also written for this readership. It is interesting to recall that although the need for engineers to become competent applied mathematicians was widely recognized in the recent past, this need is not so often expressed, at least in some countries, today. It will be interesting to compare future performance in the field of design and innovation, and thus in economic performance, between countries which adopt different educational strategies.

The subject matter of both parts of the book is largely self-contained, with Part I aimed primarily at readers with no previous knowledge of graphs and networks. The approach is one of problem solving, with theory developed as appropriate and suitable references for further study cited for the reader who desires a deeper insight into particular subject areas. To make the algorithms of Part I more accessible, they are written in ordinary language rather than pseudocode, thereby providing a ready-made set of exercises for the computer buff.

Part II assumes that the reader will have completed a first course in mathematical methods as given for engineering students in UK polytechnics and universities. The style adopted in this part is an attempt to capture that established for textbooks in other areas of applied mathematics with an appropriate, but not overwhelming, level of mathematical rigour. We have derived results, but avoided theorems almost everywhere!

Many books on applied mathematics seem to concentrate almost exclusively on the *analysis* of 'given' sytems or configurations. In producing this text we have attempted to demonstrate the use of mathematics as a design or *synthesis* tool. Before such a task may be undertaken it is necessary for the user or designer to achieve a considerable degree of experience of his field by the careful analysis of the relevant types of system or structure, and we have attempted to provide a suitable vehicle for this experience to be gained. Nevertheless, it has been at the forefront of our thinking as we have approached our task that the aim of many readers will eventually be the production of network or system designs of their own. We cannot, in a book such as this, hope to give a sufficiently full treatment of any one topic area to satisfy this aim entirely. However, by focusing on the design task, we hope to demonstrate to the reader that an understanding of the underlying mathematics is an essential prerequisite for such work.

Most of the material of both parts has been taught as a single course for students of mathematics at Coventy Polytechnic, where student reaction has been favourable. All the material of Part I and much of the material of Part II, to a suitable engineering interface, has been given to students of Information Systems Engineering, again with encouraging results. Engineering students have generally acknowledged that the course provided an essential complement to concurrent courses in both the area of information systems and networks, and the area of signals and systems, from a systems engineering viewpoint.

OUTLINE OF THE BOOK

Part I

Chapter 1 lists basic results about graphs and also considers what an algorithm is and how the efficiency of an algorithm may be measured.

Chapters 2 and 3 are concerned with design problems. In Chapter 2 the minimum connector problem is examined together with a method for extending a minimum spanning tree to enable site and/or line failures of a certain kind to be overcome. In Chapter 3 exact and heuristic algorithms for solving the minimum connector problem with added constraints are considered.

Chapter 4 describes routing algorithms, those applicable to networks with positive arc weights only, and those applicable to networks with both positive and negative arc weights.

Chapter 5 examines first the Ford–Fulkerson algorithm for calculating the maximum flow in a network. Various associated problems are then considered, in particular the construction of an optimum communication spanning tree and the synthesis of a communication network in the time-independent case.

Chapter 6 is concerned with line capacity assignment. Under certain conditions, which are highlighted in the text, different line capacity assignment strategies for star, tree and distributed networks are compared and contrasted.

Part II

Chapter 7 introduces the concepts of signals and linear systems. Mathematical models of some simple circuits are constructed, and the Laplace transform is introduced as a method of describing the input–output relationship. Block diagrams are also discussed.

Chapters 8 and 9 provide much of the technique and analytical experience necessary for our later work. Chapter 8 is concerned with system responses. By examining the type of response which can be obtained from a linear, time invariant system, concepts of stability are developed. A brief introduction to generalized functions and the convolution operation precedes a discussion of the frequency response. Chapter 9 is devoted to the harmonic decomposition of signals by use of the Fourier transform, leading to the idea of the frequency spectrum of a signal. The effect on the spectrum of sampling a continuous-time signal is first discussed here.

Chapter 10 deals with the design of analogue filters. Based on the analytical experience gained in the previous three chapters, the task of designing a low-pass filter is addressed first. Butterworth filters emerge as one solution to the design task, and the question of their realization using elementary circuits is considered. Transformations which produce band-pass, band-reject and high pass filters are investigated, and a brief introduction is given to Chebyshev designs.

Chapter 11 provides an introduction to discrete-time signals and systems. Difference equations, the Z-transform and the extension of Fourier techniques to discrete time are all discussed in some detail. The need for a fast, computationally efficient, algorithm for Fourier analysis in discrete time rapidly emerges, and the fast Fourier transform algorithm is developed here. This chapter presents several opportunities for those readers with access to a personal computer to conduct their own investigations into the subject area, and a BASIC code for the FFT algorithm is contained in the Appendix.

Chapter 12 returns to the theme of design. Building on the material in the earlier chapters, it is now possible to see how digital filters can be designed either to emulate the analogue designs of Chapter 10, or from an *ab initio* basis. Infinite-impulse and finite-impulse response designs are developed, together with their realizations as difference equations. Here again, readers with access to a personal computer, together with minimal coding skill, will find their study considerably enhanced.

PREREQUISITES

In Chapters 1 and 5, knowledge of what a set and function are and an ability to perform simple matrix calculations are sufficient. In Chapter 6, familiarity with elementary statistics and the method of Lagrange multipliers would be an advantage, but the capacity assignment strategies described there can be appreciated by a reader lacking this background knowledge.

Chapter 7 onwards assumes a knowledge of elementary calculus, and a familiarity with the Laplace transform would be helpful, but is not essential. In Chapter 8, we delve into a little analysis in connection with the discussion on generalized functions. The interested reader who wishes to develop his understanding further should consult the excellent text by Hoskins, cited in the references, for a full and clearly presented account.

EXERCISES

These are designed principally to test the reader's understanding of the material, but there are, in addition, some more testing exercises.

NOTATION

N is the set of positive, and N_0 the set of non-negative, integers. All other symbols are defined in the text. In Part II, we have adopted the convention that if $f(t)$ is a time signal, then *F(s)* denotes its Laplace transform. If this signal is sampled and the *Z*-transform taken of the resulting sequence, then this will be denoted by $\mathscr{F}(z)$.

ACKNOWLEDGEMENTS

First and foremost we should like to thank our wives for their support and encouragement during the production of this book. The children of one of us (RHJ), in their inimitable way, ensured that at least one part of the manuscript was produced on time, and their encouragement is appreciated.

We have benefited from discussions with a number of our colleagues, in particular with Barrie Baker, David Goodall, Peter Humphries, Ian Jacques, Peter Lockett, Robert Low, Sandra Prince and Jim Tabor. Much of the material on the realization of analogue filters in Chapter 10 is due to Mike Chapman, and his contribution to Part II in one form or another has been considerable. Ann Round generously read much of the typescript for Part II, and we are grateful for her comments and corrections. In addition, the encouragement of colleagues in other institutions, particularly that of Tom Høholdt, of the Danish Technical University, Inger Larsen of the Danish Engineering Academy, and Bob Critchley of the Technical University, Limerick, is acknowledged.

Andrea Cox has somehow produced a clear typescript from semi-legible manuscript for most of the text; the remainder has been produced using a personal computer with the encouragement and considerable support of Colin Judd and David Butterfield.

The contribution of our students who have sat through earlier versions of the text and who have asked useful questions and provided helpful comments is also acknowledged.

Finally, we must thank our respective cats. In each case they have sat with us during the hours of writing and examined each page with great interest, pouncing on those errors they detected. Those errors which remain are our fault, since they must be beyond feline comprehension.

Part I
Graphs in communications

1

Graphs and algorithms

1.1 INTRODUCTION

The simplest notation of a graph is that of a set of points located in the plane and a set of lines joining some, or all, of them. Examples which immediately spring to mind are road maps and electrical networks. Other, perhaps less obvious, examples are the relations between activities in a large construction project, the management structure in an organization and a chemical molecule.

Note that in some cases the lines a definite direction associated with them; for example, in a graph representing management structure, if X is Y's manager then Y cannot be X's manager and we would normally indicate this fact when depicting the structure by drawing the line thus $X \to Y$. Such a structure is called a directed graph.

On the other hand, a chemical bond between atoms has no definite direction associated with it and we would depict the ethyl alcohol molecule, to take one at random, without arrows (see Fig. 1.1). Such a structure is called an undirected graph,

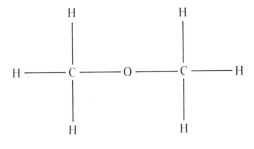

Fig. 1.1

or just simply a graph. Accepting, then, that many practical problems may be modelled using graphs, we now proceed to give some formal definitions.

1.2   UNDIRECTED GRAPHS

1.2.1   Basic definitions

An *undirected graph*, or, more simply, a *graph* G is a pair (N,E) of finite sets. N is called the *node set* and E, which consists of unordered pairs of elements of N, the *edge set*.

We write $G = (N,E)$ and, if $|N| = n$, we say that G is a graph of *order n*. The elements of N and E are called *nodes* and *edges* respectively. Note: An edge of the form (i,i) is called a loop. We shall not consider graphs containing loops in this book.

It is usual to depict G using circles for nodes and lines for edges. For example, if

$$G = (\{1,2,3,4,5\},\{(1,2),(1,3),(1,5),(2,3),(2,4),(2,5),(3,4),(3,5),(4,5)\})$$

we may depict G as in Fig. 1.2.

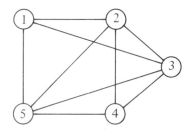

Fig. 1.2

When depicting a graph we may exhibit the configuration in any way we like. For instance, in Fig. 1.2 we could, if we wished, replace the straight line joining nodes 1 and 3 by a curved line passing above node 2. Also, that particular arrangement of nodes may be replaced by any other that seems appropriate.

Note that, because the pairs are unordered, we may also say that among many others,

$$G = (\{1,2,3,4,5\},\{(1,2),(3,1),(5,1),(2,3),(4,2),(2,5),(3,4),(5,3),(4,5)\})$$

If $i \in N$ the *degree*, $d(i)$, of i is the number of edges of G incident to i. For example, in Fig. 1.2, $d(1) = d(4) = 3$, $d(2) = d(3) = d(5) = 4$.

If $d(i)$ is even (odd), i is called an *even (odd)* node.

Because every edge contributes 2 to the degree sum we have the equation

$$\sum_{i \in N} d(i) = 2|E|$$

from which we may make the deduction that in any undirected graph, the number of odd nodes must be even.

1.2.2 Paths and cycles, connectivity

If $i,j \in N$ we say that i and j are *adjacent* if $(i,j) \in E$. For example, in Fig. 1.2, nodes 2 and 5 are adjacent whereas 1 and 4 are not.

If $i_1, i_q \in N$ a *path* joining i_1 to i_q is a sequence $i_1, i_2, \ldots, i_q$ of nodes such that i_r and i_{r+1} are adjacent for $1 \leqslant r \leqslant q-1$.

We may equally think of a path as a sequence $(i_1,i_2), (i_2,i_3), \ldots, (i_{q-1},i_q)$ of edges of G.

A *simple path* is one which does not use the same edge more than once; an *elementary path* is one which does not visit the same node more than once. Clearly an elementary path is simple, but the converse is not necessarily true. For example, in Fig. 1.2, $(1,5), (5,2),(2,4),(4,3)$ is a path joining node 1 to node 3 which is elementary (and hence simple). $(1,2),(2,5),(5,4),(4,2),(2,3)$ is a path joining node 1 to node 3 which is simple but not elementary. $(1,2),(2,5),(5,4),(4,2),(2,5),(5,3)$ is a path joining node 1 to node 3 which is neither simple nor elementary.

If $i_1, i_2, \ldots, i_{q-1}, q > 3$, is an elementary path, and i_1 and i_{q-1} are adjacent, we call $i_2, i_2, \ldots, i_{q-1}, i_1$ a *cycle*. For example, in Fig. 1.2, $(1,3),(3,2),(2,1)$ is a cycle.

If every pair of nodes of G can be joned by a path, G is called a *connected graph*. For example the graph of Fig. 1.2 is connected whereas the graph $G = (\{1,2,3,4,5,6\},\{(1,3),(2,4),(3,6),(4,5),(6,1)\})$ depicted in Fig. 1.3 is not. Here G is

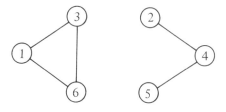

Fig. 1.3

composed of two *components*, G_1 and G_2, where $G_1 = (\{1,3,6\},\{(1,3),(3,6),(6,1)\})$ and $G_2 = (\{2,4,5\},\{(2,4),(4,5)\})$. In general there could be more than two components.

There is a path joining every pair of nodes in the same component but no path joining a node to any node in a different component. It is clear that a connected graph has just one component.

An algorithm for determining whether a graph is connected is given in section 2.3.3.

1.2.3 Partial graphs and subgraphs

Given a graph $G = (N,E)$

(i) a *partial graph* of G is a graph $G_p = (N,E_p)$, where $E_p \subset E$, and
(ii) a *subgraph* of G is a graph $G_s = (N_s,E_s)$, where $N_s \subset N$ and
     $E_s = \{(i,j) | i,j \in N_s, (i,j) \in E\}$.

The two definitions above many be combined to give a *partial subgraph* of *G*.
   Referring to the graph depicted in Fig. 1.2, Fig. 1.4 shows a partial graph of that

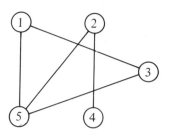

Fig. 1.4

graph, Fig. 1.5 a subgraph and Fig. 1.6 a partial subgraph.

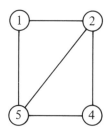

Fig. 1.5

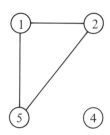

Fig. 1.6

1.3 DIRECTED GRAPHS

1.3.1 Basic definitions

A *directed graph*, or *digraph*, *G* is a pair (*N*,*A*) of finite sets. *N* is called the *node set*
and *A*, which consists of ordered pairs of elements of *N*, the *arc* set.

We write $G = (N,A)$ and, if $|N| = n$, we say that G is of *order n*. The elements of N and A are called *nodes* and *arcs* respectively, and arcs of the form (i,i) are not allowed.

If G is, for example, the digraph $(\{1,2,3,4,5\},$ $\{(1,2),(1,3)(2,1),(2,3)(2,4),(2,5)(3,4)(3,5)(4,3)(4,5)(5,1)\})$ we may depict G as in Fig. 1.7. The pairs are ordered, so we indicate this in the figure by means of an arrow.

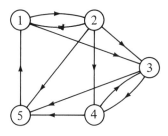

Fig. 1.7

If $(i,j)\in A$ we draw it as $\textcircled{i}\longrightarrow\textcircled{j}$; i is called the *start node*, and j the *end node*, of the arc. Note that in some cases the arcs (i,j) and (j,i) exist. When this happens we shall normally adopt the convention of drawing $\textcircled{i}\!-\!\textcircled{j}$ rather than $\textcircled{i}\rightleftharpoons\textcircled{j}$. This should cause no problem to the intelligent reader.

If $i\in N$ the number of arcs of G having i as start node is called the *outdegree*, $d_o(i)$, of node i and the number of arcs having node i as end node is called the *indegree*, $d_t(i)$, of i.

Referring to Fig. 1.7, $d_o(1) = d_t(1) = 2$, $d_o(2) = 4$, $d_t(2) = 1$, etc.

It is easy to see that, for an arbitrary digraph G,

$$\sum_{i\in N}d_o(i) = \sum_{i\in N}d_t(i) = |A| \ .$$

1.3.2 Paths, chains and cycles. Connectivity

If $i,j\in N$ we say that i and j are *adjacent* if either $(i,j)\in A$ or $(j,i)\in A$ (or both).

If $i_1, i_q\in N$ a *path* joining i_1 to i_q is a sequence $(i_2,i_2),(i_2,i_3), \ldots, (i_{q-1},i_q)$ of arcs of G. A *simple path* is one which does not use the same arc more than once; an *elementary path* is one which does not visit the same node more than once.

If $(i_1,i_2), \ldots, (i_{q-2},i_{q-1}), q>3$, is an elementary path, and $(i_{q-1},i_1)\in A$, we call $(i_1i_2), \ldots, (i_{q-2},i_{q-1}), (i_{q-1}i_1)$ a *cycle*.

A *chain* joining i_1 to i_q is a sequence $i_1, i_2, \ldots, i_q$ of nodes of G such that i_r and i_{r+1} are adjacent for $1\leqslant r\leqslant q-1$.

A chain differs from a path in that we do not have to traverse the arcs in the 'correct' direction — that is in the directions of the arrows. In a chain, the arcs traversed in the directions of the arrows are called *forward arcs*, the others *reverse arcs*. For example, in Fig. 1.7 (1,2), (2,4),(4,5) is a path from node 1 to node 5 which is both simple and elementary. (1,2),(2,5),(5,1),(1,3) is a path from node 1 to node 3 which is simple but not elementary. (1,2),(2,4),(4,5),(5,1),(1,2),(2,3) is a path from node 1 to node 3 which is neither simple nor elementary. (5,1),(1,2),(2,4),(4,5) is a cycle. (4,5),(3,5),(2,3),(2,1) is a chain joining node 4 to node 1. (4,5) and (2,1) are forward arcs, (3,5) and (2,3) reverse arcs.

G is said to be *strongly connected* if, for all $i,j \in N$, there is a path from i to j and from j to i. For example, the digraph depicted in Fig. 1.8 is strongly connected, but

Fig. 1.8

that depicted in Fig. 1.9 is not, there being no path from any of nodes 1, 4 and 5 to

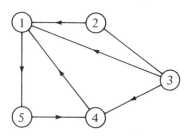

Fig. 1.9

either of nodes 2 or 3. An algorithm for determining whether a digraph is strongly connected is given in the Appendix to Chapter 4.

1.3.3 Partial graphs and subgraphs
Given a digraph $G = (N,A)$,

(i) a *partial graph* of G is a digraph $G_p = (N,A_p)$, where $A_p \subset A$, and
(ii) a *subgraph* of G is a digraph $G_s = (N_s,A_s)$, where $N_s \subset N$ and
$A_s = \{(i,j)|i,j \in N_s, (i,j) \in A\}$.

We may again combine the two to give a *partial subgraph* of *G*.

Referring to the digraph *G* depicted in Fig. 1.7, Fig. 1.10 shows a partial graph of

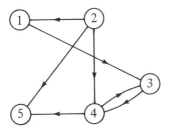

Fig. 1.10

G, Fig. 1.11 a subgraph and Fig. 1.12 a partial subgraph.

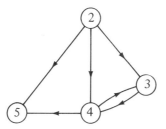

Fig. 1.11

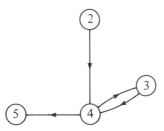

Fig. 1.12

1.4   COMPUTER REPRESENTATION OF GRAPHS

To solve problems involving large graphs, the use of a computer is essential. We therefore need a method of representing a graph for computational purposes. One way is to use matrix notation as follows.

If G is a directed graph, the *adjacency matrix*, $A = [a_{ij}]$, of G is defined by

$$a_{ij} = \begin{cases} 1 & \text{if } (i,j) \text{ is an arc of } G \\ 0 & \text{otherwise} \end{cases}.$$

For example, the adjacency matrix of the digraph in Fig. 1.7 is

$$\begin{bmatrix} 0 & 1 & 1 & 0 & 0 \\ 1 & 0 & 1 & 1 & 1 \\ 0 & 0 & 0 & 1 & 1 \\ 0 & 1 & 1 & 0 & 1 \\ 1 & 0 & 0 & 0 & 0 \end{bmatrix}.$$

If G is an undirected graph, we define the adjacency matrix of G by considering each edge as a pair of oppositely directed arcs. Thus, if G is undirected, its adjacency matrix is symmetric. For example, the adjacency matrix of the graph in Fig. 1.2 is

$$\begin{bmatrix} 0 & 1 & 1 & 0 & 1 \\ 1 & 0 & 1 & 1 & 1 \\ 1 & 1 & 0 & 1 & 1 \\ 0 & 1 & 1 & 0 & 1 \\ 1 & 1 & 1 & 1 & 0 \end{bmatrix}.$$

This is the representation which we shall use, but it is worth noting that if A is sparse we can achieve a more efficient representation by only retaining information about those a_{ij} which are non-zero. This information is held in the form of a list, for each node, of those nodes adjacent to it. Such a list is called an *adjacency list*, and more information about adjacency lists can be found in references [1] and [2] at the end of this chapter.

1.5 ALGORITHMS

The majority of problems in graph theory are solved using algorithms. What, then, do we understand by the term algorithm?

To give a precise definition is difficult; in this book we shall think of an *algorithm* as being a sequence of instructions, the performance of which, in the order given, will lead to a solution of the problem.

When using a computer it is usually helpful to have an idea of the relationship between the computational effort required to solve a problem and the size of the problem. To that end we say that the *efficiency* of an algorithm is the number, $f(n)$, of (mathematical) operations required to solve a problem of size n *in the worst case*.

Clearly, for an algorithm to be of practical use, $f(n)$ must be finite and must not increase too rapidly with n. To make the idea of efficiency more precise, let f and g be functions from N to N and c, $n_1 \in$ N be constants.

We say that $f(n)$ is $O(g(n))$ if $f(n) \leqslant c.g(n)$ for all $n \geqslant n_1$. ($O(g(n))$: read big-oh of $g(n)$.) Note that we are normally interested in the order of magnitude of $f(n)$ for large n so that we can afford to ignore the behaviour of $f(n)$ when n is small; if there is a positive integer n_1 such that the inequality holds for $n = n_1, n_1 + 1, n_1 + 2, \ldots$ that is sufficient.

If $g(n) = n^p$ (p a constant > 1) we say that the algorithm is a *polynomial time algorithm* whereas if $g(n) = p^n$ we say that it is an *exponential time algorithm*.

Now suppose that we have two algorithms for solving a particular problem: algorithm 1 with efficiency $O(g_1(n))$ and algorithm 2 with efficiency $O(g_2(n))$. Then, if $g_1(n) \leqslant g_2(n)$ for all n sufficiently large, we say that algorithm 1 is better than algorithm 2.

$a^n/n^b \to \infty$ as $n \to \infty$ $(a,b \in N, a > 1)$ so a polynomial time algorithm is better than an exponential time algorithm for the same problem. Indeed exponential time algorithms can take many years to run for comparatively small values of n.

As an *example*, consider the following algorithm which examines sums of powers of an $n \times n$ matrix A.

```
step 0:   Let R = A and p = 1
step 1:   If r_ij ≠ 0 for all i and j, go to step 4
step 2:   Let p = p + 1
          If p < n + 1, let R = R + A^p and go to step 1
step 3:   Print R
step 4:   Stop.
```

Let us now examine its efficiency. In the worst case step 1 is performed n times and step 2, $n - 1$ times. Step 1 requires a maximum of n^2 comparisons. Step 2 involves multiplying A^{p-1} by A and adding A^p to R. Multiplication of two $n \times n$ matrices needs $(2n - 1)n^2$ operations — addition and multiplication — and the addition of two $n \times n$ matrices needs a further n^2 additions.

Thus, at worst, the total number of operations needed is

$$f(n) = (n - 1)((2n - 1)n^2 + n^2) + n.n^2 = 2n^4 - n^3 < 2n^4 \ .$$

Hence $f(n)$ is $O(n^4)$, that is the efficiency of this algorithm is $O(n^4)$.

An algorithm similar to this is used to test whether a digraph is strongly connected — see the Appendix to Chapter 4.

If it is relatively easy to do so, the efficiency of each algorithm used in the text will be established at the time. Failing that, a suitable reference will be given.

FURTHER READING

Discrete mathematics

[1] N. L. Biggs, *Discrete Mathematics*, Oxford University Press, 1985.
     A beautifully written book which every undergraduate studying mathematics,
     statistics or electronics/systems engineering ought to read.
[2] J. L. Gersting, *Mathematical Structures for Computer Science*, W. H. Freeman,
     2nd edn, 1987.
[3] O. Nicodemi, *Discrete Mathematics*, West, 1987.

Graphs and networks

[4] T. B. Boffey, *Graph Theory in Operations Research*, Macmillan, 1982.
[5] N. Christofides, *Graph Theory: an Algorithmic Approach*, Academic Press,
     1975.
[6] N. Deo, *Graph Theory with Applications to Engineering and Computer Science*,
     Prentice-Hall, 1974.
[7] T. C. Hu, *Combinatorial Algorithms*, Addison-Wesley, 1982.
[8] T. C. Hu, *Integer Programming and Network Flows*, Addison-Wesley, 1969.
[9] D. K. Smith, *Network Optimisation Practice: a Computational Guide*, Ellis
     Horwood, Chichester, 1982.
     A nice introduction to the subject which contains programs, in BASIC and
     PASCAL, for all algorithms considered.

Computer communication networks

[10] M. Schwartz, *Computer-communication Network Design and Analysis*, Pren-
     tice-Hall, 1977.
[11] M. Schwartz, *Telecommunication Networks: Protocols, Modeling and Analysis*,
     Addison-Wesley, 1987.
[12] A. Tanenbaum, *Computer Networks*, Prentice-Hall, 1981.

EXERCISES

1. (a) If we wish to construct a graph with 24 edges and with all nodes of degree 3,
       how many nodes must the graph have?
   (b) Is it possible to have a group of 15 people such that each person knows exactly
       3 other people in the group?
   (c) If $G = (N,E)$ the complement, $\overline{G}$, of G is the graph whose node set is N and
       whose edges join those pairs of nodes which are not joined in G. Obtain the
       complement of the graph G depicted in Fig. 1.2.

2. A digraph may be used to model a flowchart. (A,B) is an arc of the digraph if the
   execution of instruction B can follow directly after the execution of instruction A.
   An execution sequence is a path from the start to the stop instruction.
       Consider the following simple program:

   Input: Non-zero real numbers a, b, c.
   Output: Solutions of $ax^2 + bx + c = 0$.

Draw up a flowchart and depict the corresponding digraph. Obtain all execution sequences.

3. If $G = (N,E)$, the edge connectivity of G is the smallest number of edges the removal of which would disconnect G.

   The node connectivity of G is the smallest number of nodes the removal of which, together with all edges incident to them, would disconnect G. Prove that

   (a) The edge connectivity of G cannot exceed the degree of the node with the smallest degree.

   (b) The node connectivity of G cannot exceed the edge connectivity.

   (c) The maximum node connectivity which can be achieved is $\left[\dfrac{2|E|}{|N|}\right]$, where $[s]$ denotes the integer part of s.

4. If $G = (\{1,2,3,4,5,6,7\}, \{(1,2), (1,3), (1,4), (1,7), (2,3), (3,4), (4,5), (4,7), (5,6),$ $(5,7), (6,7)\})$ depict G and hence verify, by inspection, that the edge and node connectivities of G are both 2.

   Determine the greatest node connectivity which can be achieved with a graph having 7 nodes and 11 edges and construct such a graph. (A suitable reference for the material in questions 3 and 4 is M. N. S. Swamy and K. Thulasiraman, *Graphs, Networks and Algorithms*, Wiley, 1981.)

5. G is a digraph of order n. If i and j are nodes of G we say that j is reachable from i if there is a path in G from i to j. The reachability matrix of G is an $n \times n$ matrix $R = [r_{ij}]$, where $r_{ij} = 1$ if j is reachable from i and 0 otherwise. G is strongly connected if, and only if, $r_{ij} = 1$ for all i and j, $1 \leqslant i, j \leqslant n$. If A is the adjacency matrix of G, $R = A \oplus A^2 \oplus \ldots \oplus A^n$, where A^p, $2 \leqslant p \leqslant n$ is given by $A^p = A^{p-1} \otimes A$. That is, ordinary multiplication and division are replaced by Boolean addition and multiplication $\oplus$ and $\otimes$ defined by

$$0 \oplus 0 = 0, \quad 0 \oplus 1 = 1 \oplus 0 = 1 \oplus 1 = 1 \ .$$
$$1 \otimes 1 = 1, \quad 1 \otimes 0 = 0 \otimes 1 = 0 \otimes 0 = 0 \ .$$

Details of the above may be found in [3]. Obtain the reachability matrix of the graph depicted in Fig. 1.9.

2

Trees

2.1 INTRODUCTION AND BASIC DEFINITIONS

A *tree* is an undirected, connected graph that contains no cycles.

If G is an undirected graph of n nodes then the following statements are equivalent.

(1) G is a tree.
(2) G is connected and has $n - 1$ edges.
(3) G has no cycles and has $n - 1$ edges.
(4) There is a unique elementary path joining any pair of nodes of G.

Proofs of equivalence can be found in [3].

Trees are used in, among other applications, statistics (decision trees), computer science (sorting and searching) and coding theory (weighted tree prefix codes). See [1], [3], [6], [7] for examples.

Of special importance in what follows is a tree which may be described as a skeleton of a graph.

If G is an undirected, connected graph, a *spanning tree*, T, of G is a partial graph of G which forms a tree.

It is clear that every such graph G has at least one spanning tree. For, if G has no cycles, then it is its own spanning tree. If, however, G does possess a cycle, then we may delete an edge from the cycle, and the resulting graph will still be connected. If there are other cycles, continuing in this way we finally arrive at a cycle-free graph containing all the nodes of G — that is, at a spanning tree of G. For example, the graphs in Figs 2.2 and 2.3 are both spanning trees of the graph in Fig. 2.1.

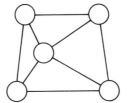

Fig. 2.1

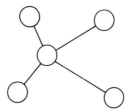

Fig. 2.2

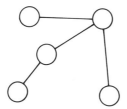

Fig. 2.3

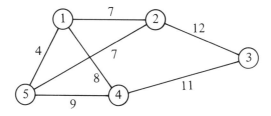

Fig. 2.4

If $G = (N,E)$, a function w which associates with each edge, e_j, a positive integer, $w(e_j)$, is called a *weight function* and G, together with w, is called a *weighted graph*, or a *network*. We write $W = (N,F,w)$ to denote G together with w.

The *weight of a spanning tree*, T, of W is the sum of the weights of all edges of T. It is denoted by $w(T)$. A weight function may be defined in a similar way for a directed graph $G = (N,A)$.

Among all spanning trees of W, the one with the smallest weight (there may be more than one) is of practical value.

Given a network W, a spanning tree of W with the smallest weight is called a *minimum spanning tree*. This is of importance in solving the *minimum connector* problem. Suppose that we have n communication sites $1, 2, \ldots, n$ and that we know the cost, c_{ij}, of building a communication line between sites i and j. What is the least expensive network which connects all n sites?

The required network must be a tree — otherwise we could remove any edge forming part of a cycle to obtain a connected network with a smaller weight. Thus, to solve the minimum connector problem, we need an algorithm to calculate a minimum spanning tree for a given network.

2.2   MINIMUM SPANNING TREE ALGORITHMS

Two such algorithms are well known.

2.2.1   Kruskal's algorithm [8]

The edges of the given network are ranked in ascending order of weight and are added to the edge set of the tree we are constructing if they do not form a cycle with those edges already in the set. Initially the edge set is $\emptyset$. The efficiency of Kruskal's algorithm is — see [2] — $O(|E|\log|E|)$, so it is especially appropriate when the network is sparse. (A graph (or network) is *sparse* if the number of edges it possesses is very much closer to the minimum possible — $(n-1)$ of there are n nodes — than to the maximum possible — $\frac{1}{2}n(n-1)$.) If, however, n is large and the network is not sparse, the ranking step is very expensive computationally and Kruskal's algorithm should not be used.

In that case, when $|E|$ is close to $\frac{1}{2}n(n-1)$, we may say that the efficiency of Kruskal's algorithm is $O(n^2 \log n)$.

KRUSKAL'S ALGORITHM

step 0: Initialize T with n nodes and no edges.

step 1: Draw up a list $\mathscr{L}$ of edges of the given network in ascending order of weight (rank arbitrarily any of equal weight).

step 2: If the first entry in $\mathscr{L}$ does not complete a cycle in T, transfer it from $\mathscr{L}$ to T. Otherwise delete it from $\mathscr{L}$ and repeat step 2.

step 3: If T is a spanning tree (has $(n-1)$ edges), stop. Otherwise repeat step 2.

Example 2.1 (see Fig. 2.4)   ·
step 0: $T = (\{1,2,3,4,5\}\emptyset)$.

step 1: $\mathscr{L}$ is $(1,5),(1,2),(2,5),(1,4),(4,5),(3,4),(2,3)$.

step 2: (1,5) is transferred from $\mathscr{L}$ to T.
         Edge set of T is {(1,5)}.
         $\mathscr{L}$ is now (1,2),(2,5),(1,4),(4,5),(3,4),(2,3).

step 3: T is not a spanning tree so repeat step 2.

step 2: (1,2) is transferred from $\mathscr{L}$ to T.
         Edge set of T is {(1,5),(1,2)}.
         $\mathscr{L}$ is (2,5),(1,4),(4,5),(3,4),(2,3).

step 3: T is not a spanning tree so repeat step 2.

step 2: (2,5) would complete a cycle in T so delete from $\mathscr{L}$.
         $\mathscr{L}$ is now (1,4),(4,5),(3,4),(2,3).
         (1,4) is transferred from $\mathscr{L}$ to T.
         Edge set of T is {(1,5),(1,2),(1,4)}.
         $\mathscr{L}$ is (4,5),(3,4),(2,3).

step 3: T is not a spanning tree so repeat step 2.

step 2: (4,5) would complete a cycle in T so delete from $\mathscr{L}$.
         $\mathscr{L}$ is now (3,4),(2,3).
         (3,4) is transferred from $\mathscr{L}$ to T.
         Edge set of T is {(1,5),(1,2),(1,4),(3,4)}.
         $\mathscr{L}$ is (2,3).

step 3: T is a spanning tree, so stop.

A minimum spanning tree for the given network is shown in Fig. 2.5. It is left

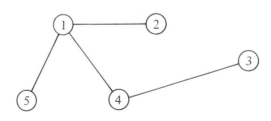

Fig. 2.5

to the reader to verify that, if the edges (2,5) and (1,2) are listed in reverse order, a different minimum spanning tree is obtained.

2.2.2 Prim's algorithm [9]

Prim's algorithm is a *greedy algorithm*, one that makes what seems to be the best choice at each step without looking ahead to see if that choice will cause problems subsequently. It grows the spanning tree from one initial edge and, at each stage, the edge added is the shortest edge remaining which has one mode in the tree. The efficiency of Prim's algorithm is $O(n^2)$ — see [1] for a neat way of proving this — and it should be preferred to Kruskal's algorithm if the given network is not sparse. The calculations are most efficiently performed using matrix notation; an alternative way of setting them out may be found in [10].

PRIM'S MATRIX ALGORITHM

step 0: Define the $n \times n$ matrix $[w_{ij}]$, where

$$w_{ij} = \begin{cases} \text{weight of } (i,j) \text{ if } (i,j) \text{ exists} \\ \infty \text{ otherwise} \end{cases}$$

Initialize T to consist of node k and no edges. (Any node will do.)

step 1: Cross out all entries in column k and make a mark on row k.

step 2: If all entries in marked rows have been crossed out, stop. Otherwise scan all marked rows and select the minimum entry (any minimum entry in the case of ties; crossed out entries are ignored).

step 3: Ir w_{rs} is the minimum entry, add s to the node set of T and (r,s) to the edge set.
Cross out column s and make a mark on row s.
Go to step 2.

Let us redo Example 2.1 using Prim's algorithm.

steps 0, 1, 2: $T = (\{1\}, \emptyset)$

$$\begin{bmatrix} \cancel{\infty} & 7 & \infty & 8 & \boxed{4} \\ \cancel{7} & \infty & 12 & \infty & 7 \\ \cancel{\infty} & 12 & \infty & 11 & \infty \\ \cancel{8} & \infty & 11 & \infty & 9 \\ \cancel{4} & 7 & \infty & 9 & \infty \end{bmatrix} \text{ x}$$

Entry selected in step 2 enclosed in □.

step 3: $T = (\{1,5\}, \{(1,5)\})$

$$\begin{bmatrix} \cancel{\infty} & 7 & \infty & 8 & \boxed{\cancel{4}} \\ \cancel{7} & \infty & 12 & \infty & \cancel{7} \\ \cancel{\infty} & 12 & \infty & 11 & \cancel{\infty} \\ \cancel{8} & \infty & 11 & \infty & \cancel{9} \\ \cancel{4} & 7 & \infty & 9 & \cancel{\infty} \end{bmatrix} \begin{matrix} \text{x} \\ \\ \\ \\ \text{x} \end{matrix}$$

step 2:

$$\begin{bmatrix} \infty & \boxed{7} & \infty & 8 & \boxed{4} \\ 7 & \infty & 12 & \infty & 7 \\ \infty & 12 & \infty & 11 & \infty \\ 8 & \infty & 11 & \infty & 9 \\ 4 & 7 & \infty & 9 & \infty \end{bmatrix} \begin{matrix} x \\ \\ \\ \\ x \end{matrix}$$

There is a tie for minimum entry. Selecting the entry in position (5,2) will lead to a different minimum spanning tree.

It is left to the reader to complete the working. Once the method is grasped, all the calculations can be done using just one matrix, and the complete solution to this example is shown below.

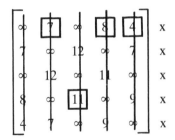

$T = (\{1,2,3,4,5\}, \{(1,5),(1,2),(1,4),(4,3)\})$.

The members of the edge set are listed in the order in which they were added to T.

2.3 ASSOCIATED PROBLEMS

2.3.1 Maximum spanning trees

We can, in a similar manner, define the *maximum spanning tree* of a given network. Either of the two algorithms above may be used to find this tree.

Using Kruskal's algorithm we rank the edges in descending order in step 1 and then proceed as before.

Using Prim's algorithm we replace each ∞ in step 0 by $-\infty$ and, in step 2, select the maximum entry.

2.3.2 Optimization of a communication network

n individuals are to receive confidential messages. Consider the connected, undirected network W whose nodes correspond to the n individuals and where there is an edge joining nodes i and j if the two individuals can communicate with each other.

The weight of edge (i,j) is the probability that a message transmitted along it will be intercepted.

Assuming that interceptions on different edges are independent events from a probabilistic point of view, how should a confidential message be circulated among the n individuals so as to minimize the probability of its becoming known to an outsider?

It is shown in [2] that this problem reduces to finding a minimum spanning tree. The interested reader should consult this book for the details and a worked example.

2.3.3 Connectivity

We adapt Prim's algorithm to obtain an algorithm of efficiency $O(n^2)$ for determining whether a graph is connected.

CONNECTIVITY ALGORITHM

step 0 Define $W = [W_{ij}]$ to be the adjacency matrix of the graph.
   Initialize the node set of T to consist of node k (any node will do).

step 1: Cross out all entries in column k and make a mark on row k.

step 2: If all entries in marked rows have been crossed out, stop. The graph is connected.
   If all entries remaining in marked rows are 0, stop. The graph is not connected.
   Otherwise scan all marked rows and select any non-zero entry.

step 3: If w_{rs} is the entry selected, add s to the node set of T. Cross out column s, make a mark on row s and go to step 2.

If the graph is not connected, the node set of T at the point where all remaining entries in marked rows are 0 will be the node set of the first component of the graph. To find the next component we could, instead of stopping, cross out a further column, make a (different) mark on the corresponding row and continue as before.

If the graph is connected, then when the algorithm terminates, the node set of T will coincide with the node set of the graph.

2.4 NETWORKS IMMUNE TO ISOLATED FAILURES

2.4.1 Isolated failure immune (IFI) networks

The ideas in the remainder of this chapter first appeared in papers by Farley and others [4], [5],]11]. We include some details here, a full account can be found in those papers.

Thus far we have constructed communication networks as cheaply as possible. The tree networks so constructed have the minimum number of lines and, as there is only one elementary path between any pair of sites, this simplifies the drawing up of routing tables for calls. Also, in broadcasting, where one site is the sender of a message which has to be received by all other sites, a tree network allows the process to be completed in $n - 1$ calls (for n sites), each site receiving the message calling all other sites to which it is directly linked.

Tree networks do, however, have some disadvantages. Blockages can occur with no alternative routes being available for message transfer, and, perhaps most important, tree networks are very vulnerable to network failures.

We assume that two types of network failure are possible: an inoperative communication line — a *line failure*, and an operative communication site — a *site failure*.

We say that a network is *immune* to a set of failures if all operative sites remain connected.

A tree network is not immune to a set consisting of a single failure so there is a need to add extra lines to the network to provide alternative routes.

We must first decide what combinations of line and/or site failures it is realistic to expect a network to overcome and, in the light of that, determine how many extra lines need to be added and where.

Let us assume that we are able to schedule maintenance of the network so as to minimize the probability of network failures occurring 'near to one another'. Network failures which do not occur 'near to one another' are called isolated failures and we make the idea clear by means of the following formal definition.

A set of network failures is said to be *isolated* if all possible pairs of failures are isolated.

(i) *Two line failures are isolated* if the inoperative lines are not incident to a common site.
(ii) *Two site failures are isolated* if the two inoperative sites are not neighbours — that is not connected by a line.
(iii) *A line failure and a site failure are isolated* if the inoperative line is not incident to a neighbour of the inoperative site.

A network is an *isolated failure immune (IFI) network* if message transfers between operative sites can be completed provided that the set of network failures is isolated.

In Fig. 2.6 the three failures denoted $\times$ form an isolated set and all operative

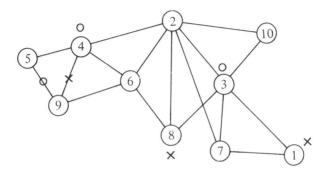

Fig. 2.6

sites are connected. The three denoted ○ do not form an isolated set, and we see that site 5 cannot be reached from the other operative sites.

Before stating an algorithm which will convert a tree network into an IFI network we present some of the relevant ideas and results.

An IFI network on two sites has the sites joined by a pair of lines. In proving Theorems 2.1–2.4 we assume that we have a set S of sites and a set E of lines with $|S| \geqslant 3$.

The subnetwork *induced* by a subset S' of S is what we understood by a subnetwork (or subgraph) in Chapter 1.

Given a network W, let $S(i)$, $i \in S$, be the set of neighbouring sites of i in N. Then W is *neighbourly* if, for every $i \in S$, the subnetwork induced by $S(i)$ is connected and contains at least two sites.

Theorem 2.1
If W is neighbourly, W is an IFI network.

Proof.   Suppose that an inoperative site is encountered during message transfer. Then all sites and lines in the subnetwork induced by $S(i)$ will be operative if failures are isolated, which means that the failure can be overcome by appropriate message routing through $S(i)$.

Suppose now that a line failure is encountered. In that case a neighbour of the intended recipient of the call can be contacted if failures are isolated. That neighbour can then call the original recipient. Thus W is an IFI network.

By Theorem 2.1, complete networks (each site directly connected to all others) are IFI networks. We seek IFI networks having as few lines as possible.

A 2-*tree* may be defined recursively as follows.

(i)   A triangle is a 2-tree.
(ii) Given a 2-tree and any line (i,j) of it we can add a new site k which is a neighbour of both i and j; the result is a 2-tree.

Figs 2.7, 2.8 and 2.9 are examples of 2-trees on 3, 4 and 5 sites.

Fig. 2.7

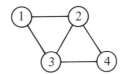

Fig. 2.8

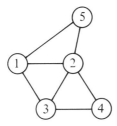

Fig. 2.9

Theorem 2.2
If a network is a 2-tree, it is an IFI network.

Proof.   By induction on the number of sites.

If the network W has 3 sites then it is neighbourly (and hence IFI). Assume that W is neighbourly if it has $\leqslant n$ sites and consider the addition of a further site. The neighbourhood of the new site consists of two sites and is connected. Furthermore this new site becomes connected to the neighbourhoods of the two sites and therefore a 2-tree on $n + 1$ sites is neighbourly.

In fact a much stronger result may be proved.

An IFI network is *minimal* if, on removal of an arbitrary line, the resulting network is not IFI.

Theorem 2.3
W is a minimal IFI network$\Leftrightarrow W$ is a 2-tree.

Proof. $\Leftarrow$ [4], $\Rightarrow$ [11].

Theorem 2.4
If W is a minimal IFI network on n sites, W has $2n - 3$ lines.

Proof. [4].

2.4.2   Algorithm to convert a tree network to a minimal IFI network
step 0: Obtain a tree network T connecting the sites.

step 1: Create a LIST $\mathscr{L}$ of all sites in T having more than one neighbour.

step 2: For the first entry i in $\mathscr{L}$, list the neighbours $i_1, i_2, \ldots, i_k$ of i in T.

step 3: For $2 \leqslant j \geqslant k$, add (i_1, i_j) to the network.
         Delete site i from $\mathscr{L}$.

step 4: If $\mathscr{L}$ is empty, stop. Otherwise repeat step 2.

Notes
(1) The algorithm is extracted from that given in [4] which includes, in addition, a method for updating a given routing table (q.v.).
(2) We would naturally like to construct an IFI network as cheaply as possible. The tree network in step 0 is then normally a minimum spanning tree and, in step 3, if there is a choice, we add that set of lines having the smallest total cost.

Example 2.2
Given the cost matrix below, construct a minimal IFI network linking the ten sites.

$$
\begin{bmatrix}
-- & 75 & 80 & 72 & 45 & 49 & 40 & 84 & 90 & 60 \\
75 & -- & 28 & 54 & 40 & 36 & 42 & 32 & 45 & 49 \\
80 & 28 & -- & 77 & 63 & 63 & 40 & 54 & 60 & 35 \\
72 & 54 & 77 & -- & 48 & 36 & 49 & 56 & 36 & 77 \\
45 & 40 & 63 & 48 & -- & 50 & 48 & 42 & 35 & 40 \\
49 & 36 & 63 & 36 & 50 & -- & 48 & 54 & 49 & 36 \\
40 & 42 & 40 & 49 & 48 & 48 & -- & 50 & 49 & 80 \\
84 & 32 & 54 & 56 & 42 & 54 & 50 & -- & 63 & 56 \\
90 & 45 & 60 & 36 & 35 & 49 & 49 & 63 & -- & 56 \\
60 & 49 & 35 & 77 & 40 & 36 & 80 & 56 & 56 & --
\end{bmatrix}
$$

We shall attempt to minimize cost by adopting the strategies outlined in note (2) above.

step 0: A minimum spanning tree, cost 318 units, is shown in Fig. 2.10.

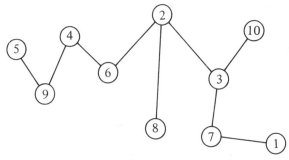

Fig. 2.10

step 1: $\mathscr{L}$ is 2, 3, 4, 6, 7, 9.

step 2: Neighbours of site 2 in T are 3, 6, 8.

step 3: We have a choice of lines to add depending upon which neighbour is chosen as 2_1. (3,6) and (3,8) cost 117; (6,3) and (6,8) cost 117; (8,3) and (8,6) cost 108. We therefore add this last pair to the network.
$\mathscr{L}$ is now 3, 4, 6, 7, 9.

step 4: $\mathscr{L}$ is not empty so repeat step 2.

step 2: Neighbours of site 3 in T are 2, 7, 10.

step 3: We again have a choice. The cheapest pair is (2,7) and (2,10), cost 91, so add these two lines to the network.
$\mathscr{L}$ is now 4, 6, 7, 9.

step 4: $\mathscr{L}$ is not empty so repeat step 2.

step 2: Neigbours of site 4 in T are 6,9.

step 3: Add (6,9), cost 49, to the network.
$\mathscr{L}$ is now 6, 7, 9.

step 4: $\mathscr{L}$ is not empty so repeat step 2.

step 2: Neighbours of site 6 in T are 2,4.

step 3: Add (2,4), cost 54, to the network.
$\mathscr{L}$ is now 7,9.

step 4: $\mathscr{L}$ is not empty so repeat step 2.

step 2: Neighbours of site 7 are 1,3.

step 3: Add (1,3), cost 80, to the network.
$\mathscr{L}$ is now 9.

step 4: $\mathscr{L}$ is not empty so repeat step 2.

step 2: Neighbours of site 9 in T are 4,5.

step 3: Add (4,5), cost 48, to the network.
$\mathscr{L}$ is now empty.

step 4: Stop.

We have added 8 lines to the 9 already present, giving 17 in all which is $2n - 3$ with $n = 10$ (Theorem 2.4). If we add those lines to Fig. 2.10 we will obtain the network drawn in Fig. 2.6.

The cost of building this IFI network is 748 units.

It is possible, however, that a different minimum spanning tree in step 0 would lead to a cheaper answer. If every penny is important — that is if we are spending our own money rather than public money — then we may, for instance, use the construction due to Gabow outlined in the next chapter to obtain all spanning trees in increasing order of weight and use the first few in the list as the starting tree in step 0.

2.4.3 Isolated line failure immune (ILFI) networks

We turn now to the special case where the only failures which can (or which are likely to) occur are line failures. We recall that a set of line failures is isolated if no two of the failing lines are incident to the same site.

A network immune to a set of isolated line failures is called an *isolated line failure immune (ILFI) network*.

If the lines of a given tree are duplicated we obtain a *double tree* (Fig. 2.11) having $2n - 2$ lines (for n sites). A double tree is clearly an ILFI network since, if line failures

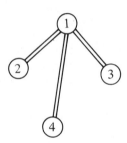

Fig. 2.11 — A double tree.

are isolated, at most one of each pair of duplicate lines can fail.

A double tree is a recursive network in that a double tree on $n + 1$ sites can be constructed from a double tree on n sites by the addition of a new site connected to an existing site by two lines. We can generalize this construction by eliminating the restriction that both new lines are connected to the same existing site.

A *2-recursive network* (Fig. 2.12) is a single site or, given any 2-recursive network

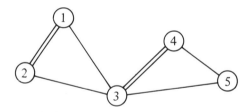

Fig. 2.12 — A 2-recursive network

on n sites, a 2-recursive network on $n + 1$ sites is obtained by connecting the new site by a total of two lines to one or two of the existing sites.

Theorem 2.5
If W is a 2-recursive network, W is an ILFI network.

Proof.   By induction on the number of sites.

The result is obvious if the network has just one site, so assume that the result is true for networks with $< n$ sites.

Let W be a 2-recursive network on n sites. Then, because of the recursive construction rule, there is a site, i say, in W of degree 2. The subnetwork induced in W by $S — \{i\}$ is 2-recursive, has $n - 1$ sites, and hence is ILFI.

If line failures are isolated, only one line connecting site i to the subnetwork can be down. Since the subnetwork remains connected under a set of isolated line failures, so does W.

Theorem 2.5 shows that an existing ILFI network can easily be expanded to include new sites. To add a new site, connect it to any one or two existing sites using a total of two lines. The decision as to which lines are to be built is generally taken on cost grounds.

A *triangle* is a cycle of three sites and three lines. A *triangled network* (Fig. 2.13) is a network in which every line is part of a triangle.

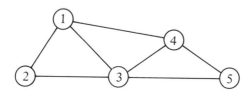

Fig. 2.13 — A triangled network.

Theorem 2.6
If W is a triangled network, W is an ILFI network.

Proof.   [5].

As we have seen, double trees and 2-recursive networks require $2n - 2$ lines (for n sites). This is not, however, the minimum number of lines required for a network to be ILFI — see, for example, the ILFI network in Fig. 2.13.

An ILFI network is *minimal* if, on removal of an arbitrary line, the resulting network is not ILFI.

We now define a class of ILFI networks which turn out to be minimal. An *abc-network* is a single site or, given by an abc-network W, a larger abc-network can be obtained by applying one of the following rules:

(a) if W has an odd number of sites, connect a new site to one or two sites of W by a total of two lines;
(b) connect two new sites, themselves connected by a line, to a site of W, thereby forming a triangle;
(c) replace a line of W by adding two new sites, each connected to both ends of the removed line, thereby forming a 4-cycle.

An important subclass of abc-networks is formed if rule (b) only is used during construction. Any network obtained in this way is called a *triangle cactus*. Note that a triangle cactus must have an odd number of sites. We look at some results concerning triangle cacti.

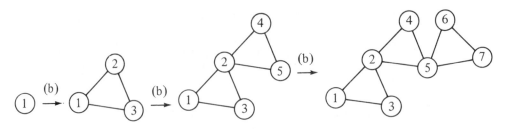

Fig. 2.14 — Example of the construction of a triangle cactus.

Theorem 2.7
If W is a triangle cactus, W is an ILFI network.

Proof. A triangle cactus is a special case of a triangled network in which every line belongs to exactly one triangle. Hence, by Theorem 2.6, W is an ILFI network.

Further, noting that at each stage in the construction of a triangle cactus we add two sites and three lines, the following result becomes evident.

Theroem 2.8
If W is a triangle cactus on n sites, W has $\frac{3}{2}(n-1)$ lines.
   [5] proves Theorems 2.7 and 2.8 for abc-networks. Finally

Theorem 2.9
If W is an abc-network (and, in particular, a triangle cactus), W is a minimal ILFI network.

Proof. [5].

2.4.4 Minimal ILFI networks from tree networks
We present here an algorithm (extracted from that given in [5] which includes, in addition, a method for updating the routing table) which converts a given tree network on an odd number of sites in a minimal ILFI network by adding lines to produce a triangle cactus.
   The sites of the tree are assumed to be numbered in *father array* — that is, if i and j are two sites, father $(i) = j$ if $j < i$ and (i,j) is a line of the tree. {In more detail, choose any site to be site 1 (usually called the root of the tree in this content). If site 1 is directly connected to s other sites, number these $2, 3, \ldots, s + 1$. Site 1 is the father of these sites; they are all brothers.
   Suppose site 2 is directly connected to t other sites. Number them $s + 2, s + 3, \ldots,$ $s + t + 1$. Site 2 is the father of these sites, site 1 their grandfather.

Suppose site 3 is directly connected to u other sites. Number them $s + t + 2$, $s + t + 3, \ldots, s + t + u + 1$. And so on.}

ALGORITHM TO CONVERT A TREE NETWORK ON AN ODD NUMBER OF SITES TO A MINIMAL ILFI NETWORK

step 0: Initialize. Put the tree into father array.
List sites. S:[$n, n - 1, \ldots, 2, 1$].
List fathers. F: [$f(n), f(n - 1), \ldots, f(2)$].
List marks. M:[$m(n), m(n - 1), \ldots, m(2), m(1)$].
Initially all marks are set to 0.
Let $i = n$.

step 1: If $m(i) = l \neq 0$, add line ($f(i)$, l) to the network and reset $m(i) = 0$, *or*
    if $m(i) = 0$ and $m(f(i)) = 0$, set $m(f(i)) = i$, *or*
    if $m(i) = 0$ but $m(f(i)) = k \neq 0$, add line (i,k) to the network and reset $m(f(i)) = 0$.

step 2: Let $i = i - 1$.
    If $i = 1$, stop. Otherwise repeat step 1.

Example 2.3
Given the cost matrix in Example 2.2 with the last row and column removed, construct a minimal ILFI network linking the nine sites.

We shall attempt to minimize cost, so our first job is to find a minimum spanning tree for the network. Such a tree is shown below in Fig. 2.15; its cost is 283 units. It

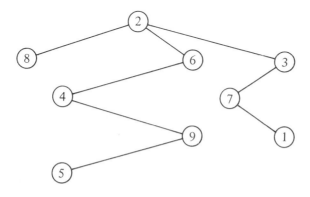

Fig. 2.15

must now be put into father array. Many such relabellings are possible; one is shown
below.

step 0:

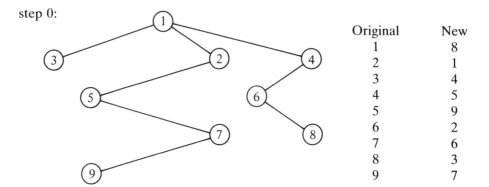

Original	New
1	8
2	1
3	4
4	5
5	9
6	2
7	6
8	3
9	7

Fig. 2.16

S:[9, 8, 7, 6, 5, 4, 3, 2, 1]
F:[7, 6, 5, 4, 2, 1, 1, 1,]
M:[0, 0, 0, 0, 0, 0, 0, 0, 0].
Let $i = 9$.

step 1: Set $m(f(9)) = 9$, i.e. $m(7) = 9$.
M:[0, 0, 9, 0, 0, 0, 0, 0, 0].
(S and F do not change so will not be listed each time.)

step 2: $i = 8 \neq 1$ so repeat step 1.

step 1: Set $m(f(8)) = 8$, i.e. $m(6) = 8$.
M:[0, 0, 9, 8, 0, 0, 0, 0, 0,].

step 2: $i = 7 \neq 1$ so repeat step 1.

step 1: $m(7) = 9$ so add line $(f(7),9)$, i.e. line (5,9), to the network.
Reset $m(7) = 0$.
M:[0, 0, 0, 8, 0, 0, 0, 0, 0,].

step 2: $i = 6 \neq 1$ so repeat step 1.

step 1: $m(6) = 8$ so add line $(f(6),8)$, i.e. line (4,8), to the network.
Reset $m(6) = 0$.
M:[0, 0, 0, 0, 0, 0, 0, 0, 0].

step 2: $i = 5 \neq 1$ so repeat step 1.

step 1: Set $m(f(5)) = 5$, i.e. $m(2) = 5$.
M:[0, 0, 0, 0, 0, 0, 0, 5, 0].

step 2: $i = 4 \neq 1$ so repeat step 1.

step 1: Set $m(f(4)) = 4$, i.e. $m(1) = 4$.
M:[0, 0, 0, 0, 0, 0, 0, 5, 4].

step 2: $i = 3 \neq 1$ so repeat step 1.

step 1: $m(3) = 0$ but $m(f(3)) = 4$ so add line (3,4) to the network.
Reset $m(f(3)) = 0$.
M:[0, 0, 0, 0, 0, 0, 0, 5, 0].

step 2: $i = 2 \neq 1$ so repeat step 1.

step 1: $m(2) = 5$ so add line $(f(2),5)$, i.e. line (1,5), to the network.
Reset $m(2) = 0$.
M:[0, 0, 0, 0, 0, 0, 0, 0, 0].

step 2: $i = 1$ so stop.

Adding the extra lines to Fig. 2.16 gives Fig. 2.17. Then using the original

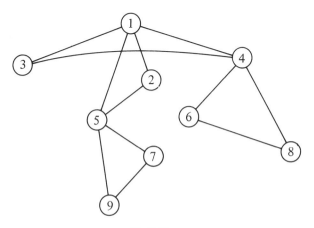

Fig. 2.17

labelling of the nodes and altering the configuration slightly to bring out the triangle cactus shape, the required ILFI network is shown in Fig. 2.18. Its

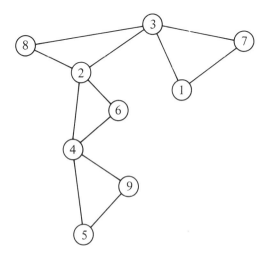

Fig. 2.18

cost is 519 units. Again different starting configurations can lead to different final answers.

    We have only scratched the surface of network reliability. For an in-depth account, see: C. J. Colbourn, *The Combinatorics of Network Reliability*, Oxford University Press, 1987.

REFERENCES

[1] N. L. Biggs, *Discrete Mathematics*, Oxford University Press, 1985.
[2] N. Christofides, *Graph Theory*: *an Algorithmic Approach*, Academic Press, 1975.
[3] N. Deo, *Graph Theory with Applications to Engineering and Computer Science*, Prentice-Hall, 1974.
[4] A. M. Farley, Networks Immune to Isolated Failures, *Networks*, **11**, 255–268, (1981).
[5] A. M. Farley and A. Proskurowski, Networks Immune to Isolated Line Failures, *Networks*, **12**, 393–403, (1982).
[6] R. P. Grimaldi, *Discrete and Combinatorial Mathematics*: *an Applied Introduction*, Addison-Wesley, 1985.
[7] D. E. Knuth, *The Art of Computer Programming*, Volume 3, Addison-Wesley, 1973.
[8] J. B. Kruskal, On the Shortest Spanning Subtree of a Graph and the Travelling Salesman Problem, *Proc. AMS*, **7**, 48–50, (1956).
[9] R. C. Prim, Shortest Connection Networks and some Generalisations, *Bell Systems Technical Journal*, **36**, 1389–1401, (1957).
[10] D. K. Smith, *Network Optimisation Practice*: *a Computational Guide*, Ellis Horwood, Chichester, 1982.
[11] J. A. Ward and C. J. Colbourn, Steiner Trees, Partial 2-trees and Minimum IFI Networks, *Networks*, **13**, 159–167, (1983).

EXERCISES

1. The (i,j) entry in the matrix below denotes the cost (in suitable units) of building a communication line linking sites i and j.

$$
\begin{bmatrix}
- & 72 & 57 & 92 & 42 & 29 & 33 \\
72 & - & 60 & 49 & 37 & 77 & 62 \\
57 & 60 & - & 55 & 53 & 39 & 59 \\
92 & 49 & 55 & - & 44 & 54 & 47 \\
42 & 37 & 53 & 44 & - & 65 & 58 \\
29 & 77 & 39 & 54 & 65 & - & 70 \\
33 & 62 & 59 & 47 & 58 & 70 & -
\end{bmatrix}
$$

   (i) Find a minimum cost spanning tree linking the sites.

(ii) Find a minimum cost spanning tree given the additional constraint that a communication line linking sites 1 and 2 must be built.

(iii) Convert each of the trees in (i) and (ii) to minimal IFI networks. Minimize cost wherever possible.

(iv) Relabel each of the trees in (i) and (ii) into father array and then convert to minimal ILFI networks.

2. In an attempt to persuade the English to speak to each other, nine major centres of population are to be linked by a new communication system. The costs of building the lines are given (in suitable units) in the matrix below.

$$
\begin{bmatrix}
- & 75 & 80 & 72 & 45 & 49 & 40 & 84 & 90 \\
75 & - & 28 & 54 & 40 & 36 & 42 & 32 & 45 \\
80 & 28 & - & 77 & 63 & 63 & 40 & 54 & 60 \\
72 & 54 & 77 & - & 48 & 36 & 49 & 56 & 36 \\
45 & 40 & 63 & 48 & - & 50 & 48 & 42 & 35 \\
49 & 36 & 63 & 36 & 50 & - & 48 & 54 & 49 \\
40 & 42 & 40 & 49 & 48 & 48 & - & 50 & 49 \\
84 & 32 & 54 & 56 & 42 & 54 & 50 & - & 63 \\
90 & 45 & 60 & 36 & 35 & 49 & 49 & 63 & -
\end{bmatrix}
$$

Minimizing cost wherever possible, construct: (i) a minimal IFI, and (ii) a minimal ILFI, network linking the sites.

3. Is the following procedure for calculating a minimum spanning tree T of a network $W = (N,E,w)$ correct?

(i) Form the subnetworks $W_1 = (N_1, W_1, w)$ and $W_2 = (N_2, E_2, w)$, where N_1 and N_2 form a partition of N. ($N_1 \cap N_2 = \emptyset$, $N_1 \cup N_2 = N$.)

(ii) Calculate the minimum spanning trees T_1 snd T_2 respectively of W_1 and W_2.

(iii) Connect T_1 and T_2 by adding the edge of least weight in E not belonging to E_1 or E_2. The resulting tree is T.

Provide a proof or a counterexample.

4. It is intended to build a communication system linking 9 population centres in Transylvania. The distances, in Transylvanian leagues, between the centres are given in the matrix below.

$$\begin{bmatrix} — & 31 & 28 & 37 & 19 & 11 & 18 & 21 & 23 \\ 31 & — & 35 & 34 & 20 & 12 & 13 & 16 & 15 \\ 28 & 35 & — & 25 & 29 & 15 & 17 & 26 & 15 \\ 37 & 34 & 25 & — & 33 & 19 & 20 & 12 & 21 \\ 19 & 20 & 29 & 33 & — & 22 & 25 & 24 & 26 \\ 11 & 12 & 15 & 19 & 22 & — & 29 & 27 & 28 \\ 18 & 13 & 17 & 20 & 25 & 29 & — & 16 & 21 \\ 21 & 16 & 26 & 12 & 24 & 27 & 16 & — & 23 \\ 23 & 15 & 15 & 21 & 26 & 28 & 21 & 23 & — \end{bmatrix}.$$

Centres 1–5 are separated from centres 6–9 by a mountain range. A communication line which crosses the mountain range costs twice as much per league to build as a line which does not. In addition, because of opposition from a local Count, a line directly linking sites 1 and 6 cannot be built.

(i) Starting with a minimum cost spanning tree, and minimizing cost wherever possible, construct a minimal IFI network linking the population centres.

(ii) Because of the nature of this particular problem it is possible to build a cheaper minimal IFI network starting with a spanning tree whose cost is close to minimum. Determine a suitable spanning tree and hence construct a minimal IFI network costing less than that constructed in (i). [Hint: see question 3.]

3

Some network design algorithms

3.1 MULTIPOINT CONNECTIONS IN CENTRALIZED NETWORKS

3.1.1 Constrained and unconstrained problems

Suppose that we have n concentrators, or minicomputers, $1, 2, \ldots, n$, with concentrator 1 a CPU receiving messages from the remainder and suppose, further, that the following two constraints apply:

(i) all lines have capacity M (*Capacity constraint*)
(ii) no more than m concentrators should be unable to communicate with the CPU if any line is down (*Reliability constraint*).

If the message rate for each concentrator and the cost of linking each pair are known, the problem is to design a least-cost network linking the concentrators and satisfying (i) and (ii). This is called a *constrained* minimum spanning tree problem to distinguish it from the unconstrained minimum spanning tree problem of the previous chapter.

The following example illustrates the difference between the two problems.

Example 3.1
Suppose c_{ij} is the cost of linking concentrators i and j, where

$$C = [c_{ij}] = \begin{bmatrix} - & 15 & 19 & 12 & 10 & 7 \\ 15 & - & 18 & 17 & 20 & 14 \\ 19 & 18 & - & 16 & 22 & 24 \\ 12 & 17 & 16 & - & 11 & 13 \\ 10 & 20 & 22 & 11 & - & 21 \\ 7 & 14 & 24 & 13 & 21 & - \end{bmatrix}.$$

A solution of the unconstrained problem is given by the (unconstrained) minimum spanning tree whose edge is {(6,1),(5,1),(4,5),(2,6),(3,4)} and whose cost is 58 units.

Now suppose that (i) every line has capacity 500 bps, and (ii) no more than 2 concentrators should be unable to communicate with the CPU if any line is down. Then, if the message rates for concentrators 2–6 are, respectively, 150, 150, 250, 200, 200 bps, we see from Fig. 3.1 that this spanning tree is an infeasible solution of the

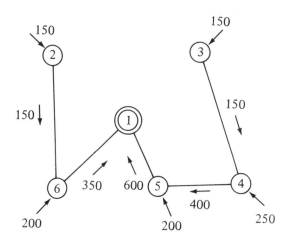

Fig. 3.1 — (Arrows denote direction of message flow).

constrained problem, for the message rate in line (5,1) exceeds the line capacity and, in addition, if this line were to fail, 3 concentrators would be unable to communicate with the CPU. The cost of the (unconstrained) minimum spanning tree does, however, provide a lower bound for the cost of a solution of the constrained problem. We will call a solution of the constrained problem an *optimum feasible tree* — that is, a least-cost tree satisfying the capacity and reliability constraints.

3.1.2 Solution of the constrained problem
To obtain an optimum feasible tree we use a branch-and-bound algorithm devised by Chandy and Russell [1]. It starts with a solution of the unconstrained problem and searches for an optimum feasible tree in a systematic manner by subdividing the set of feasible solutions into smaller subsets. The way in which the partitioning is done is illustrated using the example started earlier.

We first note that the number of feasible solutions which have to be considered can be reduced by the following theorem.

Theorem 3.1
If a solution of the unconstrained problem contains the lines $(i,1)$, $(j,1)$, ..., $(k,1)$, there is a solution of the constrained problem containing them.

Proof. [1].

Thus, in our example, (5,1) and (6,1) will form part of the optimum feasible tree we are seeking.

FIRST SUBDIVISION

Divide the set S of feasible solutions into subsets S_1 and S_2 where $S_1 = \{$feasible solutions containing (6,1) and (5,1)$\}$ and $S_2 = S - S_1$. The optimum solution we are seeking must be in S_1. Therefore discard S_2.

SECOND SUBDIVISION

(a) *Divide S_1 into subsets S_{11} and S_{12}*
This is achieved by making S_{11} contain another line — the inclusion of which does not breach the constraints — and taking S_{12} to be $S_1 - S_{11}$. Suppose we take $S_{11} = \{$feasible solutions containing (6,1), (5,1) and (4,5)$\}$. Then $S_{12} = S_1 - S_{11} = \{$feasible solutions containing (6,1), (5,1) but not (4,5)$\}$.

(b) *Find lower bounds on the costs of any solutions in S_{11} and S_{12}*
S_{11}: Find a minimum cost spanning tree containing the lines (5,1), (6,1) and (4,5). We may use Prim's algorithm with the costs of these lines put to 0 (to ensure that they are selected).

Note
We can, in general, speed up the algorithm by realizing that the lines which must be included can rule out others. Thus, if we must include (5,1), (6,1) and (4,5), we can eliminate from consideration lines (2,4) and (3,4), as including either would then breach both constraints. To ensure that they are rejected, put the cost of each to ∞. The adjusted cost matrix for step 0 of Prim's algorithm is then

$$
\begin{bmatrix}
\infty & 15 & 19 & 12 & 0 & 0 \\
15 & \infty & 18 & \infty & 20 & 14 \\
19 & 18 & \infty & \infty & 22 & 24 \\
12 & \infty & \infty & \infty & 0 & 13 \\
0 & 20 & 22 & 0 & \infty & 21 \\
0 & 14 & 24 & 13 & 21 & \infty
\end{bmatrix}
$$

As may be easily verified, we obtain a spanning tree consisting of the lines (3,1), (6,1), (4,5), (2,6), (3,2); cost 60 units.

S_{12}: Find a minimum cost spanning tree containing the lines (5,1) and (6,1) but not the line (4,5). In this case the cost matrix is

$$\begin{bmatrix} \infty & 15 & 19 & 12 & 0 & 0 \\ 15 & \infty & 18 & 17 & 20 & 14 \\ 19 & 18 & \infty & 16 & 22 & 24 \\ 12 & 17 & 16 & \infty & \infty & 15 \\ 0 & 20 & 22 & \infty & \infty & 21 \\ 0 & 14 & 24 & 13 & 21 & \infty \end{bmatrix}$$

Using Prim's algorithm we obtain a spanning tree consisting of the lines (3,1), (6,1), (4,1), (2,6), (3,4); cost 59 units.

(c) *Retain the subset having the smaller bound; discard the other*
Retain S_{12}; discard S_{11}.

(d) *Determine whether the subset retained has a feasible solution whose cost is equal to the lower bound*
If one exists it is an optimum feasible solution, [1]. If one does not exist we begin a third subdivision by dividing S_{12} into subsets S_{121} and S_{122} in the way described in (a).
   The spanning tree, cost 59 units, just constructed is drawn in Fig. 3.2. It satisfies constraints (i) and (ii) and so is a solution of the constrained problem.

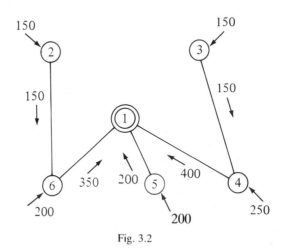

Fig. 3.2

   A general statement of the steps in the Chandy–Russell algorithm may be found in their paper and also in [10].

3.1.3 An alternative approach
Gabow [4] gives an algorithm for generating a list of all spanning trees of a network in increasing order of weight. The constraints could be checked and the first member of

the ordered list satisfying them would be an optimum feasible tree. A full description of the method is given in the paper; we extract brief details here. The algorithm generates the list by means of *T-exchanges*. If T is a spanning tree of a network, a *T-exchange* is a pair e, f of edges where $e \in T$, $f \notin T$, and $(T - e) \cup f$ is a spanning tree.

The *weight of the exchange* is $w(f) - w(e)$ and the weight of the tree $(T - e) \cup f$ is $w(T) - w(e) + w(f)$.

If T is a minimum spanning tree, a spanning tree with the next smallest weight is $(T - e) \cup f$ where e, f is a T-exchange of minimum weight.

Let us apply this method to our example. We start with the tree of Fig. 3.1 repeated, for convenience, in Fig. 3.3.

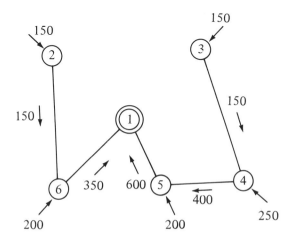

Fig. 3.3

We look now for a T-exchange of minimum weight (cost).

Consider (2,6). In order for the new network to be a tree concentrator 2 must be connected to one of concentrators 1, 3, 4, 5. Comparing the cost of line (2,6) with those of (2,1), (2,3), (2,4) and (2,5) we find that a T-exchange of minimum cost is (2,6), (2,1) with cost $15 - 14 = 1$. This, however, leads to an infeasible solution, so we reject it.

Considering the remaining lines, there is a T-exchange of cost 1 giving a feasible solution, namely (4,5), (4,1).

This is, then, an optimum feasible tree (and coincides with the one found by the Chandy–Russell algorithm).

3.2 HEURISTIC ALGORITHMS

Optimal algorithms have only limited practical usefulness owing to the large number of iterations usually needed for convergence. There are heuristic algorithms due to Esau and Williams [2], Kruskal [7] and Prim [9], and a unified algorithm due to

Kershenbaum and Chou [6], which produce near-optimal solutions — usually within 5% of the optimal — very much faster. [6] has a discussion of the efficiency of these heuristic algorithms.

We present Kruskal's algorithm below. The interested reader can find descriptions of the other algorithms in the papers or in [10].

3.2.1 Kruskal's heuristic algorithm

step 0: Define $C = [C_{ij}]$ where

$$C_{ij} = \begin{cases} \text{cost of building line } (i,j); \ i \neq j \\ \infty \ \ if \ i = j \end{cases}.$$

Initialize the tree T to consist of n sites and no lines.

step 1: Select the smallest entry in C (any one in case of ties). Let this be C_{kl}.

step 2: If the addition of (k,l) to T breaks at least one constraint, set $C_{kl} = C_{lk} = \infty$ and go to step 1.
Otherwise add this line and set $C_{kl} = C_{lk} = \infty$.

step 3: If T has $n-1$ lines, stop.
Otherwise go to step 1.

[This is an alternative way of expressing Kruskal's algorithm. It can be used in the unconstrained case — there is then just one constraint to check, namely that a cycle is not formed by the addition of a particular line.]

Let us apply this algorithm to our example.
The first three iterations lead to the addition, in turn, of (6.1), (5,1) and (4,5).
Then T is currently (see Fig. 3.4)

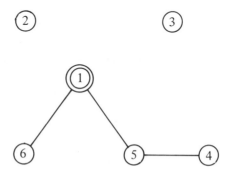

Fig. 3.4

and C is currently

$$\begin{bmatrix} \infty & 15 & 19 & \infty & \infty & \infty \\ 15 & \infty & 18 & 17 & 20 & \infty \\ 19 & 18 & \infty & 16 & 22 & 24 \\ \infty & 17 & 16 & \infty & \infty & \infty \\ \infty & 20 & 22 & \infty & \infty & 21 \\ \infty & \infty & 24 & \infty & 21 & \infty \end{bmatrix}$$

step 1: Minimum entry in C is $C_{14}(=C_{41})=12$.

step 2: The addition of $(4,1)$ would form a cycle.
Set $C_{14}=C_{41}=\infty$ and go to step 1.

step 1: Minimum entry in C is $C_{46}(=C_{64})=13$.

step 2: The addition of $(4,6)$ would form a cycle.
Set $C_{46}=C_{64}=\infty$ and go to step 1.

step 1: Minimum entry in C is $C_{26}(=C_{62})=14$.

step 2: The addition of $(2,6)$ breaks no constraint so add this line to T. Let $C_{26}=C_{62}=\infty$

step 3: T has 4 lines so go to step 1.
T is currently (see Fig. 3.5)

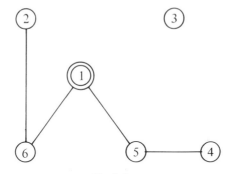

Fig. 3.5

and

$$C = \begin{bmatrix} \infty & \infty & \infty & \infty & \infty & \infty \\ \infty & \infty & \infty & \infty & 20 & \infty \\ \infty & \infty & \infty & \infty & 22 & 24 \\ \infty & \infty & \infty & \infty & \infty & \infty \\ \infty & 20 & 22 & \infty & \infty & 21 \\ \infty & \infty & 24 & \infty & 21 & \infty \end{bmatrix}$$

step 1: Minimum entry in C is $C_{12}(=C_{21})=15$.

step 2: The addition of $(2,1)$ would form a cycle.

Set $C_{21} = C_{12} = \infty$ and go to step 1.

step 1: Minimum entry in C is $C_{34}(=C_{43}) = 16$.

step 2: The addition of (3,4) breaks both the reliability and the capacity constraints.
Set $C_{34} = C_{43} = \infty$ and go to step 1.

step 1: Minimum entry in C is $C_{42}(=C_{24}) = 17$.

step 2: The addition of (2,4) would form a cycle.
Set $C_{42} = C_{24} = \infty$ and go to step 1.

step 1: Minimum entry in C is $C_{32}(=C_{23}) = 18$.

step 2: The addition of (3,2) breaks the reliability constraint.
Set $C_{32} = C_{23} = \infty$ and go to step 1.

step 1: Minimum entry in C is $C_{31}(=C_{13}) = 19$.

step 2: The addition of (3,1) breaks no constraints so add this line to T.
Set $C_{31} = C_{13} = \infty$.

step 3: T has 5 lines so stop.

The solution obtained is shown in Fig. 3.6. Its cost is 61 units.

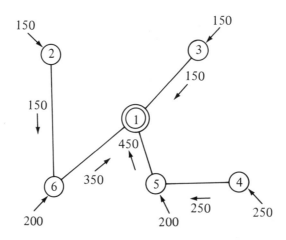

Fig. 3.6

3.3   TERMINAL CONNECTIONS AND CONCENTRATOR SITES IN CENTRALIZED NETWORKS

3.3.1   Description of the problem

In this problem, terminals may be connected directly to the CPU or to concentrators which are in turn connected to the CPU. We assume that terminal locations are known, as are possible sites for concentrators. We must decide which concentrators to use and which terminals are to be connected to which concentrator. (This is the warehouse location problem of Operational Research.)

More formally assume that we have n terminals $T_1, \ldots, T_n$ and m concentrators $C_2, C_3, \ldots, C_{m+1}$ at specified locations. C_1 is again the CPU. With each concentrator $C_j, 2 \leqslant j \leqslant m+1$, there is associated a fixed cost f_j made up of hardware costs plus the cost of connecting C_j to C_1 and a terminal capacity e_j — that is, e_j is the maximum number of terminals which may be connected to C_j. For $C_1, f_1 = 0$ and $e_1 \geqslant n$.

We say that C_j is open if it is in use, closed otherwise.

Let $\alpha_{ij} = 1$ if T_i is connected to C_j and 0 otherwise. Let $\beta_j = 1$ if C_j is open and 0 otherwise. Then the total cost function $\mathscr{C}$ is given by

$$\mathscr{C} = \sum_{j=1}^{m+1} \beta_j f_j + \sum_{i=1}^{n} \sum_{j=1}^{m+1} \alpha_{ij} C_{ij} \; ,$$

where C_{ij} is the cost of connecting T_i to C_j.

We wish to minimize $\mathscr{C}$ subject to the constraints

$$\sum_{j=1}^{m+1} \alpha_{ij} = 1 \; , \qquad 1 \leqslant i \leqslant n \quad \text{and} \quad \sum_{i=1}^{n} \alpha_{ij} \leqslant e_j \; , \qquad 2 \leqslant j \leqslant m+1 \; .$$

This is a 0–1 integer programming problem. There are $2^{(m+1)n}$ possible assignments of 0 and 1 to the α's, so exact solutions are of limited practical usefulness. We look instead at two heuristic algorithms, the ADD [8] and DROP [3] algorithms.

3.3.2 ADD algorithm

step 0: Connect all terminals to C_1
(all concentrators are closed initially).

step 1: For each closed concentrator C_j open C_j and connect up to e_j terminals to it — those giving biggest decrease in cost.
Calculate $\mathscr{C}_j$, the cost of the new configuration obtained by opening C_j.

step 2: Find the smallest $\mathscr{C}_j$ — say $\mathscr{C}_p$. If $\mathscr{C}_p \geqslant$ cost of the current configuration the algorithm terminates.
Otherwise open C_p and repeat step 1.

Example 3.2
Five terminals are to be connected to two concentrators or directly to the CPU as shown in Fig. 3.7. Assume that $e_1 = 5$, $e_2 = e_3 = 2$ and $f_2 = 9$, $f_3 = 8$.

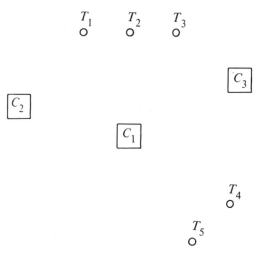

Fig. 3.7

The terminal concentrator connection costs are given in the matrix below.

$$
\begin{array}{c c c c}
 & C_1 & C_2 & C_3 \\
T_1 & 9 & 11 & 12 \\
T_2 & 15 & 10 & 9 \\
T_3 & 16 & 13 & 13 \\
T_4 & 12 & 11 & 13 \\
T_5 & 16 & 14 & 17
\end{array}
$$

step: 0:

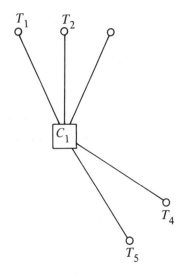

Fig. 3.8

The cost of this configuration is 68 units.

FIRST ITERATION

step 1: Open C_2 {adding 9 units ($=f_2$) immediately to the cost}.
$C_{12} - C_{11} = 2$, $C_{22} - C_{21} = -5$, $C_{32} - C_{31} = -3$, $C_{42} - C_{41} = -1$,
$C_{52} - C_{51} = -2$.
Connecting T_2 and T_3 to C_2 would reduce the cost by 8 units.
Thus $\mathscr{C}_2 = 68 + 9 - 8 = 69$.
Open C_3 {adding 8 units to the cost}.
$C_{13} - C_{11} = 3$, $C_{23} - C_{21} = -6$, $C_{33} - C_{31} = -3$, $C_{42} - C_{41} = 1$,
$C_{53} - C_{51} = 1$.
Connecting T_2 and T_3 to C_3 would reduce the cost by 9 units.
Thus $C_3 = 68 + 8 - 9 = 67$.

step 2: Leave C_3 open. The current configuration is now (see Fig. 3.9)

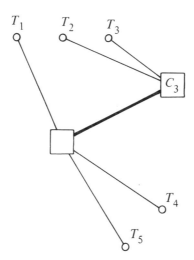

Fig. 3.9

SECOND ITERATION

step 1: Open C_2 {adding 9 to cost}.
$C_{12} - C_{11} = 2$, $C_{42} - C_{41} = -1$, $C_{52} - C_{51} = -2$ and $C_{22} - C_{23} = 1$,
$C_{32} - C_{33} = 0$.

No improvement is possible so the algorithm terminates with the configuration of Fig. 3.9.

3.3.3 DROP algorithm

step 0: For $i = 1, 2, \ldots, n$ connect T_i to one of $C_1, C_2, \ldots, C_{m+1}$ as cheaply as possible.

step 1: For each open concentrator C_j, close C_j and redistribute any terminals connected to it among the remainder (including C_1) in such a way as to decrease cost as much as possible.

Calculate $\mathscr{C}_j$, the cost of the new configuration obtained by closing C_j.

step 2: Find the smallest $\mathscr{C}_j$ — say $\mathscr{C}_p$.

If $\mathscr{C}_p \geq$ cost of the current configuration, the algorithm terminates. Otherwise close C_p and repeat step 1.

Let us redo the above example using this algorithm.

step 0: (see Fig. 3.10).

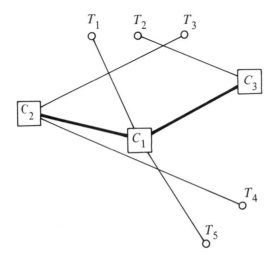

Fig. 3.10

$[T_3$ could be connected to C_2 or C_3; an arbitrary choice was made.$]$

$$\mathscr{C} = C_{11} + C_{23} + C_{32} + C_{42} + C_{51} + f_2 + f_3 = 75 .$$

FIRST ITERATION

step 1 Close C_2 {this subtracts 9 from the cost}.

$C_{31} - C_{32} = 3$, $C_{33} - C_{32} = 0$; $C_{41} - C_{42} = 1$, $C_{43} - C_{42} = 2$.

If we connect T_3 to C_3 and T_4 to C_1, total decrease in cost is 8 units. Thus $\mathscr{C}_2 = 67$.

Close C_3 {subtracting 8 from the cost}.

$C_{21} - C_{23} = 6$ We cannot connect T_2 to C_2 because this would exceed e_2.

If we connect T_2 to C_1, total decrease in cost is 2 units.

Thus $\mathscr{C}_3 = 73$.

step 2: $\mathscr{C}_p$ is $\mathscr{C}_2$ so close C_2.

Configuration is now (see Fig. 3.11)

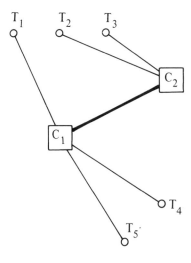

Fig. 3.11

SECOND ITERATION

step 1: If we close C_3 we have the configuration in step 0 of the ADD algorithm, Fig. 3.8, cost 68 units.

Hence the algorithm terminates with the configuration of Fig. 3.11.

Note that, in this simple example, the ADD and DROP algorithms give identical answers.

REFERENCES

[1] K. M. Chandy and R. C. Russell, The Design of Multipoint Linkages in a Teleprocessing Tree Network, *IEEE Transactions on Computing*, **C-21**, 1062–1066 (1972).

[2] L. R. Esau and K. C. Williams, A Method for Approximating the Optimal Network, *IBM Systems Journal*, **5**, 142–147 (1966).

[3] E. Fedlman, F. A. Lehner and T. L. Ray, Warehouse Location under Continuous Economies of Scale, *Management Science*, **12**, 670–684 (1966).

[4] H. N. Gabow, Two Algorithms for Generating Weighted Spanning Trees in Order, *SIAM Journal of Computing*, **6**, 139–150 (1977).

[5] A. Kershenbaum and R. R. Boorstyn, Centralised Teleprocessing Network Design, *Networks*, **13**, 279–293 (1983).

[6] A. Kershenbaum and W. Chou, A Unified Algorithm for Designing Multidrop Teleprocessing Networks, *IEEE Transactions on Communication*, **COM-22**, 1762–1772 (1974).

[7] J. B. Kruskal, On the Shortest Spanning Subtree of a Graph and the Travelling Salesman Problem, *Proc. AMS*, **7**, 48–50 (1965).

[8] A. Kuehn and M. Hamburger, A Heuristic Algorithm for Locating Warehouses, *Managment Science*, **9**, 643–666 (1963).

[9] R. C. Prim, Shortest Connection Networks and some Generalisations, *Bell Systems Technical Journal*, **36**, 1389–1401 (1957).

[10] M. Schwartz, *Computer-communication Network Design and Analysis*, Prentice-Hall, 1977.

EXERCISES

1. Given the cost matrix below, find a minimum cost spanning tree linking the six sites.

$$\begin{bmatrix} - & 12 & 15 & 17 & 24 & 20 \\ 12 & - & 19 & 25 & 22 & 23 \\ 15 & 19 & - & 29 & 27 & 21 \\ 17 & 25 & 29 & - & 18 & 16 \\ 24 & 22 & 27 & 18 & - & 26 \\ 20 & 23 & 21 & 16 & 26 & - \end{bmatrix}$$

Now assume that site 1 is a CPU receiving messages from the other sites and that the traffic generated at sites 2–6 is 40, 25, 25, 20 and 20 data units/sec respectively.

If every line has capacity 50 data units/sec, and if any line is down then no more than two sites are to be unable to communicate with the CPU, verify that the minimum cost spanning tree obtained is an infeasible solution of the constrained problem.

Use the Chandy–Russell algorithm to find an optimum feasible tree and Kruskal's heuristic algorithm to find a near-optimal solution.

2. Given the cost matrix below, find a minimum cost spanning tree linking the seven sites.

$$\begin{bmatrix} - & 7 & 8 & 5 & 24 & 10 & 17 \\ 7 & - & 9 & 15 & 13 & 18 & 14 \\ 8 & 9 & - & 16 & 12 & 6 & 19 \\ 5 & 15 & 16 & - & 20 & 25 & 21 \\ 24 & 13 & 12 & 20 & - & 22 & 27 \\ 10 & 18 & 6 & 25 & 22 & - & 23 \\ 17 & 14 & 19 & 21 & 27 & 23 & - \end{bmatrix}$$

Find an optimum feasible tree and a near-optimal solution to the constrained problem.

The added constraints are:

(i) site 1 is the CPU and the traffic generated at sites 2–7 is 5, 4, 5, 3, 4 and 2 data units/sec. respectively, and

(ii) every line has capacity 10 data units/sec. and, if any line fails no more than two sites are to be unable to communicate with the CPU.

3. Five terminals are to be connected to two concentrators or directly to the CPU as shown in Fig. 3.12. Assume that, in the usual notation, $e_1 = 5$, $e_2 = e_3 = 2$, $f_2 = 11$, $f_3 = 15$.

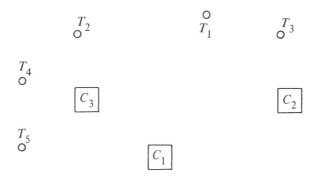

Fig. 3.12

The terminal–concentrator connection costs are given in the matrix below.

$$
\begin{array}{c}
\quad\quad C_1 \quad C_2 \quad C_3 \\
\begin{array}{c}
T_1 \\
T_2 \\
T_3 \\
T_4 \\
T_5
\end{array}
\left[
\begin{array}{ccc}
15 & 12 & 18 \\
11 & 12 & 10 \\
14 & 14 & 12 \\
15 & 11 & 16 \\
19 & 16 & 20
\end{array}
\right].
\end{array}
$$

(i) Use the ADD and DROP algorithms to find near-optimal solutions to this terminal connector problem.

(ii) Repeat if, now, $f_2 = 5$ and $f_3 = 6$.

4

Routing

4.1 INTRODUCTION

The problem of efficient message routing in a communication network is a complex one — see, for example, [1] and [10].

We shall concentrate in this chapter on what is normally referred to as shortest-path, or least-cost, routing. Even with this restriction there are choices to be made, for instance whether the algorithm is to be run centrally by a Network Control Centre or whether each site is to run the algorithm separately. A critical choice is that of the weight function; the weights could be the lengths of the communication lines, measures of congestion in the lines, costs of using the lines, etc. or, more usually, a combination of a number of factors. Schwartz and Stern [11] provide an overview of routing techniques in a variety of networks, and the interested reader is referred to this paper. We shall concentrate on presenting basic routing algorithms in a straightforward way.

If (i_1,i_2), (i_2,i_3), . . . , (i_{r-1},i_r) is a path in the given network (consisting of arcs or edges, depending on whether the network is directed or undirected) from i_1 to i_r, the *weight* of the path is $w(i_1,i_2) + w(i_2,i_3) + \ldots + w(i_{r-1},i_r)$. We shall normally be looking for paths of minimum weight from a given start node, s, to all other nodes in the network.

4.2 NETWORKS WITH ALL ARC (OR EDGE) WEIGHTS POSITIVE

In this case it is normal to use length instead of weight and shortest path instead of minimum weight path.

4.2.1 Dijkstra's algorithm [4]

The algorithm assigns a label $l(i)$ to each node i in the network. The label can be *permanent* — in which case it is the length of the shortest path from s to i, or *temporary* — in which case the length of the shortest path from s to i is less than or equal to $l(i)$.

Suppose that we know that the shortest path from s to j is of length $l(j)$, that is $l(j)$ is a permanent label, and that k is a neighbour of j for which the label $l(k)$ is temporary. The shortest path from s to k via j has length $l(j) + w(j,k)$ and, if this is less than $l(k)$, we can replace $l(k)$ by this number.

This process is repeated until every node in the network has a permanent label.

The algorithm is another example of a greedy algorithm.

We may state Dijkstra's algorithm as follows.

DIJKSTRA'S ALGORITHM

step 0: Assign a temporary label $l(i) = \infty$ to all nodes $i \neq s$.

Set $l(s) = 0$ and $p = s$. Make $l(p)$ permanent.

step 1: For each node i with a temporary label,

$$\text{let } l(i) = \begin{cases} \min \{l(i), l(p) + w(p,i)\} & \text{if } (p,i) \text{ exists} \\ l(i) & \text{otherwise} \end{cases}.$$

step 2: Find the node j with the smallest temporary label. (Any one in case of ties.)

Set $p = j$; make $l(p)$ permanent.

step 3: If all labels are permanent, stop.

Otherwise go to step 1.

To estimate the efficiency of Dijkstra's algorithm we note that step 1 is performed $n - 1$ times.

There are, in the worst case, $(n - 1)$ additions and $(n - 1)$ comparisons the first time, $(n - 2)$ of each the second time and so on. The total number of additions and comparisons is, therefore, $2((n - 1) + (n - 2)2 + \ldots + 1) = n(n - 1)$. Thus the efficiency of Dijkstra's algorithm is $O(n^2)$.

If we require the length of the shortest path from s to some specific node t, say, we terminate the algorithm when t has a permanent label.

If we wish to construct the shortest paths rather than just calculate their lengths, we can achieve this by assigning a second label to every node other than s.

Initially, this label is set to 0. If $l(p) + w(p,i) < l(i)$, the second label is changed to p. When the algorithm terminates, if, for example, the second label on node t is u, the penultimate node to be visited on the shortest path from s to t is u. In this context, node u is called the *predecessor node* of node t. The shortest paths are thus constructed from back to front.

Example 4.1

Find the shortest paths from node 1 to all other nodes in the network of Fig. 4.1. (Note that we adopt the conversion that two arcs (i,j) and (j,i) of equal length are drawn as an edge (i,j) of that length.)

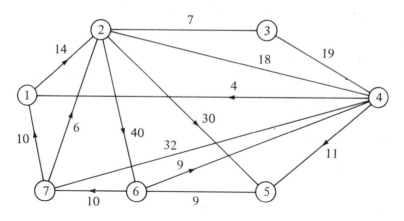

Fig. 4.1

The working is shown on Fig. 4.2.

The second label is shown as a subscript to the first and, when labels are made permanent, they are enclosed in a box.

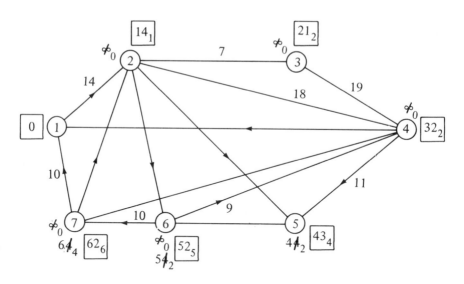

Fig. 4.2.

If, for example, we want the shortest path from node 1 to node 7, it is of length 62 units and, using the subscripts, the path is

$$(1,2), (2,4), (4,5), (5,6), (6,7) \ .$$

The calculations may also be carried out using matrix notation. This form of Dijkstra's algorithm may be stated as follows.

DIJKSTRA'S MATRIX ALGORITHM

step 0: Initialize. Let $W = [w_{ij}]$ be defined by

$$w_{ij} = \begin{cases} w(i,j) \text{ if } (i,j) \text{ exists} \\ \infty \text{ otherwise} \end{cases}.$$

step 1: Cross out all entries in column s and make a mark on row s.

step 2: Scan all marked rows and select the minimum entry.
(Any one in case of ties, crossed out entries are ignored.)

step 3: If w_{kl} is the minimum entry, cross out column l and make a mark on row l.
Add w_{kl} to each entry in row l.

step 4: If all columns are crossed out, stop.
Otherwise go to step 2.

When the algorithm terminates, if w_{kl} is an entry selected in step 2, w_{kl} is the length of the shortest path from node s to node l and node k is the predecessor node of node l.
 Example 2.2 is redone below by this method.

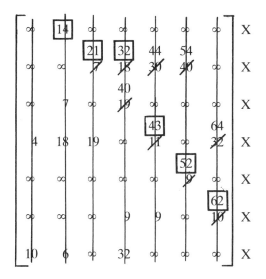

It can be easily be seen that the answers are identical with those obtained previously. For example, the shortest path from node 1 to node 7 is of length 62 units and, as the entry 62 is in the (6,7) position in the matrix, the predecessor node of node 7 is node 6.

4.2.2   Associated problems

There are two path problems which are closely related to the shortest-path problem and we examine them now before proceeding.

(i)   *The most reliable path*

Suppose that $w(i,j)$ is a measure of the *reliability* of (i,j) — normally the probability that the line is operational. Then, assuming that reliabilities of different arcs (or edges) are independent events from a statistical viewpoint, we define the *reliability* $R(P)$ of a path P by

$$R(P) = \prod_{(i,j)\in P} w(i,j)$$

and require the paths from s to all other nodes which have the greatest reliability. Taking logs:

$$\log(R(P)) = \sum_{(i,j)\in P} \log(w(i,j)) .$$

If we substitute $v(i,j) = -\log(w(i,j))$ we may use Dijkstra's algorithm to find the shortest paths from s to all other nodes in the network with weight function v. $(0 < w(i,j) < 1$ so $\log w(i,j)$ is negative. We can multiply all the logs, appropriately rounded, by a power of 10 sufficient to make v an integer-valued weight function.) These correspond to the most reliable paths in the original network. See [3].

(ii)   *The bottleneck problem*

We define the *bottleneck* of a path to be the weight of the least-weight arc (or edge) in the path.

If $w(i,j)$ is a measure of the capacity of (i,j), the paths of greatest capacity — or best bottleneck paths — from s to all other nodes are those which allow the greatest amount of information per unit time to be sent from node s to the remainder.

We can obtain an algorithm for this problem by making suitable adjustments to Dijkstra's algorithm. The weight of a path is now obtained by minimization rather than by addition, and one path is preferred to another if its weight is larger rather than if its weight is smaller.

We may state the Best Bottleneck algorithm as follows:

BEST BOTTLENECK ALGORITHM

step 0:   Assign a temporary label $l(i) = 0$ to all nodes $i \neq s$.
Set $l(s) = \infty$ and $p = s$.
Make $l(p)$ *permanent*.

step 1:   For each i with a temporary label,

$$\text{let } l(i) = \begin{cases} \max\{l(i), \min(l(p), w(p,i))\} \text{ if } (p,i) \text{ exists} \\ l(i) \text{ otherwise} \end{cases}$$

step 2:   Find the node j with the largest temporary label.
          (Any one in case of ties.)
          Set $p = j$; make $l(p)$ permanent.

step 3:   If all labels are permanent, stop.
          Otherwise go to step 1.

If we wish to construct the best bottleneck paths then we can, as before, assign a second label to each node.
    Clearly the efficiency of this algorithm is also $O(n^2)$.

Example 4.2
Find the best bottleneck paths from node 1 to all other nodes in the network of Fig. 4.3. The arc weights are measures of capacity.

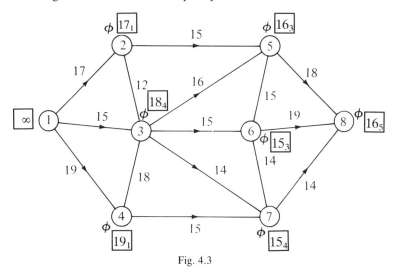

Fig. 4.3

    The best bottleneck path from node 1 to node 8, for example, has bottleneck 16 and is (1,4), (4,3) (3,5), (5,8).

Note
This algorithm may also be carried out using matrix notation. The restatement is left as an exercise. (i) and (ii) may be combined to give the path of *greatest expected capacity*. See [3] for worked example.

4.2.3 Pollack's algorithm [8]

It is often useful to know not just the shortest path from s to some other node t, say, of the network but also the second, third, etc. in case one or more paths are unusable owing to line and/or site failures. In addition, if a path with a particular property is required — for example, one which must visit a specified intermediate node — it is generally easier to list the paths in ascending order of length until one with the required property is encountered than to try to include extra conditions in Dijkstra's algorithm. (We shall, however, look briefly in the appendix to this chapter at a search tree method which can be used in simple cases.)

Pollack's algorithm for finding the second shorthest path is based on the (obvious) result that it must differ from the shortest path in at least one arc (or edge) and will be the shortest path satisfying this extra condition.

To determine the second shortest path from s to t, Dijkstra's algorithm is first used to find the shortest path from s to t. Each arc (or edge) on this path is omitted in turn, and the shortest path from s to t is found in each of the modified networks. The shortest of the paths obtained is the second shortest path through the original network.

We may state Pollack's algorithm as follows:

POLLACK'S ALGORITHM

step 0:   Find, using Dijkstra's algorithm, the shortest path from s to t.
Suppose the path is (i_0,i_1), (i_1,i_2), $\ldots$, (i_{q-1},i_q),
where $i_0 = s$ and $i_q = t$.
Call (i_{j-1},i_j) arc (or edge) j; $1 \leqslant j \leqslant q$.
Let $j = 1$ and $L = \infty$.

step 1:   Omit arc (or edge) j and find, using Dijkstra's algorithm, the shortest path from s to t in the modified network.
Denote the length of this path by l_j.

step 2:   If $l_j < L$, put $L = l_j$ and store this path.

step 3:   If $j = q$, stop.
Otherwise let $j = j + 1$ and go to step 1.

When the algorithm terminates, L is length of the second shortest path and the path itself is the one stored.

In the worst case the shortest path from s to t would consist of $n - 1$ arcs (or edges) meaning that Dijkstra's algorithm would have to be employed n times in all.

Thus the efficiency of Pollack's algorithm is $O(n^3)$.

Example 4.3
Find the second shortest path from node 1 to node 7 in the network of Fig. 4.1.

We recall that the shortest path from node 1 to node 7 is $(1,2)$, $(2,4)$, $(4,5)$, $(5,6)$, $(6,7)$.

Omitting arc 1: there is no path from node 1 to node 7.
Omitting arc 2: shortest path is (1,2), (2,5), (5,6), (6,7); length 63
Omitting arc 3: shortest path is also (1,2), (2,5), (5,6), (6,7); length 63
Omitting arc 4: shortest path is (1,2), (2,4), (4,7); length 64
Omitting arc 5: shortest path is also (1,2), (2,4), (4,7); length 64.

Thus the second shortest path from node 1 to node 7 is of length 63 units and is (1,2), (2,5), (5,6), (6,7). The reader is invited to supply the details of the above calculations.

If we wish to find the third shortest path from node s to node t we can use the same approach as above, but this time omitting two arcs (or edges) each time — one from the shortest, and one from the second shortest, path. To find the fourth shortest we omit three arcs (or edges) and so on. This method is only suitable for finding the kth shortest path where k is at most 3. If $k > 3$ it is better to use a more sophisticated approach; see, for example, [7], [9] or [12].

4.3 NETWORKS WITH POSITIVE AND NEGATIVE ARC WEIGHTS

4.3.1 The need for a new algorithm

In this case $w(i,j)$ could, for instance, represent the cost of using (i,j); then, if using (i,j) is profitable, $w(i,j)$ would be negative. Alternatively, $w(i,j)$ could measure the energy absorbed in transforming state i to state j in a physical system; then, if energy is released in transforming i to j, $w(i,j)$ is negative. In this context we usually talk of the least-cost path and its cost rather than the shortest path and its length.

Dijkstra's algorithm can fail if $w(i,j) < 0$ for at least one pair of nodes i and j.

As a simple counterexample, consider the network in Fig. 4.4. The least-cost path

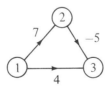

Fig. 4.4

from node 1 to node 3 is (obviously) (1,2), (2,3), cost 2 units, but, it we use Dijkstra's algorithm, node 3 is labelled permanently with the label 4 at the first stage. As the reader may easily verify, adding a number to each arc weight to make them all positive and then applying Dijkstra's algorithm will not work either. The trouble is that Dijkstra's algorithm fixes labels as permanent too soon. We need, therefore, a new algorithm to solve this problem. One such is as follows.

4.3.2   Ford's algorithm [6]

This allows negative arc costs provided that there are no cycles in the network around which the cost is negative. For, if such a cycle exists, the cost of any path which includes a node of the cycle could be made smaller than any negative number we choose by traversing the cycle as many times as necessary. It follows, then, that an undirected network *cannot* include edges with negative costs.

In Ford's algorithm we again assign a label to each node and attempt to decrease it. The difference here is that no label is considered permanent until no label can be decreased further. The algorithm, then, necessarily finds the least-cost paths from s to every other node.

We may state Ford's algorithm as follows.

FORD'S ALGORITHM

step 0:   Assign labels $l(s) = 0$, $l(i) = \infty$ for $i \neq s$.

step 1:   For each node i and each node p for which an arc (p,i) exists in the network, determine $\min\{l(i), l(p) + w(p,i)\}$.

step 2:   If, for all i and p, $\min\{l(i), l(p) + w(p,i)\} = l(i)$, stop.
Otherwise, for the first pair (p,i) for which this is not true, set $l(i) = l(p) + w(p,i)$ and go to step 1.

When the algorithm terminates, $l(i)$ is the cost of the least-cost path from s to i. If we wish to determine the path itself we can assign, as in Dijkstra's algorithm, a second label to each node.

It is essential, especially when using a computer, to determine any negative cost cycle as early as possible because, if any exist, the algorithm will not terminate. If node s lies on such a cycle then, at some stage, $l(s) < 0$ and we would then stop. For the remaining nodes, if there is no negative cost cycle in the network, the maximum number of times a label can change is $n - 1$ — the least-cost path from s to that node could pass through every other node and contain $n - 1$ arcs. Thus we also stop if any label is changed n times.

The efficiency of Ford's algorithm is — see for example [2] — O(n^3).

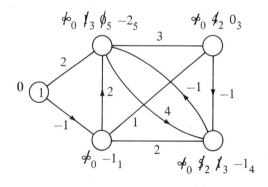

Fig. 4.5

Example 4.4

Find the least-cost path from node 1 to all other nodes in the network of Fig. 4.5.

The working is shown in Fig. 4.5 and we see that the least-cost path from node 1 to node 2, for example, is (1,3), (3,4), (4,5), (5,2), cost -2 units.

4.3.3   Floyd's algorithm [5]

This is a method of solving the *multiterminal path problem* — that is, the problem of finding the least-cost paths between every pair of nodes in the network. Clearly, we can achieve this by running one of the earlier algorithms n times with a different node each time as s, but that approach turns out to be less efficient.

We number the nodes $1, 2, \ldots, n$, and for any pair i and j, we compare the least-cost path from i directly to j with, successively, that obtained by visiting node 1 also, that obtained by visiting node 1 and/or node 2, and so on.

The costs are stored in a matrix and, at a stage $k \geqslant 1$, the entry $w_k(i,j)$ in the matrix $W_k = [w_k(i,j)]$ is the cost of the least-cost path from node i to node j visiting some or all of the nodes $1, 2, \ldots, k$.

We may state Floyd's algorithm thus

FLOYD'S ALGORITHM

step 0:   Initialize. Define $W_0 = [w_0(i,j)]$ by

$$w_0(i,j) = \begin{cases} w(i,j) \text{ if } (i,j) \text{ exists} \\ 0 \text{ if } i = j \\ \infty \text{ otherwise} \end{cases}$$

and $P = [p_{ij}]$ by $p_{ij} = i$; $1 \leqslant i,j \leqslant n$.
Let $k = 0$.

step 1:   Obtain W_{k+1} by the rule
$$w_{k+1}(i,j) = \min\{w_k(i,j), w_k(i,k+1) + w_k(k+1,j)\}.$$

If $w_{k+1}(i,j) < w_k(i,j)$, let $p_{ij} = p_{k+1j}$.

step 2:   If $k = n - 1$, stop. Otherwise, let $k = k + 1$ and go to step 1.

When the algorithm terminates, $w_n(i,j)$ is the cost of the least-cost path from node i to node j and p_{ij} is the predecessor node of node j on the least-cost path from i to j. The final P matrix is often called the *predecessor matrix*.

The number of operations required to carry out step 1 is of the order of n^2 making the efficiency of Floyd's algorithm O(n^3).

[Note that this is certainly an improvement on running Ford's algorithm n times.]

Example 4.5
Find the least-cost paths between all pairs of nodes in the network of Fig. 4.6.

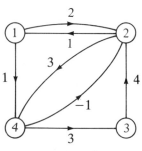

Fig. 4.6

$$
\text{step 0:} \quad W_0 = \begin{bmatrix} 0 & 2 & \infty & 1 \\ 1 & 0 & \infty & 3 \\ \infty & 4 & 0 & \infty \\ \infty & -1 & 3 & 0 \end{bmatrix} \qquad P = \begin{bmatrix} 1 & 1 & 1 & 1 \\ 2 & 2 & 2 & 2 \\ 3 & 3 & 3 & 3 \\ 4 & 4 & 4 & 4 \end{bmatrix}
$$

$k = 0$.

step 1: $\quad w_1(i,j) = \min\{w_0(i,j), w_0(i,1) + w_0(1,j)\}$.

$w_1(1,1) = \min\{0, 0 + 0\} = 0$. $\qquad w_1(1,3) = \min\{\infty, 0 + \infty\} = \infty$.
$w_1(1,2) = \min\{2, 0 + 2\} = 2$. $\qquad w_1(1,4) = \min\{1, 0 + 1\} = 1$.

$w_1(2,1) = \min\{1, 1 + 0\} = 1$.

$w_1(2,2) = \min\{0, 1 + 2\} = 0$. $\qquad w_1(2,3) = \min\{\infty, 1 + \infty\} = \infty$.
$\qquad\qquad\qquad\qquad\qquad\qquad\qquad w_1(2,4) = \min\{3, 1 + 1\} = 2$.

Change p_{24} to p_{14}, that is, change the entry 2 in the (2,4) position in P to 1, the entry in the (1,4) position.

$w_1(3,1) = \min\{\infty, \infty + 0\} = \infty$. $\quad w_1(3,3) = \min\{0, \infty + \infty\} = 0$.
$w_1(3,2) = \min\{4, \infty + 2\} = 4$. $\qquad w_1(3,4) = \min\{\infty, \infty + 1\} = \infty$.

$w_1(4,1) = \min\{\infty, \infty + 0\} = \infty$.

$w_1(4,2) = \min\{-1, \infty + 2\} = -1$. $\quad w_1(4,3) = \min\{3, \infty + \infty\} = 3$.
$\qquad\qquad\qquad\qquad\qquad\qquad\qquad w_1(4,4) = \min\{0, \infty + 1\} = 0$.

$$
\text{Then } W_1 \begin{bmatrix} 0 & 2 & \infty & 1 \\ 1 & 0 & \infty & 2 \\ \infty & 4 & 0 & \infty \\ \infty & -1 & 3 & 0 \end{bmatrix} \text{ and } P = \begin{bmatrix} 1 & 1 & 1 & 1 \\ 2 & 2 & 2 & 1 \\ 3 & 3 & 3 & 3 \\ 4 & 4 & 4 & 4 \end{bmatrix}
$$

step 2: $k = 0 \neq 3$. Let $k = 1$ and go to step 1.

step 2: $w_2(i,j) = \min\{w_1(i,j), w_1(i,2) + w_1(2,j)\}$.

$w_2(1,1) = \min\{0, 2 + 1\} = 0.$ $w_2(1,3) = \min\{\infty, 2 + \infty\} = \infty$.
$w_2(1,2) = \min\{2, 2 + 0\} = 2.$ $w_2(1,4) = \min\{1, 2 + 2\} = 1.$

$w_2(2,1) = \min\{1, 0 + 1) = 1.$ $w_2(2,3) = \min\{\infty, 0 + \infty\} = \infty$.
$w_2(2,2) = \min\{0, 0 + 0\} = 0.$ $w_2(2,4) = \min\{2, 0 + 2\} = 2.$

$w_2(3,1) = \min\{\infty, 4 + 1\} = 5.$ $w_2(3,3) = \min\{0, 4 + \infty\} = 0.$
Change p_{31} to p_{21} (3 to 2). $w_2(3,4) = \min\{\infty, 4 + 2\} = 6.$
$w_2(3,2) = \min\{4, 4 + 0\} = 4.$ Change p_{34} to p_{24} (3 to 1).

$w_2(4,1) = \min\{\infty, -1 + 1\} = 0.$ $w_2(4,3) = \min\{3, -1 + \infty\} = 3.$
Change p_{41} to p_{21} (4 to 2). $w_2(4,4) = \min\{0, -1 + 2\} = 0.$
$w_2(4,2) = \min\{-1, -1 + 0\} = -1.$

Then $W_2 = \begin{bmatrix} 0 & 2 & \infty & 1 \\ 1 & 0 & \infty & 2 \\ 5 & 4 & 0 & 6 \\ 0 & -1 & 3 & 0 \end{bmatrix}$ and $P = \begin{bmatrix} 1 & 1 & 1 & 1 \\ 2 & 2 & 2 & 1 \\ 2 & 3 & 3 & 1 \\ 2 & 4 & 4 & 4 \end{bmatrix}$.

step 2: $k = 1 \neq 3$. Let $k = 2$ and go to step 1.

step 1: $w_3(i,j) = \min\{w_2(i,j), w_2(i,3) + w_2(3,j)\}$.

$w_3(1,1) = \min\{0, \infty + 5\} = 0.$ $w_3(1,3) = \min\{\infty, \infty + 0\} = \infty$.
$w_3(1,2) = \min\{2, \infty + 4\} = 2.$ $w_3(1,4) = \min\{1, \infty + 6\} = 1.$

$w_3(2,1) = \min\{1, \infty + 5\} = 1.$ $w_3(2,3) = \min\{\infty, \infty + 0\} = \infty$.
$w_3(2,2) = \min\{0, \infty + 4\} = 0.$ $w_3(2,4) = \min\{2, \infty + 6\} = 2.$

$w_3(3,1) = \min\{5, 0 + 5\} = 5.$ $w_3(3,3) = \min\{0, 0 + 0\} = 0.$
$w_3(3,2) = \min\{4, 0 + 4\} = 4.$ $w_3(3,4) = \min\{6, 0 + 6\} = 6.$

$w_3(4,1) = \min\{0, 3 + 5\} = 0.$ $w_3(4,3) = \min\{3, 3 + 0\} = 3.$
$w_3(4,2) = \min\{-1, 3 + 4) = -1.$ $w_3(4,4) = \min\{0, 3 + 6\} = 0.$

Then $W_3 = \begin{bmatrix} 0 & 2 & \infty & 1 \\ 1 & 0 & \infty & 2 \\ 5 & 4 & 0 & 6 \\ 0 & -1 & 3 & 0 \end{bmatrix}$ and $P = \begin{bmatrix} 1 & 1 & 1 & 1 \\ 2 & 2 & 2 & 1 \\ 2 & 3 & 3 & 1 \\ 2 & 2 & 4 & 4 \end{bmatrix}$.

step 2: $k = 2 \neq 3$. Let $k = 3$ and go to step 1.

step 1: $w_4(i,j) = \min\{w_3(i,j), w_3(i,4) + w_3(4,j)\}.$

$w_4(1,1) = \min\{0, 1+0\} = 0.$ $w_4(1,3) = \min\{\infty, 1+3\} = 4.$

$w_4(1,2) = \min\{2, 1+(-1)\} = 0.$ Change p_{13} to p_{43} (1 to 4)
Change p_{12} to p_{42} (1 to 4). $w_4(1,4) = \min\{1, 1+0\} = 1.$

$w_4(2,1) = \min\{1, 2+0\} = 1.$ $w_4(2,3) = \min\{\infty, 2+3\} = 5.$
$w_4(2,2) = \min\{0, 2+(-1)\} = 0.$ Change p_{23} to p_{43} (2 to 4).
                                           $w_4(2,4) = \min\{2, 2+0\} = 2.$

$w_4(3,1) = \min\{5, 6+0\} = 5.$ $w_4(3,3) = \min\{0, 6+3\} = 0.$
$w_4(3,2) = \min\{4, 6+(-1)\} = 4.$ $w_4(3,4) = \min\{6, 6+0\} = 6.$

$w_4(4,1) = \min\{0, 0+0\} = 0.$ $w_4(4,3) = \min\{3, 0+3\} = 3.$
$w_4(4,2) = \min\{-1, 0+(-1)\} = -1.$ $w_4(4,4) = \min\{0, 0+0\} = 0.$

Then $W_4 = \begin{bmatrix} 0 & 0 & 4 & 1 \\ 1 & 0 & 5 & 2 \\ 5 & 4 & 0 & 6 \\ 0 & -1 & 3 & 0 \end{bmatrix}$ and $P = \begin{bmatrix} 1 & 4 & 4 & 1 \\ 2 & 2 & 4 & 1 \\ 2 & 3 & 3 & 1 \\ 2 & 4 & 4 & 4 \end{bmatrix}.$

step 2: $k = 3$, stop.

W_4 is the matrix whose (i,j) entry is the cost of the least-cost path from node i to node j. Any such path may be constructed using the predecessor matrix P. For example, the least-cost path from node 3 to node 4 costs 6 units — $w_4(3,4) = 6$. To construct the path, $p_{34} = 1$ so the predecessor node of node 4 is node 1. Now look at the entry p_{31}; this is 2 so the predecessor node of node 1 is node 2. Finally p_{32} is 3 so the path is (3,2), (2,1), (1,4).

Notes
(i) It is again important to determine any negative cost cycles which may exist. If $w_k(i,i) < 0$ for some k and i it means that node i lies on a negative cost cycle; stop.
(ii) Once the algorithm is clearly understood we may perform the calculations quite easily on the W matrices. For instance, when forming W_1 from W_0 we compare the (i,j) entry in W_0 with the sum of the entries in the $(i,1)$ and $(1,j)$ positions. If, then, we highlight row 1 and column 1 of W_0 we compare any non-highlighted entry with the sum of the highlighted entries in its row and its column. (Highlighted entries remain unchanged.)

$$
\begin{bmatrix}
0 & 2 & \infty & \underline{1} \\
\underline{1} & 0 & \infty & \underline{3} \\
\infty & 4 & 0 & \infty \\
\infty & -1 & 3 & 0
\end{bmatrix}.
$$

In general, when forming W_{k+1} from W_k, highlight row $(k+1)$ and column $(k+1)$ in W_k and proceed as explained above for the formation of W_1 from W_0.

APPENDIX A: WARSHALL'S ALGORITHM [12]

This algorithm constructs the reachability matrix of a directed graph more efficiently than by calculating power of the adjacency matrix. We may state it as follows.

WARSHALL'S ALGORITHM

step O: Initialize. Let $W_0 = [w_0(i,j)]$ be the adjacency matrix of the graph.
Let $k = 0$.

step 1:   Obtain W_{k+1} by the rule
$$w_{k+1}(i,j) = w_k(i,j) \oplus (w_k(i,k+1) \otimes w_k(k+1,j)) .$$

step 2:   If $k = n - 1$, stop.
Otherwise, let $k = k + 1$ and go to step 1.

We see that, for $k \geq 1$, $w_k(i,j)$ is equal to 1 if, and only if, there is a path from node i to node j visiting some or all of the nodes, 1, 2, ..., k. Thus, when the algorithm terminates, W_n is the reachability matrix of the graph.

The efficiency of Warshall's algorithm is also $O(n^3)$.

Example 4.6
Use Warshall's algorithm to determine whether the directed graph whose adjacency matrix is given below is strongly connected.

step 0: $W_0 = A = \begin{bmatrix} 0 & 0 & 0 & 0 & 1 \\ 1 & 0 & 1 & 0 & 0 \\ 1 & 1 & 0 & 1 & 0 \\ 1 & 0 & 0 & 0 & 0 \\ 0 & 0 & 0 & 1 & 0 \end{bmatrix}$ Let $k = 0$.

step 1: $\underline{w_1(i,j) = w_0(i,j)\oplus(w_0(i,1)\otimes w_0(1,j)).}$

At each iteration of step 1 we shall list only those entries which change.

$$w_1(2,5) = w_0(2,5)\oplus(w_0(2,1)\otimes w_0(1,5)) = 0\oplus(1\otimes1) = 1.$$
$$w_1(3,5) = w_0(3,5)\oplus(w_0(3,1)\otimes w_0(1,5)) = 0\oplus(1\otimes1) = 1.$$
$$w_1(4,5) = w_0(4,5)\oplus(w_0(4,1)\otimes w_0(1,5)) = 0\oplus(1\otimes1) = 1.$$

$$\text{Then } W_1 = \begin{bmatrix} 0 & 0 & 0 & 0 & 1 \\ 1 & 0 & 1 & 0 & 1 \\ 1 & 1 & 0 & 1 & 1 \\ 1 & 0 & 0 & 0 & 1 \\ 0 & 0 & 0 & 1 & 0 \end{bmatrix}.$$

step 2: $k = 0 \neq 4$. Let $k = 1$ and go to step 1.

step 1: $\underline{w_2(i,j) = w_1(i,j)\oplus(w_1(i,2)\otimes w_1(2,j)).}$
$$w_2(3,3) = w_1(3,3)\oplus(w_1(3,2)\otimes w_1(2,3)) = 0\oplus(1\oplus1) = 1.$$

$$\text{Then } W_2 = \begin{bmatrix} 0 & 0 & 0 & 0 & 1 \\ 1 & 0 & 1 & 0 & 1 \\ 1 & 1 & 1 & 1 & 1 \\ 1 & 0 & 0 & 0 & 1 \\ 0 & 0 & 0 & 1 & 0 \end{bmatrix}.$$

step 2: $k = 1 \neq 4$. Let $k = 2$ and go to step 1.

step 2: $\underline{w_3(i,j) = w_2(i,j)\oplus(w_2(i,3)\otimes w_2(3,j)).}$
$$w_3(2,2) = w_2(2,2)\oplus(w_2(2,3)\otimes w_2(3,2)) = 0\oplus(1\otimes1) = 1.$$
$$w_3(2,4) = w_2(2,4)\oplus(w_2(2,3)\otimes w_2(3,4)) = 0\oplus(1\otimes1) = 1.$$

$$\text{Then } W_3 = \begin{bmatrix} 0 & 0 & 0 & 0 & 1 \\ 1 & 1 & 1 & 1 & 1 \\ 1 & 1 & 1 & 1 & 1 \\ 1 & 0 & 0 & 0 & 1 \\ 0 & 0 & 0 & 1 & 0 \end{bmatrix}.$$

step 2: $k = 2 \neq 4$. Let $k = 3$ and go to step 1.

step 1: $w_4(i,j) = w_3(i,j) \oplus (w_3(i,4) \otimes w_3(4,j))$.

$w_4(5,1) = w_3(5,1) \oplus (w_3(5,4) \otimes w_3(4,1)) = 0 \oplus (1 \otimes 1) = 1$.

$w_4(5,5) = w_3(5,5) \oplus (w_3(5,4) \otimes w_3(4,5)) = 0 \oplus (1 \otimes 1) = 1$.

Then $W_4 = \begin{bmatrix} 0 & 0 & 0 & 0 & 1 \\ 1 & 1 & 1 & 1 & 1 \\ 1 & 1 & 1 & 1 & 1 \\ 1 & 0 & 0 & 0 & 1 \\ 1 & 0 & 0 & 1 & 1 \end{bmatrix}$.

step 2: $k = 3 \neq 4$. Let $k = 4$ and go to step 1.

step 1: $w_5(i,j) = w_4(i,j) \oplus (w_4(i,5) \otimes w_4(5,j))$.

$w_5(1,1) = w_4(1,1) \oplus (w_4(1,5) \otimes w_4(5,1)) = 0 \oplus (1 \otimes 1) = 1$.

$w_5(1,4) = w_4(1,4) \oplus (w_4(1,5) \otimes w_4(5,4)) = 0 \oplus (1 \otimes 1) = 1$.

$w_5(4,4) = w_4(4,4) \oplus (w_4(4,5) \otimes w_4(5,4)) = 0 \oplus (1 \otimes 1) = 1$.

Then $W_5 = \begin{bmatrix} 1 & 0 & 0 & 1 & 1 \\ 1 & 1 & 1 & 1 & 1 \\ 1 & 1 & 1 & 1 & 1 \\ 1 & 0 & 0 & 1 & 1 \\ 1 & 0 & 0 & 1 & 1 \end{bmatrix}$.

step 2: $k = 4$, stop.

$R = W_5$ and, since R does not consist entirely of ones, the graph is not strongly connected.

The reader should draw the digraph and verify by observation that it is not strongly connected.

Note

We may again perform the calculations on the W matrices. When forming W_{k+1} from W_k, highlight row $(k + 1)$ and column $(k + 1)$ in W_k and consider any non-highlighted 0 entry. If the highlighted elements in its row and its column are both 1, the 0 may be changed to 1; otherwise it remains 0.

APPENDIX B

As mentioned in section 4.3 it is possible in simple cases to use a search tree method
to obtain a path from *s* to *t* having a particular property — usually visiting a specified
intermediate node.

All arc weights are positive and the network is directed.

Example 4.7
By drawing up a search tree, find the shortest path from node 1 to node 8 in the
network of Fig. 4.7 which includes node 4. The search tree is shown in Fig. 4.8.

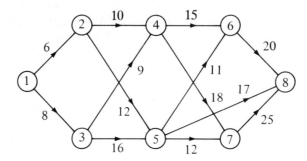

Fig. 4.7

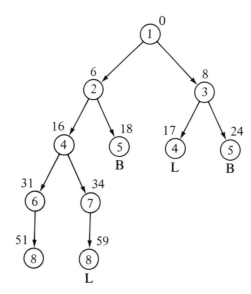

Fig. 4.8

A node superscript shows the length of the shortest path from node 1 to that node
by following the arrows. The letter L under a node means that that particular branch
of the tree will not lead to the required shortest path and that there is, therefore, no
point in continuing with it. For example, (1,3),(3,4) is of length 17 whereas

(1,2),(2,4) is of length 16. Thus node 4, which lies on the particular shortest path we are seeking, must be reached via node 2 rather than node 3.

The letter B under a node means that that particular branch of the tree has by-passed the node whose inclusion is necessary — node 4 in this example.

From Fig. 4.8 the shortest path from node 1 to node 8 which includes node 4 is (1,2),(2,4),(4,6),(6,8), length 51 units.

REFERENCES

[1] D. Bertsekas and R. Gallager, *Data Networks*, Prentice-Hall, 1987.

[2] T. B. Boffey, *Graph Theory in Operations Research*, Macmillan, 1982.

[3] N. Christofides, *Graph Theory: an Algorithmic Approach*, Academic Press, 1975.

[4] E. W. Dijkstra, A Note on Two Problems in Connection with Graphs, *Num. Math.*, **1**, 269–271 (1959).

[5] R. W. Floyd, Algorithm 97 (Shortest Path), *Comm. of Assoc. for Computing Machinery*, **5**, 345 (1962).

[6] L. R. Ford, Network Flow Theory, Rand Corp. Report P-923 (1956).

[7] N. Katoh, T. Ibaraki and H. Mine, An Efficient Algorithm for k Shortest Simple Paths, *Networks*, **12**, 411–427 (1982).

[8] M. Pollack, The kth Best Route through a Network, *Operations Research*, **9**, 578–580 (1961).

[9] M. Pollack, Solutions of the kth Best Route through a Network — a Review, *Journal of Math. Analysis and Applications*, **3**, 547–559 (1961).

[10] M. Schwartz, *Computer-communication Network Design and Analysis*, Prentice-Hall, 1977.

[11] *M. Schwartz and T. E. Stern, Routing Techniques used in Computer Communication Networks, IEEE Trans. on Comm.*, **COM-28**, 539–552 (1980).

[12] J. Y. Yen, Finding the kth Shortest Loopless Paths in a Network, *Mangement Sci.*, **17** 712–716 (1971).

[13] S. Warshall, A Theorem on Boolean Matrices, *J. ACM*, **9**, 11–12 (1962).

EXERCISES

1. The distance matrix of a communication network is shown below.

$$
\begin{bmatrix}
- & 5 & 8 & 6 & \infty & \infty & \infty & \infty \\
5 & - & 2 & \infty & 9 & \infty & \infty & \infty \\
8 & 2 & - & 3 & 7 & 6 & 5 & \infty \\
6 & \infty & 3 & - & \infty & 6 & 8 & \infty \\
\infty & 9 & 7 & \infty & - & 1 & \infty & 7 \\
\infty & \infty & 6 & 6 & 1 & - & 1 & 8 \\
\infty & \infty & 5 & 8 & \infty & 1 & - & 6 \\
\infty & \infty & \infty & \infty & 7 & 8 & 6 & -
\end{bmatrix}
$$

Find the shortest, and the second shortest, route from site 1 to site 8.

2. The (i,j)-entry in the matrix below represents the time taken to traverse the arc (i,j) in some communication network.

$$
\begin{bmatrix}
- & 4 & 6 & 7 & \infty & \infty & \infty & \infty \\
\infty & - & 1 & \infty & 8 & \infty & \infty & \infty \\
\infty & \infty & - & \infty & 5 & 7 & 9 & \infty \\
\infty & \infty & 2 & - & \infty & \infty & 6 & \infty \\
\infty & \infty & \infty & \infty & - & 1 & \infty & 4 \\
\infty & \infty & \infty & \infty & \infty & - & \infty & 2 \\
\infty & \infty & \infty & \infty & \infty & 2 & - & 3 \\
\infty & \infty & \infty & \infty & \infty & \infty & \infty & -
\end{bmatrix}
$$

(a) Find the shortest, and the second shortest, route from site 1 to site 8.
(b) By drawing up a search tree, or otherwise, find the shortest route from site 1 to site 8 that includes site 7.
(c) Find the shortest route from site 1 to site 8 if there is a delay at each of sites 2–7 equal to the time taken to reach that site.

3. The capacity matrix of a communication network is shown below.

$$
\begin{bmatrix}
- & 16 & 18 & 0 & 0 & 0 & 0 & 0 \\
0 & - & 0 & 10 & 12 & 0 & 0 & 0 \\
0 & 0 & - & 9 & 16 & 0 & 0 & 0 \\
0 & 0 & 0 & - & 0 & 15 & 18 & 0 \\
0 & 0 & 0 & 0 & - & 11 & 12 & 17 \\
0 & 0 & 0 & 0 & 0 & - & 0 & 20 \\
0 & 0 & 0 & 0 & 0 & 0 & - & 25 \\
0 & 0 & 0 & 0 & 0 & 0 & 0 & -
\end{bmatrix}
$$

(a) Find the best bottleneck, or maximum capacity, path from site 1 to site 8.
(b) What is the best bottleneck path from site 1 to site 8 if now nodes 2–7 have capacities as given in the table?

node	2	3	4	5	6	7
capacity	15	12	14	8	9	14

4. The (i,j) entry in the matrix below represents the reliability of arc (i,j) in some communication network.

$$\begin{bmatrix} - & 0.9 & 0.8 & 0.7 & 0 & 0 & 0 & 0 \\ 0 & - & 0.7 & 0 & 0 & 0.6 & 0 & 0 \\ 0 & 0 & - & 0.6 & 0.7 & 0.8 & 0 & 0 \\ 0 & 0 & 0 & - & 0.5 & 0 & 0.8 & 0 \\ 0 & 0 & 0 & 0 & - & 0.9 & 0.7 & 0.9 \\ 0 & 0 & 0 & 0 & 0 & - & 0 & 0.7 \\ 0 & 0 & 0 & 0 & 0 & 0 & - & 0.8 \\ 0 & 0 & 0 & 0 & 0 & 0 & 0 & - \end{bmatrix}$$

Find the most reliable path from site 1 to site 8.

5. If the union of all the shortest paths from s to every other node in a network is taken, the result is a (directed) tree called the shortest path, or skim, tree for node s.

To construct such a tree, each time a node j receives a permanent label add the arc (u,j) to the tree, where u is the predecessor node of node j.

Using the network of question 2, construct the shortest path tree for node 1.

6. In the cost matrix $C = [c_{ij}]$, c_{ij} represents the cost incurred, if positive, or the profit made, if negative, in using arc (i,j).

$$C = \begin{bmatrix} -1 & 2 & -1 & \infty & \infty \\ 2 & - & \infty & 3 & 4 \\ \infty & 3 & - & 1 & 2 \\ \infty & 3 & 1 & - & -1 \\ \infty & -1 & 2 & \infty & - \end{bmatrix}.$$

Draw the network, and, using Ford's algorithm, find the least-cost path from node 1 to node 2.

7.

$$\text{Given } W_0 = \begin{bmatrix} 0 & 7 & 10 & 5 \\ 7 & 0 & 20 & 13 \\ 10 & 20 & 0 & 19 \\ 5 & 13 & 19 & 0 \end{bmatrix}$$

use Floyd's algorithm to obtain W_1 writing out the calculations in full.
    Then obtain W_2 W_3, and W_4 but do not write out the calculations in full each time.

$$\text{Repeat if } W_0 = \begin{bmatrix} 0 & 7 & \infty & 5 \\ \infty & 0 & 20 & 13 \\ 10 & \infty & 0 & \infty \\ \infty & \infty & 19 & 0 \end{bmatrix}$$

this time including the matrix, P, of predecessors in the calculations.

8. Use Warshall's algorithm to determine whether the directed graph whose adjacency matrix is given below is strongly connected.

$$\begin{bmatrix} 0 & 1 & 0 & 1 & 1 \\ 0 & 0 & 0 & 1 & 0 \\ 0 & 1 & 0 & 0 & 0 \\ 0 & 0 & 1 & 0 & 0 \\ 1 & 0 & 0 & 1 & 0 \end{bmatrix}.$$

9. Are the following results true? In each case, provide a proof or counterexample.

   (a) Obtain the shortest path tree for every node in a network. At least one of these trees will be a minimum spanning tree.

   (b) In order to find the longest path from s to t in a network with no cycles, proceed as follows. If the length of arc (i,j) is d_{ij}, define d'_{ij} by $d_{ij}' = K - d_{ij}$, where $K > d_{ij}$ for all i and j, and find the shortest path from s to t in the adjusted network. This corresponds to the longest path from s to t in the original network.

5

Flows in networks

5.1 INTRODUCTION

It is often important to know the information-carrying capacity of a communication network. We assume that the network is directed with a particular node s, the *source*, such that all arcs incident to s have s as start node and a particular node t, the *sink*, such that all arcs incident to t have t as end node.

The arc weights denote the *capacities* of the arcs — usually the amounts of information per unit time which can be transmitted along the arcs — and we wish to know the maximum amount of information which can be transmitted, per unit time from s to t. s, it is assumed, can transmit, and t can receive an unlimited amount of information per unit time. If this is not the case, the network can be adjusted as described in section 5.3.1.

Let $W = (N,A,c)$, where $c:A \rightarrow N$ is the capacity function. If $(i,j) \in A$, we denote the capacity of (i,j) by $c(i,j)$.

A function $f:A \rightarrow N_0$ (the flow in an arc could be 0) is said to be a *flow* for W if

(i) $f(i,j) \leqslant c(i,j)$ for each $(i,j) \in A$, $\qquad\qquad\qquad\qquad$ (5.1)

$\qquad\qquad\qquad\qquad\qquad\qquad\qquad\qquad$ *Feasibility condition*

$\qquad$ and

(ii) $\displaystyle\sum_{(u,j)\in A} f(u,j) = \sum_{(j,v)\in A} f(j,v)$ for each $j \neq s$ or t.

$\qquad\qquad\qquad\qquad\qquad\qquad\qquad\qquad\qquad\qquad\qquad\qquad$ (5.2)

$\qquad\qquad\qquad\qquad\qquad\qquad\qquad\qquad\qquad$ *Consistency condition*

The *value*, F, of the flow is given by

$$F = \sum_{(u,t)\in A} f(u,t) = \sum_{(s,v)\in A} f(s,v).$$

$\qquad\qquad\qquad\qquad\qquad\qquad\qquad\qquad\qquad\qquad\qquad\qquad$ (5.3)

(If we have to consider an undirected network, we replace every edge (i,j) by a pair of arcs (i,j) and (j,i), each with capacity equal to that of the edge (i,j). Then if, for example, there is a flow of 5 units in the arc (i,j) and a flow of 2 units in the arc (j,i), we say there is a net flow of 3 units from i to j. See [3].)

Equation (5.3) follows immediately from (5.2), as nothing is gained or lost at intermediate nodes.

Suppose now that S and T are subsets of N satisfying $s \in S$, $t \in T$, $S \cap T = \emptyset$ and $S \cup T = N$. We call the pair (S,T) a *cut* and the set of arcs $\{(i,j) | i \in S, t \in T \text{ or } i \in T, j \in S\}$ a *cut set of arcs* separating, or cutting off, s from t. If they are removed, the network is disconnected into two or more components.

Further, the *capacity*, $c(S,T)$ *of the cut* (S,T) is given by

$$c(S,T) = \sum_{\substack{i \in S \\ j \in T}} c(i,j). \tag{5.4}$$

Note that the net flow from S to T is, by equation (5.2), the same as the flow from s to t. Thus

$$F = \sum_{\substack{i \in S \\ j \in T}} f(i,j) - \sum_{\substack{u \in T \\ v \in S}} f(u,v)$$

so

$$F \le \sum_{\substack{i \in S \\ j \in T}} f(i,j).$$

But $f(i,j) \le c(i,j)$ for each $(i,j) \in A$ by equation (5.1).

Hence

$$F \le \sum_{\substack{i \in S \\ j \in T}} c(i,j) = c(S,T). \tag{5.5}$$

This is true for any flow f and any cut (S,T), so the value of the maximum flow in the network cannot exceed the capcity of the cut whose capacity is least. We usually express this result by saying max flow $\le$ min cut.

We shall show later that these two quantities are equal, but look first at an example to illustrate the ideas involved. Consider the network in Fig. 5.1 where node 1 is the source and node 6 the sink. The number in boxes are the flows along the arcs; the other numbers are the capacities of the arcs. The value, F, of the flow is 14 units. Note that the flow in some arcs is equal to the capacity of the arc. If that occurs we say taht the arc is *saturated*. (1,2) and (4,6), for example, are saturated arcs.

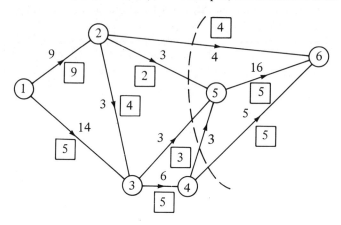

Fig. 5.1.

Let a cut (S,T) be defined by $S = \{1,2,3,4\}$ and $T = \{5,6\}$. The arcs in the cut set are those intersected by the dashed line in Fig. 5.1 and

$$c(S,T) = c(2,5) + c(2,6) + c(3,5) + c(4,5) + c(4,6) = 18 \geqslant F.$$

Before proving the fundamental theorem in this subject we need to introduce one further concept, that of the flow-augmenting chain.

Suppose that, in a particular network, we have the chain given in Fig. 5.2. For any

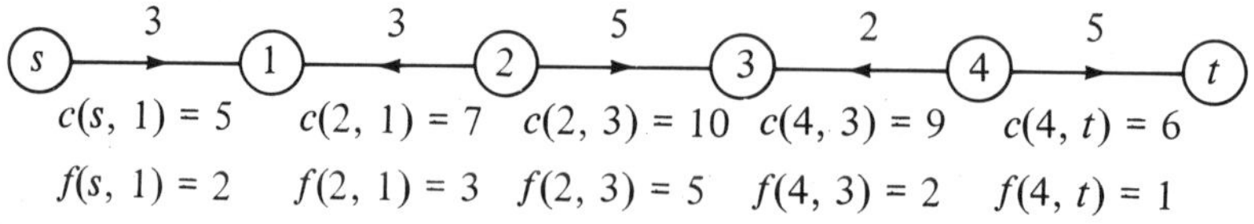

Fig. 5.2.

such chain, let

$$a_{st} = \min \begin{cases} c(i,j) - f(i,j) & \text{for all forward arcs } (i,j) \text{ in the chain} \\ f(j,i) & \text{for all reverse arcs } (j,i) \text{ in the chain.} \end{cases} \quad \text{and}$$

We can then augment, or increase, the current value of the flow from s to t by adding a_{st} to the flow in each forward arc and subtracting it from the flow in each reverse arc. The new flow is still consistent and feasible.

The relevant numbers are shown above the arcs in Fig. 5.2 and we see that $a_{st} = 2$. We can then augment the flow in that network by 2 units by adding 2 to the flow in arcs $(s,1)$, $(2,3)$ and $(4,t)$ and subtracting 2 from the flow in arcs $(2,1)$ and $(4,3)$.

Such a chain is called a *flow-augmenting chain*.

A chain whose initial node is s but whose final node is not t is called an *incomplete flow-augmenting chain*.

Now we may prove the following.

Theorem 5.1

The maximum value of a flow from s to t is equal to the minimum capacity of any cut separating s from t.

Proof. Let $\overline{F}$ be the value of the maximum flow from s to t, S the set of nodes u for which there is an incomplete flow-augmenting chain from s to u and $T = N - S$.

$t \notin S$ otherwise the flow could be augmented contrary to our initial assumption that it is maximum. Thus (S,T) is a cut separating s from t.

Now let (i,j) be any arc of the network with $i \in S, j \in T$. There is an incomplete flow-augmenting chain from s to i but, because $j \in T$, it follows that $f(i,j) = c(i,j)$.

Similarly, if (k,l) is any arc of the network with $k \in T, l \in S$, there is an incomplete flow-augmenting chain from s to l which cannot be extended to k because $k \in T$. Hence $f(k,l) = 0$.

Thus

$$\overline{F} = \sum_{\substack{i \in S \\ j \in T}} f(i,j) - \sum_{\substack{k \in T \\ l \in S}} f(k,l) = \sum_{\substack{i \in S \\ j \in T}} c(i,j) = c(S,T).$$

If (S_1, T_1) is any other cut separating s from t, it follows from equation (5.5) and the above that $c(S_1, T_1) \geqslant \overline{F} = c(S,T)$.

Hence (S,T) must be a minimum cut. (A network could have more than one minimum cut.)

5.2   THE FORD–FULKERSON ALGORITHM FOR MAXIMUM FLOW [3]

We start with a consistent, feasible flow obtained by inspection — if desired we can start with a zero flow in every arc — and, by a labelling process, construct flow—augmenting chains.

We state the algorithm below. (Slightly different statements may be found in [1], [2], [3], [8].)

FORD FULKERSON ALGORITHM

step 0: Obtain a consistent, feasible flow.

step 1: Assign the pair of labels $(0, \infty)$ to s.

step 2: Select any labelled node j and examine all arcs (i,j) and (j,k) where i and k are unlabelled nodes.

    (i) For any such arc (i,j) with $f(i,j) > 0$, assign the pair of labels $(j, f(i,j))$ to node i.

    (ii) For any such arc (j,k) with $c(j,k) - f(j,k) > 0$, assign the pair of labels $(j, c(j,k) - f(j,k))$ to node k.

step 3: Repeat step 2 until no more labelling is possible.

    (i) If t is unlabelled, stop.
        The current flow is a maximum and, if S denotes the set of labelled nodes and $T = N - S$, (S,T) is a minimum cut.

    (ii) If t is labelled, construct, using the first of the pair of labels, a flow-augmenting chain. a_{st} will be the smallest of the second labels of all nodes in the chain. Augment the flow by a_{st}, erase all labels and go to step 1.

For discussion of the efficiency of this algorithm, see [6] and [7].

Example 5.1
Find the maximum flow from node 1 to node 6 in the network of Fig. 5.1 using the flow depicted there for step 0.

FIRST ITERATION

Steps 1 *and* 2:

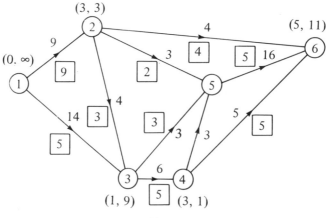

Fig. 5.3

Note: There is generally a choice of nodes to be taken as node j each time step 2 is repeated. For the labelling in Fig. 5.3 the order was $j = 1, j = 3, j = 4, j = 5$. If we had chosen $j = 2$ rather than $j = 4$ we would have constructed a different flow-augmenting chain.

Whatever choices we make, the value of the maximum flow will be the same but, in general, flows in individual arcs may be different.

step 3: Node 6 is labelled.

Constructing the chain (from back to front as in Dijkstra's algorithm) $a_{st} = 1$. Add 1 to the flows in each of the arcs above, erase all labels and go to step 1.

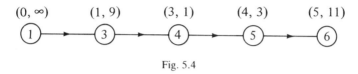

Fig. 5.4

SECOND ITERATION

steps 1 *and* 2:

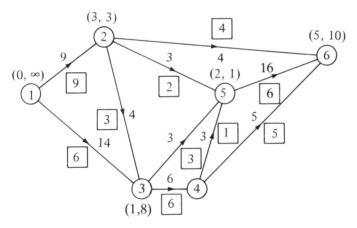

Fig. 5.5

$$[j = 1, j = 3, j = 2, j = 5]$$

step 3: Node 6 is labelled.
Constructing the chain we obtain $a_{st} = 1$. Subtract 1 from the flow in (2,3) and add 1 to the flow in the other arcs of the chain. Erase all labels and go to step 1.

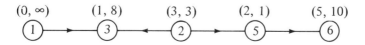

Fig. 5.6

THIRD ITERATION

steps 1 *and* 2:

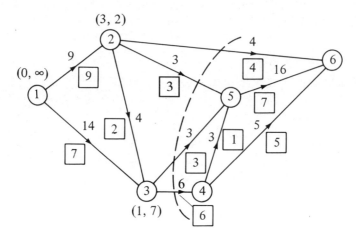

Fig. 5.7

$$[j = 1, j = 3, j = 2]$$

step 3: Node 6 is unlabelled; stop.
        The value of the maximum flow from node 1 to node 6 is 16 units and
        $(\{1,2,3\}, \{4,5,6\})$ is a minimum cut. The arcs intersected by the dashed line
        form a minimum cut set. As may be easily verified, in this example there is a
        unique minimum cut set.

5.3 ASSOCIATED PROBLEMS
5.3.1 Networks with many sources and sinks

Suppose that a communication network has p source nodes $s_1, s_2, \ldots, s_p$ with s_i capable
of transmitting an amount c_i, $1 \leqslant i \leqslant p$, of information per unit time and q sink nodes
$t_1, t_2, \ldots, t_q$ with t_j capable of receiving an amount d_j, $1 \leqslant j \leqslant q$, of information per unit
time.

      If any source may transmit to any sink, the problem is to find the maximum
amount of information per unit time it is possible to transmit from all the sources to
all the sinks.

      To solve this problem we add to the network a supersource s together with arcs
(s,s_i) of capacity c_i, $1 \leqslant i \leqslant p$, and a supersink t together with arcs (t_j,t) of capacity d_j,
$1 \leqslant j \leqslant q$. The required maximum flow is the maximum flow from s to t in the adjusted
network.

5.3.2   Networks with arc and node capacities

Suppose that a particular node j ($\neq s$ or t) has capacity c_j. We replace such a node by two nodes j_1 and j_2 linked by an arc (j_1, j_2) of capacity c_j. Any arc which had j as end node now has j_1 as end node and any arc which had j as start node now has j_2 as start node. The adjusted network has only arc capacities and the Ford-Fulkerson algorithm may now be used to calculate maximum flow.

5.3.3   Networks with upper and lower bounds on flow

It is possible that some arcs of the network have a required minimum flow value. Denoting this required minimum flow in (i,j) by $r(i,j)$, the feasibility condition becomes

$$0 < r(i,j) \leqslant f(i,j) \leqslant c(i,j). \tag{5.6}$$

The question is whether there is a flow from s to t which satisfies equations (5.2) and (5.6).

To answer the question we introduce an artificial source s' and an artificial sink, t' into the network. For every arc (i,j) for which $r(i,j) > 0$ we add arcs (s',j) and (i,t'), each with capacity $r(i,j)$, and decrease the capacity of (i,j) to $c(i,j) - r(i,j)$. Finally, we add the arc (t,s) with capacity ∞ .

For example, referring to the network of Fig. 5.1, if $r(2,3) = 3$ and $r(5,6) = 5$, we would adjust the network as in Fig. 5.8(a). If the value of the maximum flow from s' to t' in the adjusted network is $\Sigma r(i,j)$ — that is, all arcs with s' as start node, and all arcs with t' as end node, are saturated and the flow in (t,s) is $\Sigma r(i,j)$ — there is a flow with this value in the original network satisfying equations (5.2) and (5.6). Otherwise, no such flow exists.

A maximum flow, value 8 units, is shown in Fig. 5.8(a). There is, therefore, a flow, value 8 units, in the original network with $3 \leqslant f(2,3) \leqslant 4$ and $5 \leqslant f(5,6) \leqslant 16$.

If, for each arc (i,j) with $r(i,j) > 0$, we add $r(i,j)$ to the flow along (i,j) in the adjusted network and delete the arcs (s',j) and (i,t'), and, after all such arcs are considered, delete s' and t' and (t,s), then we will have constructed a flow of value $\Sigma r(i,j)$ in the original network satisfying equations (5.2) and (5.6).

These adjustments are shown in Fig. 5.8(b). The pairs of numbers by arcs (2,3) and (5,6) denote the maximum and minimum flow values possible along these arcs.

The above feasible flow may be increased as before provided that we are 'careful' with arcs (2,3) and (5,6). For example, at the moment (2,3) cannot appear as a reverse arc in a flow-augmenting chain, as the current flow in this arc cannot be decreased. (Clearly (5,6) could never appear as a reverse arc in such a chain.)

It should also be noted that, in a problem of this sort, the definition of the capacity of a cut (S,T) must be adjusted to read

$$c(S,T) = \sum_{\substack{i \in S \\ j \in T}} c(i,j) - \sum_{\substack{i \in T \\ j \in S}} r(i,j).$$

(a)

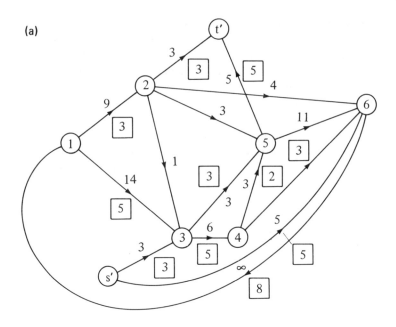

(b)

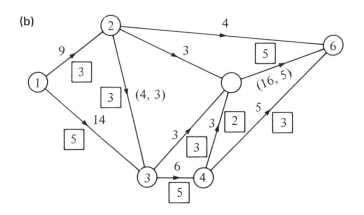

Fig. 5.8

5.3.4   The maximum flow between every pair of nodes

We assume that, at any given time, just one node in the network can act as source (s) and one as sink (t). The problem can be solved by doing $\frac{1}{2}n(n-1)$ s to t computations, but there is a more efficient method due to Gomory and Hu [4],[7] which requires only $(n-1)$ such computations.

   In the applications of this technique the networks are usually undirected and we make this assumption here.

   Then, if $\overline{F}_{ij}$ is the value of the maximum flow from node i to node j, $\overline{F}_{ji} = \overline{F}_{ij}$.

Gomory and Hu's method constructs a tree network T^* flow — equivalent to the original network. This tree is called, not unreasonably, a *Gomory–Hu tree*. Two networks are said to be *flow-equivalent* to each other if the maximum flow values between all pairs of nodes are the same.

There is a formal statement of the algorithm, together with a worked example, in [2]; we will illustrate the method here by means of an example.

Example 5.2

Find the maximum flow between every pair of nodes in the undirected network of Fig. 5.9.

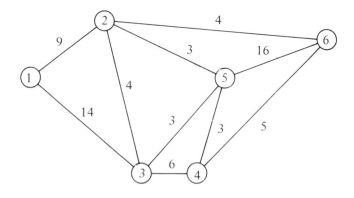

Fig. 5.9

The astute reader will spot that this is the undirected counterpart of the network in Fig. 5.1.

step 1: *Pick any node as s and any other as t. Find the maximum flow from s to t and a minimum cut (S,T).*

Let us take node 1 to be s and node 6 to be t. Then, as may easily be verified, the maximum flow from s to t again has value 16, and a minimum cut is $(\{1,2,3\},\{4,5,6\})$.

step 2: *Represent the cut symbolically by $S\overset{\bar{F}}{\text{———}}T$.*

That is, in one circle, all the nodes of S are listed, and in the other, all the nodes of T. The edge joining them, with weight $\bar{F}$, is one of the edges of T^*. We have

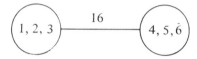

Fig. 5.10

We now focus attention on one of the subsets forming the cut — let us focus attention on *T*.

step 3: *Select any circle in the tree network obtained so far which contains more than one node of T. Pick one of the nodes as s, another as t, and find the maximum flow from s to t in the network adjusted from the original by condensing nodes in the following way; if the circle containing s and t were to be removed (together with all incident edges) from the tree so far constructed, this tree would be reduced to one or more subtrees; condense the nodes of each subtree into single nodes.*

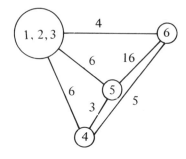

Fig. 5.11

In Fig. 5.11, ((1,2,3) ,5) has capacity 6, the sum of the capacities of (2,5) and (3,5). Take *s* to be node 4 and *t* to be node 5.

   In this very simple network we see by inspection that the maximum flow from node 4 to node 5 has value 14 and a minimum cut is ({4},{1,2,3,5,6}).

step 4: *Represent this cut symbolically, in a way similar to that in step 2, to give another edge of T*.*

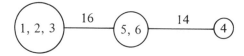

Fig. 5.12

Note
Nodes 5 and 6 are placed in the same circle because they belong to the same subset in the minimum cut. Also the circle containing them is placed next to the circle containing 1,2,3 because these five nodes belong to the same subset in the minimum cut.

step 5: *Repeat steps 3 and 4 until no circle of the tree network we are constructing contains more than one node of T.*
We now find the maximum flow from node 5(*s*) to node 6(*t*) using again the network of Fig. 5.11.

We see, again by inspection, that the maximum flow from node 5 to node 6 has value 25 and a minimum cut in ({1,2,3,4,5},{6}). Representing the cut symbolically gives

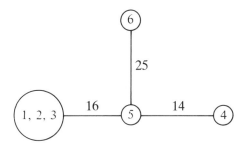

Fig. 5.13

No node of the tree network we are constructing now contains more than one node of *T*.

step 6: *Repeat steps 3, 4 and 5, this time focusing attention on the nodes of S rather than the nodes of T.*
Take *s* to be node 2 and *t* to be node 3. The adjusted network is that depicted in Fig. 5.14.

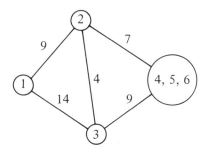

Fig. 5.14

By inspection the maximum flow from node 2 to node 3 has value 20 and a minimum cut is ({2},{1,3,4,5,6}).
Representing this cut symbolically gives

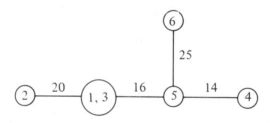

Fig. 5.15

Now, taking s to be node 1 and t to be node 3 we find, from Fig. 5.14, that the maximum flow from s to t has value 23 and a minimum cut is $(\{1\},\{2,3,4,5,6\})$.

Representing this last cut symbolically, we obtain finally a Gomory–Hu tree T^* flow-equivalent to the original network of Fig. 5.9. T^* is depicted in Fig. 5.16.

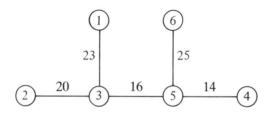

Fig. 5.16

The value of the maximum flow node i to node j in the network of Fig. 5.9 is obtained by taking the minimum value of the edge weights on the unique elementary path from node i to node j in the tree network of Fig. 5.16. For example, $\overline{F}_{24}(=\overline{F}_{42}) = \min(20, 16, 14) = 14$.

5.3.5 Minimum cost flow from s to t
The best-known method for the solution of this problem is the *out-of-kilter* algorithm devised by Ford and Fulkerson [3]. It is, however, rather tedious for hand calculation. A description of it, together with a worked example, may be found in [8]. See also [2] for an alternative approach.

5.4   APPLICATIONS
5.4.1   The optimum communication spanning tree
Suppose we have to build a telephone system linking n sites. Given the cost of building a line between sites i and j, the cheapest network is given by a minimum spanning tree connecting the sites. Now assume that we know the number, k_{ij}, of telephone calls that were made between sites i and j before the new network was built and that we expect the new k_{ij} values to be close to the old. We would like, naturally,

to minimize communication costs in the new network and, if we make the assumption that the cost of placing a call between sites i and j is proportional to, or, more simply, equal to the minimum number, l_{ij}, of lines along which the call must be transmitted, then the communication cost of any network built is given by

$$\sum_{\substack{1 \le i,j \le n \\ i<j}} k_{ij}.l_{ij}.$$

The best network, constructed using the above cost assumption, would not, in general, be a tree. We would build a line along the shortest — taking the length of each line to be 1 — path between any two sites and then superpose all these paths to obtain the best network. (An example of this technique can be found in section 5.5.2.) It would normally contain more than $n-1$ lines and so its construction cost would be larger than that of a tree. To try to achieve a balance we construct a tree, called by Hu the *optimum communication spanning tree*, which is the spanning tree having the smallest communication cost.

The following algorithm [7] constructs such a tree.

OPTIMUM COMMUNICATION SPANNING TREE ALGORITHM

step 0: Given $k_{ij} \ge 0$, construct an undirected network W such that the capacity of edge (i,j) is k_{ij}.

step 1: Construct a Gomory–Hu tree T^* of W.

T^* is the required optimum communication spanning tree, and the communication cost may be obtained by summing the edge weights of T^*.

Example 5.3
Given the matrix $K = [k_{ij}]$ below, construct a corresponding optimum communication spanning tree.

$$K = \begin{bmatrix} 0 & 9 & 14 & 0 & 0 & 0 \\ 9 & 0 & 4 & 0 & 3 & 4 \\ 14 & 4 & 0 & 6 & 3 & 0 \\ 0 & 0 & 6 & 0 & 3 & 5 \\ 0 & 3 & 3 & 3 & 0 & 16 \\ 0 & 4 & 0 & 5 & 16 & 0 \end{bmatrix}.$$

A zero off-diagonal entry indicates that the number of telephone calls placed between these sites is negligible.

step 0: W is the network of Fig. 5.9.

step 1: T^* is the tree network of Fig. 5.16.

The communication cost of this network is 98.

(We may check this figure by calculating $\sum_{\substack{1 \leqslant i,j \leqslant 6 \\ i < j}} k_{ij} \cdot l_{ij}$.

Writing out the sum gives $k_{12} \cdot l_{12} + k_{13} \cdot l_{13} + k_{14} \cdot l_{14} + k_{15} \cdot l_{15} + k_{16} \cdot l_{16} + k_{23} \cdot l_{23} + k_{24} \cdot l_{24} + k_{25} \cdot l_{25} + k_{26} \cdot l_{26} + k_{34} \cdot l_{34} + k_{35} \cdot l_{35} + k_{36} \cdot l_{36} + k_{45} \cdot l_{45} + k_{46} \cdot l_{46} + k_{56} \cdot l_{56} = 9.2 + 14.1 + 0.3 + 0.2 + 0.3 + 4.1 + 0.3 + 3.2 + 4.3 + 6.2 + 3.1 + 0.2 + 3.1 + 5.2 + 16.1 = 98$.)

5.4.2 The number of arc-disjoint paths

Two paths in a directed network are said to be *arc-disjoint* if they have no arcs in common. (They may have nodes in common.) If there are m arc-disjoint paths from a source s to a sink t then at least m arcs must fail before it becomes impossible to transmit information from s to t.

To calculate the number of such paths we set the capacity of each arc equal to 1 and use the Ford–Fulkerson algorithm to find the maximum flow from s to t.

It is left as an exercise for the reader to show that, in the network of Fig. 5.1, there are two arc-disjoint paths from node 1 to node 6.

5.5 MULTICOMMODITY FLOW

5.5.1 Introduction

We have again many sources and sinks, but now there is the added restriction that information transmitted from a particular source must be directed to a particular sink. If we think of information flowing from a specified source to a specified sink as the flow of a certain commodity, the network then has many different commodities flowing simultaneously. If we denote the value of the flow of commodity a by F_a, and its source and sink by s_a and t_a, then, if the portion of it flowing in (i,j) is denoted by $f_a(i,j)$, equations (5.1), (5.2) and (5.3) become, respectively,

$$\sum_a f_a(i,j) \leqslant c(i,j), \tag{5.7}$$

$$\sum_{(u,j) \in A} f_a(u,j) = \sum_{(j,v) \in A} f_a(j,v), \quad j \neq s_a \text{ or } t_a, \tag{5.8}$$

$$F_a = \sum_{(s_a,v)} f_a(s_a,v) = \sum_{(u,t_a)} f_a(u,t_a). \tag{5.9}$$

The problem of maximizing the sum of the flows of the different commodities is a very difficult one — see [6] — and we shall not attempt it here. Instead we look at a particular application. This account is rather terse; for a fuller explanation, see Chapter 11 of [6].

5.5.2   The synthesis of a communication network [5]

Suppose that there is a (constant) minimum flow requirement r_a for commodity a. (For cases where r_a is time dependent, see [6].)

Then, if the network is to be able to handle all such flow requirements simultaneously,

$$F_a \geqslant r_a \quad \text{for each } a. \tag{5.10}$$

We must find a set of capacities $c(i,j)$, or c_{ij} say, such that equations (5.7), (5.8) and (5.10) are satisfied with the total cost

$$\sum_{i,j} c_{ij}.d_{ij}$$

a minimum, where d_{ij} is the cost of building a unit capacity arc from site i to site j.

We may synthesize such a network in the following way, [5],[7]. Using the d_{ij} as lengths, we find, using Floyd's algorithm, the shortest paths between every pair of nodes. We then construct arcs with just enough capacity to carry the required flow along these paths. The final network is obtained by superposing all the arc capacities along all the shortest paths.

5.5.3   Algorithm to synthesize, at minimum cost, an n-node network with given flow requirement matrix R and cost matrix D

step 0   Obtain, using Floyd's algorithm, the predecessor matrix P.
Define $C = [c_{ij}]$ by $c_{ij} = 0$, $1 \leqslant i,j \leqslant n$.
Set $i = 1$.

step 1:   For each j, $1 \leqslant j \leqslant n$, $j \neq i$, obtain from P the shortest path from node i to node j and, from R, the required flow of the commodity with source node i and sink node j. For each arc (u,v) on the shortest path, let $c_{uv} = c_{uv} + r_{ij}$.

step 2:   If $i = n$, stop.
Otherwise let $i = i + 1$ and go to step 1.

Using the final capacity matrix C and the given cost matrix D,

$$\text{cost}_{\min} = \sum_{i,j} c_{ij}.d_{ij}.$$

Example 5.4
Synthesize, at minimum cost, a 4-node network with flow requirement and cost matrices R and D, respectively, below.

$$R = \begin{bmatrix} 0 & 5 & 4 & 2 \\ 3 & 0 & 5 & 8 \\ 4 & 4 & 0 & 7 \\ 6 & 2 & 5 & 0 \end{bmatrix} \qquad D = \begin{bmatrix} 0 & 12 & 20 & 5 \\ 12 & 0 & 4 & 5 \\ 20 & 4 & 0 & 13 \\ 5 & 5 & 13 & 0 \end{bmatrix}.$$

step 0: $P = \begin{bmatrix} 1 & 4 & 2 & 1 \\ 4 & 2 & 2 & 2 \\ 4 & 3 & 3 & 2 \\ 4 & 4 & 2 & 4 \end{bmatrix}$ and $C = \begin{bmatrix} 0 & 0 & 0 & 0 \\ 0 & 0 & 0 & 0 \\ 0 & 0 & 0 & 0 \\ 0 & 0 & 0 & 0 \end{bmatrix}.$

Obtaining P is left as an exercise.
Denote the shortest path from node i to node j by S_{ij}.
Let $i = 1$.

step 1: $j = 2$: $r_{12} = 5$: S_{12} is (1,4),(4,2). Let $C_{14} = C_{14} + 5$,
$C_{42} = C_{42} + 5$.
$j = 3$: $r_{13} = 4$: S_{13} is (1,4),(4,2),(2,3). Let $C_{14} = C_{14} + 4$,
$C_{42} = C_{42} + 4$, $C_{23} = C_{23} + 4$.
$j = 4$: $r_{14} = 2$: S_{14} is (1,4). Let $C_{14} = C_{14} + 2$.

Then C is $\begin{bmatrix} 0 & 0 & 0 & 11 \\ 0 & 0 & 4 & 0 \\ 0 & 0 & 0 & 0 \\ 0 & 9 & 0 & 0 \end{bmatrix}.$

step 2: $i = 1 \neq 4$. Let $i = 2$ and go to step 1.

step 1: $j = 1$: $r_{21} = 3$: S_{21} is (2,4),(4,1). Let $C_{24} = C_{24} + 3$, $C_{41} = C_{41} + 3$.
$j = 3$: $r_{23} = 5$: S_{23} is (2,3). Let $C_{23} = C_{23} + 5$.
$j = 4$: $r_{24} = 8$: S_{24} is (2,4). Let $C_{24} = C_{24} + 8$.

C is now $\begin{bmatrix} 0 & 0 & 0 & 11 \\ 0 & 0 & 9 & 11 \\ 0 & 0 & 0 & 0 \\ 3 & 9 & 0 & 0 \end{bmatrix}.$

step 2: $i = 2 \neq 4$. Let $i = 3$ and go to step 1.

step 1: $j = 1$: $r_{31} = 4$: S_{31} is $(3,2)$, $2,4)$, $(4,1)$.
  Let $C_{32} = C_{32} + 4$, $C_{24} = C_{24} + 4$, $C_{41} = C_{41} + 4$.
  $j = 2$: $r_{32} = 4$: S_{32} is $(3,2)$. Let $C_{32} + C_{32} + 4$.
  $j = 4$: $r_{34} = 7$: S_{34} is $(3,2),(2,4)$. Let $C_{32} = C_{32} + 7$, $C_{24} = C_{24} + 7$.

$$\text{So } C \text{ is} \begin{bmatrix} 0 & 0 & 0 & 11 \\ 0 & 0 & 9 & 22 \\ 0 & 15 & 0 & 0 \\ 7 & 9 & 0 & 0 \end{bmatrix}.$$

step 2: $i = 3 \neq 4$. Let $i = 4$ and go to step 1.

step 1: $j = 1$: $r_{41} = 6$: S_{41} is $(4,1)$. Let $C_{41} = C_{41} + 6$.
  $j = 2$: $r_{42} = 2$: S_{42} is $(4,2)$. Let $C_{42} = C_{42} + 2$.
  $j = 3$: $r_{43} = 5$: S_{43} is $(4,2),(2,3)$. Let $C_{42} = C_{42} + 5$, $C_{23} = C_{23} + 5$.

$$\text{Finally, } C \text{ is} \begin{bmatrix} 0 & 0 & 0 & 11 \\ 0 & 0 & 14 & 22 \\ 0 & 15 & 0 & 0 \\ 13 & 16 & 0 & 0 \end{bmatrix}.$$

step 2: $i = 4$, stop.

The final version of C above gives the minimum capacities necessary to satisfy the flow requirements. The cost of this network is $(11 + 13)5 + (15 + 14)4 + (22 + 16)5 = 426$ units.

REFERENCES

[1] N. Biggs, *Discrete Mathematics*, Oxford University Press, 1987.
[2] N. Christofides, *Graph Theory: an Algorithmic Approach*, Academic Press, 1975.
[3] L. R. Ford Jr and D. R. Fulkerson, *Flows in Networks*, Princeton University Press, 1962.
[4] R. E. Gomory and T. C. Hu, Synthesis of a Communication Network, *J. Siam*, **12**, 348–369 (1964).
[5] R. E. Gomory and T. C. Hu, Multi-terminal Network Flows, *J. Siam*, **9**, 551–570 (1961).
[6] T. C. Hu, *Combinatorial Algorithms*, Addison-Wesley, 1982.

[7] T. C. Hu, *Integer Programming and Network Flows*, Addison-Wesley, 1969.
[8] D. K. Smith, *Network Optimisation Practice*: *a Computational Guide*, Ellis Horwood, Chichester, 1982.

EXERCISES

In the networks of Figs 5.17—5.19, arc weights denote capacities in data units/sec.

1. Find the maximum flow from node 1 to node 7 in the network of Fig. 5.17 given

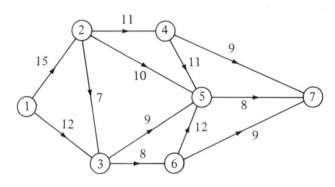

Fig. 5.17

the initial flows below (all in data units/sec.) and identify a minimum cut.
(1,2):13, (1,3):8, (2,4):5, (2,5):8
(3,6): 8, (4,7):5, (5,7):8, (6,7):8.

2. Starting with a zero flow in every arc and using the labelling procedure, find the maximum flow from node 1 to node 7 in the network of Fig. 5.18 and identify a minimum cut.

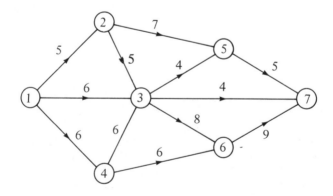

Fig. 5.18

3. Find the number of arc-disjoint paths from node 1 to node 10 in the digraph whose adjacency matrix is given below.

$$\begin{bmatrix} 0 & 1 & 1 & 1 & 1 & 0 & 0 & 0 & 0 & 0 \\ 0 & 0 & 0 & 0 & 0 & 1 & 0 & 0 & 0 & 0 \\ 0 & 1 & 0 & 0 & 0 & 1 & 0 & 0 & 0 & 0 \\ 0 & 0 & 1 & 0 & 1 & 0 & 0 & 0 & 0 & 0 \\ 0 & 0 & 0 & 0 & 0 & 0 & 0 & 0 & 1 & 0 \\ 0 & 0 & 0 & 1 & 0 & 0 & 1 & 0 & 0 & 1 \\ 0 & 0 & 0 & 0 & 1 & 0 & 0 & 1 & 0 & 1 \\ 0 & 0 & 0 & 0 & 0 & 0 & 0 & 0 & 0 & 1 \\ 0 & 0 & 0 & 1 & 0 & 1 & 0 & 1 & 0 & 1 \\ 0 & 0 & 0 & 0 & 0 & 0 & 0 & 0 & 0 & 0 \end{bmatrix}.$$

4. In the network of Fig. 5.19, nodes 2 and 3 are source nodes capable of transmitting

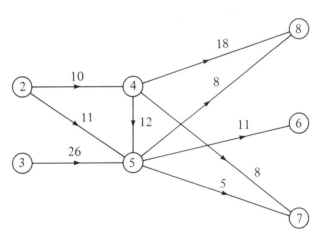

Fig. 5.19

14 and 23 data units/sec. respectively while nodes 6, 7 and 8 are sink nodes capable of receiving 15, 6 and 20 units/sec. respectively. Arc weights denote capacities in data units/sec.

If any source can transmit to any sink, find the maximum flow from all sources to all sinks given the initial flows below (all in data units/sec.) and identify a minimum cut.

(2,4):10, (3,5):16, (4,7):2, (4,8):8, (5,6):4,
(5,7): 4, (5,8): 8.

If there is now the added constraint that node 5 has a capacity of 18 data units/sec., what is the maximum flow from all sources to all sinks?

5. Given the matrix

$$K = \begin{bmatrix} 0 & 9 & 6 & 0 & 0 & 0 \\ 9 & 0 & 3 & 5 & 2 & 0 \\ 6 & 3 & 0 & 0 & 3 & 0 \\ 0 & 5 & 0 & 0 & 8 & 8 \\ 0 & 2 & 3 & 8 & 0 & 7 \\ 0 & 0 & 0 & 8 & 7 & 0 \end{bmatrix}$$

find a corresponding optimum communication spanning tree.

6. Synthesize, at minimum cost, a 4-node network with flow requirement matrix R and cost matrix D, where

$$R = \begin{bmatrix} 0 & 2 & 3 & 5 \\ 3 & 0 & 1 & 6 \\ 4 & 2 & 0 & 5 \\ 2 & 3 & 4 & 0 \end{bmatrix} \quad \text{and} \quad D = \begin{bmatrix} 0 & 7 & 10 & 5 \\ 7 & 0 & 20 & 13 \\ 10 & 20 & 0 & 19 \\ 5 & 13 & 19 & 0 \end{bmatrix}.$$

6

An introduction to line capacity assignment

6.1 BASIC ASSUMPTIONS

We focus attention in this chapter on another design problem, namely what capacities should be assigned to the communication lines of a network in order to achieve a certain specified level of network performance. The network is assumed to be one of message-switched type where a particular message is routed from start site (s) to terminal site (t) via intermediate sites. A concentrator, or minicomputer, is located at each site to decide (among other questions) how messages are to be processed. It is clear that queues develop at each concentrator as messages arrive and wait to be processed.

The delay, T, for a specific message is given by

$$T = \text{waiting time} + \text{processing time} \ . \tag{6.1}$$

If we suppose that, on average, λ messages per second arrive at a specific concentrator, that the average message length is $1/\mu$ data units per second, and that the outgoing communication line is of capacity C data units per second, then, if a message arrives and n messages are waiting ahead of it to be processed,

$$T = \frac{n}{\mu C} + \frac{1}{\mu C} \ , \tag{6.2}$$

on the assumption that messages are processed on a first-come first-served basis.

The *average message delay time*, $E(T)$, is given by

$$E(T) = \frac{E(n)}{\mu C} + \frac{1}{\mu C} \ . \tag{6.3}$$

In order to determine $E(T)$ we have to make some assumptions about message statistics. We shall adopt the simplest model assuming the following throughout the chapter.

(i) The message arrival rate is Poisson, that is

$$P \text{ (} k \text{ arrivals in } \tau \text{ seconds)} = \frac{(\lambda\tau)^k \, e^{-\lambda\tau}}{k!}$$

$E(k) = \lambda\tau$ so λ is the average message arrival rate. Then the time between arrivals is shown, for example in [1], to be an exponential random variable — see below — and the average time between arrivals is $1/\lambda$.

(ii) The message lengths are exponentially distributed with mean $1/\mu$. Thus, if we denote message length by r, the probability density function of r is $f(r) = \mu e^{-\mu r}$ and $E(r) = 1/\mu$.

At first sight this assumption seems inappropriate because the exponential is a continuous distribution whereas message length is a discrete variable. However, it does allow us to obtain reasonably good design results quite easily.

(iii) Messages are transmitted along a single outgoing line of capacity C. In that case the processing time distribution is given by $f(t) = \mu C e^{-\mu C t}$, with $E(t) = 1/(\mu C)$ the average time taken to transmit a message.

(iv) As many messages as necessary may be stored in the concentrator to await processing.

Such a model is usually referred to as an *M/M/1 queue*. (The notation *X/Y/s* is normally used in the queueing literature; X denotes the probability density function of the time between arrivals, Y the probability density function of the processing time distribution and s the number of servers. M denotes the exponential probability density — M for Markov.)
   With these assumptions it can be shown that

$$E(T) = \frac{1}{\mu C - \lambda} . \tag{6.4}$$

Excellent detailed presentations of the material in this section with equation (6.4) derived carefully may be found in the two books by Schwartz [6] and [7], and in Kleinrock [3]. The reader who wishes to know more about the underlying assumptions is advised to consult them.

6.2 CAPACITY ASSIGNMENT IN CENTRALIZED NETWORKS

6.2.1 Star networks

A *star network* is one in which each concentrator has a direct line to a central processing unit, all messages being directed to the said CPU.

We proceed by considering an illustrative example.

Example 6.1

Consider the star network of Fig. 6.1. The numbers in parentheses denote the

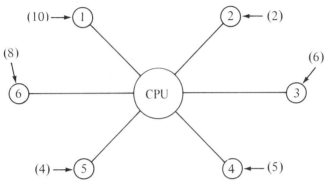

Fig. 6.1

number of terminals connected to each concentrator. Each terminal transmits, on average, 3 messages per minute, and the average message length is 100 bits.

The capacity of line i, from concentrator i to the CPU, will be denoted by C_i and the average message rate for that line by λ_i.

Some capacity assignment strategies will now be examined and compared.

We assume that, for each i, concentrator i receives the messages as they arrive from the terminals and, after processing any queues that form, forwards them along line i to the CPU. (Our interest is in line capacity assignment so we shall not concern ourselves with the details of these procedures. The reader who wishes to learn about, for example, statistical multiplexing should consult one of the three books referred to at the end of the previous section.)

Then λ_i, in messages per second, is given by

$$\lambda_i = \tfrac{1}{20} \times \text{number of terminals connected to concentrator } i.$$

Thus $\lambda_i = \tfrac{1}{20} \times 10 = 0.5$ and, similarly, $\lambda_2 = 0.1$, $\lambda_3 = 0.3$, $\lambda_4 = 0.25$, $\lambda_5 = 0.2$ and $\lambda_6 = 0.4$.

Denoting the average time delay in seconds incurred by a message on line i by T_i, then, from equation (6.4),

$$T_i = \frac{1}{\mu_i C_i - \lambda_i} \ . \tag{6.5}$$

Note that, in this example, $1/\mu_i = 100$ ($= 1/\mu$ say) for each i but, in general, this need not be the case. Here, then, we may write

$$T_i = \frac{1}{\mu C_i - \lambda 2_i'} \quad .$$
(6.5)

We must now decide what our measure of network performance is to be. We first make the assumption that cost is linearly proportional to capacity. Then, if there is a fixed budget available — which, in practice, is usually the case — this is equivalent to having a fixed total capacity available for distribution among the communication lines. Denote the total available capacity by C.

We define the *average message delay*, $\overline{T}$, for the network by

$$\overline{T} = \frac{1}{\Lambda} \sum_j \lambda_j T_j \quad ,$$
(6.6)

and it is $\overline{T}$ that we accept as an appropriate measure of network performance. (Equation (6.6) was first used by Kleinrock in his classic book [3]. It can also be shown [6] to follow in a natural way from a well-known result in queuing theory due to Little [5].)

Λ is the total incoming (average) message rate for the network; for a star network

it follows that $\Lambda = \sum \lambda_j$.

To minimize $\overline{T}$ subject to the constraint that the total capacity be fixed is a Lagrange multiplier problem. Before obtaining the optimizing (minimizing) values of the line capacities, we look at two simpler strategies. The first is an *equal assignment strategy*, each line receiving, in this example, one sixth of the total available capacity, and a *proportional assignment strategy* where, for each i.

$$C_i = \frac{\lambda_i C}{\sum_j \lambda_j} \quad .$$

These assignments, together with their average message delays and the corresponding values of $\overline{T}$, are shown in Table 6.1 on the assumption that $C = 2,400$ bits per second.

If we examine the two strategies we see that the equal assignment strategy favours the light users at the expense of the heavy users whereas the proportional assignment strategy has the opposite effect.

Table 6.1

	Equal assignment		Proportional assignment	
λ_i	C_i^E (bps)	T_i^E(sec.)	C_i^P(bps)	T_i^P(sec.)
0.5	400	0.286	686	0.157
0.1	400	0.256	137	0.787
0.3	400	0.270	411	0.262
0.25	400	0.267	343	0.314
0.2	400	0.263	274	0.394
0.4	400	0.278	549	0.196
$\sum_j \lambda_j = 1.75$	$\overline{T}^E = 0.274$		$\overline{T}^P = 0.269$	

We now look at the *optimal assignment strategy*. It can be shown that C_i^o, the optimal value of C_i, is given by

$$C_i^o = \frac{\lambda_i}{\mu_i} + \frac{C(1-\rho)\sqrt{\dfrac{\lambda_i}{\mu_i}}}{\sum_j \sqrt{\dfrac{\lambda_j}{\mu_j}}}, \tag{6.7}$$

and, in the special case where $\mu_i = \mu$ for each i,

$$C_i^o = \frac{\lambda_i}{\mu} + \frac{C(1-\rho)\sqrt{\lambda_i}}{\sum_j \sqrt{\lambda_j}}, \tag{6.7}'$$

where $C\rho = \sum_j \dfrac{\lambda_i}{\mu_j}$ in (6.7) and $\dfrac{1}{\mu}\sum_j \lambda_j$ in (6.7)'.

We may calculate $\overline{T}^o$, the corresponding minimum value of $\overline{T}$, using (6.6) or, if we wish, we may use one of the formulae below.

Using (6.7):

$$\overline{T}^o = \frac{\left(\sum_j \sqrt{\dfrac{\lambda_j}{\mu_j}}\right)^2}{\Lambda C(1-\rho)}. \tag{6.8}$$

Using (6.7)':

$$\overline{T}^{\circ} = \frac{\left(\sum_j \sqrt{\lambda_j}\right)^2}{\Lambda\mu C(1-\rho)} \ . \tag{6.8}$$

Some of the details of the derivation of these formulae, and an interpretation of ρ, are given in the Appendix to this chapter.

The optimal capacity assignments are shown in Table 6.2 together with the line

Table 6.2

λ_i	Optimal assignment		Discrete assignment	
	C_i° (bps)	T_i°(sec.)	C_i^P(bps)	T_i^P(sec.)
0.5	549	0.200	600	0.182
0.1	233	0.448	200	0.526
0.3	417	0.258	400	0.270
0.25	378	0.283	400	0.267
0.2	336	0.316	300	0.357
0.4	487	0.224	500	0.217
	$\overline{T}^{\circ} = 0.255$		$\overline{T}^D = 0.257$	

capacities we might have to use in practice. For it seems unlikely that we would be able to lease lines of exactly the capacities we require; it is far more likely that we would have to use the nearest available size. If we suppose that line capacities are available only in integer multiples of 100 bps then, remembering that the total capacity available is 2,400 bps, we might make the assignments, C_i^P, shown in Table 6.2. Note the corresponding small increase in the average message delay. (The same remarks apply here to the proportional assignment strategy.)

If we examine equation (6.7) we see that the optimal capacity C_i°, is composed of two parts.

The first part, λ_i/μ_i, is the minimum necessary to allow message transmission along line i; the remaining part is assigned using a square root assignment strategy. This approach, while avoiding the extremes of favouritism and penalty of the equal and proportional assignment strategies, still tends to favour the heavy user at the expense of the light.

If we examine equation (6.8) we see that we can decrease $\overline{T}$ by increasing C — that is, by spending more. This fact is no doubt obvious to any mathematician or engineer, though perhaps not to graduates in some other disciplines. The choice of C

as 2,400 bps was an arbitrary one. In practice we could try various values of C and determine the corresponding values of $\overline{T}^\circ$. We should then be able to determine, by plotting a graph of $\overline{T}^\circ$ against C and interpolating, what the value of C must be in order to achieve a desired average message delay.

We have made a number of simplifying assumptions in order to obtain answers quickly and easily. Nevertheless, the values of C_i° do give us a sensible point from which to start discussions of suitable choices of capacity for the communication lines.

6.2.2   Tree networks

If all messages are directed to a CPU, a star network yields the smallest possible value of $\overline{T}$. However, if most of the concentrators are sited a long way from the CPU, the total line length of such a network could be very large. In practice, lines are leased from British Telecom, or some equivalent organization abroad, and the cost is normally directly proportional to the capacity and the length of the line. The use of a tree network instead can cut down the number of long lines which have to be used and so can lead to a substantial saving in leasing costs; the drawback is that the value of $\overline{T}$ is greater. To illustrate this latter fact, consider the tree network of Fig. 6.2. The capacity of line i is again denoted by C_i.

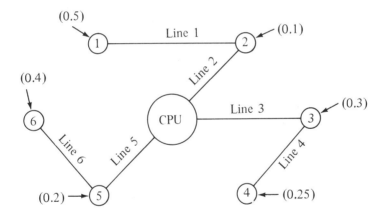

Fig. 6.2

The analysis of this model is more complicated. For example, at concentrator 2 we have messages arriving along line 1 in addition to those generated by the terminals. Similarly for concentrators 3 and 5.

Experience has, however, shown that we may assume *independence of queues*. Therefore, to obtain λ_2 we add the average message rate for the messages arriving along line 1 to that for the messages generated by the two terminals connected to concentrator 2. Similarly for λ_3 and λ_5. (This assumption is certainly valid if the network traffic is light, or if the messages generated by the terminals far outnumber the messages arriving along a communication line. In any case, these calculations can provide only an approximate answer — we have made a number of simplifying assumptions and the traffic statistics cannot be known precisely.)

Then, for the network of Fig. 6.2,

$$\lambda_2 = 0.5 + 0.1 = 0.6, \quad \lambda_3 = 0.25 + 0.3 = 0.55 \text{ and } \lambda_5 = 0.4 + 0.2 = 0.6.$$

$$\lambda_1 = 0.5, \quad \lambda_4 = 0.25 \text{ and } \lambda_6 = 0.4$$

just as they were in the star network. Note that, in a tree network, $\Lambda \neq \sum_j \lambda_j$.

In such a network, Λ is the sum, taken over all concentrators, of the average message rates for the messages generated by the terminals. Thus the value of Λ will be the same for a star network and a tree network connecting a given set of concentrators to a CPU.

Under the independence assumption, the optimum capacity assignments are also given by equation (6.7)′ and the corresponding minimum value of T by equation (6.8)′. The optimal assignments are shown in Table 6.3. The reader is invited to

Table 6.3

	Optimal assignment	
λ_i	C_i^o(bps)	T_i^o (sec.)
0.5	411	0.277
0.6	456	0.253
0.55	434	0.264
0.25	280	0.392
0.6	456	0.253
0.4	363	0.310
		$\overline{T}^o = 0.462$

produce the corresponding discrete assignments and to verify that the average time delays for the equal and proportional assignment strategies are 0.478 and 0.471 sec. respectively. In this constructed example it is not possible to determine the leasing costs for the two networks. In practice, however, we would be able to consider not only the star network but, in addition, a number of tree networks and their corresponding leasing costs and minimum average time delays. (Exercise 2 at the end of the chapter contains information enabling such comparisons to be made.)

As decision balancing cost against network performance — and perhaps taking into account other factors — could then be taken.

6.3 CAPACITY ASSIGNMENT IN DISTRIBUTED NETWORKS

We now look at a more general case where messages are exchanged among the concentrators.

Consider the illustrative example below.

Example 6.2

Concentrators at five sites, connected as shown in Fig. 6.3, exchange messages. The

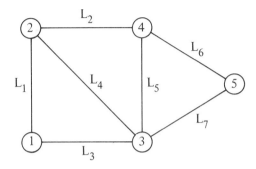

Fig. 6.3

number of messages per second sent, on average, from concentrator s to concentrator t is given by the entry m_{st} in the message (or traffic) matrix M. L_i denotes line i whose capacity will again be denoted by C_i.

$$M = \begin{bmatrix} - & 1.0 & 0.6 & 0.7 & 0.5 \\ 1.0 & - & 0.55 & 0.9 & 0.8 \\ 0.6 & 0.55 & - & 0.5 & 0.45 \\ 0.7 & 0.9 & 0.5 & - & 0.8 \\ 0.5 & 0.8 & 0.45 & 0.8 & - \end{bmatrix}$$

In order to determine the capacities to be assigned to the communication lines of Fig. 6.3 we must first know how messages are to be routed. In practice the shortest route is normally used and we shall assume that the relevant calculations have been done for the five sites. Rather than include information about distances we shall assume that the shortest route from s to t in Fig. 6.3 is that which uses the smallest number of lines. All shortest routes, with the exception of those from 1 to 4 and 2 to 5, may then be determined easily from the figure. If, now, we are given the additional information that the shortest route from 1 to 4 is (1,2),(2,4) and that from 2 to 5 is (2,4),(4,5), our routing information is complete.

The next problem is to determine the average message rate, λ_i, for each i. Once again, experience has shown that we may assume *independence of queues*, so λ_i is the sum of the average message rates for all messages routed along line i.

To simplify the calculations still further we assume that all lines have the same capacity in each direction. In addition M is symmetric so the average message rate on any line will be the same in each direction. Thus we may concentrate on message flow *in one direction only*, let us say from s to t, where $s < t$. Then the average *one-way* message rates for lines 1 to 7 are

$$
\begin{aligned}
L_1&: \lambda_1 = m_{12} + m_{14} & = 1.0 + 0.7 & = 1.7 \\
L_2&: \lambda_2 = m_{14} + m_{24} + m_{25} & = 0.7 + 0.9 + 0.8 & = 2.4 \\
L_3&: \lambda_3 = m_{13} + m_{15} & = 0.6 + 0.5 & = 1.1 \\
L_4&: \lambda_4 = m_{23} & = 0.55 & = 0.55 \\
L_5&: \lambda_5 = m_{34} & = 0.5 & = 0.5 \\
L_6&: \lambda_6 = m_{25} + m_{45} & = 0.8 + 0.8 & = 1.6 \\
L_7&: \lambda_7 = m_{15} + m_{35} & = 0.5 + 0.45 & = 0.95 \quad.
\end{aligned}
$$

If we are given the information that all messages have average length $1/\mu = 100$ bits, equation $(6.7)'$ may be used to calculate the optimal one-way capacity assignments and equation $(6.8)'$ the corresponding value of $\overline{T}^{\circ}$. The total one-way incoming (average) message rate for the network is now given by $\Lambda = \frac{1}{2} \sum_{s,t} m_{st}$; all other quantities in these two equations are calculated in the same way as before.

Table 6.4 compares the optimal assignments with the equal and proportional

Table 6.4

λ_i	Equal assignment		Proportional assignment		Optimal assignment	
	C_i^{E} (bps, 1-way)	T_i^{E} (msec.)	C_i^{P} (bps, 1-way)	T_i^{P} (msec.)	C_i° (bps, 1-way)	T_i° (msec.)
1.7	2000	54.6	2705	39.4	2424	44.4
2.4	2000	56.8	3818	27.9	2918	37.3
1.1	2000	52.9	1750	61.0	1923	55.2
0.55	2000	51.4	875	122.0	1337	78.0
0.5	2000	51.3	795	134.2	1272	81.8
1.6	2000	54.3	2545	41.9	2347	45.7
0.95	2000	52.5	1511	70.6	1780	59.3
	$\overline{T}^{E} = 70.3$		$\overline{T}^{P} = 69.0$		$\overline{T}^{\circ} = 64.6$	

$(1 \text{ msec.} = 10^{-3} \text{ sec.})$

assignment strategies on the assumption that the total capacity available is 14,000 bps — once more an arbitrary choice. Again the optimal assignment strategy avoids the extremes of the equal and proportional strategies whilst still favouring the heavy, rather than the light, user.

The above is an artificial example, but the approach used has been found useful in the design of large networks. See [4].

6.4 SOME GENERALIZATIONS

(1) Choose line capacities to minimize

$$T^{(k)} = \left\{ \frac{1}{\Lambda} \sum_j \lambda_j\, T_j^k \right\}^{\frac{1}{k}}. \tag{6.9}$$

This is a generalization of our previous performance criterion as equation (6.9) reduces to (6.6) if $k = 1$.

If we allow $k \to \infty$ in (6.9) we see the largest time delay on any of the lines becomes dominant and this time delay is then minimized subject to the total capacity being fixed. In this case it turns out [6] that the average time delay is the same for each line.

As no user is treated more (or less) favourably than any other, this approach is often referred to as a user-oriented approach to design.

(2) In a centralized network where cost is not linearly proportional to capacity, we wish to assign capacities — chosen from a finite number of available capacities — to the communication lines in order to minimize the maximum, average time delay from any site in the network to the CPU. An heuristic approach is used in practice, and the reader who wishes for details is referred to the paper by Frank *et al.* [2], which describes, for a given tree network, a method of selecting (globally) least-cost line capacities when a maximum average time delay is specified for each site.

(3) If we make the more realistic assumption that the processing time distribution is a general one, we then have an M/G/1 queuing model. The analysis of this model is more complicated and the interested reader is referred to [3], [6] and [7].

APPENDIX

(1) *The derivation of equations (6.7) and (6.8)*
Suppose there are n communication lines. Then

$$\overline{T} = \frac{1}{\Lambda} \sum_{j=1}^{n} \lambda_j\, T_j = \frac{1}{\Lambda} \sum_{j=1}^{n} \frac{\lambda_j}{\mu_j C_j - \lambda_j}.$$

The function to be optimized is

$$F(C_1, \ldots, C_n, \alpha) = \frac{1}{\Lambda} \sum_{j=1}^{n} \frac{\lambda_j}{\mu_j C_j - \lambda_j} + \alpha\left(\sum_{j=1}^{n} C_j - C \right)$$

where α is a Lagrange multiplier.

Then, differentiating partially with respect to each of the variables in turn and putting the results equal to zero, we have

$$\frac{-\lambda_1\mu_1}{\Lambda(\mu_1 C_1 - \lambda_1)^2} + \alpha = 0 \ , \tag{i}$$

$$\cdots$$

$$\frac{-\lambda_i\mu_i}{\Lambda(\mu_i C_i - \lambda_i)^2} + \alpha = 0 \ , \tag{ii}$$

$$\cdots$$

$$\frac{-\lambda_n\mu_n}{\Lambda(\mu_n C_n - \lambda_n)^2} + \alpha = 0 \ , \tag{iii}$$

$$\sum_{j=1}^{n} C_j - C = 0 \ . \tag{iv}$$

From (ii)

$$C_i = \frac{\lambda_i}{\mu_i} + \sqrt{\left(\frac{\lambda_i}{\mu_i}\right)\left(\frac{1}{\alpha\Lambda}\right)} \ . \tag{v}$$

Rearranging:

$$C_i - \frac{\lambda_i}{\mu_i} = \sqrt{\left(\frac{\lambda_i}{\mu_i}\right)}\sqrt{\left(\frac{1}{\alpha\Lambda}\right)} \ .$$

Similarly,

$$C_1 - \frac{\lambda_1}{\mu_1} = \sqrt{\left(\frac{\lambda_1}{\mu_1}\right)}\sqrt{\left(\frac{1}{\alpha\Lambda}\right)}$$

$$\cdots$$

$$C_n - \frac{\lambda_n}{\mu_n} = \sqrt{\left(\frac{\lambda_n}{\mu_n}\right)}\sqrt{\left(\frac{1}{\alpha\Lambda}\right)} \ .$$

Adding:

$$\sum_{j=1}^{n} C_j - \sum_{j=1}^{n} \frac{\lambda_j}{\mu_j} = \left(\sum_{j=1}^{n} \sqrt{\left(\frac{\lambda_j}{\mu_j}\right)} \right) \sqrt{\left(\frac{1}{\alpha \Lambda}\right)} \ .$$

Writing $\sum_{j=1}^{n} \frac{\lambda_j}{\mu_j}$ as ρC and rearranging,

$$\sqrt{\frac{1}{\alpha \Lambda}} = \frac{C(1-\rho)}{\sum_{j=1}^{n} \sqrt{\left(\frac{\lambda_j}{\mu_j}\right)}} \ .$$

Substitute in (v) to give

$$C_i^o = \frac{\lambda_i}{\mu_i} + \frac{C(1-\rho) \sqrt{\left(\frac{\lambda_i}{\mu_i}\right)}}{\sum_{j=1}^{n} \sqrt{\left(\frac{\lambda_j}{\mu_j}\right)}} \ . \tag{6.7}$$

(We shall not attempt to show that these values of the C_i do yield a minimum.)
Then, substituting for C_i in equation (6.5), we have

$$T_i = \left[\lambda_i + \frac{C(1-\rho)\sqrt{(\lambda_i \mu_i)}}{\sum_{j=1}^{n} \sqrt{\left(\frac{\lambda_j}{\mu_j}\right)}} - \lambda_i \right]^{-1}$$

that is,

$$T_i = \frac{\sum_{j=1}^{n} \sqrt{\left(\frac{\lambda_j}{\mu_j}\right)}}{C(1-\rho)\sqrt{(\lambda_i \mu_i)}} \ .$$

Substituting in equation (6.6) gives

$$\overline{T} = \frac{\sum\limits_{i=1}^{n} \sqrt{\left(\frac{\lambda_j}{\mu_j}\right)}}{\Lambda C(1-\rho)} \left(\sum\limits_{j=1}^{n} \sqrt{\left(\frac{\lambda_j}{\mu_j}\right)} \right)$$

or

$$\overline{T} = \frac{\left(\sum\limits_{j=1}^{n} \sqrt{\left(\frac{\lambda_j}{\mu_j}\right)} \right)^2}{\Lambda C(1-\rho)} . \tag{6.8}$$

If $\mu_i = \mu$ for all i then, in (6.7), we have

$$C_i^{\circ} = \frac{\lambda_i}{\mu} + \frac{C(1-\rho) \sqrt{\left(\frac{\lambda_i}{\mu}\right)}}{\frac{1}{\sqrt{\mu}} \sum\limits_{j=1}^{n} \sqrt{\lambda_j}}$$

or

$$C_i^{\circ} = \frac{\lambda_i}{\mu} + \frac{C(1-\rho)\sqrt{\lambda_i}}{\sum\limits_{j=1}^{n} \sqrt{\lambda_j}} \tag{6.7'}$$

and, in (6.8),

$$\overline{T} = \frac{\left(\sum\limits_{j=1}^{n} \sqrt{\lambda_j} \right)^2}{\Lambda \mu C(1-\rho)} . \tag{6.8'}$$

(2) *Traffic intensity parameters*

It is clear from equation (6.5) that, as λ_j approaches $\mu_i C_i$, the average time delay, T_i, on line i becomes very large. $1/(\mu_i C_i)$ is the time taken to process an average message, so it is reasonable to think of $\lambda_i \times 1/(\mu_i C_i)$, that is, $\lambda_i/\mu_i C_i$ as a measure of the intensity of the traffic on line i. We therefore define ρ_i, the *traffic intensity parameter* for line i, by $\rho_i = \lambda_i/\mu_i C_i$. Then, in terms of ρ_i, we may express the average time delay on line i by

$$T_i = \frac{1}{\mu_i C_i (1 - \rho_i)} \ .$$

(6.5)'

Further, $C_i \rho_i = \lambda_i/\mu_i$ so we may think of ρ, defined by $C\rho = \sum\limits_{j=1}^{n} (\lambda_j/\mu_j)$, as being a traffic intensity parameter for the whole network. In Example 6.1, $\rho = \frac{175}{2400} = 0.073$ for the star network and $\frac{290}{2400} = 0.121$ for the tree network. Thus the traffic in each is very light.

REFERENCES

[1] D. R. Cox and W. L. Smith, *Queues*, Chapman & Hall, 1961.
[2] H. Frank, I. T. Frisch, R. van Slyke and W. S. Chou, Optimal Design of Centralized Computer Networks, *Networks*, **1**, 43–58 (1971).
[3] L. Kleinrock, *Communication Nets*; *Stochastic Message Flow and Delay*, McGraw-Hill, 1964. Reprinted, Dover Publications, 1972.
[4] L. Kleinrock, Models for Computer Networks, *Proc. IEEE International Conference on Communications*, June (1969), pp. 21.9–21.16.
[5] D. C. Little, A Proof of the Queuing Formula: $L = \lambda W$, *Operations Research*, **9**, 383–387 (1961).
[6] M. Schwartz, *Computer Communication Network Design and Analysis*, Prentice-Hall, 1977.
[7] M. Schwartz, *Telecommunication Networks: Protocols, Modelling and Analysis*, Addison-Wesley, 1987.

EXERCISES

1. Refer to Example 6.1.

   (a) For the star network, calculate $\bar{T}^{\circ}$ for $C = 1200, 1500, 1800, 2100, 2400, 2700, 3000$ bps, and plot a graph of $\bar{T}^{\circ}$ against C.
   (b) If the number of terminals connected to each concentrator is doubled, and if the total capacity available is 1800 bps, obtain the values of $\bar{T}^{\mathrm{E}}$, $\bar{T}^{\mathrm{P}}$ and $\bar{T}^{\circ}$ for both the star and the tree networks.

2. Concentrators at six sites are connected to a CPU forming a star network. (Assume that the arrangement is the same as in Example 6.1.) The number of terminals connected to each connector is shown below.

Concentrator	1	2	3	4	5	6
Terminals	10	8	8	6	12	4

Each terminal transmits, on average, three messages per minute and the average message length is 100 bits. The total capacity available is 1800 bps.

(a) Calculate $\overline{T}^{E}$, $\overline{T}^{P}$ and $\overline{T}^{\circ}$.

(b) If now the only lines available for leasing have capacity $B \times 100$ bps, where $B = 1, 2, \ldots, 6$, adjust the optimal capacity assignments to the closest of these available capacities — remembering that the total capacity must not exceed 1800 bps — and calculate $\overline{T}^{D}$.

(c) If the distances of concentrators 1–6 from the CPU are, respectively, 25, 60, 80, 20, 30 and 70 miles, and if the cost of leasing a $B \times 100$ bps line is B cost units per mile per week, calculate the leasing cost of the star network whose line capacities are as in (b).

(d) The distances of the concentrators from each other are given (in miles) in the matrix below.

$$\begin{bmatrix} — & 19 & 40 & 60 & 39 & 33 \\ 19 & — & 21 & 55 & 44 & 60 \\ 40 & 21 & — & 50 & 68 & 72 \\ 60 & 55 & 50 & — & 62 & 68 \\ 39 & 44 & 68 & 62 & — & 23 \\ 33 & 60 & 72 & 68 & 23 & — \end{bmatrix}.$$

Find a minimum spanning tree connecting the seven sites.

(e) For this tree, obtain $\overline{T}^{\circ}$, $\overline{T}^{D}$ and the leasing cost, and compare with the answers obtained for the star network. Repeat for any other tree you deem worthy of consideration.

3. Refer to Example 6.2.
   If messages from site 1 to site 4 are now routed via site 3 — with all other routes unchanged — find the new value of $\overline{T}^{\circ}$.

4. A model of communication network connecting five sites is shown in Fig. 6.4. The

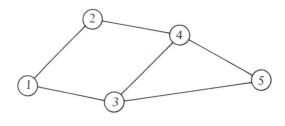

Fig. 6.4

message (or traffic) matrix for the network is

$$
M = \begin{bmatrix}
- & 0.33 & 0.17 & 0.17 & 0.33 \\
0.33 & - & 0.33 & 0.17 & 0.33 \\
0.17 & 0.33 & - & 0.5 & 0.33 \\
0.17 & 0.17 & 0.5 & - & 0.5 \\
0.33 & 0.33 & 0.33 & 0.5 & -
\end{bmatrix}.
$$

Assume that the route to be taken by a message from site i to site j is that which traverses the smallest number of lines. All message routes, with the exception of those from site 1 to site 4 and site 2 to site 3, may then be determined from the figure. To complete the routing information, assume that messages from 1 to 4 are routed via 2 and messages from 2 to 3 via 4.

The average message length is 200 bits and the total capacity available is 6000 bps.

Assuming that all communication lines have the same capacity in each direction, and using the fact that M is symmetric, obtain the one-way capacity assignments for the equal, proportional and optimal strategies.

The calculate $\overline{T}^{\mathrm{E}}$, $\overline{T}^{\mathrm{P}}$ and $\overline{T}^{\mathrm{O}}$.

ANSWERS TO SELECTED EXERCISES

Chapter 1.
1. (a) 16.
   (b) No.
4. 3.

Chapter 2.
The edge sets only will be given.

1. (i) {(1,5),(1,6),(1,7),(2,5),(3,6),(4,5)}; cost 224 units.
   (ii) {(1,2),(1,6),(1,7),(2,5),(3,6),(4,5)}; 254.
   (iii) Edges in (i) plus {(1,2),(1,3),(2,4),(5,6),(5,7)}; 525.
         Edges in (ii) plus {(1,3),(1,5),(2,4),(2,7),(6,7)}; 534.
   (iv) Edges in (i) plus {(1,3),(2,4),(5,7)}; 388.
        Edges in (ii) plus {(1,3),(2,4),(2,7)}; 422.
2. MST is {(2,3),(2,6),(2,8),(3,7),(7,1),(6,4),(4,9),(9,5)}; cost 283 units.
   (i) Edges in MST plus {(1,3),(2,4),(2,7),(4,5),(6,8),(6,9),(3,8)}; 664.
   (ii) Edges in MST plus {(1,3),(2,4),(3,8),(4,5)}; 519.
3. No.
4. (i) Cost 424 units on the assumption that construction costs are 1 cost unit per league for lines not crossing the mountain range.
   (ii) MST for centres 1–5 is {(1,3),(1,5),(2,5),(3,4)} and for centres 6–9 is

$\{(6,8),(7,8),(7,9)\}$. Connect these two trees by the line $(2,6)$ to give a spanning tree of cost 180. IFI network consists of these plus $\{(1,2),(1,4),(2,8),(3,5),(5,6),(6,7),(8,9)\}$; 405.

Chapter 3.
Again edge sets only will be given.
1. C–R: $\{(1,2),(1,3),(1,4),(1,6),(4,5)\}$; cost 82 units.
   K: $\{(1,2),(1,3),(1,4),(1,5),(4,6),\}$; 84.
2. $\{(1,2),(1,3),(1,4),(1,7),(2,5),(3,6)\}$; 56.
3. (i) All terminal connected to C_1; 74.
   (ii) ADD: T_4 and T_5 connected to C_2, remainder to C_1; 72.
   DROP: T_1 and T_4 connected to C_2, remainder to C_1; 72.

Chapter 4.
1. $(1,2),(2,3),(3,7),(7,8)$; length 18 units.
   $(1,4),(4,6),(6,7),(7,8)$; 19.
2. (a) $(1,2),(2,3),(3,5),(5,6),(6,8)$; 13 time units.
   $(1,2),(2,3),(3,5),(5,8)$; 14.
   (b) $(1,4), (4,7), (7,8)$; 16.
   (c) $(1,2),(2,5),(5,8)$; 36.
3. (a) $(1,3),(3,5),(5,8)$; bottleneck 16 units.
   (b) $(1,2),(2,4),(4,7),(7,8)$; 10
4. $(1,3),(3,5),(5,8)$; reliability 0.504.
6. $(1,3),(3,4),(4,5),(5,2)$; profit 2 units.

7.
$$W_4 = \begin{bmatrix} 0 & 7 & 10 & 5 \\ 7 & 0 & 17 & 12 \\ 10 & 17 & 0 & 15 \\ 5 & 12 & 15 & 0 \end{bmatrix}.$$

$$W_4 = \begin{bmatrix} 0 & 7 & 24 & 5 \\ 30 & 0 & 20 & 13 \\ 10 & 17 & 0 & 15 \\ 29 & 36 & 19 & 0 \end{bmatrix}, \quad P = \begin{bmatrix} 1 & 1 & 4 & 1 \\ 3 & 2 & 2 & 2 \\ 3 & 1 & 3 & 1 \\ 3 & 1 & 4 & 4 \end{bmatrix}.$$

8. Not strongly connected.
9. Both false.

Chapter 5.
1. $\bar{F} = 25$ data units/sec., $(\{1,2,3,4,5\}, \{6,7\})$.
2. $\bar{F} = 17$, $(\{1\}, \{2,3,4,5,6,7\})$.
3. 3 arc disjoint paths.

4. $\bar{F} = 34$, ({2,3,5}, {4,6,7,8}), $\bar{F} = 28$.
5. See Fig. 5.20.

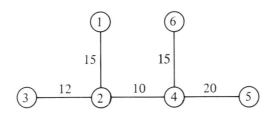

Fig. 5.20

6.

$$C = \begin{bmatrix} 0 & 7 & 8 & 16 \\ 10 & 0 & 0 & 0 \\ 11 & 0 & 0 & 0 \\ 9 & 0 & 0 & 0 \end{bmatrix}, \qquad \text{cost 434 units.}$$

Chapter 6.
1. (b) $\bar{T}^{E} = 0.440$, $\bar{T}^{P} = 0.414$, $\bar{T}^{o} = 0.391$ sec. (STAR) $\bar{T}^{E} = 0.851$, $\bar{T}^{P} = 0.816$, $\bar{T}^{o} = 0.800$ sec. (TREE).
2. (a) $\bar{T}^{E} = 0.392$, $\bar{T}^{P} = 0.385$, $\bar{T}^{o} = 0.374$ sec.
   (b) $\bar{T}^{D} = 0.378$.
   (c) 815 cost units.
   (e) $\bar{T}^{o} = 0.609$, $\bar{T}^{D} = 0.637$; 426.
3. 66.8 msec.
4. $\bar{T}^{E} = 0.323$, $\bar{T}^{P} = 0.319$, $\bar{T}^{o} = 0.314$ sec.

Part II
Signals, systems and the filtering process

7

Signals and linear system fundamentals

7.1 INTRODUCTION

In this and later chapters of this book we will be concerned with signals and operations on signals. The first task is to define what is meant by a signal and then to classify signals into different types according to their nature. When this has been achieved, the concept of a system is introduced by the consideration of some elementary ideas from the theory of electrical circuits. Useful ideas and insight can be obtained from block diagrams representing circuits (or systems) and these are discussed for the time domain. Laplace transforms are reviewed, with their role seen as that of system representation rather than as a method for the solution of differential equations.

7.2 SIGNALS AND SYSTEMS

A signal is a time-varying quantity, used to cause some effect or produce some action. Mathematically we describe a signal as a function of time used to represent a variable of interest associated with a system, and we classify signals according to both the way in which they vary with time and the manner of that variation. The classification which we shall use discriminates between continuous-time or discrete-time signals and thereafter between deterministic or stochastic signals, although we will be concerned only with deterministic signals. Deterministic signals can be modelled or represented using completely specified functions of time, for example

(1) $f_1(t) = a\sin(\omega t)$, with a and ω constant and $-\infty < t < \infty$,
(2) $f_2(t) = ce^{-dt}$, with c and d constant and $t \geqslant 0$,

(3) $f_3(t) = \begin{cases} 1 & |t| \leqslant A, \text{ with } A \text{ constant and } -\infty < t < \infty \\ 0 & |t| > A \end{cases}$.

Each signal $f_1(t)$, $f_2(t)$ and $f_3(t)$ above is a function of the continuous-time variable t, and are thus continuous-time signals. Notice that although $f_3(t)$ is a continuous-time signal, it is not a continuous function of time.

In some applications, notably in connection with digital computers, signals are only represented at discrete (or separated) values of the time variable (or index). Between these discrete-time instants the signal may take the value zero, be undefined or simply of no interest. Examples of discrete time signals are

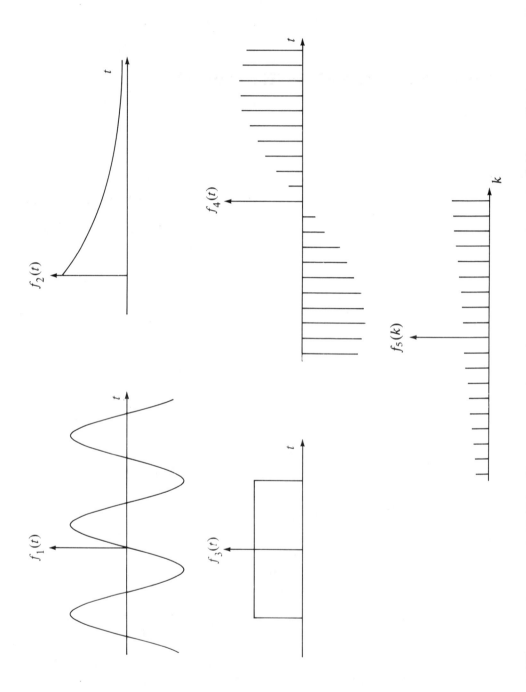

Fig. 7.1 — Graphs of $f_1(t)$, $f_2(t)$, $f_3(t)$, $f_4(t)$ and $f_5(k)$.

(1) $f_4(nT) = a \sin nT$, with a and T constant and
         $n = \ldots -2, -1, 0, 1, 2, \ldots$, an integer or zero.
(2) $f_5(k) = bk + c$, with b and c constants and $k = 0, 1, 2, \ldots$, a positive integer
         or zero.

The signals $f_4(nT)$ and $f_5(k)$ are functions of nT and k respectively, where n and k may take only integer values or zero. Thus values of the signal are only defined at discrete points. The two notations have been used for a purpose: the origin of many discrete-time signals is in the 'sampling' of continuous signal $f(t)$ at (usually) equal intervals, T. If n represents a sampling index or counter, then this process generates the sequence of values $\{f(nT)\}$ with each term $f(nT)$ generated by a formula as in $f_4(nT)$ above. Using the notation as in $f_5(k) = bk + c$ merely suppresses the information on sampling interval and uses instead the index of position, k, in the sequence $\{f(k)\}$ as the independent variable. Fig. 7.1 exhibits the graphs of some of these signals.

Stochastic signals, either continuous time or discrete time, cannot be so represented and their description has to be in terms of average properties. The analysis and processing of such signals is an important part of communication theory, but depends on an understanding of deterministic signal processing. This book concentrates on deterministic signals, and thus may serve as an introduction to the more advanced texts in this area.

A dictionary definition of a system is a set of things considered as a collective whole. Restricting the scope somewhat, we will consider systems to be processors which operate on input signals to produce output signals. Since we are working with representations or mathematical models of signals, our systems will be mathematical models of real systems. Input and output signals may be of any of the types discussed and we will think of our mathematical models of systems as models of systems which have the purpose of processing signals. The continuous-time systems we will consider have their origin in simple electrical circuits which can be modelled quite simply using a differential equation.

7.3   *L–C–R* CIRCUITS

We will consider circuits which are configurations of three basic elements and which are driven by a voltage source. We will discover that from these basic building blocks, systems can be constructed which are capable of performing useful tasks in the field of signal processing. First, we must define the circuit elements and the manner of their interaction. The three elements are

(1) a resistor
(2) an inductance
(3) a capacitor.

The effect of each of these devices in a loop of a circuit in which a current $i(t)$ flows is expressed in terms of the voltage drop measured across each device. This is illustrated for each case in Figs. 7.2–7.4.

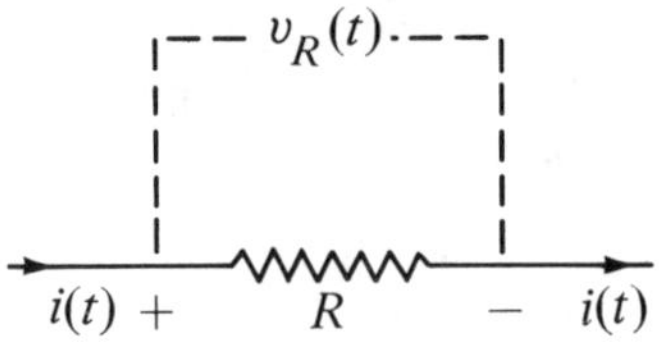

$$v_R(t) = Ri(t) \tag{7.1}$$

(1) Resistor, with constant resistance R (ohms)

Fig. 7.2

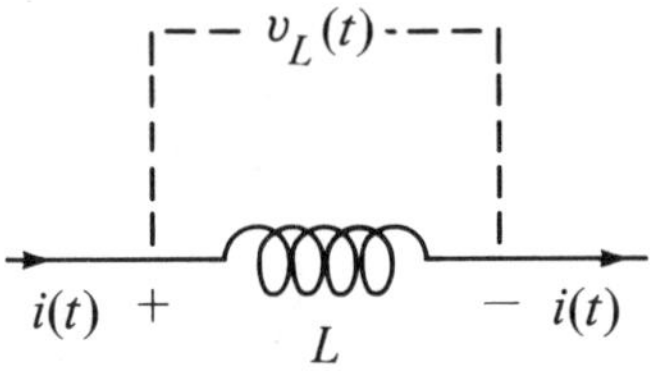

$$v_L(t) = L\,\frac{di(t)}{dt} \tag{7.2}$$

(2) Inductor, with constant inductance L (Henrys)

Fig. 7.3

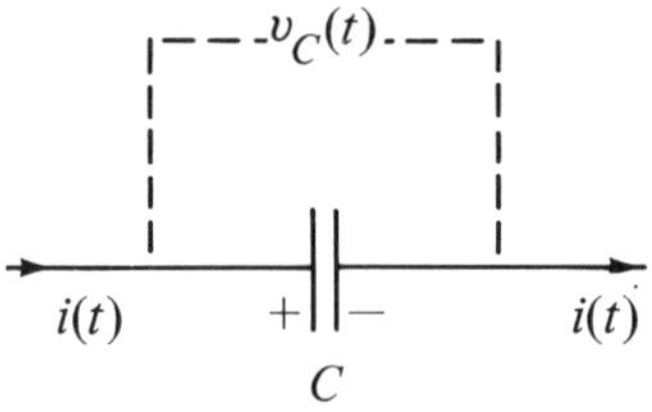

$$v_C(t) = \frac{1}{C}\int_{t_0}^{t} i(\tau)d\tau + v(t_0) \tag{7.3}$$

(3) Capacitor, with constant capacitance C (Farads)

Fig. 7.4

In equation (7.3), $v(t_0)$ is the voltage measured across the capacitor at time t_0. An alternative form of this relation is obtained by differentiation with respect to time as

$$i(t) = C\,\frac{dv_c(t)}{dt}\ . \tag{7.4}$$

The relations (7.1)–(7.3) are the component constitutive equations, and we note that the loop current measured on each side of each device is the same. Circuits containing the above components will be driven by a voltage source, delivering a voltage $e(t)$ independent of the current $i(t)$. Such a device is shown at the left-hand side of Fig. 7.5 in Example 7.1.

Equations describing circuit behaviour are obtained by using Kirchhoff's laws. These are simply stated as:

(A) Kirchhoff's voltage law: the sum of the voltage drops around a closed loop of a circuit is zero.

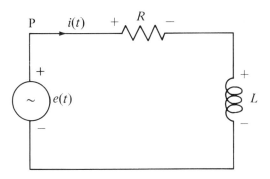

Fig. 7.5 — The *L–R* circuit of Example 7.1

(B) Kirchhoff's current law: the algebraic sum of the currents at a junction is zero.

The use of these laws and the formation of circuit equations for simple cases will be demonstrated using some examples. The interested reader seeking a more advanced discussion of circuits is referred to Papoulis [5] and Adby [1].

Example 7.1   *The L–R circuit*
Fig. 7.5 shows a circuit containing a resistor with constant resistance R and an inductor with constant inductance L, in future referred to as a resistor R and an inductor L. There are no junctions in this circuit and we have only Kirchhoff's voltage law available to determine the behaviour of this circuit when driven by the voltage source $e(t)$ and with an assumed current $i(t)$ flowing.

Taking as our starting point P as shown in Fig. 7.5 we must have, progressing in a clockwise sense,

$$v_R(t) + v_L(t) - e(t) = 0 \ . \tag{7.5}$$

The last term has the form shown, $-e(t)$, since with conditions as shown and passing through the source $e(t)$ in the sense described, there is a presumed voltage rise. In fact, whether there is actually a voltage rise or a voltage drop at this stage, equation (7.5) still represents conditions correctly because the system is *linear*. It now remains to rearrange (7.5) and use the appropriate constitutive equations (7.1) and (7.2) to obtain

$$Ri(t) + L\frac{di(t)}{dt} = e(t)$$

or

$$\frac{di(t)}{dt} + \frac{Ri(t)}{L} = \frac{1}{L}e(t) \ . \tag{7.6}$$

The solution of this differential equation will produce $i(t)$, the current in the circuit given the input $e(t)$ and an initial condition, $i(t_0)$ say. It may not be that $i(t)$ is the desired output for the system; other possibilities might be $v_R(t)$ or $v_L(t)$, the voltages measured across R and L respectively. However, a knowledge of $i(t)$ is easily seen to be sufficient to obtain either of these quantities.

Example 7.2   The C–R circuit (Fig. 7.6)

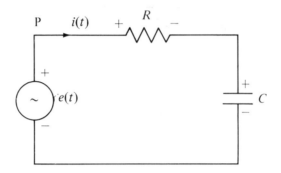

Fig. 7.6 — The C–R circuit.

Using the same technique as in Example 7.1 we quickly obtain

$$v_R(t) + v_C(t) - e(t) = 0 \tag{7.7}$$

and using (7.1) and (7.3) we have

$$Ri(t) + \frac{1}{C}\int_{t_0}^{t} i(\tau)\,d\tau + v(t_0) = e(t) \ . \tag{7.8}$$

To remove the integral in (7.8) we could differentiate with respect to time to produce

$$R\frac{di(t)}{dt} + \frac{1}{C}i(t) = \frac{de(t)}{dt} \ . \tag{7.9}$$

Equation (7.9) is an acceptable form of circuit equation, but the presence of the time derivative of the input, $de(t)/dt$, could produce difficulties.

An alternative approach is to return to equation (7.7) and make use of the alternative form of the constitutive equation for the capacitor, (7.4), i.e.

$$i(t) = C\frac{dv_C(t)}{dt} \ .$$

Since $v_R(t) = Ri(t)$, this means that

$$v_R(t) = RC\frac{dv_C(t)}{dt}$$

and (7.7) becomes

$$RC\frac{dv_C(t)}{dt} + v_C(t) = e(t)$$

or

$$\frac{dv_C(t)}{dt} + \frac{1}{RC}v_C(t) = \frac{1}{RC}e(t) \ . \tag{7.10}$$

Thus, by choice of the quantity $v_C(t)$ as the variable to describe the behaviour of this circuit, we have avoided the occurrence of the term $de(t)/dt$. The solution of (7.10) will produce $v_C(t)$, the voltage drop measured across the capacitor, given the input $e(t)$ and the initial condition $v_C(t_0)$, say.

It is interesting to observe the similar forms of (7.6) and (7.10), and to note that the form in (7.10) was obtained after the choice of $v_C(t)$ as dependent variable. There is a physical reason for this, and an account using the concept of state variables, which is discussed below, may be found in Gabel and Roberts [3]. Our next step is to ask what happens in a circuit which contains all three elements connected in series. Such a circuit is illustrated in Fig. 7.7, and in this case Kirchhoff's voltage law yields

$$v_R(t) + v_L(t) + v_C(t) = e(t) \tag{7.11}$$

and use of the constitutive laws (7.1)–(7.3) would yield a circuit equation in the manner of Examples 7.1 and 7.2. We do not do this at once; instead we observe that if we use the constitutive equations (7.1) and (7.2) we obtain

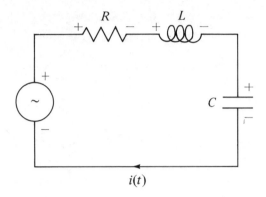

Fig. 7.7 — The L–C–R circuit.

$$Ri(t) + L\frac{di(t)}{dt} + v_C(t) = e(t) \ . \tag{7.12}$$

Writing the constitutive equation (7.4) for the capacitor C as

$$\frac{dv_c(t)}{dt} - \frac{1}{C}i(t) = 0 \ , \tag{7.13}$$

we see that (7.12) and (7.13) form a pair of coupled differential equations which describe the behaviour of the circuit in Fig. 7.7. This pair of equations determines the behaviour of the two quantities $i(t)$ and $v_C(t)$ which emerged as 'natural' when discussing circuits with either an inductor or a capacitor respectively. These two quantities are called state variables for the L–C–R circuit, and when we know the value of both of these quantities for all time t, we say we know the state of the circuit at any time, implying a complete knowledge of its behaviour.

It is natural, since the values of L, C and R are constant, to consider a matrix representation of the system of equations (7.12) and (7.13). To do this, define a state vector $\mathbf{x}(t) = [v_C(t) \ i(t)]^T$ and rearranging (7.12) as

$$\frac{di(t)}{dt} = -\frac{1}{L}v_C(t) - \frac{R}{L}i(t) + e(t)$$

leads to the form

$$
\begin{bmatrix} \dfrac{dv_C(t)}{dt} \\[3mm] \dfrac{di(t)}{dt} \end{bmatrix} = \begin{bmatrix} 0 & \dfrac{1}{C} \\[3mm] -\dfrac{1}{L} & -\dfrac{R}{L} \end{bmatrix} \begin{bmatrix} v_C(t) \\[3mm] i(t) \end{bmatrix} + \begin{bmatrix} 0 \\[3mm] 1 \end{bmatrix} e(t)
$$

or

$$\dot{\mathbf{x}}(t) = \mathbf{A}\mathbf{x}(t) + \mathbf{b}u(t) \tag{7.14}$$

where

$$
\mathbf{A} = \begin{bmatrix} 0 & \dfrac{1}{C} \\[3mm] -\dfrac{1}{L} & -\dfrac{R}{L} \end{bmatrix}, \qquad \mathbf{b} = \begin{bmatrix} 0 \\[3mm] 1 \end{bmatrix}, \qquad u(t) = e(t)
$$

If the output is to be $y(t) = i(t)$, then we can write $y(t) = [0\ 1]\,\mathbf{x}(t)$.

The form (7.14) is known as the state-space representation of the circuit and generalizes to

$$\dot{\mathbf{x}}(t) = \mathbf{A}\mathbf{x}(t) + \mathbf{B}\mathbf{u}(t)$$

$$\mathbf{y}(t) = \mathbf{C}\mathbf{x}(t) + \mathbf{D}\mathbf{u}(t)$$

where $\mathbf{B}$ is now a matrix and $\mathbf{u}(t) = [u_1(t) \dots u_m(t)]^T$ is a vector of inputs. $\mathbf{y}(t) = [y_1(t) \dots y_p(t)]^T$ is a vector of outputs, and $\mathbf{C}$ and $\mathbf{D}$ are matrices of appropriate dimension. This generalization provides a useful method for modelling systems with more than one input, and is exploited particularly in the field of control theory. For more details, see Burghes and Graham [2].

7.4 LINEAR SYSTEMS

So far in our development we have identified the concept of a system and looked in some detail at systems which take the form of simple electric cicruits. 'Linear' was only mentioned in passing during the derivation of a particular circuit equation, and as yet the concept has not been explained. To rectify this, we consider first an ordinary differential equation of the form

$$\frac{d^n y(t)}{dt^n} + a_{n-1}(t)\frac{d^{n-1}y(t)}{dt^{n-1}} + \dots a_0(t)y(t) = b_0(t)\frac{d^m u(t)}{dt^m} \dots b_m(t)u(t) \tag{7.15}$$

which relates the input $u(t)$ to the output $y(t)$, and where the coefficients $a_i(t)$, $i = 0$ ...$n - 1$ and $b_j(t), j = 0, \ldots m$, are functions of time t. We write (7.15) in the compact form

$$L_1[y(t)] = L_2[u(t)] \tag{7.16}$$

where L_1 and L_2 are operators defined by

$$L_1 \equiv \left[\frac{d^n}{dt^n} + a_{n-1}(t)\frac{d^{n-1}}{dt^{n-1}} \ldots + a_0(t) \right] ,$$

$$L_2 \equiv \left[b_0(t)\frac{d^m}{dt^m} + \ldots b_m(t) \right] .$$

An operator L is said to be linear if

$$L[au(t) + bv(t)] = aL[u(t)] + bL[v(t)]$$

where $u(t)$ and $v(t)$ are two functions with derivatives to a sufficient order, and a and b are any constants. It is easy to see that L_1 and L_2 as defined above are linear operators under this definition.

The differential equation (7.16) which contains only linear operators is then known as a linear ordinary differential equation, and, by association, the system which it models is called a linear system. We note the differential equations (7.6) and (7.11) which represented the $L–R$ circuit and the $C–R$ circuit respectively are of the form (7.15) and hence that of (7.16), whilst each of the pair (7.12) and (7.13) describing the $L–C–R$ circuit were also of this form. In fact, each of these equations had a further property, in that all the coefficients were constants, that is, non-time-varying. Such linear systems are called linear time invariant systems, indicating physically that the circuit parameters are fixed for all time.

Example 7.3
Show that the system represented by the differential equation

$$\frac{d^2y(t)}{dt^2} + 3t\frac{dy(t)}{dt}4e^{-t}y(t) = \frac{du(t)}{dt} \tag{7.17}$$

is linear.
    We write the differential equation as

$$L_1[y(t)] = L_2[u(t)] \ ,$$

where

$$L_1 \equiv \left[\frac{d^2}{dt^2} + 3t\frac{d}{dt} + 4e^{-t} \right] \qquad \text{and} \qquad L_2 = \left[\frac{d}{dt} \right] .$$

Now

$$L_1[\alpha y_1(t) + \beta y_2(t)] = \left[\frac{d^2}{dt^2} + 3t\frac{d}{dt} + 4e^{-t} \right] [\alpha y_1(t) + \beta y_2(t)]$$

$$= \frac{d^2}{dt^2}(\alpha y_1(t) + \beta y_2(t)) + 3t\frac{d}{dt}(\alpha y_1(t) + \beta y_2(t)) + 4e^{-t}(\alpha y_1(t) + \beta y_2(t))$$

$$= \alpha\left(\frac{d^2y_1(t)}{dt^2} + 3t\frac{dy_1(t)}{dt} + 4e^{-t}y_1(t) \right) + \beta\left(\frac{d^2y_2(t)}{dt^2} + 3t\frac{dy_2(t)}{dt} + 4e^{-t}y_2(t) \right)$$

$$= \alpha L_1[y_1(t)] + \beta L_1[y_2(t)] \ .$$

So L_1 is a linear operator. Similarly

$$L_2[au_1(t) + bu_2(t)] = \left[\frac{d}{dt} \right] [au_1(t) + bu_2(t)]$$

$$= \frac{d}{dt}(au_1(t) + bu_2(t))$$

$$= a\frac{du_1(t)}{dt} + b\frac{du_2(t)}{dt} = aL_2[u_1(t)] + bL_2[u_2(t)] \ ,$$

and thus L_2 is also a linear operator and (7.17) is a linear differential equation. Although the system represented by (7.17) is linear, it is not time invariant.

We can now infer a most useful result for linear systems, known as the principle of superposition, which finds considerable application. Suppose we have a linear system modelled by the differential equation.

$$L_1[y(t)] = L_2[u(t)] \ ,$$

where L_1 and L_2 are linear operators and $y(t)$ is the output or response corresponding to the input $u(t)$, with zero initial conditions. Suppose that a second input $v(t)$ produces the response $x(t)$ when also subject to zero initial conditions. That is

$$L_1[x(t)] = L_2[v(t)] \ .$$

The response or output corresponding to the linear combination of these two inputs

$$w(t) = au(t) + bv(t) \ , \qquad \text{with } a \text{ and } b \text{ constant,}$$

and also with zero initial conditions, will be the solution of

$$L_1[z(t)] = L_2[w(t)] \tag{7.18}$$

Now

$$\begin{aligned}
L_2[w(t)] &= L_2[au(t) + bv(t)] \\
&= aL_2[u(t)] + bL_2[v(t)] \\
&= aL_1[y(t)] + bL_1[x(t)] \\
&= L_1[ay(t) + bx(t)] \ .
\end{aligned}$$

That is, $L_1[ay(t) + bx(t)] = L_2[w(t)]$; in other words, $z(t) = ay(t) + bx(t)$ is a solution of (7.18), and the fact that $z(t)$ satisfies the requirement of zero initial conditions ensures uniqueness.

These ideas may be clarified in the following examples.

Example 7.4
Suppose a linear time invariant system is modelled as

$$\frac{dy(t)}{dt} + 2y(t) = u(t) \ , \qquad t \geq 0 \ .$$

Demonstrate the principle of superposition.

Let us take two input signals $u_1(t) = 1$ and $u_2(t) = e^{-t}$ with $t \geq 0$, and find the output or responses when $y(0) = 0$. This is the so-called zero-state response of the system.

When $u(t) = u_1(t) = 1$, we must find the response $y_1(t)$ given by

$$\frac{dy_1(t)}{dt} + 2y_1(t) = 1 \qquad \text{with } y_1(0) = 0 \ .$$

By inspection (or otherwise!) we see that

$$y_1(t) = Ae^{-2t} + \tfrac{1}{2}$$

where A is an arbitrary constant. But $y_1(0) = 0$ and so $A = -\tfrac{1}{2}$ and thus $y_1(t) = \tfrac{1}{2}(1 - e^{-2t})$. On the other hand, with $u(t) = u_2(t) = e^{-t}$, we find that

$$\frac{dy_2(t)}{dt} + 2y_2(t) = e^{-t} ,$$

which implies that

$$y_2(t) = Be^{-2t} + e^{-t} ,$$

with B determined from $y_2(0) = 0$ as $B = -1$, so that

$$y_2(t) = e^{-t} - e^{-2t} .$$

Now, with the composite input $w(t) = au_1(t) + bu_2(t) = a + be^{-t}$ where a and b are constant, we must solve for the output $z(t)$, where

$$\frac{dz(t)}{dt} + 2z(t) = a + be^{-t} \qquad \text{with } z(0) = 0 .$$

We find that $z(t) = Ce^{-2t} + (a/2) + be^{-t}$ and $z(0) = 0$ determines the arbitrary constant C as $C = -(a/2) - b$ and thus

$$z(t) = \frac{a}{2}(1 - e^{-2t}) + b(e^{-t} - e^{-2t})$$

$$= a[\tfrac{1}{2}(1 - e^{-2t})] + b[e^{-t} - e^{-2t}]$$

$$= ay_1(t) + by_2(t) .$$

As we have noted, the response of a linear system to a particular input when all initial conditions are zero, is called the zero-state response. We have shown that if the zero-state responses to two different inputs are known, then the zero-state response to a linear combination of these inputs is the same linear combination of the individual responses. Clearly this can be generalized to any number of different inputs and their zero-state responses.

7.5 BLOCK DIAGRAMS

Before dealing with this topic, we consider an alternative form of the circuit diagram which highlights the concept of the circuit processing an input signal to produce an output signal. Consider again the C–R circuit in Example 7.2. The input to this circuit is $e(t)$ and if the desired output, $y(t)$, is the voltage $v_c(t)$ measured across the capacitor, we can represent this situation in the re-drawn form given in Fig. 7.8. It is

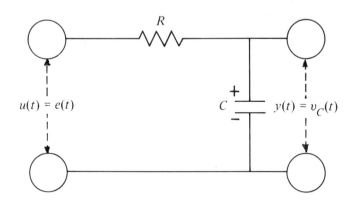

Fig. 7.8 — The C–R circuit.

assumed that the readings obtained for $y(t)$ are exactly the values of $v_c(t)$, implying that an ideal measuring device is used, taking no current. In fact this is not physically possible! However, the current through the measuring device is assumed to be so small that the presence of the device may be ignored in the analysis of the circuit.

Although the representation of the circuit above is helpful, block diagrams can give further insight. Block diagrams focus on the mathematical model of the circuit or system and are formed from four basic building blocks. For continuous time systems these blocks represent the operations of:

(1) multiplication by a constant,
(2) time differentiation,
(3) time integration, and
(4) summation, including the possibility of sign reversal.

Diagrammatically these are represented in Fig. 7.9. In fact (2), time differentiation, rarely appears, and frequently initial conditions are zero with this information conveyed in (3) — time integration — by the absence of the vertical arrow.

In Example 7.2 we saw that the C–R circuit of Fig. 7.8 could be modelled by the differential equation

$$\frac{dy(t)}{dt} + \frac{1}{RC}y(t) = \frac{1}{RC}u(t)$$

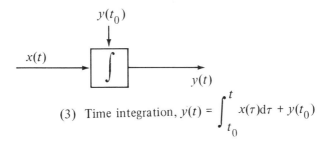

(1) Multiplication, $y(t) = ax(t)$

(2) Time differentiation, $y(t) = \dfrac{\mathrm{d}x(t)}{\mathrm{d}t}$

(3) Time integration, $y(t) = \displaystyle\int_{t_0}^{t} x(\tau)\mathrm{d}\tau + y(t_0)$

(4) Summation, $y(t) = x_1(t) - x_2(t)$

Fig. 7.9 — Block diagram operations.

when $y(t) = v_C(t)$, the voltage drop measured across C, is the output and $u(t) = e(t)$ is the input. Now solve this equation for $\mathrm{d}y(t)/\mathrm{d}t$, the highest occurring derivative, to obtain

$$\frac{\mathrm{d}y(t)}{\mathrm{d}t} = \frac{1}{RC}(u(t) - y(t)) \ . \tag{7.19}$$

Suppose for a moment that we had somehow formed a signal to represent $dy(t)/dt$, then one integration together with a specified initial condition would generate $y(t)$. When $y(t_0) = 0$ we can illustrate this as in Fig. 7.10. We now see (7.19) as a

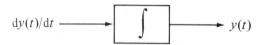

Fig. 7.10 — Integration of $dy(t)/dt$ to produce $y(t)$ with $y(t)_0) = 0$.

'prescription' for generating the signal $dy(t)/dt$ as a scaled sum of the input $u(t)$ and $- y(t)$, and this leads to the system block diagram of Fig. 7.11. Fig. 7.11 gives us more

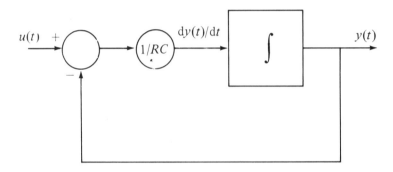

Fig. 7.11 — Block diagram for the C–R circuit.

insight into how the system processes the input signal. The input $u(t)$ is combined with a negative feedback of the system output; the composite signal is then scaled (amplifed if $1/RC > 1$, or attenuated if $1/RC < 1$) and integrated to form the output. The block diagram as built up for this example illustrates the processing effect of the circuit rather more clearly by showing the path (and the construction) of signals within the system. We will make use of this visualization in conjunction with the Laplace transform version of signals and blocks in the next section.

7.6 THE LAPLACE TRANSFORMATION

Readers are assumed to be familiar with an elementary treatment of the Laplace transformation. It is likely that such treatment will have focused on the transformation as a solution technique for linear ordinary differential equations with constant coefficients. We will show that there is a wider role to be played by the transform, and that we can generate a useful tool for the analysis of linear time invariant systems.

Initially we take a slightly wider view of the topic and first define the two-sided or bilateral Laplace transform of a continuous function of time, $f(t)$, defined on $-\infty < t < \infty$. We then define

$$F(s) = \int_{-\infty}^{\infty} f(t)\,e^{-st}\,dt \qquad\qquad (7.20)$$

$$= \mathscr{L}_B\{f(t)\} \; ,$$

where s is a complex number, as the bilateral Laplace transform of $f(t)$. The transform is said to exist whenever (7.20) exists, that is when the integral takes a finite value. Most of the time, the functions we are concerned with will represent time-varying signals, which are causal, that is $f(t) = 0$ for $t < 0$. Under these circumstances, (7.20) *reduces* to

$$F(s) = \int_0^{\infty} f(t)\,e^{-st}\,dt \; , \qquad\qquad (7.21)$$

and $F(s)$ is called the one-sided, or unilateral, Laplace transform of the causal function $f(t)$.

Example 7.5
Find the unilateral Laplace transform of $f(t)$ when $f(t) = e^{-at}\xi(t)$, where

$$\xi(t) = \begin{cases} 0 & t < 0 \\ 1 & t \geqslant 0 \end{cases}$$

is the Heaviside step function and $a > 0$. Here we observe that $f(t)$ is causal, because

$$f(t) = \begin{cases} 0 & t < 0 \\ 1 & t \geqslant 0 \end{cases} \; .$$

Using (7.21)

$$F(s) = \int_0^{\infty} e^{-at}e^{-st}dt = \int_0^{\infty} e^{-(s+a)t}\,dt$$

$$= \frac{1}{s+a} \; , \qquad \text{if } \mathrm{Re}(s) > -a \; . \qquad\qquad (7.22)$$

We note that $f(t)$ is causal in view of the presence of $\xi(t)$, and it is easy to see from (7.20) that $g(t) = e^{-at}$, $-\infty < t < \infty$, does not have a bilateral transform. It is important to note that in view of causality, (7.21) can be rewritten as

$$F(s) = \int_{0^-}^{\infty} f(t)e^{-st}\,dt \ , \tag{7.23}$$

where 0^- is defined by $0^- = -\sigma^2$, where σ is real, so that $\sigma^2 > 0$. This modification will be used freely at a later stage. Table 7.1 lists frequently occurring causal functions

Table 7.1 — Laplace transforms of elementary causal functions.

$f(t)$	$F(s)$
$a\xi(t)$	a/s
$t\xi(t)$	$1/s^2$
$t^n\xi(t)$	$n!/s^{n+1}$
$\sin(at)\xi(t)$	$a/(s^2 + a^2)$
$\cos(at)\xi(t)$	$s/(s^2 + a^2)$
$e^{-at}\xi(t)$	$1/(s + a)$
$e^{-at}\sin(bt)\xi(t)$	$(s + a)/((s + a)^2 + b^2)$
$e^{-at}\cos(bt)\xi(t)$	$b/((s + a)^2 + b^2)$

and their Laplace transforms. To avoid repeated use of the term, we will drop the word unilateral unless needed, and assume that all signals are causal.

7.7 A SUMMARY OF PROPERTIES OF THE TRANSFORM

We summarize here the most immediately applicable results from the theory; for a fuller discussion, see Gabel and Roberts [3], or O'Neil [4].

(1) Linearity: If the Laplace transforms of two continuous-time signals $f_1(t)$ *and* $f_2(t)$ are $F_1(s)$ and $F_2(s)$ respectively, then

$$\mathcal{L}\{af_1(t) + bf_2(t)\} = aF_1(s) + bF_2(s) \ ,$$

where a and b are any constants. The proof of this result is immediate:

$$\mathcal{L}\{af_1(t) + bf_2(t)\} = \int_0^{\infty} (af_1(t) + bf_2(t))e^{-st}\,dt$$

$$= a \int_0^\infty f_1(t) e^{-st} \, dt + b \int_0^\infty f_2(t) e^{-st} \, dt$$

$$= a F_1(s) + b F_2(s) \ .$$

(2) Time differentiation: If the Laplace transform of $f(t)$,

$$\mathcal{L}\{f(t)\} = F(s) \ ,$$

then

$$\mathcal{L}\left\{ \frac{df(t)}{dt} \right\} = sF(s) - f(0) \ . \tag{7.24}$$

The proof is by direct calculation; by definition

$$\mathcal{L}\left\{ \frac{df(t)}{dt} \right\} = \int_0^\infty e^{-st} \frac{df(t)}{dt} \, dt = f(t) e^{-st} \Big|_0^\infty + s \int_0^\infty f(t) e^{-st} \, dt \ ,$$

$$= sF(s) - f(0) \ ,$$

since from the existence of $F(s)$, $f(t)e^{-st} \to 0$ as $t \to \infty$.
     Repeated integration by parts, or an inductive proof, shows that

$$\mathcal{L}\left\{ \frac{d^n f(t)}{dt^n} \right\} = s^n F(s) - s^{n-1} f(0) - s^{n-2} f^1(0) \ \ldots \ -f^{n-1}(0) \tag{7.25}$$

where

$$f^n(0) = \frac{d^n f(t)}{dt^n} \bigg|_{t=0} \ .$$

(3) Time integration: If $\mathcal{L}\{f(t)\} = F(s)$, where $f(t)$ is a continuous-time function of exponential order. That is, $f(t) \leqslant M e^{\alpha t}$ as $t \to \infty$, so that both $f(t)$ and its integral possess Laplace transforms, then

$$\mathcal{L}\left\{\int_0^t f(\tau)\,d\tau\right\} = \frac{F(s)}{s} \ .$$

Again the proof follows from the definition,

$$\mathcal{L}\left\{\int_0^t f(\tau)\,d\tau\right\} = \int_0^\infty \left(\int_0^t f(\tau)\,d\tau\right) e^{-st}\,dt$$

$$= -\frac{e^{-st}}{s}\int_0^t f(\tau)\,d\tau \bigg|_0^\infty + \frac{1}{s}\int_0^\infty f(t)e^{-st}\,dt \ .$$

Examining the first term in detail, as $t \to \infty$, we have that

$$\lim_{t\to\infty}\left(\frac{e^{-st}}{s}\int_0^t f(\tau)\,d\tau\right)$$

$$\leq \lim_{t\to\infty}\left(\frac{e^{-st}}{s}\frac{Me^{\alpha t}}{\alpha}\right)$$

$$= \frac{M}{\alpha s}\lim_{t\to\infty}(e^{-(s-\alpha)t}) = 0 \qquad \text{if Re}(s) > \alpha \ .$$

Also, at $t = 0$

$$\frac{e^{-st}}{s}\int_0^t f(\tau)\,d\tau = 0 \ ,$$

and so

$$\mathcal{L}\left\{\int_0^t f(\tau)\,d\tau\right\} = \frac{F(s)}{s} \ .$$

(4) Convolution: If $\mathcal{L}\{f(t)\} = F(s)$ and $\mathcal{L}\{g(t)\} = G(s)$, then

$$\mathcal{L}\{f(t)*g(t)\} = F(s)G(s) \ ,$$

where $f(t)*g(t)$ is the time convolution of $f(t)$ and $g(t)$, defined by the convolution integrals

$$f(t)*g(t) = \int_0^t f(\tau)g(t-\tau)\,d\tau = \int_0^t g(\tau)f(t-\tau)\,d\tau \ .$$

This result is proved in, for example, Poularikas and Seely [6].
    Also of use are the two so-called shift theorems.

(5)   First shift theorem: if $\mathscr{L}\{f(t)\} = F(s)$, then $\mathscr{L}\{e^{at}f(t)\} = F(s-a)$.

(6)   Second shift theorem: if $\mathscr{L}\{f(t)\} = F(s)$, then $\mathscr{L}\{f(t-\tau)\} = e^{-\tau s}F(s)$.

Both of these theorems are straightforward to establish, and are left as exercises.

    We observed in (7.23), that the lower limit of integration could be taken as $0^- = -\sigma^2 < 0$. This can be used in all of the above results; in particular (7.24) becomes

$$\mathscr{L}\left\{\frac{df(t)}{dt}\right\} = sF(s) - f(0^-) \ , \tag{7.26}$$

with a similar form for (7.25).
    We are then lead to think of 'initial conditions' as those which obtain for all time $t \leqslant 0$ (actually $t < 0$ in certain cases — see Chapter 8) instead of at $t = 0$ only.

7.8   APPLICATION TO LINEAR TIME INVARIANT SYSTEMS

Let us return to our C–R circuit of Example 7.2, for which the output $y(t)$ is given by

$$\frac{dy(t)}{dt} + \frac{1}{RC}y(t) = \frac{1}{RC}u(t) \ .$$

Taking transforms with $\mathscr{L}\{u(t)\} = U(s)$ and $\mathscr{L}\{y(t)\} = Y(s)$ and $y(0) = 0$, that is an initially relaxed system, we have

$$sY(s) + \frac{1}{RC}Y(s) = \frac{1}{RC}U(s) \tag{7.27}$$

or

$$(1 + RCs)Y(s) = U(s) \ . \tag{7.28}$$

Using (7.28) and solving for the term containing the highest power of s, we obtain

$$sY(s) = \frac{1}{RC}(U(s) - Y(s)) \ .$$ (7.29)

Proceeding as for (7.19) previously, we suppose that in the transform domain we have generated the transformed signal $sY(s)$. Then multiplication by $1/s$ will generate $Y(s)$, the transform of the output.

Finally we recognize (7.29) as a 'recipe' for generating $sY(s)$ and draw the Laplace transform domain block diagram representation of the C–R circuit as in Fig. 7.12. The similarity with Fig. 7.11 is obvious, with the '$1/s$ block' serving as the

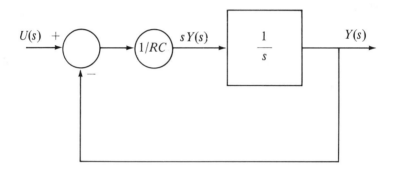

Fig. 7.12 — Transform domain block diagram of C–R circuit.

transformed integrator, clearly in line with property (3) of the **Laplace** transformation.

An even simpler form can be deduced, which suppresses structural information but contains all the information for its reconstruction. Equation (7.28) can be represented by a single block operating on the transform of the input signal to yield the transformed output signal; see Fig. 7.13. The diagram leads naturally to the idea

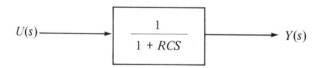

Fig. 7.13 — Single block representation of C–R circuit.

of the system Laplace transfer function $H(s)$. Writing (7.28) as

$$Y(s) = H(s)U(s)$$ (7.30)

We see that in the transform domain, the entire action of the circuit or system, on the input signal transform $U(s)$, is achieved by multiplication by $H(s)$. The convolution theorem allows us to invert (7.30) as

$$y(t) = h(t)*u(t)$$

$$= \int_0^t h(t-\tau)u(\tau)\,d\tau \tag{7.31}$$

where $h(t) = \mathscr{L}^{-1}\{H(s)\}$ is the (time-domain) transfer function. Notice that (7.31) makes an important statement for linear time invariant systems; if we know the transfer function $h(t)$, then we can express the zero-state system response corresponding to an arbitrary input as an integral. We will discuss this point later; meanwhile we will illustrate the use of (7.31) by an example.

Example 7.6
Find the response of the system with transfer function

$$h(t) = \beta e^{-\alpha t}\xi(t)\ ,\qquad \alpha,\ \beta > 0\ ,$$

to a step input signal, $u(t) = \xi(t)$.
    Using (7.31), the step response, which is understood to mean from the zero initial state, will be $y_s(t)$, where

$$y_s(t) = \int_0^t \beta e^{-\alpha(t-\tau)}1\,d\tau$$

$$= \int_0^t \beta e^{-\alpha\tau}\,d\tau\ .$$

Here we have used the commutative property for time convolution: $h(t)*u(t) = u(t)*h(t)$. Thus

$$y_s(t) = -\frac{\beta}{\alpha}e^{-\alpha\tau}\bigg|_0^t = \frac{\beta}{\alpha}(1-e^{-\alpha t})\ .$$

(See Fig. 7.14.)
    As a further demonstration of these ideas we will examine the L–C–R circuit discussed in section 7.3. Our analysis produced the pair of coupled first-order, linear, constant coefficient differential equations (7.12) and (7.13) repeated here:

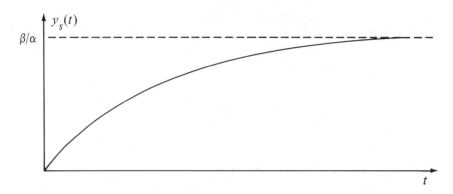

Fig. 7.14 — Step response for Example 7.6.

$$Ri(t) + L\frac{di(t)}{dt} + v_C(t) = e(t) \ ,$$

$$\frac{dv_C(t)}{dt} - \frac{1}{C}i(t) = 0 \ .$$

Take the Laplace transform, with $\mathcal{L}\{e(t)\} = E(s)$, $\mathcal{L}\{i(t)\} = I(s)$, $\mathcal{L}\{v_C(t)\} = V_C(s)$ with $i(0) = v(0) = 0$, corresponding to an initial zero state, to obtain

$$RI(s) + LsI(s) + V_C(s) = E(s)$$

$$sV_C(s) = \frac{1}{C}I(s) \ .$$

Proceeding as before we solve for $sI(s)$ and $sV_C(s)$ (already done) as the terms in the highest power of s in each equation, that is

$$sI(s) = \frac{1}{L}\{E(s) - V_C(s) - RI(s)\} \ , \tag{7.32}$$

$$sV_C(s) = \frac{1}{C}I(s) \ . \tag{7.33}$$

Considering (7.32) first, we easily determine the structure of Fig. 7.15. We see that we need to have available the transformed signal $V_C(s)$, but since $sV_C(s) = I(s)/C$, scaling the signal $I(s)$ by a factor $1/C$ and then passing it through a second '1/s block' will generate $V_C(s)$. We can then produce the final diagram as in Fig. 7.16. Referring to the diagram, we might be interested in either $I(s)$ or $V_C(s)$, or rather the inverse of

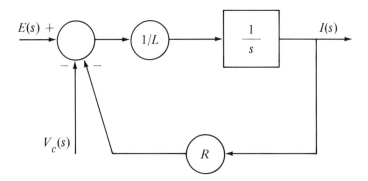

Fig. 7.15 — First stage in the development of the $L-C-R$ circuit block diagram.

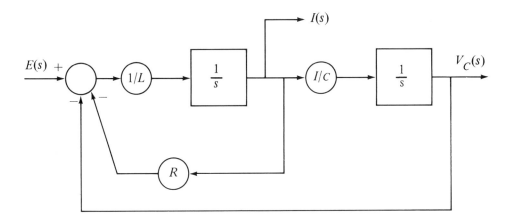

Fig. 7.16 — The complete $L-C-R$ block diagram.

these transforms, as the output corresponding to an input voltage $e(t)$. We thus seek the appropriate Laplace transfer functions. Evidently the transformed signal $I(s)$ is generated as

$$I(s) = \frac{1}{s} \times \frac{1}{L} \times \{E(s) - RI(s) - V_C(s)\}$$

$$= \frac{1}{sL} \left\{ E(s) - RI(s) - \frac{1}{C} \times \frac{1}{s} I(s) \right\} .$$

Therefore,

$$I(s)\left\{\frac{LCs^2 + RCs + 1}{LCs^2}\right\} = \frac{1}{Ls}E(s)$$

or

$$I(s) = \frac{Cs}{LCs^2 + RCs + 1}E(s) = H_1(s)E(s) \ . \tag{7.34}$$

Also, since

$$V_C(s) = \frac{1}{Cs}I(s) \ ,$$

$$V_C(s) = \frac{1}{LCs^2 + RCs + 1}E(s) = H_2(s)E(s) \ . \tag{7.35}$$

Thus depending on the desired output we can generate the two Laplace transfer functions $H_1(s)$ and $H_2(s)$. Although these are not identical, there are clearly some similarities, and as an indication of the origin of the similarities, we can construct differential equations for each output provided that the restriction to zero initial conditions is observed.

From (7.34)

$$(LCs^2 + RCs + 1)I(s) = CsE(s) \ ,$$

and if initial conditions on $i(t)$, $di(t)/dt$ and $e(t)$ are zero, this is the Laplace transform of the differential equation

$$LC\frac{d^2i(t)}{dt^2} + RC\frac{di(t)}{dt} + i(t) = C\frac{de(t)}{dt} \ . \tag{7.36}$$

On the other hand, from (7.35) we easily obtain the differential equation for $v_C(t)$ as the output in the form

$$LC\frac{d^2v_C(t)}{dt^2} + RC\frac{dv_C(t)}{dt} + v_C(t) = e(t) \ . \tag{7.37}$$

The two equations (7.36) and (7.37) are alternative forms of the circuit equation for the L–C–R circuit, which could in fact have been inferred by elimination between (7.12) and (7.13).

7.9 TRANSFER FUNCTIONS

We conclude this chapter by reviewing our ideas on system transfer functions for linear time invariant (LTI) systems. Such a system, including any of the above circuits, can be modelled by a differential equation of the form

$$\frac{d^n y(t)}{dt^n} + a_{n-1}\frac{d^{n-1}y(t)}{dt^{n-1}} \ldots + a_0 y(t) = b_m \frac{d^m x(t)}{dt^m} + \ldots + b_0 x(t) \tag{7.38}$$

where $x(t)$ is the input and $y(t)$ the output and where $a_0 \ldots a_{n-1}, b_0 \ldots b_m$ are constants.

LTI systems which have been modelled using a system of n first-order equations can be represented in the form (7.38) after elimination, which may be performed directly or using block diagrams, following the method in section 7.8.

With an initially relaxed system, meaning that all conditions on $y(t)$ and $x(t)$ and their derivatives at $t = 0$ are zero, taking the Laplace transform of (7.38), with $\mathscr{L}\{x(t)\} = X(s)$, and $\mathscr{L}\{y(t)\} = Y(s)$, we obtain

$$(s^n + a_{n-1}s^{n-1} + \ldots + a_0)Y(s) = (b_m s^m + \ldots + b_0)X(s) \ .$$

Thus,

$$Y(s) = \frac{b_m s^m + \ldots + b_0}{s^n + a_{n-1}s^{n-1} + \ldots + a_0} X(s) \tag{7.39}$$

i.e.

$$Y(s) = H(s)X(s) \ , \tag{7.40}$$

where

$$H(s) = \frac{b_m s^m + \ldots + b_0}{s^n + a_{n-1}s^{n-1} + \ldots + a_0} \ . \tag{7.41}$$

Here $H(s)$, as previously identified, is the Laplace transfer function, and if $m \leqslant n$ (the usual situation), $H(s)$ is said to be 'proper'. The denominator of $H(s)$, that is

$$s^n + a_{n-1}s^{n-1} + \ldots + a_0 \; ,$$

is called the characteristic polynomial of the system, and we observe that in the different representations (7.36) and (7.37) above of the same system, then we would obtain the same characteristic polynomial. This is not a coincidence, and a proof that the characteristic equation is independent of the particular representation of the system chosen is suggested in the exercises.

$H(s)$, defined by (7.41), can be inverted to yield

$$h(t) = \mathscr{L}^{-1}\{H(s)\} \tag{7.42}$$

as the (time-domain) transfer function. Recalling ideas of section 7.8, we can express the zero-state response of a linear time invariant system for a given input $x(t)$ in a compact form. From (7.40), using the convolution theorem for Laplace transforms, we have

$$y(t) = \int_0^t h(t-\tau)x(\tau)\,d\tau$$

$$= \int_0^t h(\tau)x(t-\tau)\,d\tau \; ,$$

where $h(t)$ is obtained from (7.42). At this point, if the numerator of $H(s)$ in (7.41) is other than a constant, i.e. $b_i = 0$, $i \neq 0$, we are restricted to inputs $x(t)$ which have zero initial conditions. Later we will consider this point again.

Finally we demonstrate these and earlier ideas by means of an example.

Example 7.7
Consider the circuit shown in Fig. 7.17. Find the Laplace transfer function between the input voltage $x(t)$ and output voltage $y(t) = v_2(t)$, the voltage drop measured across C_2. Notice how we have chosen to denote the current in the branches of the circuit; the effect of this is to automatically satisfy Kirchoff's current law at the junctions P and Q. Remember also that, by assumption, the measuring device, used to obtain $y(t)$, is assumed to draw a negligible current, which is ignored. The output $y(t)$ is thus $v_2(t)$, the voltage drop across the capacitor C_2.

Using our procedure for analysing circuits, we first consider the circuit APQBA, a loop in the overall circuit, and with the usual notation Kirchhoff's voltage law for this loop gives

$$v_R(t) + v_1(t) - x(t) = 0 \; . \tag{7.43}$$

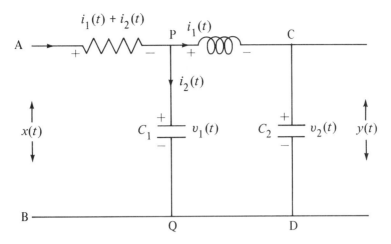

Fig. 7.17 — Circuit for Example 7.7.

Clearly (7.43) does not involve the output $y(t) = v_2(t)$, and we need a second 'loop' equation. There are two candidates, the loop APCDQBA or the loop PCDQP, and either may be chosen. Having used either of these loops, we will have traversed every route in the entire network at least once and have thus extracted all the information available. We select for our second loop PCDQP and obtain

$$v_L(t) + v_2(t) - v_1(t) = 0 \ . \tag{7.44}$$

Writing down the component constitutive equations, we obtain

$$\text{for } R \qquad v_R = (i_1(t) + i_2(t))R \ , \tag{7.45}$$

$$\text{for } C_1 \qquad i_2(t) = C_1 \frac{\mathrm{d}v_1(t)}{\mathrm{d}t} \ , \text{ using the derivative form,} \tag{7.46}$$

$$\text{for } L \qquad v_L(t) = L \frac{\mathrm{d}i_1(t)}{\mathrm{d}t} \ , \tag{7.47}$$

$$\text{for } C_2 \qquad i_1(t) = C_2 \frac{\mathrm{d}v_2(t)}{\mathrm{d}t} \ . \tag{7.48}$$

Viewing the system (7.43)–(7.48) as a whole, we see that (7.46)–(7.48) is a set of 3 simultaneous linear differential equations with constant coefficients, whereas

(7.43)–(7.45) provide a set of algebraic (or static) equations. Equations (7.46)–(7.48) imply that the variables $v_1(t)$, $v_2(t)$, $i_1(t)$ may be used to describe the circuit behaviour (in other words, provide a set of state variables), whereas the static equations (7.43)–(7.45) link the state variables, both to each other, and via the auxilliary variables $i_2((t)$, $v_L(t)$ and $v_R(t)$ to the input $x(t)$.

Our aim is to obtain the Laplace transfer function for the circuit, and this task can be achieved by eliminating the auxiliary variables as follows.

Using (7.46), we have

$$\frac{dv_1(t)}{dt} = \frac{1}{C_1} i_2(t) \ ,$$

but from (7.45)

$$i_2(t) = \frac{1}{R} v_R(t) - i_1(t)$$

$$= \frac{1}{R}(x(t) - v_1(t)) - i_1(t), \text{ from (7.43)}.$$

Thus (7.46) becomes

$$\frac{dv_1(t)}{dt} = \frac{1}{RC_1} x(t) - \frac{1}{RC_1} v_1(t) - \frac{1}{C_1} i_1(t) \ , \tag{7.49}$$

with the right-hand side involving only state variables and the input $x(t)$.

Also (7.47) becomes, using (7.44),

$$\frac{di_1(t)}{dt} = \frac{1}{L} v_1(t) - \frac{1}{L} v_2(t) \ , \tag{7.50}$$

wheras (7.48) is in the desired form when written as

$$\frac{dv_2(t)}{dt} = \frac{1}{C_2} i_1(t) \quad . \tag{7.51}$$

The time domain block diagrams for the circuit could now be built up in stages as before, but as our aim is the system transfer function, we now transform our equations from the time domain to the Laplace transform domain. We obtain, with zero initial conditions,

$$sV_1(s) = \frac{1}{RC_1} X(s) - \frac{1}{RC_1} V_1(s) - \frac{1}{C_1} I_1(s) \quad , \tag{7.52}$$

$$sI_1(s) = \frac{1}{L} V_1(s) - \frac{1}{L} V_2(s) \quad , \tag{7.53}$$

$$sV_2(s) = \frac{1}{C_2} I_1(s) \quad . \tag{7.54}$$

Obviously, algebraic elimination yields the transfer function readily at this stage. However, we first construct the transform domain block diagram in stages as illustrated in Fig. 7.18(a)–(d).

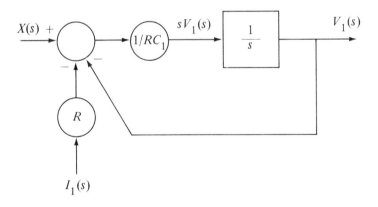

Fig. 7.18(a) — Block diagram for (7.52): $I_1(s)$ is needed.

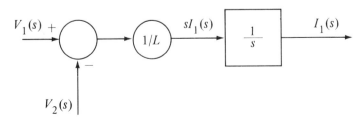

Fig. 7.18(b) — Block diagram for (7.53): $V_1(s)$ is available from (a) above; $I_1(s)$ is now available; $V_2(s)$ is needed.

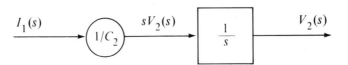

Fig. 7.18(c) — Block diagram for (7.54): $I_1(s)$ is available from (b) above; $V_2(s)$ is now available.

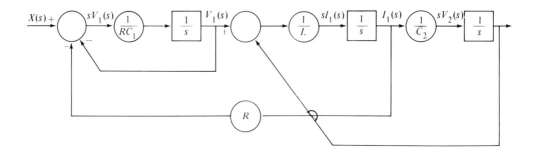

Fig. 7.18(d) — Block diagram for Example 7.7.

From (7.52)–(7.54) (or reading from the diagram),

$$Y(s) = \frac{1}{C_2 s} I_1(s) \tag{7.55}$$

$$I_1(s) = \frac{1}{Ls}(V_1(s) - Y(s)) \tag{7.56}$$

$$V_1(s) = \frac{1}{RC_1 s}(X(s) - V_1(s) - RI_1(s)) \tag{7.57}$$

$$Y(s) = \frac{1}{LC_2 s^2}(V_1(s) - Y(s))$$

from (7.55) and (7.56), or

$$Y(s)\left\{1 + \frac{1}{LC_2 s^2}\right\} = \frac{1}{LC_2 s^2}V_1(s) \ .$$

That is,

$$Y(s)\{1 + LC_2 s^2\} = V_1(s) \ . \tag{7.58}$$

But

$$V_1(s)\left\{1 + \frac{1}{RC_1 s}\right\} = \frac{1}{RC_1 s}(X(s) - RI_1(s))$$

from (7.57)

$$= \frac{1}{RC_1 s}\left(X(s) - \frac{R}{Ls}(V_1(s) - Y(s))\right) \ .$$

That is,

$$V_1(s)\left\{1 + \frac{1}{RC_1 s} + \frac{1}{LC_1 s^2}\right\} = \frac{1}{RC_1 s}\left\{X(s) + \frac{R}{Ls}Y(s)\right\} \ ,$$

so that

$$V_1(s)\{LC_1 R s^2 + Ls + R\} = Ls\left\{X(s) + \frac{R}{Ls}Y(s)\right\}$$

$$= LsX(s) + RY(s) \ .$$

Thus, using (7.58)

$$Y(s)\{LC_2s^2 + 1\}\{LC_1Rs^2 + Ls + R\} = LsX(s) + RY(s) \ ,$$

so

$$Y(s)\{L^2C_1C_2Rs^4 + L^2C_2s^3 + RL(C_1 + C_2)s^2 + Ls\} = LsX(s)$$

or

$$Y(s) = \frac{\dfrac{1}{LC_1C_2R}X(s)}{s^3 + \dfrac{1}{C_1R}s^2 + \dfrac{(C_1 + C_2)}{LC_1C_2}s + \dfrac{1}{LC_1C_2R}} \tag{7.59}$$

$$= H(s)X(s) \ . \tag{7.60}$$

From (7.59) the Laplace transfer function for the system is

$$H(s) = \frac{\dfrac{1}{LC_1C_2R}}{s^3 + \dfrac{1}{C_1R}s^2 + \dfrac{(C_1 + C_2)}{LC_1C_2}s + \dfrac{1}{LC_1C_2R}} \tag{7.61}$$

and we note that this is 'proper' in the sense defined.

Finally we note that by inverting (7.60), using (7.61), we obtain as the time-domain representation of this system

$$\frac{d^3y(t)}{dt^3} + \frac{1}{C_1R}\frac{d^2y(t)}{dt^2} + \frac{(C_1 + C_2)}{LC_1C_2}\frac{dy(t)}{dt} + \frac{1}{LC_1C_2R}y(t) = \frac{x(t)}{LC_1C_2R} \ , \tag{7.62}$$

where $x(t)$ is the input voltage and $y(t) = v_2(t)$ is the output voltage measured across the capacitor C_2.

In this chapter, we have examined the concepts of signals and linear systems. We have seen that simple electrical circuits can be used to perform operations on input signals to produce output signals, and we have developed a method for the analysis of such systems. The Laplace transform, with its associated block diagrams, has been shown to be a useful tool in such analysis, and we have observed the duality between time and transform domains. In the next chapter we examine some specific responses of linear systems which will help us to understand system characteristics and system behaviour. In later chapters we shall develop methods for the design of systems which will perform specific operations on input signals.

REFERENCES

[1] P. R. Adby, *Applied Circuit Theory*, Ellis Horwood, Chichester, 1980.
[2] D. N. Burghes and A. Graham, *Introduction to Control Theory, including Optimal Control*, Ellis Horwood, Chichester, 1980.
[3] R. A. Gabel and R. A. Roberts, *Signals and Linear Systems*, Wiley, New York, 1987.
[4] P. V. O'Neil, *Advanced Engineering Mathematics*, Wadsworth, Belmont, 1983.
[5] A. Papoulis, *Circuits and Systems: a Modern Approach*, Holt, Rinehart and Winston, New York, 1980.
[6] A. D. Poularikas and S. Seely, *Elements of Signals and Systems*, PWS-Kent, Boston, 1988.

EXERCISES

1. If the desired output of the system of Example 7.1 is v_L, obtain a corresponding differential equation representation.

2. $\mathbf{M}$ is a non-singular matrix, and $\mathbf{B} = \mathbf{M}^{-1}\mathbf{AM}$. Show that $\det(\lambda\mathbf{I} - \mathbf{A}) = \det(\lambda\mathbf{I} - \mathbf{B})$. A system is described in state-space form as

$$\frac{\mathrm{d}}{\mathrm{d}t}\mathbf{x}(t) = \mathbf{A}\mathbf{x}(t) + \mathbf{b}u(t)$$

$$y(t) = \mathbf{c}^{\mathrm{T}}\mathbf{x}(t) \ ,$$

and a transformation of state is defined by $\mathbf{z}(t) = \mathbf{M}\mathbf{x}(t)$. Show that

$$\frac{\mathrm{d}}{\mathrm{d}t}\mathbf{z}(t) = \mathbf{M}^{-1}\mathbf{AM}\mathbf{z}(t) + \mathbf{M}^{-1}\mathbf{b}u(t)$$

$$y(t) = \mathbf{c}^{\mathrm{T}}\mathbf{M}^{-1}\mathbf{z}(t)$$

and hence deduce that the characteristic equation of the system is independent of any such transformation.

3. Prove the two shift theorems for the Laplace transform given in section 7.7.

4. Obtain the transfer function for the system represented by the differential equation

$$\frac{d^2y(t)}{dt^2} + 5\frac{dy(t)}{dt} + 6y(t) = u(t) \ .$$

5. What is the transfer function for the system

$$\frac{d^3y(t)}{dt^3} + 4\frac{d^2y(t)}{dt^2} + y(t) = u(t) - 3\frac{du(t)}{dt} \ ?$$

6. The convolution operation is defined as

$$f(t)*g(t) = \int_{-\infty}^{\infty} f(\tau)g(t-\tau)\,d\tau \ .$$

Show that if $f(t)$ and $g(t)$ are both causal functions, then

$$f(t)*g(t) = \int_0^t f(\tau)g(t-\tau)\,d\tau$$

$$= \int_0^t f(t-\tau)g(\tau)\,d\tau \ .$$

Hence calculate $f(t)*g(t)$ when $f(t) = e^{-2t}\xi(t)$, and $g(t) = t\xi(t)$, where

$$\xi(t) = \begin{bmatrix} 0, t<0 \\ 1, t\leq0 \end{bmatrix},$$ is the Heaviside step function. If $f(t) = e^{-t}$ and $g(t) = t\xi(t)$, evaluate $f(t)*g(t)$.

7. Obtain a state-space representation, that is, find a matrix $\mathbf{A}$ and vectors $\mathbf{b}$ and $\mathbf{c}$, for the third-order system of Example 7.7. Evaluate $\det(\lambda\mathbf{I} - \mathbf{A})$ for the matrix $\mathbf{A}$.

8. Use the method of Example 7.3 to show that

$$e^{-2t}\frac{d^2y(t)}{dt^2} + 3e^{-t}\frac{dy(t)}{dt} + y(t) = u(t)$$

represents a linear system.

9. Determine the solution of the differential equation

$$\frac{d^2y(t)}{dt^2} + 7\frac{dy(t)}{dt} + 12\,y(t) = u(t)$$

when (i) $u(t) = \sin t$, and (ii) when $u(t) = \sin 2t$. What is the long-term behaviour of these solutions, and does this depend on the initial conditions? What would be the long-term behaviour of the solution when $u(t) = \sin t + \sin 2t$?

8

System responses

8.1 INTRODUCTION

In Chapter 7 we showed that some elementary electrical circuits could be modelled by linear differential equations or systems of linear differential equations. The idea of system response was introduced, in passing, as the output of a system subjected to an input signal. In the model, the differential equation was set up so that the output was given by (or derivable from) the solution. The first section of this chapter will look at factors which govern some important aspects of response behaviour. After developing some mathematical techniques we consider particular responses which serve to characterize a linear system and we conclude with a discussion of responses as viewed in the frequency domain

8.2 STABILITY OF LINEAR TIME INVARIANT SYSTEMS

Before defining what is meant by stability for linear time invariant systems we will examine the output of two such systems which are both initially relaxed and subject to a step input. First, consider the system with Laplace transfer function.

$$H_1(s) = \frac{1}{(s+1)(s+2)} \ .$$
(8.1)

Now $Y(s) = H_1(s)X(s)$, where $Y(s) = \mathcal{L}\{y(t)\}$ is the Laplace transform of the output, and $X(s) = \mathcal{L}\{x(t)\}$ is the Laplace transform of the input. With $x(t) = \xi(t)$, the step function, $X(s) = 1/s$ and

$$Y(s) = \frac{1}{s(s+1)(s+2)} \ ;$$

thus

$$Y(s) = \frac{\frac{1}{2}}{s} - \frac{1}{s+1} + \frac{\frac{1}{2}}{s+2}$$

and so inverting,

$$y(t) = (\tfrac{1}{2} - e^{-t} + \tfrac{1}{2} e^{-2t}) \, \xi(t) \ . \tag{8.2}$$

Fig. 8.1 shows the graph of $y(t)$, the response of the system (8.1) to the step input.

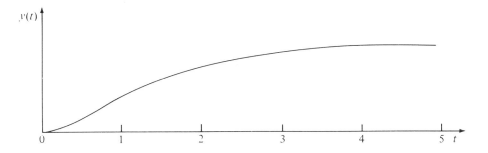

Fig. 8.1 — Response of system (8.1) to a step input.

Secondly, consider the system with Laplace transfer function

$$H_2(s) = \frac{1}{(s-1)(s+2)} \tag{8.3}$$

subject to the same input. The output is then given by

$$y(t) = \mathcal{L}^{-1} \left\{ \frac{1}{s(s-1)(s+2)} \right\}$$

$$= \mathcal{L}^{-1} \left\{ \frac{\frac{1}{3}}{s-1} - \frac{\frac{1}{2}}{s} + \frac{\frac{1}{6}}{s+2} \right\}$$

$$= (\tfrac{1}{3} e^t - \tfrac{1}{2} + \tfrac{1}{6} e^{-2t}) \, \xi(t) \ . \tag{8.4}$$

Fig. 8.2 illustrates the graph of $y(t)$ in this case.

We observe drastically different behaviour of the output signals as given in (8.2) and (8.4): in the former case we see a rise to a bounded limiting value of $\frac{1}{2}$, whereas the solution in (8.4) increases without bound. In the two chosen examples, the reason for the differing behaviour is easy to locate. For system (8.3), the term $(s-1)$ in the denominator of $H_2(s)$ generates a term in e^t in the solution, which produces the unbounded behaviour of the output. We see that this behaviour is inherent in the system Laplace transfer function, and is not dependent in any way on the input signal. We say that system (8.1) is a stable system, meaning that a bounded input signal produces a bounded output signal, whereas (8.3) is unstable. We thus are led to examine system Laplace transfer functions in order to determine conditions for system stability.

In the last chapter we saw that linear time invariant systems generated Laplace transfer functions of the form (7.41), that is

$$H(s) = \frac{b_m s^m + b_{m-1} s^{m-1} \ldots + b_0}{s^n + a_{n-1} s^{n-1} + \ldots + a_0} .$$

The examples we considered all lead to 'strictly proper' transfer functions $H(s)$, for which $m < n$, and we will only consider these here. The denominator of $H(s)$, $g(s)$ given by

$$g(s) = s^n + a_{n-1} s^{n-1} + \ldots + a_0$$

is the characteristic polynomial of the system, and may be factorized into complex factors, so that

$$g(s) = \prod_{i=1}^{n} (s - \lambda_i) , \tag{8.5}$$

where λ_i, $i = 1, 2, \ldots, n$, are the roots of the characteristic equation

$$g(s) = 0 ,$$

and are called the poles of the system.

We consider the case when the λ_i, $i = 1, 2, \ldots, n$, are distinct, i.e.

$$\lambda_i \neq \lambda_j , \qquad i \neq j ,$$

when $H(s)$ can be decomposed into partial fractions in the form

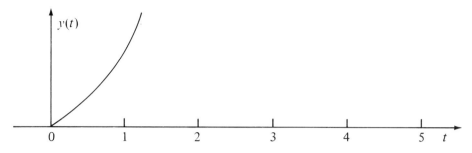

Fig. 8.2 — Response of system (8.3) to a step input.

$$H(s) = \sum_{j=1}^{n} \frac{\alpha_j}{s - \lambda_j} \; . \tag{8.6}$$

Inverting (8.6) we obtain

$$\mathcal{L}^{-1}\{H(s)\} = h(t)$$

$$= \sum_{j=1}^{n} \alpha_j \, e^{\lambda_j t} \; . \tag{8.7}$$

Now λ_j, $j = 1, 2, \ldots, n$, is in general a complex number so that

$$\lambda_j = a_j + i b_j \; , \qquad \text{with } a_j, \, b_j \text{ both real} \; ,$$

and

$$e^{\lambda_j t} = e^{(a_j + i b_j)t} = e^{a_j t} (\cos b_j t + i \sin b_j t) \; . \tag{8.8}$$

Clearly as $t \to \infty$, $|e^{\lambda_j t}| \to \infty$ (implying that $|h(t)| \to \infty$) if $a_j > 0$, for *any* $j = 1, 2, \ldots, n$, whereas if $a_j < 0$ for *all* $j = 1, 2, \ldots, n$, then $|h(t)| \to 0$ as $t \to \infty$.

We define a stable system as a system for which all the poles, that is, the λ_j, $j = 1$, $2, \ldots, n$, and where $\lambda_j \neq \lambda_k$, $j \neq k$, lie in left half-plane. If $\lambda_j = a_j + i b_j$ then this means that $a_j < 0$ for all $j = 1, 2, \ldots, n$. The extension to the case when there are repeated roots of the characteristic equation is straightforward.

With this definition of stability it is possible to deduce that a system which satisfies the definition will yield a bounded output in response to a bounded input.

Example 8.1
Examine the stability of the systems with transfer functions:

(i) $H_1(s) = \dfrac{1}{s^2 + \sqrt{2}s + 1}$ (ii) $H_2(s) = \dfrac{1}{s(s+1)}$.

In each case, system stability will be determined by the location of the poles of $H(s)$ (see Fig. 8.3).

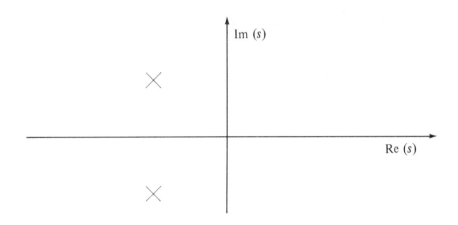

Fig. 8.3 — Locations of poles of $H_1(s) = s^2 + \sqrt{2}s + 1$.

In case (i), solving $s^2 + \sqrt{2}s + 1 = 0$, we obtain

$$s = -\frac{\sqrt{2} \pm \sqrt{(2-4)}}{2} = -\frac{\sqrt{2} \pm \sqrt{2}i}{2} = \frac{\sqrt{2}}{2}(-1 \pm i) \ .$$

Thus we see that the poles of $H_1(s)$, λ_1 and λ_2 are given by

$$\lambda_1 = \frac{\sqrt{2}}{2}(-1+i) \quad \text{and} \quad \lambda_2 = \frac{\sqrt{2}}{2}(-1-i)$$

both of which lie on the left half-plane, that is $\mathrm{Re}(\lambda) < 0$. Thus the system is stable. In case (ii) solving for the poles we have $s(s+1) = 0$. That is $\lambda_1 = 0$ and $\lambda_2 = -1$. Clearly λ_2 is in the left half-plane $\mathrm{Re}(\lambda) < 0$; however, λ_1 is not. By the definition of stability, the system with transfer function $H_2(s) = 1/s(s+1)$ is not stable. Systems of this type with simple (non-repeated) poles on the imaginary axis are classified as marginally stable. This point will be explored in section 8.4.

8.3   INTRODUCTION TO GENERALIZED FUNCTIONS

We have seen in an earlier section that in the Laplace transform domain the input–output relationship for linear time invariant systems is

$$Y(s) = H(s)X(s) \ . \tag{8.9}$$

In (8.9), $Y(s)$ is the transform of the output, $H(s)$ the system transfer function $X(s)$ the transform of the input. In section 8.2 we considered outputs of two systems in response to a step input. The output included terms arising from the form of the input and also terms representing the dynamics contained in the system transfer function itself. In producing a definition of system stability we focused only on the dynamics of the system so that the definition would be independent of any particular input. The *system* dynamics are determined by the time domain function, or response,

$$y_\delta(t) = \mathcal{L}^{-1}\{H(s)\} \ ,$$

which is just the inverse Laplace transform of the transfer function. This response would be generated, from the input–output relationship (8.9), by that input whose Laplace transform $X(s)$ satisfied $X(s) = 1$. Up to this point we have not seen any function $x(t)$ with this property, but does such an entity exist? In the 'ordinary' sense the answer is 'no'; however, if we are prepared to generalize our idea of a function, then we can achieve our objective.

We define the (generalized) impulse function, $\delta(t)$ — also called the Dirac δ-function — in terms of the property

$$\int_{-\infty}^{\infty} f(t) \ \delta(t - b) \ \mathrm{d}t = f(b) \ , \tag{8.10}$$

if $f(t)$ is continuous at $t = b$. From (8.10) it follows that

(1) $\delta(t) = 0 \quad t \neq 0$

$$\tag{8.11}$$

(2) $\delta(t)$ is undefined at $t = 0$.

We see from (8.11) that we cannot define $\delta(t)$ point by point as we do for 'ordinary' functions. We can, however, give an interpretation which may help in understanding. For a fuller treatment, the reader should consult Hoskins [2], who uses a similar development.

Consider the sequence of functions $\{p_n(t)\}$, defined by

$$p_n(t) = \begin{cases} 0 & |t| > \dfrac{1}{2n} \\[2ex] n & |t| < \dfrac{1}{2n} \ . \end{cases} \tag{8.12}$$

A typical member of this sequence is illustrated in Fig. 8.4.

From (8.12), taking the limit as $n \rightarrow \infty$, we see that

$$\lim_{n \rightarrow \infty} p_n(t) = \begin{cases} \text{undefined} & t = 0 \\ 0 & t \neq 0 \end{cases}.$$

Thus the limit of the sequence of functions $p_n(t)$ as $n \rightarrow \infty$ has just those properties which were ascribed to $\delta(t)$ in (8.11). Now if $f(t)$ is continuous in some region including $t = 0$ we have

$$\lim_{n \rightarrow \infty} \int_{-\infty}^{\infty} f(t) \, p_n(t) \, dt$$

$$= \lim_{n \rightarrow \infty} \int_{-\frac{1}{2}n}^{\frac{1}{2}n} f(t) \, p_n(t) \, dt$$

$$= \lim_{n \rightarrow \infty} f(\varepsilon_n) , \qquad -\frac{1}{2n} < \varepsilon_n < \frac{1}{2n} \quad \text{(1st mean-value theorem for integrals)}$$

$$= f(0) ,$$

which is (8.10) with $b = 0$.

From this, we may infer that $\delta(t)$ may be interpreted as the limit of a sequence of 'ordinary' functions $\{p_n(t)\}$. The process of generalization of the concept of a function, then, means that we admit such 'generalized functions', defined as limits of sequences of ordinary functions, to our function (or signal) space. The reader who is familiar with the proof of the existence of the real number $\sqrt{2}$ may see a similarity of concept here.

In describing $\delta(t)$ as the limit of a sequence of ordinary functions, it is apparent that there may be more than one suitable sequence of functions whose limit is $\delta(t)$. We thus need to give a definition of equivalence for such generalized functions. Such a definition is possible if we introduce the concept of a *testing function*. Testing functions are continous, have continuous derivatives of all orders, and are zero outside a finite interval. An example of a class of testing functions is

$$\theta_a(t) = \begin{cases} e^{-a^2/(a^2 - t^2)} & |t| < a \\ 0 & |t| > a \end{cases}.$$

where a is a parameter.

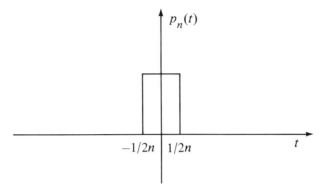

Fig. 8.4 — Graph of $p_n(t)$.

Suppose $g_1(t)$ and $g_2(t)$ are two generalized functions (or combinations of 'ordinary' functions and generalized functions); then $g_1(t)$ is equivalent to $g_2(t)$ if

$$\int_{-\infty}^{\infty} g_1(t)\,\theta(t)\,\mathrm{d}t = \int_{-\infty}^{\infty} g_2(t)\,\theta(t)\,\mathrm{d}t \tag{8.14}$$

for all testing functions $\theta(t)$.

A helpful interpretation of the relationship (8.14) is given in Gabel and Roberts [1], where the process of 'examining' $g_1(t)$ and $g_2(t)$ by multiplication by $\theta(t)$ and integration is likened to the use of a measuring instrument. Essentially the definition of equivalence means that two generalized functions are equivalent if the measuring instrument cannot detect any differences between them. One is quite used to this idea elsewhere: two electrical supplies are deemed equivalent if measurements of the voltage, current and frequency yield equal values, irrespective of their source.

Example 8.2

Show that $\delta(t) = \mathrm{d}\xi(t)/\mathrm{d}t$, where $\xi(t) = \begin{cases} 1 & (t \geqslant 0) \\ 0 & (t < 0) \end{cases}$ is the Heaviside step function and $\mathrm{d}\xi(t)/\mathrm{d}t$ is the generalized derivative.

Before demonstrating the equivalence of $\delta(t)$ and $\mathrm{d}\xi(t)/\mathrm{d}t$ under the definition (8.14), we demonstrate the plausibility of the result. First of all, note that in the pointwise sense,

$$\frac{d\xi(t)}{dt} = \begin{cases} 0 & t \neq 0 \\ \text{undefined} & t = 0 \end{cases}.$$

Also, if $f(t)$ is any function continuous in a region containing the origin $-\alpha < t < \alpha$ say,

$$\int_{-\infty}^{\infty} f(t) \frac{d\xi(t)}{dt} \, dt = \int_{-\alpha}^{\alpha} f(t) \frac{d\xi(t)}{dt} \, dt$$

$$= \int_{-\alpha}^{\alpha} f(t) \lim_{\Delta t \to 0} \frac{\xi(t + \Delta t) - \xi(t)}{\Delta t} \, dt$$

$$= \lim_{\Delta t \to 0} \frac{1}{\Delta t} \int_{-\Delta t}^{0} f(t) \, dt,$$

assuming the interchange of order is permissible

$$= \lim_{\Delta t \to 0} \frac{1}{\Delta t} \, \Delta t \, f(\varepsilon_n) \qquad -\Delta t < \varepsilon_n < 0 \text{ (First MVT for integrals)}$$

$$= f(0) \, ,$$

from the continuity of $f(t)$ on $(-\alpha, \alpha)$.

Thus we see that $d\xi(t)/dt$ has the properties required of $\delta(t)$, and we now establish the equivalence formally.

Using (8.14), we must show that

$$\int_{-\infty}^{\infty} \frac{d\xi(t)}{dt} \, \theta(t) \, dt = \int_{-\infty}^{\infty} \delta(t) \, \theta(t) \, dt \qquad (8.15)$$

for all testing functions $\theta(t)$.

From (8.10), with $b = 0$, the right-hand side of (8.15) is

$$\int_{-\infty}^{\infty} \delta(t) \, \theta(t) \, dt = \theta(0) \, .$$

On the other hand, the left-hand side can be integrated by parts, that is,

$$\int_{-\infty}^{\infty} \frac{d\xi(t)}{dt}\,\theta(t)\,dt = [\xi(t)\theta(t)]\,\Big|_{-\infty}^{\infty} - \int_{-\infty}^{\infty} \xi(t)\,\frac{d\theta(t)}{dt}\,dt \ .$$

The first term vanishes by the properties of testing functions (zero outside a finite interval, $(-\alpha, \alpha)$ say) and we are similarly guaranteed the existence of $d\theta(t)/dt$ as a continuous function. Thus

$$\int_{-\infty}^{\infty} \frac{d\xi(t)}{dt}\,\theta(t)\,dt = -\int_{-\infty}^{\infty} \xi(t)\,\frac{d\theta(t)}{dt}\,dt$$

$$= -\int_{0}^{\infty} \frac{d\theta(t)}{dt}\,dt$$

$$= -(\theta(t))\,\Big|_{0}^{\infty} = \theta(0) \ ,$$

since $\theta(t) = 0$, $|t| > \alpha$.

Thus both left- and right-hand sides of (8.15) yield the same number $\theta(0)$ for every testing function $\theta(t)$. We have thus established the equivalence of

$$\delta(t) \quad \text{and} \quad \frac{d\xi(t)}{dt}$$

where $d\xi(t)/dt$ denotes the generalized derivative of $\xi(t)$.

Example 8.3
Let $f(t)$ define the causal function

$$f(t) = e^{-at}\,\xi(t) \qquad a > 0$$

Then

$$\frac{df(t)}{dt} = -a e^{-at}\,\xi(t) + e^{-at}\,\frac{d\xi(t)}{dt}$$

$$= -a e^{-at}\,\xi(t) + e^{-at}\,\delta(t) \ .$$

As shown in Fig. 8.5, $f(t)$ has a jump discontinuity at $t = 0$. This behaviour is contained in the generalized derivative with the appearance of a term in $\delta(t)$. Note that we cannot associate a value with $df(t)/dt$ at $t = 0$; however, we shall find that we will only need to make use of such expressions as integrands, and the difficulty will not arise.

Example 8.4
As frequently used equivalence is

$$f(t) \; \delta(t) = f(0) \; \delta(t) \tag{8.16}$$

when $f(t)$ is continuous at $t = 0$. This follows at once since

$$\int_{-\infty}^{\infty} f(t) \; \delta(t) \; \theta(t) \; dt = f(0) \; \theta(0)$$

and

$$\int_{-\infty}^{\infty} f(0) \; \delta(t) \; \theta(t) \; dt = f(0) \; \theta(0)$$

also, for all testing functions $\theta(t)$.

Example 8.5
Consider $f_1(t) = \sin \; \omega t \; \xi(t)$ and $f_2(t) = \cos \; \omega t \; \xi(t)$. At once, $df_1(t)/dt = \omega \cos \; \omega t \; \xi(t) + \sin \; \omega t \; \delta(t) = \omega \cos \; \omega t \; \xi(t)$ by (8.16).

Also $df_2(t)/dt = -\omega \sin \; \omega t \; \xi(t) + \cos \; \omega t \; \delta(t)$

$$= -\omega \sin \; \omega t \; \xi(t) + \delta(t) \qquad \text{again by (8.16)}.$$

We see that $df_1(t)/dt$ does not in fact contain a term in $\delta(t)$. This is not surprising since $f_1(t) = \sin \; \omega t \; \xi(t)$ is continuous at $t = 0$.

8.4 THE IMPULSE RESPONSE

In section 8.3 we developed a calculus of generalized functions, concentrating on the so-called delta-function, or impulse function. The name impulse function derives from applications in mechanics where $\delta(t)$ can be used to model the effect of an idealized impulsive force. That is, a force of very large magnitude applied over a very short time interval. For this reason, the response of an initially quiescent (zero-state) system to such an input is known as the impulse response.

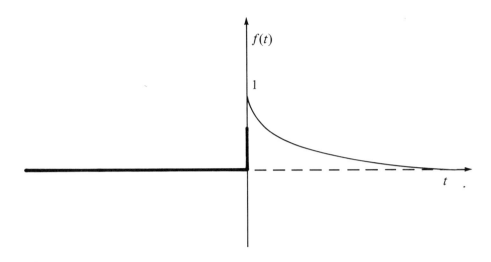

Fig 8.5 — Graph of $f(t) = e^{-at}\xi(t) = \begin{cases} e^{-at} & t<0 \\ 0 & t\geq 0 \end{cases}$, $a>0$.

For our purposes, the attractive feature of the delta- or impulse function is that it has the property discussed in section 8.3, that is

$$\mathcal{L}\{\delta(t)\} = 1 \ . \tag{8.17}$$

This result follows immediately because

$$\mathcal{L}\{\delta(t)\} = \int_{0^-}^{\infty} \delta(t)\, e^{-st}\, dt$$

$$= \int_{-\infty}^{\infty} \delta(t)\, e^{-st}\, dt = 1 \ ,$$

from (8.10), with $b = 0$.

In obtaining this result we have used (7.23) as the defining integral for the Laplace transform. This is necessary because the form (7.21) is undefined in view of the location of $\delta(t)$ at $t = 0$. (It was exactly for this purpose that (7.23) was introduced!)

Suppose we now set

$$x(t) = \delta(t)$$

as the input to the linear system with Laplace transfer function $H(s)$. Then $Y_\delta(s)$, the transform of the output, will be, from (7.40),

$$Y_\delta(s) = H(s)\ X(s)\ ,$$

but, from (8.17), $\mathcal{L}\{x(t)\} = X(s) = 1$ and so

$$Y_\delta(s) = H(s) \tag{8.18}$$

and $Y_\delta(s)$ is the Laplace transform of the impulse response. Inverting (8.18) we see that the impulse response $y_\delta(t)$, given by

$$y_\delta(t) = \mathcal{L}^{-1}\{Y_\delta(s)\} = \mathcal{L}^{-1}\{H(s)\}\ ,$$

is the inverse transform of the system transfer function. As we observed in section 8.3, the time domain function $y_\delta(t)$ determines the pure system dynamics, used in the definition of stability.

It is easy to see that a stable system, that is a system for which all the poles of $H(s)$ lie in the left half-plane, will have an impulse response which decays to zero as t increases. On the other hand, an unstable system with at least one pole of $H(s)$ in the right half-plane will have an impulse response which is unbounded as t increases. Systems with *simple* poles on the imaginary axis, the boundary between the stable and unstable regions of the plane, were classified as marginally stable in section 8.2.

For real systems, that is systems for which the characteristic polynomial $g(s)$ has real coefficients, simple poles on the imaginary axis can only occur as $s = 0$ or as the complex conjugate pair $s = \pm i\omega$, $-\infty < \omega < \infty$. Such poles will contribute terms in

$$\frac{a_1}{s} \quad \text{or} \quad \frac{a_2 s + a_3}{s^2 + \omega^2}$$

to the partial fraction expansion of the Laplace transfer function $H(s)$. Inverting these terms yields terms in the impulse response of the form

$$a_1 \xi(t) \quad \text{or} \quad \left(a_2 \cos \omega t + \frac{a_3}{\omega} \sin \omega t\right) \xi(t)\ .$$

In both cases we obtain contributions to the impulse response which do not decay to zero as t increases, but they do not become unbounded either. For this reason, such systems, which otherwise possess only stable poles in their transfer functions, are classified as marginally stable.

Example 8.6
Find the impulse response for the following systems and state whether the systems are stable, unstable or marginally stable.

(1) $\dfrac{d^2y(t)}{dt^2} + 3\,\dfrac{dy(t)}{dt} + 2y(t) = x(t)$.

(2) $\dfrac{d^2y(t)}{dt^2} + \sqrt{2}\,\dfrac{dy(t)}{dt} + y(t) = x(t)$.

(3) $\dfrac{d^2y(t)}{dt^2} + \sqrt{2}\,\dfrac{dy(t)}{dt} + y(t) = x(t) + 2\,\dfrac{dx(t)}{dt}$.

(4) $\dfrac{d^4y(t)}{dt^4} + 3\,\dfrac{d^3y(t)}{dt^3} + 3\,\dfrac{d^2y(t)}{dt^2} + 3\,\dfrac{dy(t)}{dt} + 2y(t) = x(t)$.

(5) $\dfrac{d^3y(t)}{dt^3} + \dfrac{d^2y(t)}{dt^2} = 2x(t) + \dfrac{dx(t)}{dt}$.

In each case we wish to take the Laplace transform with zero initial conditions. In view of the need to include $t = 0$ in the region of integration, we use the form (7.26), meaning that such conditions are applied at 0^-, a point to the left of the origin. This is an important point, recognizing that it is impossible to specify conditions at the moment when the impulse is applied.

(1) With $\mathcal{L}\{x(t)\} = \mathcal{L}\{\delta(t)\} = \displaystyle\int_{0^-}^{\infty} \delta(t)e^{-st}\,dt = 1$

and $\mathcal{L}\{y_\delta(t)\} = Y_\delta(s)$, the Laplace transform of the impulse response, we obtain

$$(s^2 + 3s + 2))\,Y_\delta(s) = 1 \ .$$

So

$$Y_\delta(s) = \frac{1}{s^2 + 3s + 2} = \frac{1}{(s+1)(s+2)}$$

$$= \frac{1}{s+1} - \frac{1}{s+2} \ .$$

Thus the impulse response is

$$y_\delta(t) = \mathcal{L}^{-1}\{Y_\delta(s)\}$$
$$= (e^{-t} - e^{-2t})\xi(t) \ .$$

Since $y_\delta(t) \to 0$ as $t \to \infty$ the system is stable.

(2)   With notation as above, we have

$$(s^2 + \sqrt{2}s + 1)\, Y_s(s) = 1 \ .$$

That is

$$Y_\delta(s) = \frac{1}{s^2 + \sqrt{2}s + 1}$$

$$= \frac{\sqrt{2}\left(\dfrac{1}{\sqrt{2}}\right)}{\left(s + \dfrac{\sqrt{2}}{2}\right)^2 + \left(\dfrac{\sqrt{2}}{2}\right)^2} \ ,$$

thus $y_\delta(t) = \left(\sqrt{2}\, e^{-(\sqrt{2}/2)t} \sin \dfrac{\sqrt{2}}{2} t\right) \xi(t).$

(3)   Again, with the same notation

$$(s^2 + \sqrt{2}s + 1)\, Y_\delta(s) = 2s + 1 \ . \tag{8.19}$$

So

$$Y_\delta(s) = \frac{2s + 1}{s^2 + \sqrt{2}s + 1} = \frac{2s + 1}{\left(s + \dfrac{\sqrt{2}}{2}\right)^2 + \dfrac{1}{2}}$$

$$= \frac{2\left(s + \dfrac{\sqrt{2}}{2}\right)}{\left(s + \dfrac{\sqrt{2}}{2}\right)^2 + \dfrac{1}{2}} + \frac{\dfrac{1}{\sqrt{2}}\cdot\sqrt{2}\,(1 - \sqrt{2})}{\left(s + \dfrac{\sqrt{2}}{2}\right)^2 + \dfrac{1}{2}} \ .$$

Thus $y_\delta(t) = \left[2e^{-(\sqrt{2}/2)t} \cos \dfrac{\sqrt{2}t}{2} - (2 - \sqrt{2})e^{-(\sqrt{2}/2)t} \sin \dfrac{\sqrt{2}t}{2} \right] \xi(t) \ .$

In fact we can use the following argument to obtain this response from case (2). The transform of the impulse response in that case satisfied

$$(s^2 + \sqrt{2}s + 1)\, Y_\delta(s) = 1 \ .$$

Multiply both sides by $2s + 1$ and we see that

$$(2s + 1)(s^2 + \sqrt{2}s + 1) \ Y_\delta(s) = (2s + 1) \ .$$

Since differentiation, and hence multiplication, by s is commutative we can write

$$(s^2 + \sqrt{2}s + 1)(2s + 1) \ Y_\delta(s) = (2s + 1) \ .$$

Now define $Z_\delta(s) = (2s + 1) \ Y_\delta(s)$ so that

$$(s^2 + \sqrt{2}s + 1) \ Z_\delta(s) = 2s + 1 \ ,$$

and we see that $Z_\delta(s)$ satisfies (8.19) which defines the transform of the impulse response for system (3). But $Z_\delta(s) = (2s + 1) \ Y_\delta(s)$ or in the time domain

$$z_\delta(t) = 2 \frac{dy_\delta(t)}{dt} + y_\delta(t) \ ,$$

where $y_\delta(t) = \left[\sqrt{2}e^{-(\sqrt{2}/2)t} \sin \frac{\sqrt{2}}{2} t \right] \xi(t)$ is the impulse response of system (2). Thus

$$z_\delta(t) = 2\sqrt{2} \left[-\frac{\sqrt{2}}{2} e^{-(\sqrt{2}/2)t} \sin \frac{\sqrt{2}}{2} t \ \xi(t) \right.$$

$$+ \frac{\sqrt{2}}{2} e^{-(\sqrt{2}/2)t} \cos \frac{\sqrt{2}}{2} t \ \xi(t) + e^{-(\sqrt{2}/2)t} \sin \frac{\sqrt{2}}{2} t \ \delta(t) \left. \right]$$

$$+ \sqrt{2}e^{-(\sqrt{2}/2)t} \sin \frac{\sqrt{2}}{2} t \ \xi(t) \tag{8.20}$$

That is

$$z_\delta(t) = \left[2e^{-(\sqrt{2}/2)t} \cos \frac{\sqrt{2}}{2} t - (2 - \sqrt{2})e^{-(\sqrt{2}/2)t} \sin \frac{\sqrt{2}}{2} t \right] \xi(t) \ , \tag{8.21}$$

where we have used the result that $d\xi(t)/dt = \delta(t)$ in (8.20) and the equivalence $f(t) \ \delta(t) = f(0) \ \delta(t)$ in obtaining (8.21). $z_\delta(t)$ is then the impulse response for system (3) and agrees with the result obtained by direct calculation. We see that in view of the term in $e^{-(\sqrt{2}/2)t}$, the impulse response decays to zero as t increases, meaning that the system is stable.

(4)   Again taking Laplace transforms we find that

$$(s^4 + 3s^3 + 3s^2 + 3s + 2) \, Y_\delta(s) = 1 \ .$$

That is

$$Y_\delta(s) = \frac{1}{s^4 + 3s^3 + 3s^2 + 3s + 2}$$

$$= \frac{1}{(s^2 + 1)(s^2 + 3s + 2)} \qquad\qquad (8.22)$$

$$= \frac{1}{(s + i)(s - i)(s + 1)(s + 2)} \ .$$

Thus the system has two poles in the left half-plane and two simple poles on the imaginary axis, leading us to expect marginal stability.
   Now from (8.22) we have

$$Y_\delta(s) = \frac{1}{(s^2 + 1)(s + 1)(s + 2)}$$

$$= \frac{\dfrac{1}{2}}{s + 1} - \frac{\dfrac{1}{5}}{s + 2} - \frac{\dfrac{1}{10}(3s - 1)}{s^2 + 1}$$

and so, inverting,

$$y_\delta(t) = \left[\frac{1}{2} e^{-t} - \frac{1}{5} e^{-2t} - \frac{1}{10} \sin t - \frac{3}{10} \cos t \right] \xi(t) \ .$$

So we see that the impulse response does indeed remain bounded as $t \to \infty$. It does not, however, decay to zero in view of the terms in $\sin t$ and $\cos t$. Marginal stability is thus confirmed.

(5)   On taking transforms we see that

$$(s^3 + s^2) \, Y_\delta(s) = s + 2$$

or

$$Y_s(s) = \frac{s+2}{s^2(s+1)} \ .$$

There is now a double pole at $s = 0$, on the imaginary axis, and we expect instability. Inverting, since

$$\frac{s+2}{s^2(s+1)} \equiv \frac{2}{s^2} - \frac{1}{s} + \frac{1}{s+1} \ ,$$

$$y_\delta(t) = (2t - 1 + e^{-t})\xi(t) \ .$$

We see that as $t \to \infty$, $y_\delta(t) \to \infty$ and the system is unstable. Again, we could use an alternative technique as in (3) above. If we first consider the system

$$\frac{d^3y(t)}{dt^3} + \frac{d^2y(t)}{dt^2} = x(t)$$

we see the transform of the impulse response is given by

$$Y_\delta(s) = \frac{1}{s^2(s+1)} = \frac{1}{s^2} - \frac{1}{s} + \frac{1}{s+1} \ .$$

So

$$Y_\delta(s) = (t - 1 + e^{-t}) \ \xi(t) \ .$$

By the argument of (3), the impulse response for the system

$$\frac{d^3y(t)}{dt^3} + \frac{d^2y(t)}{dt^2} = 2x(t) + \frac{dx(t)}{dt}$$

is then

$$z_\delta(t) = 2y_\delta(t) + \frac{dy_\delta(t)}{dt}$$

$$= 2(t - 1 + e^{-t})\xi(t) + (1 - e^{-t})\xi(t) + (t - 1 + e^{-t})\delta(t)$$

$$= (2t - 1 + e^{-t})\xi(t) + (t - 1 + e^{-t})\,\delta(t)$$
$$= (2t - 1 + e^{-t})\,\xi(t) \ ,$$

using the equivalence $f(t)\,\delta(t) = f(0)\,\delta(t)$.

8.5 THE STEP RESPONSE

In the last section we investigated the concept of the impulse response, finding it a useful device for 'characterizing' the system because it isolated the system dynamics. A second 'standard' response is the step response, that is, the system response from the zero state to an input.

$$x(t) = \xi(t) = \begin{cases} 0 & t < 0 \\ 1 & t \geq 0 \end{cases} \ ,$$

where $\xi(t)$ is the Heaviside step function (see Fig. 8.6). Conceptually, the step

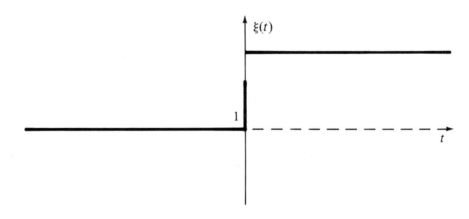

Fig. 8.6 — The step function $\xi(t)$.

function is easier than the impulse 'function', and approximations to step inputs can be made in the laboratory.

Example 8.7
Calculate the step response (see Fig. 8.7) for the system

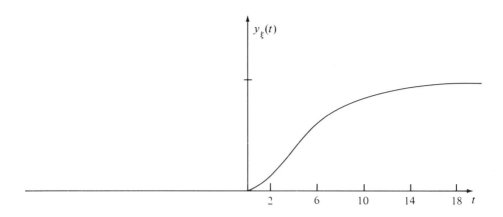

Fig. 8.7 — Step response for system of Example 8.7.

$$\frac{d^2 y(t)}{dt^2} + \frac{3}{4}\frac{dy(t)}{dt} + \frac{1}{8}y(t) = x(t) \ .$$

If the Laplace transform of the step response is $Y_\xi(s)$ we see that

$$\left(s^2 + \frac{3}{4}s + \frac{1}{8}\right) Y_\xi(s) = \mathcal{L}\{\xi(t)\} = \frac{1}{s} \ ,$$

that is

$$Y_\xi(s) = \frac{1}{s(s^2 + \frac{3}{4}s + \frac{1}{8})} = \frac{1}{s(s + \frac{1}{2})(s + \frac{1}{4})}$$

$$= \frac{8}{s} + \frac{8}{s + \frac{1}{2}} - \frac{16}{s + \frac{1}{4}} \ .$$

Thus $y_\xi(t) = 8(1 + e^{-t/2} - 2e^{-t/4})\xi(t)$.

There is a relationship between step and impulse responses. Because $d\xi(t)/dt = \delta(t)$, it follows that for linear time invariant systems, the impulse response is the derivative of the step response. Thus, for Example 8.7 we calculate the impulse response as

$$y_\delta(t) = \frac{d}{dt} y_\xi(t) = 8\left(-\tfrac{1}{2}e^{-t/2} + \tfrac{1}{2}e^{-t/4}\right)\xi(t)$$

$$+ 8(1 + e^{-t/2} - 2e^{-t/4}) \, \delta(t)$$

$$= 4(e^{-t/4} - e^{-t/2})\xi(t) \ ,$$

which can be checked by direct calculation.

Example 8.8
Determine the step and impulse response for the system

$$\frac{dy(t)}{dt} + y(t) = ax(t) + \frac{dx(t)}{dt} \qquad a \neq 1 \ .$$

With a zero initial state we have for the transform $Y_\xi(s)$ of the step response

$$Y_\xi(s) = \frac{s+a}{s+1} \cdot \frac{1}{s}$$

$$= \frac{a}{s} + \frac{1-a}{s+1} \ .$$

Thus $y_\xi(t) = (a + (1-a) \, e^{-t})\xi(t)$.
  The impulse response is found by differentiation as

$$y_\delta(t) = (a-1)e^{-t} \, \xi(t) + (a + (1-a)e^{-t})\delta(t)$$
$$= (a-1)e^{-t} \, \xi(t) + \delta(t) \ .$$

Here we see that the impulse response contains an impulse $\delta(t)$ at $t = 0$. This can be verified by direct calculation, and the block diagram for the system (Fig. 8.8)

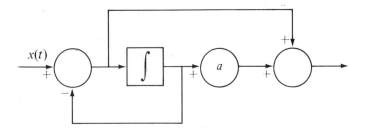

Fig. 8.8 — Block diagram for system of Example 8.8.

illustrates the reason for its presence in the output. From Fig. 8.8 we see that the impulse applied at $t = 0$ has an instantaneous path to the output $y(t)$.

8.6 SIGNAL DECOMPOSITION AND CONVOLUTION

This section focuses on a concept which, in conjunction with the ideas on impulse response developed earlier, leads to a succinct picture of signal processing using a linear time invariant system.

First we notice from (8.10) that it is true that if $x(t)$ is a continuous function

$$x(t) = \int_{-\infty}^{\infty} x(\tau)\, \delta(t - \tau) d\tau \ . \tag{8.23}$$

The interpretation of (8.23) is that $x(t)$ can be regarded as the superposition of a continuum of appropriately weighted impulse functions. In other words, $x(t)$ can be *decomposed* as a superposition of impulses. We shall see that this is a key idea in the understanding of system response.

Suppose that we subject an initially quiescent linear time invariant system to such an input $x(t)$. If $x(t)$ is bounded, continuous, and of finite support (that is, non-zero only for a finite time interval) we may approximate this signal by a train of pulses as shown in Fig. 8.9.

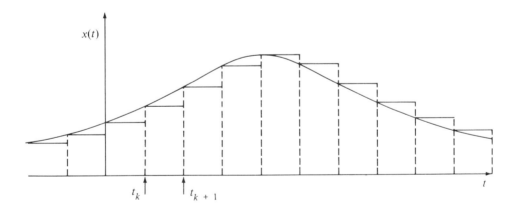

Fig. 8.9 — Rectangular pulse approximation to the signal $x(t)$.

Now, since

$$\xi(t - t_k) = \begin{cases} 0 & t < t_k \\ 1 & t \geq t_k \end{cases}$$

and

$$\xi(t - t_{k+1}) = \begin{cases} 0 & t < t_{k+1} \\ 1 & t \geq t_{k+1} \end{cases}$$

we may write for $t_k \leq t < t_{k+1}$

$$x(t) \sim x(t_k)[\xi(t - t_k) - \xi(t - t_{k+1})] \ . \tag{8.24}$$

Thus our approximation to $x(t)$ is

$$x(t) \sim \sum_k x(t_k)[\xi(t - t_k) - \xi(t - t_{k+1})] \ . \tag{8.25}$$

If we supply the scaled pulse (8.24) as the input to a quiescent linear, time invariant system, the output will be

$$y(t) = x(t_k)[y_\xi(t - t_k) - y_\xi(t - t_{k+1})] \ , \tag{8.26}$$

where $y_\xi(t)$ is the step response of the system.

Suppose that the step response $y_\xi(t)$ has a continuous derivative, $y'_\xi(t)$, then writing $p = t - t_k$ in (8.26) we have

$$\begin{aligned} y(t) &= x(t_k)[y_\xi(p) - y_\xi(p - \Delta \tau_k)] \\ &= x(t_k)[y'_\xi(p_k)]\Delta \tau_k \end{aligned} \tag{8.27}$$

where $\Delta \tau_k = t_{k+1} - t_k$ and $p - \Delta \tau_k < p_k < p$.

Result (8.27) follows from the first mean-value theorem of differential calculus, and it also follows from the assumed continuity of $y'_\xi(t)$ that

$$y'_\xi(p_k) \to y'_\xi(p) \qquad \text{as} \qquad \Delta \tau_k \to 0 \ . \tag{8.28}$$

In section 8.5 we saw that $y'_\xi(t)$, the derivative of the step response, is just the impulse response $y_\delta(t)$, discussed in section 8.4. Thus we see that (8.27) becomes

$$y(t) = x(t_k) \, y_\delta(p_k) \Delta \tau_k \ . \tag{8.29}$$

The response in (8.29) arises from the single pulse (8.24) as input to our system. If we now supply the approximating pulse train (8.25) to the system, linearity and time invariance give the output as

$$y(t) = \sum_k x(t_k) \, y_\delta(p_k) \Delta \tau_k \ .$$

Now, taking the limit as $\Delta \tau_k \to 0$, implying that the approximating pulses become smaller and smaller in duration, and with $t_k \to \tau$ a continuous variable, we see that

$$y(t) = \lim_{\Delta \tau_k \to 0} \sum_k x(t_k) \, y_\delta(p_k) \Delta \tau_k = \int_{-\infty}^{\infty} x(\tau) \, y_\delta(t - \tau) \mathrm{d}\tau \ . \tag{8.30}$$

In obtaining (8.30) we have used (8.25), enabling us to write

$$y_\delta(p_k) \to y_\delta(p) = y_\delta(t - \tau) \qquad \text{since } t_k \to \tau \ .$$

The clue to the interpretation of (8.30) lies in (8.25), which we now show leads to our starting point, (8.23).
   We may write (8.25) as

$$x(t) \sim \sum_k x(t_k) [\xi'(p_k)] \Delta \tau_k$$

with the notation as before. Taking the limit as $\Delta \tau_k \to 0$ we see that because $\xi'(t) = \delta(t)$, and proceeding as above,

$$x(t) = \int_{-\infty}^{\infty} x(\tau) \, \delta(t - \tau) \mathrm{d}\tau \ .$$

This is equation (8.23) again, and we are now able to make the interpretation that the system 'sees' $x(t)$ as a continuum of weighted impulses. The response generated, as given by (8.30), is a superposition of weighted, impulse responses, with each element of the total response delayed by an appropriate amount. Integrals of the form in (8.30) are called convolution integrals and, although not particularly easy to evaluate, provide a ready appreciation of the behaviour of linear, time invariant systems.

In fact, we generated this type of integral in section 7.9, based on the transfer function concept, and we now show that these two forms are equivalent when we are considering causal systems. Suppose that both the impulse response $y_\delta(t)$ and the input signal $x(t)$ are causal. At once we see that

$$x(t) = 0 \qquad t < 0$$

and moreover   (8.31)

$$y_\delta(t - \tau) = 0 \qquad \text{when } \tau > t .$$

Under these circumstances the output $y(t)$ is given by

$$y(t) = \int_{-\infty}^{\infty} x(\tau)\, y_\delta(t - \tau) d\tau = x(t) * y_\delta(t)$$

$$= \int_{0}^{t} x(\tau)\, y_\delta(t - \tau)\, d\tau \qquad\qquad (8.32)$$

in view of (8.31)

This is exactly the result (7.44), with $h(t)$ now identified as $y_\delta(t)$, the impulse response. The alternative form (7.45) is easily obtained by a simple change of variable.

The * notation is particularly convenient for denoting the convolution operation. We note that since

$$x(t) * y(t) = \int_{-\infty}^{\infty} x(\tau)\, y(t - \tau)\, d\tau$$

$$= \int_{-\infty}^{\infty} x(t - \tau)\, y(\tau)\, d\tau$$

$$= y(t) * x(t) ,$$

* (convolution) is commutative.

Example 8.9
For the causal, time invariant system

$$\frac{d^2 y(t)}{dt^2} + 5\frac{dy(t)}{dy} + 6y(t) = x(t) \qquad\qquad (8.33)$$

calculate the impulse response and use the convolution result to find the zero initial-state response to an input

$$x(t) = e^{-t}\xi(t) .$$

The transform of the impulse response is given by

$$Y_\delta(s) = H(s)$$

where

$$H(s) = \frac{1}{s^2 + 5s + 6} = \frac{1}{(s+3)(s+2)} .$$

$$= \frac{1}{s+2} - \frac{1}{s+3} .$$

Then $y_\delta(t) = h(t) = (e^{-2t} - e^{-3t})\xi(t) .$

Using (8.32) (or (8.30)) we see that the response to the input $x(t) = e^{-t}\xi(t)$ will be, for $t \geqslant 0$,

$$y(t) = \int_0^t x(\tau)\, y_\delta(t-\tau)\, d\tau = \int_0^t x(t-\tau) y_\delta(\tau)\, d\tau$$

$$= \int_0^t e^{-(t-\tau)}\{e^{-2\tau} - e^{-3\tau}\}\, d\tau$$

$$= e^{-t} \int_0^t (e^{-\tau} - e^{-2\tau})\, d\tau$$

$$= e^{-t}\left[-e^{-\tau} + \frac{e^{-2\tau}}{2} \right]_0^t$$

$$= e^{-t}\left[1 - e^{-t} - \frac{1}{2} + \frac{e^{-2t}}{2} \right] = \frac{1}{2}e^{-t} + \frac{e^{-3t}}{2} - e^{-2t} \qquad t \geqslant 0 .$$

Obviously $y(t) = 0$, $t < 0$. The response is thus

$$y(t) = (\tfrac{1}{2}e^{-t} + \tfrac{1}{2}e^{-3t} - e^{-2t})\xi(t)$$

and this result can be checked by direct calculation. Taking transforms in (8.33) with zero initial conditions we obtain

$$(s^2 + 5s + 6)Y(s) = X(s) = \frac{1}{s+1}.$$

That is,

$$Y(s) = \frac{1}{(s+1)(s+2)(s+3)}$$

$$= \frac{\frac{1}{2}}{s+1} - \frac{1}{s+2} + \frac{\frac{1}{2}}{s+3},$$

and so $y(t) = (\frac{1}{2}e^{-t} - e^{-2t} + \frac{1}{2}e^{-3t})\xi(t)$, as before.

Clearly, the direct calculation of the response is more efficient, and thus reinforces our point that convolution is an aid to understanding and manipulation rather than a tool for solution.

The convolution operation, with system impulse response as 'kernel', shows very clearly why the impulse response is said to characterize a linear system. Once this is known, we are able to express the response of the system for an arbitrary input $x(t)$ in the compact form (8.30). We are, of course, at this stage restricted to the zero-state response, that is, to systems which are quiescent before $t = 0$. We investigate the removal of this restriction and some other ideas in the following examples.

Example 8.10
Claculate the impulse response, and hence the step response, for the system

$$\frac{d^2y(t)}{dt^2} + 4\frac{dy(t)}{dt} + 3y(t) = 2x(t) + 3\frac{dx(t)}{dt}.$$

The impulse response has transform

$$Y_\delta(s) = \frac{2 + 3s}{s^2 + 4s + 3}$$

$$= \frac{2 + 3s}{(s+3)(s+1)} = \frac{\frac{7}{2}}{s+3} - \frac{\frac{1}{2}}{s+1}.$$

Thus the impulse response is

$$y_\delta(t) = (\tfrac{7}{2}\,e^{-3t} - \tfrac{1}{2}\,e^{-t})\xi(t) \ .$$

For the step response $y_\xi(t)$ we set $x(t) = \xi(t)$, and by convolution we see that

$$y_\xi(t) = \int_0^t 1.y_\delta(t-\tau)\,d\tau$$

$$= \int_0^t y_\delta(\tau)\,d\tau \ .$$

That is, the step response is just the integral of the impulse response. Performing the integration, we see that

$$y_\xi(t) = \int_0^t (\tfrac{7}{2}\,e^{-3\tau} - \tfrac{1}{2}\,e^{-\tau})\,d\tau$$

$$= [\tfrac{1}{2}e^{-\tau} - \tfrac{7}{6}\,e^{-3\tau}]_0^t = \tfrac{1}{2}\,e^{-t} - \tfrac{7}{6}\,e^{-3t} + \tfrac{2}{3} \qquad t \geqslant 0 \ .$$

Again the response is clearly zero for $t < 0$, and so we write

$$y_\xi(t) = (\tfrac{1}{2}\,e^{-t} - \tfrac{7}{6}\,e^{-3t} + \tfrac{2}{3})\xi(t) \ .$$

The result is easily checked by direct calculation as follows. Since $x(t) = \xi(t)$, $dx/dt = \delta(t)$ we can obtain the step response as the solution of the differential equation

$$\frac{d^2 y_\xi(t)}{dt^2} + 4\,\frac{dy_\xi(t)}{dt} + 3y_\xi(t) = 2\xi(t) + 3\delta(t) \ , \qquad t \geqslant 0 \ .$$

Taking Laplace transforms with 0^- as the lower limit of integration we find that if $\mathcal{L}\{y_\xi(t)\} = Y_\xi(s)$,

$$(s^2 + 4s + 3)Y_\xi(s) = \frac{2}{s} + 3 \ .$$

That is

$$Y_\xi(s) = \frac{2 + 3s}{s(s^2 + 4s + 3)}$$

$$= \frac{1}{s} \left[\frac{2+3s}{s^2+4s+3} \right] = \frac{1}{s} Y_\delta(s) .$$

We may infer at this stage that our result will be consistent with that obtained above in view of the $1/s$ factor. This is the transform domain integration operator, and confirms the general result that the step response is the time integral of the impulse response. Since

$$\frac{1}{s} \frac{2+3s}{s^2+4s+3} = \frac{\frac{2}{3}}{s} - \frac{\frac{7}{6}}{s+3} + \frac{\frac{1}{2}}{s+1}$$

we see that $y_\xi(t) = (\frac{1}{2} e^{-t} - \frac{7}{6} e^{-3t} + \frac{2}{3})\xi(t)$, as before.

Example 8.11
Find the response of causal system

$$\frac{d^2y(t)}{dt^2} + 3 \frac{dy(t)}{dt} + 2y(t) = 3x(t) + \frac{dx(t)}{dt}$$

to the input $x(t) = e^{-at}\xi(t)$ from the quiescent state.
    The transfer function $H(s)$ is easily seen to be

$$H(s) = \frac{s+3}{s^2+3s+2} = \frac{s+3}{(s+1)(s+2)}$$

and thus since $X(s) = \mathcal{L}\{e^{-at}\xi(t)\} = \frac{1}{s+a}$,

$$Y(s) = H(s) \ X(s)$$

$$= \frac{s+3}{(s+1)(s+2)(s+a)} \tag{8.34}$$

$$= \frac{\frac{2}{a-1}}{s+1} - \frac{\frac{1}{a-2}}{s+2} + \frac{\frac{3-a}{(1-a)(2-a)}}{s+2} .$$

Inverting, the response is seen to be

$$y(t) = \left(\frac{2}{a-1} e^{-t} - \frac{1}{a-2} e^{-2t} + \frac{3-a}{(1-a)(2-a)} e^{-at} \right) \xi(t) \ . \tag{8.35}$$

The purpose of including this example is to highlight the concept of an initial condition. In writing down the transfer function, we assumed zero initial conditions on both $y(t)$ and $dy(t)/dt$, and on $x(t)$. We are quite entitled to do this if we use the Laplace transform definition in the form (7.23), with the lower limit of integration at 0^-. The transform of $dx(t)/dt$ is then found from (7.26) as $sX(s)$, since $x(0^-) = 0$. The fact that $x(0) = 1$ does not, therefore, concern us.

The calculation can easily be checked from first principles as follows. Since $x(t) = e^{-at}\xi(t)$,

$$\frac{dx(t)}{dt} = -ae^{-at}\xi(t) + e^{-at}\xi'(t)$$

$$= -ae^{-at}\xi(t) + e^{-at}\delta(t)$$

$$= -ae^{-at}\xi(t) + \delta(t) \ .$$

We must then solve the differential equation

$$\frac{d^2y(t)}{dt^2} + 3\frac{dy(t)}{dt} + 2y(t) = \delta(t) - ae^{-at}\xi(t) + 3e^{-at}\xi(t) \ .$$

Taking transforms, again using the definition (7.23), we obtain

$$(s^2 + 3s + 2)Y(s) = 1 + \frac{(3-a)}{s+a} = \frac{s+3}{s+a} \ .$$

Thus $Y(s) = (s+3)/(s+1)(s+2)(s+a)$, which is (8.34) again, and so $y(t)$ is obtained as above in (8.35)

Example 8.12
Calculate the impulse response for the system

$$\frac{d^2y(t)}{dt^2} + 3\frac{dy(t)}{dt} + 2y(t) = x(t) \ . \tag{8.36}$$

Hence find the response to an input $x(t) = 2e^{-3t}\xi(t)$ if

$$y(t) = 1 \ , \qquad y'(t) = 0 \qquad t < 0 \ .$$

What are $y(0)$ and $y'(0)$?

In this example, the system is initiated with $y(t) = 1$ and $y'(t) = 0$. We think of these conditions as having persisted for some period before the 'clock' is started at $t = 0$. The condition is not applied suddenly at $t = 0$, a situation which would lead to a different problem.

The impulse response is defined as a response from the quiescent state, with its Laplace transform $Y_\delta(s)$ given by

$$Y_\delta(s) = H(s) = \frac{1}{s^2 + 3s + 2} = \frac{1}{(s + 2)(s + 1)} = \frac{1}{s + 1} + \frac{1}{s + 2}$$

where $H(s)$ is the transfer function. Inverting, we obtain the impulse response as

$$y_\delta(t) = \mathcal{L}^{-1} H(s)\} = (e^{-t} - e^{-2t})\xi(t) \ .$$

We now wish to calculate the response to the input $x(t) = 2e^{-3t}\xi(t)$ with the initial conditions

$$y(t) = 1 \ , \qquad y'(t) = 0 \qquad t < 0 \ .$$

Taking transforms in (8.36), as usual with 0^- as the lower limit of integration, we see that

$$s^2 Y(s) - s + 3(s Y(s) - 1) + 2Y(s) = X(s)$$

or

$$(s^2 + 3s + 2)Y(s) = 3 + s + X(s) \ .$$

That is,

$$Y(s) = (3 + s + X(s)) \frac{1}{s^2 + 3s + 2}$$

$$= (3 + s + X(s)) \ H(s)$$

$$= (3 + s + X(s)) \ Y_\delta(s)$$

where $H(s)$ is the transfer function and $Y_\delta(s)$ is the Laplace transform of the impulse response, which are, of course, equal. Thus $Y(s) = (3 + s)Y_\delta(s) + X(s)Y_\delta(s)$, and so

$$y(t) = [\mathcal{L}^{-1}(3+s)] * [y_\delta(t)] + [x(t)] * [y_\delta(t)] \ . \tag{8.37}$$

In (8.37) we see that the system response can be expressed as the sum of two convolutions, the first of which involves a time function whose Laplace transform is $F(s) = s$. We argue that, since the operation of differentiation in the time domain corresponds to multiplication by s in the Laplace transform domain, then

$$\mathcal{L}^{-1}\{s\} = \frac{d}{dt} \mathcal{L}^{-1}\{1\} = \frac{d}{dt} \delta(t)$$

$$= \delta'(t) \ .$$

We can test this conjecture as follows:

$$\mathcal{L}\{\delta'(t)\} = \int_{0^-}^{\infty} \delta'(t) e^{-st} \, dt$$

$$= e^{-st}\delta(t) \Big|_{0^-}^{\infty} + \int_{0^-}^{\infty} s e^{-st}\delta(t) \, dt$$

$$= s \ ,$$

as required.

Notice that the first term in the integration-by-parts process vanishes because $\delta(t)$ is zero everywhere except at $t = 0$.

With this result established we may perform the convolutions in (8.37), so that

$$y(t) = [3\delta(t) + \delta'(t)] * y_\delta(t) + x(t) * y_\delta(t)$$

$$= \int_{0^-}^{t} 3\delta(\tau) \, y_\delta(t-\tau) \, d\tau + \int_{0^-}^{t} \delta'(\tau) y_\delta(t-\tau) \, d\tau$$

$$+ \int_{0^-}^{t} 2e^{-3\tau} \, y_\delta(t-\tau) \, d\tau$$

$$= 3y_\delta(t) + \int_{0^-}^{t} \delta'(\tau) y_\delta(t-\tau) \, d\tau$$

$$+ \int_{0^-}^{t} 2e^{-3\tau}(e^{-(t-\tau)} - e^{-2(t-\tau)}) \, d\tau \ .$$

The second term can be integrated by parts to obtain

$$\int_{0^-}^{t} \delta'(\tau) y_\delta(t-\tau)\, d\tau = y_\delta(t-\tau)\delta(\tau)\Big|_{0^-}^{t} + \int_{0^-}^{t} y_\delta'(t-\tau)\delta(\tau)\, d\tau$$

$$= y_\delta'(t)$$

$$= \frac{d}{dt}\left[[e^{-t} - e^{-2t}]\,\xi(t) \right]$$

$$= (e^{-t} - e^{-2t})\delta(t) + (2e^{-2t} - e^{-t})\xi(t)$$

$$= (2e^{-2t} - e^{-t})\xi(t) \;,$$

using the equivalence $f(t)\delta(t) = f(0)\delta(t)$.

Finally we obtain

$$y(t) = 3(e^{-t} - e^{-2t})\xi(t) + (2e^{-2t} - e^{-t})\xi(t)$$

$$+ \int_{0^-}^{t} 2e^{-3\tau}(e^{-(t-\tau)} - e^{-2(t-r)})\, d\tau$$

$$= [3e^{-t} - 3e^{-2t} + e^{-3t}]\xi(t) \;.$$

At $t = 0$ we obtain $y(0) = 1$, and since

$$y'(t) = [-3e^{-t} + 6e^{-2t} - 3e^{-3t}]\xi(t) + [3e^{-t} - 3e^{-2t} + e^{-3t}]\delta(t)$$

$$= [6e^{-2t} - 3e^{-t} - 3e^{-3t}]\xi(t) + \delta(t) \;,$$

we see that $y'(t)$ contains an impulse at the origin.

It is obvious that a direct calculation of the system response is a more efficient solution technique: taking transforms in (8.36), with $x(t) = 2e^{-3t}\xi(t)$, we obtain

$$Y(s) = \frac{s+3}{(s+1)(s+2)} + \frac{2}{(s+3)(s+1)(s+2)}$$

$$= \frac{3}{s+1} - \frac{3}{s+2} + \frac{1}{s+3} \;.$$

Inverting, $y(t) = [3e^{-t} - 3e^{-2t} + e^{-3t}]\xi(t)$, as before.

This final example re-emphasizes our point that convolution, together with the impulse response function, is a powerful general tool for system analysis. It is not, however, a particularly efficient technique for the determination of a particular case of system response.

8.7 FREQUENCY RESPONSE

The last section considered an approach to the characterization of linear systems based upon a time domain decomposition of signals — that is, into a superposition of a continuum of impulses, with the characterization then being the system response to a single impulse input. In this section we lay the foundations for a second approach to the characterization problem, this time in the so-called frequency domain. In order to achieve this purpose we examine the response of a causal linear, time invariant system to an input of the form $x(t) = A e^{i\omega t}\xi(t)$. Such an input is a convenient form, from which responses to the real inputs $A\cos \omega t\, \xi(t)$ or $A\sin \omega t\, \xi(t)$ may be deduced easily if required. Suppose that the system has Laplace transfer function $H(s)$; then the transform $Y(s)$ of the output $y(t)$ will be given by

$$Y(s) = H(s)X(s) \tag{8.38}$$

in general. When $x(t) = A e^{i\omega t}\xi(t)$, $X(s) = \mathscr{L}\{x(t)\} = A/(s - i\omega)$ and (8.38) becomes

$$Y(s) = H(s)\,\frac{A}{s - i\omega}\,. \tag{8.39}$$

In (7.41) we saw that if $H(s)$ was of the form

$$H(s) = \frac{b_m s^m + b_{m-1}s^{m-1} + \ldots + b_0}{s^n + a_{n-1}s^{n-1} + \ldots + a_0} = \frac{P(s)}{Q(s)}$$

$H(s)$ was said to be 'proper' if $\deg P(s) \leqslant \deg Q(s)$, that is $m \leqslant n$, and $H(s)$ is strictly proper if $m < n$.

   All our examples have involved strictly proper transfer functions $H(s)$; however, there is no simplification gained by restricting ourselves beyond the requirement of a proper transfer function $H(s)$. Under these circumstances, we can decompose the right-hand side of (8.39) into partial fractions. If all the zeros λ_k, $k = 1, 2, \ldots, n$, of $Q(s)$, that is the poles of $H(s)$, are distinct and $\lambda_k \neq i\omega$, $k = 1, 2, \ldots, n$, we have

$$Y(s) = H(s)\,\frac{A}{s - i\omega} = \sum_{k=1}^{n} \frac{c_k'}{s - \lambda_k} + \frac{c}{s - i\omega}\,. \tag{8.40}$$

[The analysis is readily modified in the case of repeated zeros of $Q(s)$, and the final result is unchanged.]

   In (8.40), the constants c_k' and c are generally complex. However, inversion is straightforward and we obtain

$$y(t) = \left[\sum_{k=1}^{n} c'_k\, e^{\lambda_k t} + c e^{i\omega t} \right] \xi(t) \ .$$

From our time domain analysis of section 8.2 we infer that if the system is stable, so that all the zeros, λ_k, of $Q(s)$ lie in the left half-plane, then

$$y(t) \sim y_{ss}(t) = c\, e^{-i\omega t} \xi(t) \tag{8.41}$$

as $t \to \infty$.

In (8.41), $y_{ss}(t)$ is the 'steady-state' response of the system in response to the input $x(t) = A e^{-i\omega t} \xi(t)$. We note that such a response has physical meaning only for stable systems. Determination of the steady-state response thus requires only the determination of the constant c. This follows at once by writing (8.40) in the form

$$AH(s) = \sum_{k=1}^{n} \frac{c'_k(s - i\omega)}{s - \lambda_k} + c \ ,$$

then on putting $s = i\omega$, we see that

$$c = AH(i\omega) \ .$$

Thus, (8.41) is now

$$y(t) \sim y_{ss}(t) = AH(i\omega) e^{i\omega t} \xi(t)$$

$$= H(i\omega) x(t) \ . \tag{8.42}$$

This means that the steady-state output is just the input 'modified' by a (variable) complex scaling factor. It is significant that the steady-state response, as we have just seen, depends not at all on the initial state of the system, that is, it is independent of the initial conditions. From (8.42), $y(t)$ will be a complex signal and represents the response of the system to a complex input signal at frequency ω. Real signal responses can be obtained by taking the real or imaginary part as needed. The result (8.42) shows a further important fact. The *effect* of the system on the input signal in producing the output signal is contained in the quantity

$$H(i\omega) \ .$$

This is simply the system Laplace transfer function evaluated on the imaginary axis, which is possible when $H(s)$ exists in a region which contains this axis. This is always the case for stable systems. To analyse this effect further, write

$$H(i\omega) = |H(i\omega)|e^{i\phi_\omega} \qquad \phi_\omega \in (-\pi, \pi]$$

in recognition of the fact that $H(i\omega)$ is a complex-valued quantity. Using (8.42), we may write

$$|y_{ss}(t)| = |H(i\omega)|A.e^{i(\omega t + \phi_\omega)} \ .$$

Thus $|y_{ss}(t)| = |H(i\omega)|A = |H(i\omega)||x(t)|$ and $\arg\ (y_{ss}(t)) = \omega t + \phi_\omega = \arg\ x(t) + \arg\ H(i\omega)$. We can see that the effect of the system on the input signal $x(t) = Ae^{i\omega t}\xi(t)$ in the steady state is the generation of an output signal at the same frequency ω. This output signal is, however, scaled (amplified if $|H(i\omega)| > 1$, attenuated if $|H(i\omega)| < 1$) by the factor $|H(i\omega)|$, and is phase-shifted by an amount ϕ_ω relative to $x(t)$. Clearly the magnitude of these effects depends on the frequency ω, of the input signal, and for this reason $H(i\omega)$ is termed the system frequency response. The real quantities $|H(i\omega)|$ and $\arg\ H(i\omega)$ are then known as the amplitude and phase response respectively. $H(i\omega)$, as the frequency response, serves to characterize the system in the frequency domain, and we see that $H(i\omega)$ is closely related to the transfer function $H(s)$. Indeed $H(i\omega)$ is sometimes called the system frequency transfer function. $H(i\omega)$ is in fact a Fourier transform, and the next chapter deals with this subject in detail. When this has been completed, the full value of the frequency response as a system characteristic may be appreciated. We conclude this section with some examples of the determination of frequency domain responses.

Example 8.13
Calculate the frequency response of the causal, linear time invariant system defined by

$$\frac{d^2y(t)}{dt^2} + 2\frac{dy(t)}{dt} + 5y(t) = 5x(t) \ .$$

Find also the amplitude and phase responses.
    We first check the location of the system poles. On taking Laplace transforms, with the usual notation, we see that

$$Y(s) = H(s)X(s)$$

where $H(s) = 5/(s^2 + 2s + 5)$.
    The system poles are located at the zeros of the characteristic polynomial, $Q(s)$, where

$$Q(s) = s^2 + 2s + 5 \ .$$

Now $Q(s) = 0$ implies $s = -1 \pm \sqrt{-4} = -1 \pm 2i$, so that $\lambda_1 = -1 + 2i$ and $\lambda_2 = -1 - 2i$. Thus since $\text{Re}(\lambda_1) = \text{Re}(\lambda_2) = -1$, both poles are in the left half of the complex plane and the system is stable. The frequency response is then

$$H(i\omega) = \frac{5}{(i\omega)^2 + 2(i\omega) + 5} = \frac{5}{(5 - \omega^2) + 2i\omega}$$

$$= \frac{5((5 - \omega^2) - 2i\omega)}{(5 - \omega)^2 + 4\omega^2} \ .$$

The amplitude response follows at once as

$$|H(i\omega)| = \frac{5}{\sqrt{((5 - \omega^2)^2 + 4\omega^2)}} = \frac{5}{\sqrt{(25 - 6\omega^2 + \omega^4)}}$$

whereas the phase response is defined as

$$\phi_\omega = \arg H(i\omega) = -\tan^{-1}\frac{2\omega}{5 - \omega^2} \ , \qquad \phi_\omega \in (-\pi, \pi] \ .$$

Notice that (8.43) exhibits the manner in which input signals of different frequencies are processed by the system. When ω is 'small'

$$|H(i\omega)| \sim \frac{5}{\sqrt{25}} = 1 \ ,$$

whereas when ω is 'large', $|H(i\omega)| \sim 0$. We see that at one extreme, signals of low frequency (small values of ω) are passed unaltered in magnitude whereas at the other extreme, high-frequency (large values of ω) signals are virtually eliminated (see Fig. 8.10).

Example 8.14
Find the steady-state response of the system

$$\frac{d^2y(t)}{dt^2} + 2\frac{dy(t)}{dt} + 5y(t) = 5\left(x(t) + \frac{dx(t)}{dt}\right)$$

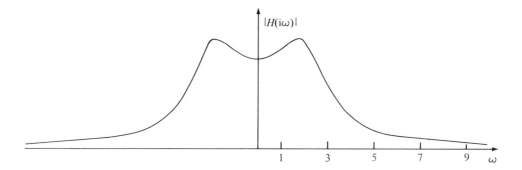

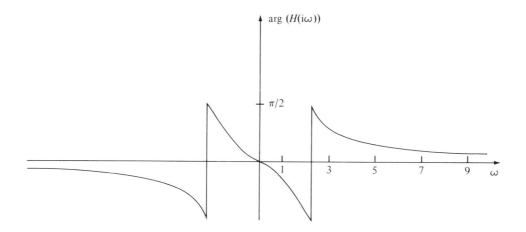

Fig. 8.10 — Amplitude and phase response for system of Example 8.13.

to the inputs $x_1(t) = 10 \cos t \, \xi(t)$ and $x_2(t) = 10 \cos 10t \, \xi(t)$.
The system transfer function is

$$H(s) = \frac{5(1+s)}{s^2 + 2s + 5}$$

and, since the pole locations are as for Example 8.13, the system is stable. There is thus a frequency response given by

$$H(i\omega) = \frac{5(1+i\omega)}{5 - \omega^2 + 2i\omega} \; .$$

Moreover, $y_{ss}(t) = H(i\omega)x(t)$, and if $x(t) = 10 \cos t \, \xi(t) = $ Re $\{10e^{it}\}$ it follows that, in this case since $\omega = 1$,

$$y_{ss}(t) = \text{Re } \{H(i)10e^{it}\}$$
$$= 10|H(i)|\{\cos (t + \phi_1)\} \quad .$$

Now

$$|H(i\omega)| = \frac{5\sqrt{(1 + \omega^2)}}{\sqrt{((5 - \omega^2)^2 + 4\omega^2)}}$$

and arg $H(i\omega) = \tan^{-1}\omega - \tan^{-1}2\omega/(5 - \omega^2) = \phi_\omega$. So with $\omega = 1$, $H(i) = \frac{5\sqrt{2}}{\sqrt{20}} = \frac{5\sqrt{2}}{2\sqrt{5}} = \sqrt{\frac{5}{2}}$

$$\phi_1 = \tan^{-1} 1 - \tan^{-1} \tfrac{1}{2}$$
$$= \frac{\pi^c}{4} - 0.4636^c = 0.3218^c \quad .$$

Thus with input $x_1(t)$

$$y_{ss}(t) = 10\sqrt{\tfrac{5}{2}} \cos (t + 0.3218) = 15.8113. \cos (t + 0.3218) \quad .$$

On the other hand, with input $x_2(t)$, we obtain

$$y_{ss}(t) = 10|H(10i)|\cos (10t + \phi_2)$$

where

$$|H(10i)| = \frac{5\sqrt{101}}{\sqrt{((95)^2 + 400)}} = 0.5176$$

and $\phi_2 = \tan^{-1} 10 + \tan^{-1} \frac{20}{95} = 1.4711^c + 0.2075^c = 1.6786^c$. Thus

$$y_{ss}(t) = 10 \times 0.5176 \times \cos (10t + 1.6786)$$
$$= 5.176 \cos 10(t + 1.6786) \quad .$$

It is now possible to see how the two input signals are processed by the system. Both inputs are subject to substantial modification, both in amplitude and in phase. In particular, the amplitude of the output signal in the second case is only about 33% of that of the first case.

The principle of superposition, as discussed in Chapter 7, ensures that the response to the composite signal $x(t) = x_1(t) + x_2(t)$ would exhibit the same type of behaviour, with one component amplified and the other attenutated.

In this last section we have developed a characterization of a linear system in terms of the frequency domain behaviour. The applicability of this characterization only becomes apparent when we consider a second form of signal decomposition, this time in the frequency domain. Achieving this decomposition is the purpose of the next chapter.

REFERENCES

[1] R. A. Gabel and R. A. Roberts, *Signals and Linear Systems*, Wiley, New York, 1987.
[2] R. F. Hoskins, *Generalised Functions*, Ellis Horwood, Chichester, 1979.

EXERCISES

1. Find the Laplace transfer functions for the following systems, and hence find the impulse response in each case. Draw a block diagram for each system.

    (a) $\dfrac{d^2y(t)}{dt^2} + 3\,\dfrac{dy(t)}{dt} + 2y(t) = u(t)$.

    (b) $\dfrac{d^2y(t)}{dt^2} + 2\,\dfrac{dy(t)}{dt} + 2y(t) = u(t)$.

    (c) $8\,\dfrac{d^2y(t)}{dt^2} + 6\,\dfrac{dy(t)}{dt} + y(t) = u(t)$.

    (d) $3\,\dfrac{d^2y(t)}{dt^2} + 2\,\dfrac{dy(t)}{dt} + 2y(t) = 2u(t) + \dfrac{du(t)}{dt}$.

2. Find the response of the system

    $$2\,\frac{d^2y(t)}{dt^2} + 3\,\frac{dy(t)}{dt} + y(t) = u(t) \ ,$$

    to an input e^{-at}, where $a > 0$, (i) directly and (ii) by first calculating the impulse response and then using the convolution integral.

3. Show that a system with a repeated pole on the imaginary axis has an unbounded impulse response, and is hence unstable.

4. Which of the following characteristic equations represent systems which are stable? Are any marginally stable?

(a) $s^2 + 4s + 5$.
(b) $s^2 + 2s + 3$.
(c) $4s^2 - s + 1$.
(d) $s^3 + s^2 + s + 1$.
(e) $s^4 + 2s^2 + 1$.

5. Calculate the step response of the system

$$4\frac{d^2y(t)}{dt^2} + 4\frac{dy}{dt} + 5y(t) = u(t) \ .$$

What is the impulse response?

6. Determine the amplitude and phase responses of the system

$$\frac{d^3y(t)}{dt^3} + 2\frac{d^2y(t)}{dt^2} + 2\frac{dy(t)}{dt} + y(t) = \frac{du(t)}{dt} \ .$$

Illustrate with a diagram, perhaps obtained using a computer.

7. Find the response of the system

$$\frac{d^2y(t)}{dt^2} + 2\frac{dy(t)}{dt} + 5y(t) = u(t),$$

if $u(t) = e^{-t}\xi(t)$, and $y(0^-) = 0$, $y'(0^-) = 1$.

8. Evaluate $d/dt\{e^{-3t}\xi(t)\}$, and also $d/dt\{\sin(at)\xi(t)\}$, where $\xi(t)$ is the Heaviside step function.
   Prove also that $d/dt\{t\xi(t)\} = \xi(t)$.

9. Use the identity $|t| = (-t)\xi(-t) + t\xi(t)$ to show that $d/dt\{|t|\} = \xi(t) - \xi(-t)$.

10. Show that

$$\int_{-\infty}^{\infty} \delta'(t) f(t) \, dt = -f'(0)$$

if $f(t)$ is continuous at $t = 0$. Show further (by induction?) that

$$\int_{-\infty}^{\infty} \delta^n(t) f(t) \, dt = (-1)^n f^n(0).$$

9

Fourier methods

9.1 INTRODUCTION

In the last chapter we examined various time-domain system responses. We saw that considerable insight could be gained using the concept of the system impulse response, because signals can be decomposed into a superposition of impulses. Later, we turned our attention to the frequency domain and we found that a so-called frequency response function could be associated with stable, causal, linear, time invariant systems. This function enabled us to predict the steady-state output of the system when the input signal was a sine or cosine wave at frequency ω. This was achieved using the complex exponential representation form rather than the trigonometric functions, sine and cosine.

The principle of superposition discussed in Chapter 7 allows us to combine together such signals of different frequencies and to again predict the steady-state response. In this chapter we examine a frequency domain decomposition of signals which will permit us to make full use of the frequency response concept in understanding the frequency domain view of signal processing.

9.2 FOURIER SERIES

We begin our treatment with a consideration of periodic functions. Our aim in this section is to achieve the decomposition of periodic signals into a form suitable for use with a frequency response function in determining the steady-state response of a system to a periodic signal as input.

Suppose that $f(t)$ is a periodic function, or signal of period $T = 2A$. Such a signal is illustrated in Fig. 9.1. Clearly, we can define this signal by the two relationships

$$f(t) = \begin{cases} 1, & -A < t < 0 \\ 0, & 0 \leqslant t \leqslant A \end{cases}$$

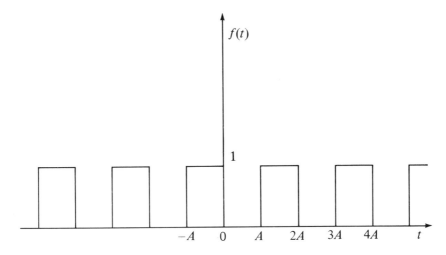

Fig. 9.1 — A periodic pulse of period $2A$.

and

$$f(t + T) = f(t),$$

where $T = 2A$ is the period.

In some applications, notably the solution of partial differential equations, it is necessary to seek a representation of such a function in terms of a combination of sine and cosine functions of different frequencies ω. Our requirements are slightly different, and we shall obtain an expansion or representation using the complex exponential function $e^{i\omega t}$ instead.

The detailed question of when such a representation exists is beyond the scope of this text. However, when the Dirichlet conditions are satisfied, we can be certain that the periodic function, or signal, $f(t)$ of period T, does possess a Fourier expansion. The Dirichlet conditions can be stated as follows

(a) Within each period, $f(t)$ is bounded, so that $f(t)$ is absolutely integrable on $[0, T]$.
(b) Within each period, there is at most a finite number of maxima and minima.
(c) Within each period, there is at most a finite number of finite discontinuities.

If these conditions, which are 'sufficient' conditions, are satisfied, then $f(t)$ has a Fourier expansion which can be expressed in the form

$$f(t) \sim \sum_{-\infty}^{\infty} A_n \exp(in\omega_0 t) \tag{9.1}$$

where $\omega_0 = 2\pi/T$.

We use the '$\sim$' notation to denote 'is represented by', and (9.1) means that the signal $f(t)$ is represented by its Fourier series expansion. This is an important idea, since it is not true that at every value of t, the left-hand side of the expression always takes the same value as the right-hand side. In particular, at a point of discontinuity, the Fourier expansion will converge to the mean of the left- and right-hand limits of $f(t)$, irrespective of any definition of the value of $f(t)$ actually at the point.

The process of determining the Fourier expansion is now reduced to the determination of the coefficient A_n for all values of n, that is, all positive and negative integers, and zero. In fact this task is not particularly onerous, and is possible in view of the 'orthogonality' relationship:

$$\frac{1}{T}\int_{t_0}^{t_0+T} e^{in\omega_0 t}\, e^{-im\omega_0 \tau}\, \mathrm{d}t = \delta_{mn} = \begin{array}{ll} 0, & m \neq n \\ 1, & m = n. \end{array} \tag{9.2}$$

The reader is invited to verify this result in the exercises at the end of this chapter.

The technique for determining the expansion now involves multiplying (9.1) by

$$\frac{1}{T} e^{-im\omega_0 t},$$

where m is a positive or negative integer or zero, and integrating over one full period. If we require that the same result be obtained for $f(t)$ or its Fourier representation, we must have

$$\frac{1}{T}\int_{t_0}^{t_0+T} f(t)\, e^{-im\omega_0 t}\, \mathrm{d}t$$

$$= \frac{1}{T}\int_{t_0}^{t_0+T}\left[\sum_{n=-\infty}^{\infty} A_n\, e^{in\omega_0 t}\right] e^{-im\omega_0 t}\, \mathrm{d}t$$

$$= \frac{1}{T}\sum_{n=-\infty}^{\infty} A_n \int_{t_0}^{t_0+T} e^{in\omega_0 t}\, e^{-im\omega_0 t}\, \mathrm{d}t\ .$$

$$= A_m,$$

in view of (9.2). We have assumed that interchanging the order of integration and summation is permissible in obtaining our result.

We have established a formula for the generation of the coefficients in the Fourier expansion of the periodic function $f(t)$ as

$$A_n = \int_{t_0}^{t_0+T} f(t)\, e^{-in\omega_0 t}\, dt$$

$$= \int_0^T f(t)\, e^{-in\omega_0 t}\, dt, \qquad (9.3)$$

where $\omega_0 = 2\pi/T$.

The method is demonstrated in the following example.

Example 9.1

Calculate the coefficients of the Fourier series which represents the periodic function of Fig. 9.1.

First, notice that we can write $f(t)$ as

$$f(t) = \begin{vmatrix} 0, & 0 < t < A \\ 1, & A \leqslant t \leqslant 2A \end{vmatrix}.$$

Now, the expansion coefficients are given by (9.3) as

$$A_n = \int_0^T f(t)\, e^{-in\omega_0 t}\, dt,$$

where $\omega_0 = 2\pi/T = \pi/A$. Thus

$$A_n = \frac{1}{2A} \int_A^{2A} e^{-in\omega_0 t}\, dt$$

$$= \frac{1}{2A(-in\omega_0)} [e^{-in\omega_0 2A} - e^{-in\omega_0 A}]$$

$$= \frac{1}{2A\, in\omega_0} e^{-in\omega_0 3A/2} [e^{-in\omega_0 A/2} - e^{-in\omega_0 A/2}]$$

$$= \frac{1/2}{An\omega_0/2} e^{-in\omega_0 3A/2} \sin(n\omega_0 A/2)$$

$$= \frac{1}{2} e^{-in\omega_0 3A/2} \frac{\sin(n\omega_0 A/2)}{(n\omega_0 A/2)}, \qquad n \neq 0. \qquad (9.4)$$

When $n = 0$, we find that

$$A_0 = \frac{1}{2A} \int_A^{2A} dt = 1/2. \tag{9.5}$$

Thus the required coefficients are given by (9.4) and (9.5), and it is now possible to write down the Fourier series which represents $f(t)$ as

$$f(t) \sim 1/2 + 1/2 \sum_{n=-\infty}^{\infty} {}' \, e^{-in\omega_0 3A/2} \, \frac{\sin{(n\omega_0 A/2)}}{(n\omega_0 A/2)} \, e^{-in\omega_0 t},$$

where the $/$ notation on the summation sign means that the value $n = 0$ is excluded. The original signal $f(t)$ is a real signal and this means that the Fourier series is in fact real, despite appearances to the contrary. The interested reader may wish to establish that this is the case.

In (9.4), we encountered the quantity $\sin(x)/x$, where $x = n\omega_0 A/2$. This quantity occurs frequently in the analysis of signals and it is useful to define the function sinc (x) as

$$\text{sinc}\,(x) = \begin{vmatrix} \sin{(x)}/x, & x \neq 0 \\ 1, & x = 0. \end{vmatrix}$$

The motivation for the value at $x = 0$ comes from the value of the limit of $\sin(x)/x$ as $x \to 0$. With this definition, and after substituting for the value of $\omega_0 = \pi/A$, we can express the coefficients of Example 9.1 as

$$A_n = \tfrac{1}{2} e^{-in3\pi/2} \, \text{sinc}\,(n\pi/2), \tag{9.6}$$

for all values of n.

In fact the coefficients of the Fourier expansion are all that is really required to convey the necessary information on the harmonic composition of a signal. The expansion itself will not generally concern us.

At this point it may be worth a short digression in the cause of better understanding. The process we have just gone through in Example 9.1 is exactly analogous to the process of computing the components of a vector in a vector space. Suppose that we have a vector **r** in a three-dimensional Euclidean space. We are familiar with the task of computing the components of such a vector relative to the orthogonal base vectors **i**, **j**, and **k**. These components are actually obtained by taking the 'dot', or scalar, product with each base vector in turn, that is we form

$$r_x = \mathbf{r} \cdot \mathbf{j}, \quad r_y = \mathbf{r} \cdot \mathbf{j} \quad \text{and} \quad r_z = \mathbf{r} \cdot \mathbf{k}.$$

The process of decomposition of a signal using the techniques of Fourier analysis can be thought of in the same way. In effect, we are treating a signal as a vector in an infinite-dimensional vector space, and computing the components of the signal in the 'harmonic directions' defined by the basis vectors $e^{in\omega_0 t}$. The scalar, or inner, product in this vector space is now

$$\frac{1}{T}\int_0^T f(t)g(t)\ dt,$$

where $f(t)$ and $g(t)$ are signals or vectors in signal space, and $1/T$ is a normalizing factor, chosen so that the inner product of a base vector with itself shall be unity. This structure is called a scalar product because the result of the calculation is a scalar, or number, exactly as we obtain from the 'dot' product of two vectors in Euclidean space.

Our previous work on frequency response can now be seen as an investigation of how a linear system processes the base vectors of our signal space. Intuitively, we can appreciate that if this is known, then it is reasonable to suppose that we can predict the response to any signal vector in the space.

Having found the Fourier coefficients of a periodic signal $f(t)$, we now interpret their meaning. Since $e^{in\omega_0 t} = \cos(n\omega_0 t) + i\sin(n\omega_0 t)$, where n is an integer, or zero, our decomposition has yielded a prescription for constructing a periodic signal $f(t)$ from the elementary harmonic functions $\cos(n\omega_0 t)$ and $\sin(n\omega_0 t)$. We have *chosen* to express this prescription using the complex exponential representation, and this choice has two implications. First, the Fourier coefficients are, in general, complex numbers, and second, we have to use both positive and negative values of the index n. It is important to appreciate that both these implications are direct consequences of our choice of basis functions used to span the signal space. From another point of view, had we chosen to use as basis functions the real set $\{\cos(n\omega_0 t), \sin(n\omega_0 t), n \geqslant 0\}$, then real signals $f(t)$ could have been 'resolved' into real components relative to these real 'harmonic directions'. Our choice of a set of complex base vectors is made in order to simplify later manipulation.

Let us now consider in more detail the Fourier coefficients relative to our chosen base set $\{e^{in\omega_0 t}, n$ a positive or negative integer or zero$\}$. First, notice that if $f(t)$ is periodic of period T, then it has frequency comnponents at the frequencies $n\omega_0$, $n = 0, \pm 1, \pm 2, \pm 3 \ldots$, and $\omega_0 = 2\pi/T$. This is a discrete set of components located at multiples of the 'fundamental' frequency ω_0, defined by the period T of $f(t)$. Each component A_n is, in general, a complex number, so that $A_n = a_n + ib_n$, say. Thus each term in the Fourier series takes the form

$$A_n e^{in\omega_0 t} = (a_n + ib_n)e^{in\omega_0 t}$$

$$= [a_n \cos(n\omega_0 t) - b_n \sin(n\omega_0 t)] + i[a_n \sin(n\omega_0 t) + b_n \cos(n\omega_0 t)]$$
$$= \sqrt{[a_n^2 + b_n^2]}\{\cos(n\omega_0 t + \phi_n) + i\sin(n\omega_0 t + \phi_n)\}$$
$$= |A_n| \; e^{i(n\omega_0 t + \phi_n)} = |A_n| \; e^{i(n\omega_0 t + \arg A_n)}$$

where $\phi_n = \arg A_n$, and $\cos(\phi_n) = a_n/(a_n^2 + b_n^2)$, $\sin(\phi_n) = b_n/(a_n^2 + b_n^2)$.

We see that each coefficient of the Fourier series provides the required information on the amplitude, $|A_n|$, and the phase, $\arg A_n$, of the corresponding harmonic. This information is displayed graphically using two diagrams. The first is called the signal amplitude spectrum, and is a specification of $|A_n|$ as a function of n, or $n\omega_0$. The second diagram is called the phase spectrum, and specifies $\arg A_n$ again as a function of n or $n\omega_0$.

We now consider these spectra for the signal $f(t)$ of Example 9.1. From (9.6), we have that

$$|A_n| = 1/2 \; |\text{sinc} \; (n\pi/2)|,$$

and

$$\arg (A_n) = \left| \begin{array}{ll} -3n\pi/2 + 2p\pi, & \text{when sinc } (n\pi/2) \geq 0 \\ \pi - 3n\pi/2 + 2p\pi, & \text{when sinc } (n\pi/2) < 0 \end{array} \right.$$

where p is an integer, chosen so that $\arg(A_n) \in (-\pi, \pi]$. (See Fig. 9.2.)

It is interesting to observe the effect of time shifting on the spectrum of periodic signals. Suppose that $f(t)$ is periodic of period T and has Fourier coefficients F_n, say, where $n = 0, \pm 1, \pm 2, \ldots$. If we calculate the coefficients G_n of the time-shifted version, $f(t + \tau)$, we find that

$$G_n = \frac{1}{T} \int_0^T f(t + \tau) e^{-in\omega_0 t} \, dt$$

$$= \frac{1}{T} \int_\tau^{\tau + T} f(u) \; e^{-in\omega_0 (u - \tau)} \, du$$

$$= \frac{e^{in\omega_0 \tau}}{T} \int_0^T f(t) \; e^{-in\omega_0 t} \, dt$$

$$= e^{in\omega_0 \tau} F_n.$$

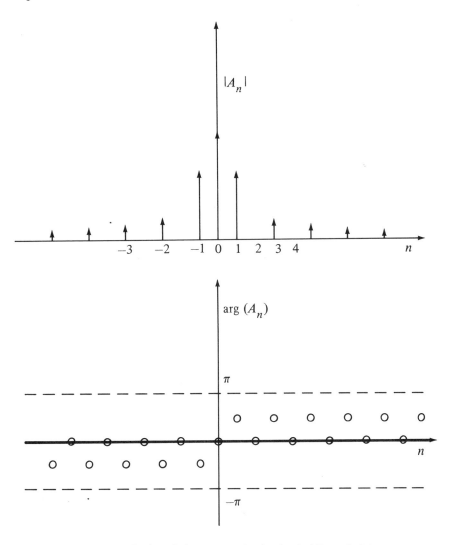

Fig. 9.2 — Amplitude and phase spectra for the signal of Example 9.1.

We see that since $|e^{in\omega_0\tau}| = 1$, $|G_n| = |F_n|$ for all n. This means that the time shift has no effect at all on the amplitude spectrum. However, $\arg G_n = \arg F_n + n\omega_0\tau$, showing a phase shift proportional to the frequency $n\omega_0$ for a given time shift τ.

9.3 THE FOURIER TRANSFORM

Having established a technique for the representation of periodic signals in the frequency domain, we must admit that not many signals of interest are likely to be periodic! It must now be our task to attempt to develop a method which will achieve a similar representation or decomposition, for non-periodic signals, defined on $-\infty < t < \infty$. Fig. 9.3 illustrates such a signal, $f(t)$, and shows a portion of the signal

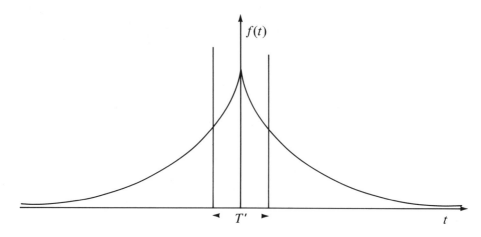

Fig. 9.3 — A non-periodic signal, and the view through the window of duration T.

as visible through a 'time window' of duration T', placed symmetrically about the origin.

Concentrating only on that portion of signal 'visible' through the window, we could pretend that outside the window our signal consisted of periodic repeats of the portion we observe through the window. This would make no different at all to the portion of signal that we can 'see', that is, the segment in the window alone. We could then go on to perform a Fourier analysis of this 'pretend' periodic function, using the methods of section 9.2. The clever part of the operation is then to investigate the behaviour of the Fourier expansion as the duration of the window, T', increases without bound. Loosely speaking, we are adopting the picture that non-periodic signals are actually periodic signals, but that their period is infinite in duration!

To explore these ideas, set

$$g(t) = \left| \begin{array}{ll} f(t), & |t| < T'/2 \\ g(t - nT'), & |t| \geqslant T'/2, \end{array} \right.$$

where n is a positive or negative integer. This defines $g(t)$ as the periodic extension of that portion of $f(t)$, visible through our window, and is illustrated in Fig. 9.4.

Clearly, when $|t| < T'/2$, the graphs of $f(t)$ and $g(t)$ are identical, but since $g(t)$ is periodic of period T' we can use the methods of section 9.1 to write

$$g(t) \sim \sum_{n=-\infty}^{\infty} G_n e^{in\omega_0 t} \tag{9.7}$$

with

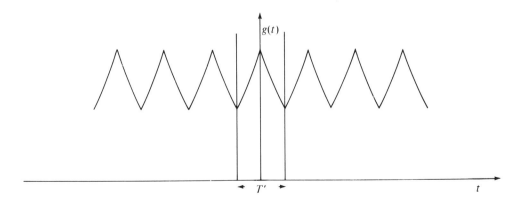

Fig. 9.4 — The periodic function $g(t)$, the periodic extension of the view through the window.

$$G_n = \frac{1}{T'} \int_{-T'/2}^{T'/2} g(\tau) \, e^{-in\omega_0\tau} \, d\tau. \tag{9.8}$$

We proceed by substituting (9.8) into (9.7) to obtain

$$g(t) \sim \sum_{n=-\infty}^{\infty} \left[\frac{1}{T'} \int_{-T'/2}^{T'/2} g(\tau) \, e^{-in\omega_0\tau} \, d\tau \right] e^{in\omega_0 t} \tag{9.9}$$

We now ask what happens as $T' \to \infty$. Obviously our window widens, so that eventually $g(t)$ agrees with $f(t)$ for all values of t. Also, the summation in (9.9) becomes an integral, a point which becomes apparent if we write (9.9) in the form

$$g(t) \sim \sum_{n=-\infty}^{\infty} \frac{\omega_0}{2\pi} e^{in\omega_0 t} \int_{-T'/2}^{T'/2} g(\tau) \, e^{-in\omega_0\tau} \, d\tau. \tag{9.10}$$

Each time the summation index n changes by 1, $n\omega_0$ changes by an amount ω_0. However, since $\omega_0 = 2\pi/T' \to 0$ as $T' \to \infty$, we are led to write $n\omega_0 = \omega$, a continuous variable, with $\omega_0 = d\omega$. Note that for non-periodic signals, the separation between harmonic components in the frequency domain goes to zero as $T' \to \infty$. Thus summation over n, corresponding to the process of summation over distinct frequency components at separation ω_0, is replaced by integration over the continuous frequency variable ω. Recall that if $T' \to \infty$, then $g(t) = f(t)$ everywhere and we can write (9.10) in the form

$$f(t) \sim \int_{-\infty}^{\infty} \frac{d\omega}{2\pi} e^{i\omega t} \int_{-\infty}^{\infty} \tilde{f}(\tau) e^{-i\omega \tau} d\tau. \tag{9.11}$$

This is known as the Fourier integral representation of $f(t)$, and if we define

$$F(i\omega) = \int_{-\infty}^{\infty} f(\tau) e^{-i\omega \tau} d\tau \tag{9.12}$$

then (9.11) can be written

$$f(t) \sim \frac{1}{2\pi} \int_{-\infty}^{\infty} F(i\omega) e^{i\omega t} d\omega. \tag{9.13}$$

Here $F(i\omega)$ is called the Fourier transform of the time signal $f(t)$. Whenever the defining integral exists, $F(i\omega)$ plays the role of the Fourier coefficients of section 9.2 and is our desired frequency domain representation of $f(t)$. We note that non-periodic signals have frequency components at all values of the continuous frequency variable ω. This is in contrast to the situation we observed for signals of finite period T', for which the frequency components occurred only at distinct values $n\omega_0$ of the frequency variable.

Equation (9.13) then shows how to construct a *representation* of the time signal $f(t)$ from a knowledge of its Fourier transform $F(i\omega)$. By retaining the '$\sim$' notation, we stress that this is a representation of $f(t)$, noting in particular the behaviour of this representation at any points of discontinuity. We recall from section 9.2 that the Fourier representation converges to the mean of left- and right-hand limits of $f(t)$ as t tends to the point of discontinuity, irrespective of any definition of $f(t)$ actually at the point.

Based on the results (9.12) and (9.13), we can construct a bi-directional path between time and frequency domains. In this connection, it is useful to have a notation for the Fourier transform operation, and we use the symbol $\mathcal{F}$ for this purpose. Thus we may write (9.12) as

$$\mathcal{F}\{f(t)\} = F(i\omega) = \int_{-\infty}^{\infty} f(t) e^{-i\omega t} dt \tag{9.14}$$

and (9.14) defines the Fourier transform of $f(t)$ whenever the integral exists. (N.B. We have not said that when the integral does not exist then there is not a Fourier transform!) The path from the frequency domain to the time domain makes use of the inverse Fourier transform, as defined by the integral on the right side of (9.13). Thus we write

$$\mathscr{F}^{-i}\{G(i\omega)\} = g(t) = \frac{1}{2\pi} \int_{-\infty}^{\infty} G(i\omega) \, e^{i\omega t} \, d\omega. \tag{9.15}$$

In (9.15) we use an ' = ' sign, because the time domain signal $g(t)$ is *defined* as the result of performing the integration on the right-hand side.

Example 9.2
Find the Fourier transform of the causal function

$$f(t) = e^{-at}\xi(t), \; a > 0.$$

Using (9.14), we have,

$$\mathscr{F}\{e^{-at}\xi(t)\} = \int_{-\infty}^{\infty} e^{-at}\xi(t) \, e^{-i\omega t} \, dt$$

$$= \int_{0}^{\infty} e^{-(a+i\omega)t} \, dt$$

$$= \frac{-1}{(a+i\omega)} \left[e^{-(a+i\omega)t} \right]_{0}^{\infty}$$

$$= \frac{1}{(a+i\omega)} = \frac{a-i\omega}{a^2+\omega^2}$$

$$= F(i\omega).$$

The Fourier transform of Example 9.2 was calculated without difficulty. However, we note that attempts to calculate the transforms of e^{at} and e^{-at}, $a > 0$, would both fail because the defining integral would not exist in either case. In fact, we find that we are unable to obtain the transforms of many 'elementary' functions by this means. Dirichlet gave a set of conditions which are sufficient for the existence of the integral in the definition of the Fourier transform of the signal $f(t)$. These are:

(a) $f(t)$ mut be absolutely integrable on $(-\infty, \infty)$, that is

$$\int_{-\infty}^{\infty} |f(t)| \, dt \text{ is finite, and}$$

(b) $f(t)$ has, at most, a finite number of finite discontinuities, and a finite number of maxima and minima in any finite interval.

These conditions are seen to be a natural extension to the conditions given earlier for the existence of a Fourier series representation of a periodic function.

In Example 9.3 we examine a function or signal which clearly satisfies these conditions.

Example 9.3
Calculate the Fourier transform of the rectangular pulse defined by

$$f(t) = \begin{vmatrix} A, & |t| \leqslant T/2 \\ 0, & |t| > T/2 \end{vmatrix}$$

and depicted in Fig. 9.5.

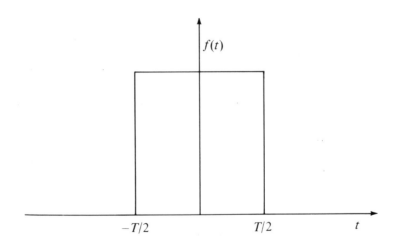

Fig. 9.5 — The rectangular pulse of Example 9.3.

Again using the defining integral, (9.14), we have

$$\mathscr{F}\{f(t)\} = \int_{-\infty}^{\infty} f(t)\, e^{-i\omega t}\, dt$$

$$= \int_{-T/2}^{T/2} A\, e^{-i\omega t}\, dt$$

$$= \frac{-A}{i\omega} \left[e^{-i\omega t} \right]_{-T/2}^{T/2} \qquad \omega \neq 0$$

$$= \frac{A}{i\omega} \left[e^{i\omega T/2} - e^{-i\omega T/2} \right] \qquad \omega \neq 0$$

$$= AT \frac{\sin (\omega T/2)}{\omega T/2} \quad \omega \neq 0.$$

Since $\mathcal{F}\{f(t)\} = 1$, when $\omega = 0$, we can express this result as

$$\mathcal{F}\{f(t)\} = AT \text{ sinc } (\omega T/2) = F(i\omega)$$

for all values of ω.

The results of Examples 9.2 and 9.3 are contained in Table 9.1, and the reader is invited to confirm the other transforms in the exercises.

Table 9.1 — Some elementary functions and their Fourier transforms

$f(t)$	Fourier transform $\mathcal{F}\{f(t)\}$
$e^{-at} \xi(t), a>0$	$\dfrac{a - i\omega}{a^2 + \omega^2}$
$te^{-at} \xi(t), a>0$	$\dfrac{1}{(a + i\omega)^2}$
$e^{-a\lvert t \rvert}, a>0$	$\dfrac{2a}{a^2 + \omega^2}$
$\begin{bmatrix} A, & \lvert t \rvert \leqslant T/2 \\ 0, & \lvert t \rvert > T/2 \end{bmatrix}$	$AT \text{ sinc } (\omega T/2)$

9.4 THE FOURIER SPECTRUM

In section 9.2, we discussed the two spectra associated with the Fourier decomposition of periodic signals. There we saw that both the amplitude and the phase spectra consisted of a discrete set of components, located at multiples of the 'fundamental' frequency ω_0. In the case of non-periodic signals, the Fourier transform takes the role of the Fourier coefficients and if $\mathcal{F}\{f(t)\} = F(i\omega)$ is the transform of a non-periodic signal $f(t)$, then $F(i\omega)$ is known as the (complex) frequency spectrum of $f(t)$. Since $F(i\omega)$ is, in general, a complex-valued function of the real frequency variable ω, we write

$$F(i\omega) = \lvert F(i\omega) \rvert e^{i\theta(i\omega)}.$$

Here, the two real-valued functions of ω, $\lvert F(i\omega) \rvert$ and $\theta(i\omega)$, are called the amplitude and phase spectra respectively.

Example 9.4

Calculate the amplitude and phase spectra for the signal of Example 9.2.

In Example 9.2, we found that if $f(t) = e^{-at} \xi(t)$, then

$$F(i\omega) = \frac{1}{a + i\omega}.$$

The amplitude spectrum is then given by

$$|F(i\omega)| = \frac{1}{\sqrt{(a^2 + \omega^2)}}$$

whereas $\theta(i\omega)$, the phase spectrum, is defined by

$$\theta(i\omega) = -\tan^{-1}(\omega/a).$$

These spectra are illustrated in Fig. 9.6. The illustrations in Fig. 9.6 serve to stress

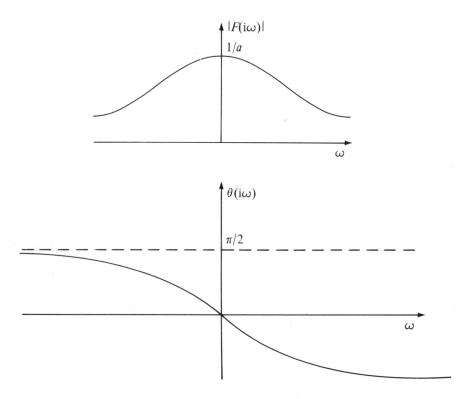

Fig. 9.6 — The amplitude and phase spectra for the signal $e^{-at} \xi(t)$ of Example 9.4.

that the amplitude and phase spectra are defined for all values of the continuous variable ω.

Sometimes, as in Example 9.3, we find that the Fourier transform is a purely real quantity. In that example, we saw that

$$\mathcal{F}\{f(t)\} = F(i\omega) = AT \text{ sinc } (\omega T/2).$$

Here, $|F(i\omega)| = AT \text{ sinc } (\omega T/2)|$,

$$\theta(i\omega) = \begin{vmatrix} 0, & \text{sinc } (\omega T/2) \geqslant 0 \\ \pi, & \text{sinc } (\omega T/2) < 0. \end{vmatrix}$$

Clearly, if we plotted the graph of the real-valued function $F(i\omega) = \text{sinc } (\omega T/2)$, then we could convey all the information in a single graph. However, this would contradict the definition of the amplitude spectrum as essentially positive. We thus do not make use of this representation, although it is in common use elsewhere.

We can make two observations based on our discussion of the Fourier transform so far. First note that in the examples so far considered, the amplitude spectrum has been an even function of the frequency variable ω. This is not a coincidence, and it can be shown that this will always be the case when the time signal $f(t)$ is a real signal, and is again a consequence of our decomposition of $f(t)$ onto a basis consisting of complex exponential functions. A second point is the behaviour of the amplitude spectra with increasing ω. In each case, the magnitude of $F(i\omega)$ falls off rapidly as ω increases. This means that most of the information on the shape of the pulse or signal $f(t)$ is conveyed in the frequency domain in an interval around the origin $\omega = 0$. For the rectangular pulse of Example 9.3, a graph of the amplitude spectrum shows that a device capable of passing accurately signals of frequencies less than about $5\pi/T$, would pass a reasonably accurate copy of the pulse. Such information on the ability of systems to pass signals of different frequencies is contained in the frequency response of the system, and it should now be apparent why this is such an important system property.

9.5 PROPERTIES OF THE FOURIER TRANSFORM

In this section we do not propose to give an exhaustive discussion of the properties of the Fourier transform. Rather, we restrict ourselves to a consideration of those properties which will assist us in our work on the processing of signals using linear systems.

(1) Linearity: The first property we will consider is the linearity property, which is vital to many applications of the theory. Suppose that two signals, $f(t)$ and $g(t)$, have Fourier transforms $F(i\omega)$ and $G(i\omega)$ respectively. The Fourier transform of linear combination of these two signals is then

$$\mathscr{F}\{\alpha f(t) + \beta g(t)\} = \int_{-\infty}^{\infty} \{\alpha f(t) + \beta g(t)\}\ e^{-i\omega t}\ dt$$

$$= \alpha \int_{-\infty}^{\infty} f(t) e^{-i\omega t}\ dt + \beta \int_{-\infty}^{\infty} g(t) e^{-i\omega t}\ dt$$

$$= \alpha F(i\omega) + \beta G(i\omega)\ . \tag{9.16}$$

Clearly, the linearity result will also apply to the inverse transform.

(2) Time Differentiation: The second important property to be discussed is the time-differentiation result. To establish this result, assume that $f(t)$ has a Fourier transform $F(i\omega)$; then from (9.15) we have

$$f(t) = \frac{1}{2\pi} \int_{-\infty}^{\infty} F(i\omega)\ e^{i\omega t}\ d\omega.$$

Differentiate this result with respect to t, and

$$\frac{df}{dt} = \frac{1}{2\pi} \int_{-\infty}^{\infty} (i\omega)\ F(i\omega)\ e^{i\omega t}\ d\omega.$$

Comparison with (9.15) shows us that this means that df/dt is the inverse Fourier transform of $(i\omega)F(i\omega)$, and thus that $\mathscr{F}\{df/dt\} = (i\omega)F(i\omega)$.

If we apply the argument n times, we see that

$$\mathscr{F}\left[\frac{d^n f}{dt^n}\right] = (i\omega)^n\ F(i\omega).$$

(3) Time Shifting: We have already discussed the effects of a time shift on the Fourier spectrum of a periodic signal. Here, we establish the general property. Suppose that a signal $f(t)$ has a Fourier transform $F(i\omega)$; the transform of the time-shifted version $f(t-\tau)$ will be

$$\mathscr{F}\{f(t-\tau)\} = \int_{-\infty}^{\infty} f(t-\tau)\ e^{-i\omega t}\ dt.$$

Writing $x = t - \tau$, we obtain

$$\mathcal{F}\{f(t-\tau)\} = e^{-i\omega\tau} \int_{-\infty}^{\infty} f(x)\, e^{-i\omega x}\, dx$$
$$= e^{-i\omega\tau}\, F(i\omega).$$

Note that $|e^{-i\omega\tau} F(i\omega)| = |F(i\omega)|$, showing that the amplitude spectrum of $f(t-\tau)$ is identical with that of $f(t)$. On the other hand, $\arg[e^{-i\omega\tau} F(i\omega)] = \arg[F(i\omega)] - \omega\tau$, and we see that there is a phase shift by an amount proportional to frequency ω.

(4) Frequency Shifting: This result is the basis of the process of modulation, by which information is transmitted using carrier signals at selected frequencies. Again, suppose that a signal $f(t)$ has Fourier transform $F(i\omega)$ and consider the transform of the signal $g(t) = e^{-i\omega_0 t} f(t)$. From the definition of the Fourier transform we have

$$\mathcal{F}\{g(t)\} = \int_{-\infty}^{\infty} f(t)\, e^{i\omega_0 t}\, e^{-i\omega t}\, dt$$
$$= \int_{-\infty}^{\infty} f(t) e^{-i(\omega-\omega_0)t}\, dt. \qquad (9.17)$$

Now, by definition,

$$F(i\omega) = \int_{-\infty}^{\infty} f(t)\, e^{-i\omega t}\, dt \qquad (9.18)$$

and since substituting $\omega - \omega_0$ for ω in (9.18) yields (9.17) we have shown that

$$\mathcal{F}\{f(t)e^{i\omega_0 t}\} = F(i[\omega-\omega_0]).$$

We can see that the effect of multiplication of $f(t)$ by $e^{i\omega_0 t}$ is to shift the spectrum of $f(t)$, so that it is centred on $\omega = \omega_0$.

(5) The Symmetry Property: This is the last property that we will consider in detail. The symmetry property reflects the symmetry which is apparent in the paths between time and frequency domain. We will make significant use of this result as we seek to enlarge our library of Fourier transforms. Suppose as usual that $F(i\omega)$ is the Fourier transform of some time signal $f(t)$. Then by (9.15) we have

$$f(t) = \frac{1}{2\pi} \int_{-\infty}^{\infty} F(i\omega)\, e^{i\omega t}\, d\omega$$

or

$$2\pi f(t) = \int_{-\infty}^{\infty} F(ix)\ e^{ixt}\ dx.$$

Thus

$$2\pi f(-t) = \int_{-\infty}^{\infty} F(ix)\ e^{-ixt}\ dx,$$

and writing ω in place of t, we obtain

$$2\pi f(-\omega) = \int_{-\infty}^{\infty} F(ix)\ e^{-i\omega x}\ dx$$

$$= \int_{-\infty}^{\infty} F(it)\ e^{-i\omega t}\ dt = \mathcal{F}\{F(it)\},$$

the Fourier transform of the time signal $F(it)$.

There is a convenient notation for conveying the implication of the symmetry result. If $F(i\omega)$ is the Fourier transform of $f(t)$, then we write

$$f(t) \leftrightarrow F(i\omega),$$

and we say that $f(t)$ and $F(i\omega)$ are a Fourier transform pair. Thus if $f(t) \leftrightarrow F(i\omega)$ is a transform pair, then the symmetry property gives us that $F(it) \leftrightarrow 2\pi f(-\omega)$ is another transform pair.

We now demonstrate these properties in the following examples.

Example 9.5

The input $u(t)$ and output $y(t)$ of a causal, linear, time-invariant system are related by

$$\frac{d^2 y(t)}{dt^2} + 3\frac{dy(t)}{dt} + 2y(t) = \frac{du(t)}{dt} + 4u(t). \tag{9.19}$$

If $u(t)$ and $y(t)$ have Fourier transforms denoted by

$$\mathcal{F}\{u(t)\} = U(i\omega) \quad \text{and} \quad \mathcal{F}\{y(t)\} = Y(i\omega),$$

find $H(i\omega)$ such that $Y(i\omega) = H(i\omega)U(i\omega)$.

At once, using the time-differentiation propety (2) above, we have that

$$\mathscr{F}\left\{\frac{du(t)}{dt}\right\} = i\omega\ \mathscr{F}\{u(t)\} = i\omega\ U(i\omega),$$

$$\mathscr{F}\left\{\frac{dy(t)}{dt}\right\} = i\omega\ Y(i\omega),\ \text{and}$$

$$\mathscr{F}\left\{\frac{d^2y(t)}{dt^2}\right\} = (i\omega)^2\ Y(i\omega).$$

Now taking Fourier transforms in (9.19), we have

$$\mathscr{F}\left\{\frac{d^2y(t)}{dt^2} + 3\ \frac{dy(t)}{dt} + 2y(t)\right\} = \mathscr{F}\left\{\frac{du(t)}{dt} + 4u(t)\right\}$$

and using the linearity property (1) above, we can write

$$\mathscr{F}\left\{\frac{d^2y(t)}{dt^2}\right\} + 3\mathscr{F}\left\{\frac{dy(t)}{dt}\right\} + 2\mathscr{F}\{y(t)\}$$

$$= \mathscr{F}\left\{\frac{du(t)}{dt}\right\} + 4\mathscr{F}\{u(t)\}.$$

That is,

$$(i\omega)^2\ Y(i\omega) + 3(i\omega)\ Y(i\omega) + 2Y(i\omega)$$
$$= (i\omega)\ U(i\omega) + 4U(i\omega),$$

so that

$$Y(i\omega) = \frac{4 + i\omega}{2 - \omega^2 + 3i\omega}\ U(i\omega).$$

Thus,

$$H(i\omega) = \frac{4 + i\omega}{2 - \omega^2 + 3i\omega}.$$

In Example 9.5 we have, in effect, obtained a Fourier transfer function for the linear system (9.19). In section 8.7, we identified the same function, $H(i\omega)$, with the Laplace transfer function of the system $H(s)$, evaluated on the imaginary axis when this was possible. Such an evaluation was shown to be possible for causal linear systems which were stable. Such systems possess impulse response functions $h(t) = \mathcal{L}^{-1}\{H(s)\} = \mathcal{F}^{-1}\{H(i\omega)\}$, which are causal, so that $h(t) = 0$, $t < 0$, and decay to zero as $t \to \infty$. By examining the defining integrals for the Laplace and Fourier transforms for such functions $h(t)$, we see that the Fourier transform (9.12) is correctly obtained in these cases, by writing $s = i\omega$ in the Laplace transform integral (7.21).

Example 9.6
Calculate the Fourier transform of the pulse of Fig. 9.7.

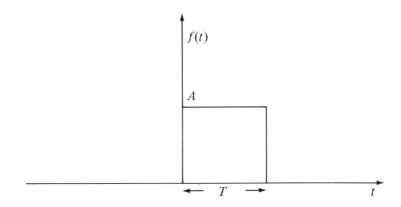

Fig. 9.7 — The shifted pulse of duration T.

This pulse is simply the pulse of Example 9.3, delayed by $T/2$ sec.. Thus, using the result of that example and the time-shifting result, (3) above, we obtain for the Fourier transform

$$F(i\omega) = e^{-i\omega T/2} AT \text{ sinc } (\omega T/2).$$

Comparing this result with that of Example 9.3, we observe that the amplitude spectrum of each pulse is identical. The phase spectra, however, exhibit a difference in line with that discussed earlier for the periodic pulse train.

Example 9.7
The signal $f(t)$ has Fourier transform $F(i\omega)$. What are the Fourier transforms of the signals

(i) $g_1(t) = f(t) \cos (\omega_c t)$ and
(ii) $g_2(t) = f(t) \sin (\omega_c t)$?

(i) Now $g_1(t) = f(t) \cos (\omega_c t) = f(t) [e^{i\omega_c t} + e^{-i\omega_c t}]/2$.

Thus we can write, using first the linearity property, and then the frequency-shifting property (4), above

$$\mathcal{F}\{g_i(t)\} = 1/2 \; \mathcal{F}\{e^{i\omega_c t} f(t)\} + 1/2 \; \mathcal{F}\{e^{-i\omega_c t} f(t)\}$$
$$= 1/2 F(i(\omega - \omega_c)) + 1/2 \; F(i(\omega + \omega_c)).$$

(ii) Similarly,

$$\mathcal{F}\{g_2(t)\} = 1/2i \; \mathcal{F}\{e^{i\omega_c t} f(t)\} + 1/2i \; \mathcal{F}\{e^{-\omega_c t} f(t)\}$$
$$= 1/2i \; F(i(\omega - \omega_c)) - 1/2i \; F(i(\omega + \omega_c)).$$

The result in part (i) of Example 9.7 provides the explanation of the process of modulation. The signal $\cos(\omega_c t)$ is a 'carrier' signal and $f(t)$ is a real, information-carrying signal, with amplitude spectrum $|F(i\omega)|$ centred on $\omega = 0$. The carrier signal $\cos(\omega_c t)$ is modulated by the process of multiplication at each instant by the signal $f(t)$ to produce the signal $g_i(t)$. We see that $G(i\omega)$, the frequency spectrum of $g(t)$, contains two copies of $F(i\omega)$, one centred on $\omega = \omega_c$, the other on $\omega = -\omega_c$, the frequency of the carrier signal. In our discussion so far, the signals we have considered have had the significant portion of their amplitude spectra restricted to a fairly small band of frequencies, centred on $\omega = 0$. If such signals were used to modulate carrier signals of different, suitably separated frequencies, then the simultaneous transmission of several such signals should be possible in such a way that the information contained in each modulating signal could be recovered. In Chapter 10 we will examine devices, called analogue filters, which will enable the necessary recovery process.

Example 9.8
Use the symmetry property and the final entry of Table 9.1 to calculate the Fourier transform of the signal

$$g(t) = \frac{1}{a^2 + t^2}.$$

Let $f(t) = e^{-a|t|}$, then $\mathcal{F}\{f(t)\} = F(i\omega) = 2a/(a^2 + \omega^2)$ from Table 9.1. That is,

$$f(t) \leftrightarrow F(i\omega)$$

is a Fourier transform pair. Using the symmetry property (5) above, we have that

$F(it) \leftrightarrow 2\pi f(-i\omega)$ is then another transform pair. Now,

$$F(it) = \frac{2a}{a^2 + t^2}$$

and $f(-\omega) = e^{-a|\omega|}$, and thus we deduce that

$$\frac{2a}{a^2 + t^2} \leftrightarrow 2\pi \, e^{-a|\omega|}$$

is a transform pair.

Writing $g(t) = 1/(a^2 + t^2)$, we then have $g(t) \leftrightarrow G(i\omega)$, where $G(i\omega) = \pi/a \, e^{-a|\omega|}$.

From Example 9.8, we see that the symmetry property provides a method of extending our library of transforms. Actually, the property also serves as an alternative expression of the path between the frequency and time domain, in place of the intgegral form (9.15). (See, for example, Lighthill [1].) We shall make considerable use of this property in the next section.

We conclude this section with an example which will motivate our study of analogue filters in Chapter 10.

Example 9.9
A signal, $f(t) = g(t) + h(t)$, consists of two elements. The first element, $g(t)$, is a symmetric unit pulse of duration 2π sec. The other element, $h(t)$, is a copy of this pulse modulating a carrier signal with carrier frequency $\omega_0 = 5$ rad/sec. Discuss the transmission of the signal $f(t)$ through the stable linear system with Laplace transfer function

$$H(s) = \frac{1}{s^2 + 2s^2 + 2s + 1}.$$

We first form the Fourier transform $\mathcal{F}\{f(t)\}$ and examine the amplitude spectrum of the input signal.

Using the result of Example 9.3, and applying the linearity and frequency-shifting properties, we obtain

$$\mathcal{F}\{f(t)\} = 2\pi \, \text{sinc} \, (\omega\pi) + \pi[\text{sinc}(\omega - 5)\pi + \text{sinc}(\omega + 5)\pi] = F(i\omega).$$

The amplitude spectrum of this signal, $|F(i\omega)|$, is depicted in Fig. 9.8.

Now we turn our attention to the linear system itself. From $H(s)$, we form $H(i\omega)$, which we can do, since we are considering a stable system. At once,

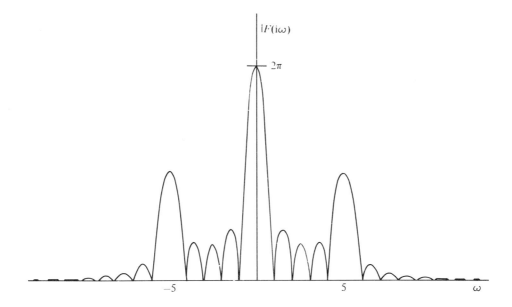

Fig. 9.8 — Amplitude spectrum of the composite signal $f(t)$ of Example 9.9.

$$H(i\omega) = \frac{1}{1 - 2\omega^2 + i(2\omega - \omega^3)}$$

and the amplitude response, $|H(i\omega)|$, is thus

$$|H(i\omega)| = \frac{1}{\sqrt{\{(1 - 2\omega^2)^2 + (2\omega - \omega^3)^2\}}}.$$

This response is illustrated in Fig. 9.9. If the output signal is $y(t)$, with Fourier transform $Y(i\omega)$, then $Y(i\omega) = H(i\omega)F(i\omega)$, and the amplitude spectrum of the output signal is

$$|Y(i\omega)| = |H(i\omega)\ F(i\omega)| = |H(i\omega)|\ |F(i\omega)|.$$

This amplitude spectrum is shown in Fig. 9.10. From Fig. 9.10, we see that the spectrum of the output signal contains a reasonably good copy of the spectrum of $g(t)$, the first element of the input signal. The second element, $h(t)$, has been 'filtered out' by the linear system. In fact, the system used to process $f(t)$ is a third-order

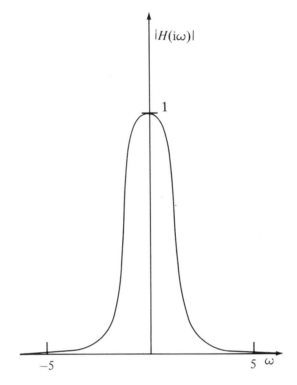

$|H(i\omega)|$

1

−5   5 ω

Fig. 9.9 — The amplitude response of the system of Example 9.9.

Butterworth low-pass filter, the design and properties of which we study in detail in
Chapter 10.

9.6 SIGNAL ENERGY AND POWER

In our discussion of non-periodic signals thus far, we have restricted attention to a
fairly small group of signals, all of which satisfy the Dirichlet conditions for the
existence of a Fourier transform. It is necessary to extend our work to include a wider
class of signals. Before attempting to do this, we introduce two quantities associated
with signals, which may be used to provide a convenient classification of signals. We
define the total energy associated with the signal $f(t)$, defined on $(-\infty, \infty)$, as

$$E = \int_{-\infty}^{\infty} |f(t)|^2 \, dt.$$

The total power associated with the signal $f(t)$ is defined as

$$P = \lim_{T \to \infty} \frac{1}{2T} \int_{-T}^{T} |f(t)|^2 \, dt. \tag{9.20}$$

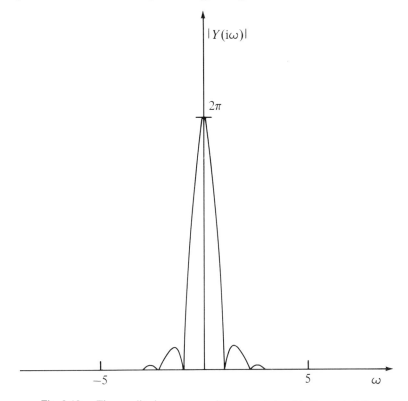

Fig. 9.10 — The amplitude spectrum of the output signal in Example 9.9.

We can make some observations based on the definition of signal energy and power for the types of signal that we have already encountered.

Non-periodic signals, which satisfy the Dirichlet conditions, are absolutely integrable on $(-\infty, \infty)$. Thus, the total energy associated with such a signal is E_0, say, where

$$E_0 = \int_{-\infty}^{\infty} |f(t)|^2 \, dt$$

and E_0 is a finite number. Clearly, the total power associated with the same signal $f(t)$ is zero, since

$$\mathbf{P} = \lim_{T \to \infty} \frac{1}{2T} E_0 = 0.$$

If we now turn our attention to periodic signals of period T_0, we notice that if we set $T = rT_0 + \tau$, where r is a positive integer and τ a constant, we can write (9.20) as

$$P = \lim_{r \to \infty} \int_{-(rT_0+\tau)}^{(rT_0+\tau)} |f(t)|^2 \, dt$$

$$= \lim_{r \to \infty} \left[\frac{1}{2(rT_0+\tau)} \, 2r \int_{\tau}^{T_0+\tau} |f(t)|^2 \, dt + \right.$$

$$\left. + \frac{1}{2(rT_0+\tau)} \int_{-\tau}^{\tau} |f(t)|^2 \, dt \right] = \frac{1}{T_0} \int_{\tau}^{T_0+\tau} |f(t)|^2 \, dt. \tag{9.21}$$

This means that the total power associated with a periodic function can be obtained by integration over a single period.

Example 9.10
Find the total power associated with the periodic signal

$$f(t) = A \, \sin \, (\omega_0 t).$$

What is the total energy? At once,

$$P = \frac{\omega_0}{2\pi} \int_{0}^{2\pi/\omega_0} A^2 \sin^2 \, (\omega_0 t) \, dt = \frac{A^2}{2}.$$

It is clear that the total energy is unbounded, since the defining integral does not tend to a finite limit.

We now have the means to establish our classification of signals, referred to above. This classification is into energy signals, which have finite energy, and zero power, and into power signals, which have unbounded energy, but finite power, associated with them. It follows that those non-periodic signals which satisfy the Dirichlet conditions for the existence of a Fourier transform will fall into the first category, whereas those periodic signals which satisfy the Dirichlet conditions for the existence of a Fourier series will be members of the second. In the next section, we will try to devise a generalization of the Fourier transform which will allow us to include signals of the second type into a single representation in the frequency domain. Before this, we draw attention to another consequence of the observed symmetry between time and frequency domains. Let us write (9.21) as

$$P = \frac{1}{T_0} \int_{0}^{T_0} |f(t)|^2 \, dt = \frac{1}{T_0} \int_{0}^{T_0} f(t) f^*(t) \, dt$$

where $f(t)$ is periodic of period T_0 and $f^*(t)$ denotes the complex conjugate signal. Replacing $f^*(t)$ with its Fourier expansion,

$$P = \frac{1}{T_0} \int_0^{T_0} f(t) \sum_{-\infty}^{\infty} F_n^* \, e^{-in\omega_0 t} \, dt$$

$$= \sum_{-\infty}^{\infty} F_n^* \left[\frac{1}{T_0} \int_0^{T_0} f(t) \, e^{-in\omega_0 t} \, dt \right]$$

$$= \sum_{-\infty}^{\infty} |F_n|^2 . \tag{9.22}$$

We have shown that for periodic signals, which possess a Fourier expansion, it is possible to obtain an expression for the power content of the signal in terms of the frequency domain represenation. The reader may wish to obtain a similar result for the energy associated with an energy signal.

Example 9.11
In this example we demonstate the use of (9.22) above for the periodic signal

$$f(t) = A \sin(\omega_0 t).$$

Now $f(t) = A/2i \, (e^{i\omega_0 t} - e^{-i\omega_0 t})$, and so

$$F_{-1} = -A/2i \quad \text{and} \quad F_1 = A/2i;$$

the total power associated with $f(t)$ is then, by (9.22),

$$P = [A^2/4 + A^2/4] = A^2/2, \text{ in agreement with our previous calculation.}$$

9.7   A GENERALIZATION OF THE FOURIER TRANSFORM

This section is devoted to an attempt to draw together our previous results into a unified treatment. The key step in our development is to examine the Fourier transform of $\delta(t)$, the Dirac delta function. By definition,

$$\mathcal{F}\{\delta(t)\} = \int_{-\infty}^{\infty} e^{-i\omega t} \, \delta(t) \, dt = 1$$

using (8.10), with $b = 0$. That is,

$$\delta(t) \leftrightarrow 1 \tag{9.23}$$

is a Fourier transform pair.

We recall that the Laplace transform of $\delta(t)$ is also 1, provided that due attention is paid to the lower limit of integration. It also follows from (8.10) that

$$\mathcal{F}\{\delta(t - t_0)\} = \int_{-\infty}^{\infty} \delta(t - t_0) \, e^{-i\omega t} \, dt = e^{-i\omega t_0},$$

or,

$$\delta(t - t_0) \leftrightarrow e^{-i\omega t_0} \tag{9.24}$$

is a Fourier transform pair.

These two transform pairs are represented pictorially in Fig. 9.11.

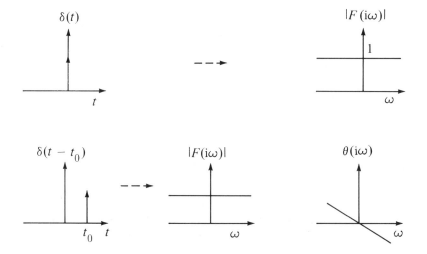

Fig. 9.11 — The Fourier transform pairs (9.23) and (9.24).

The next step is to use the symmetry property to deduce further transform pairs from (9.23) and (9.24). From (9.23), we obtain, using the symmetry property,

$$1 \leftrightarrow 2\pi \, \delta(-\omega) = 2\pi \, \delta(\omega) \tag{9.25}$$

and (9.24) leads in a similar way to

$$e^{-it t_0} \leftrightarrow 2\pi \, \delta(-\omega - t_0). \tag{9.26}$$

Writing $t_0 = -\omega_0$ in (9.26) establishes the transform pair

$$e^{i\omega_0 t} \leftrightarrow 2\pi \, \delta(\omega_0 - \omega) = 2\pi \, \delta(\omega - \omega_0). \tag{9.27}$$

Notice that the energy associated with $f(t) = 1$, and $g(t) = e^{i\omega_0 t}$, is unbounded; however, both signals possess finite power. (The calculations are left as an exercise.) In each case, we see that the transforms of the power signals $f(t)$ and $g(t)$ contain δ-functions, and are thus not transforms in the ordinary sense. For this reason, such transforms are called generalized Fourier transforms. Although we have had to follow an indirect path to obtain such generalized transforms, the reader is invited in the exercises to verify that use of the inversion result (9.15) is a straightforward operation. We give a pictorial representation of the Fourier transforms in (9.25) and (9.27) in Fig. 9.12.

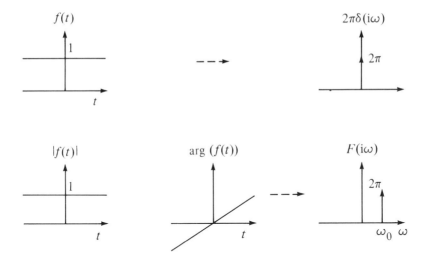

Fig. 9.12 — Representation of the generalized Fourier transforms of (9.25) and (9.27).

It is now possible to contemplate an attempt to calculate a generalized Fourier transform for the power signal $f(t) = A \cos(\omega_0 t)$.

Since $f(t) = A \cos(\omega_0 t) = A(e^{i\omega_0 t} + e^{-i\omega_0 t})/2$, we have, using linearity and (9.27),

$$\begin{aligned}
\mathcal{F}\{A \cos(\omega_0 t)\} &= A/2 \, \mathcal{F}\{e^{i\omega_0 t} + e^{-i\omega_0 t}\} \\
&= A/2\{2\pi \, \delta(\omega - \omega_0) + 2\pi \, \delta(\omega + \omega_0)\} \\
&= A\pi\{\delta(\omega - \omega_0) + \delta(\omega + \omega_0)\}
\end{aligned} \tag{9.28}$$

From (9.28), we see that the spectrum of $A\cos(\omega_0 t)$ consists of two impulses, located at $\omega = \omega_0$ and $\omega = -\omega_0$. The amplitude spectrum is thus zero everywhere except at $\omega = \pm\omega_0$, where it is undefined. We give a pictorial representation (*not*) a graph!) in Fig. 9.13.

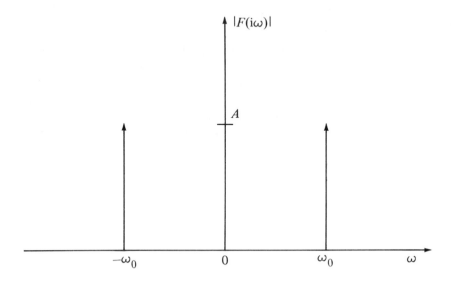

Fig. 9.13 — A pictorial representation of the amplitude spectrum of the signal $A\cos(\omega_0 t)$.

The result (9.27) provides the means of producing the Fourier transform of a periodic signal $f(t)$, of period T, which has a Fourier series representation. Suppose that the Fourier series has been calculated, so that

$$f(t) \sim \sum_{-\infty}^{\infty} A_n \, e^{in\omega_0 t}.$$

We then find the generalized Fourier transform of $f(t)$ as

$$\mathcal{F}\{f(t)\} = \mathcal{F}\left\{\sum_{-\infty}^{\infty} A_n \, e^{in\omega_0 t}\right\}$$

$$= \sum_{-\infty}^{\infty} \mathcal{F}\{A_n \, e^{in\omega_0 t}\}$$

$$= 2\pi \sum_{-\infty}^{\infty} A_n \, \delta(\omega - n\omega_0),$$

assuming that we may interchange the order of summation and transformation. The generalized Fourier transform of $f(t)$ thus consists of impulses located at multiples of the fundamental frequency $\omega_0 = 2\pi/T$. Associated with each pulse is the appropriate coefficient from the Fourier series expansion.

Example 9.12
Obtain the generalized Fourier transform for the pulse train $f(t)$ of Fig. 9.1.
    In Example 9.1, we established that

$$f(t) \sim \sum_{-\infty}^{\infty} A_n e^{in\omega_0 t}$$

where $\omega_0 = \pi/A$, and $A_n = 1/2\, e^{-in3\pi/2}\, \text{sinc}\,(n\pi/2)$.
    The generalized Fourier transform is then

$$2\pi \sum_{-\infty}^{\infty} 1/2\, e^{-in3\pi/2}\, \text{sinc}\,(n\pi/2)\, \delta(\omega - n\pi/A).$$

Clearly, all the information on the spectrum of the periodic signal of Example 9.12 is available after the Fourier series calculation. The Fourier transform also contains this same information, with each discrete spectral component now associated with an impulse located at an appropriate point on the frequency axis. In our discussion of sampling of continuous-time signals, we will need to make use of the so-called unit impulse train

$$f(t) = \sum_{-\infty}^{\infty} \delta(t - nT), \tag{9.30}$$

a representation of which is shown in Fig. 9.14. Here, $f(t)$ is periodic, of period T, and thus we represent $f(t)$ by a Fourier series of the form

$$f(t) \sim \sum_{n=-\infty}^{\infty} D_n e^{in\omega_0 t},$$

with $\omega_0 = 2\pi/T$. The coefficients D_n are then given by

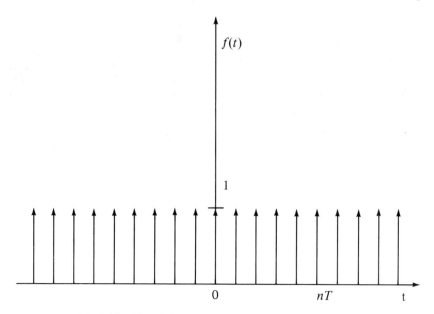

Fig. 9.14 — Pictorial representation of the unit impulse train.

$$D_n = \frac{1}{T} \int_{-T/2}^{T/2} f(t) \, e^{in\omega_0 t} \, dt.$$

Within the single period $[-T/2, T/2]$, $f(t) = \delta(t)$, and so

$$D_n = \frac{1}{T} \int_{-T/2}^{T/2} \delta(t) \, e^{-in\omega_0 t} \, dt = \frac{1}{T}.$$

It then follows from (9.29) that the generalized Fourier transform of $f(t)$ is

$$2\pi \sum_{-\infty}^{\infty} D_n \, \delta(\omega - n\omega_0) = \frac{2\pi}{T} \sum_{-\infty}^{\infty} \delta(\omega - n\omega_0).$$

Writing $\omega_0 = 2\pi/T$, we have established the transform pair

$$\sum_{n=-\infty}^{\infty} \delta(t - nT) \leftrightarrow \omega_0 \sum_{n=-\infty}^{\infty} \delta(\omega - n\omega_0), \qquad (9.31)$$

and we see that the time domain impulse train has, as its image, an impulse train in the frequency domain.

9.8 THE CONVOLUTION THEOREMS

In our discussion of the properties of the Fourier transform, we did not discuss convolution. This was a deliberate choice, because it is felt that the power of these results is easier to appreciate when their use can be demonstrated. An important use will be demonstrated in the concluding section of this chapter, when the sampling of time signals is discussed. In the meantime, we give here two convolution results, together with an outline of their proofs.

First we deal with the problem of determining the Fourier transform of the time domain convolution integral, $f(t)^*g(t)$, where

$$f(t)^*g(t) = \int_{-\infty}^{\infty} f(t-\tau)g(\tau)\ d\tau = \int_{-\infty}^{\infty} f(\tau)g(t-\tau)\ d\tau.$$

Now,

$$\mathscr{F}\{f(t)^*g(t)\} = \int_{-\infty}^{\infty} \left[\int_{-\infty}^{\infty} f(\tau)g(t-\tau)\ d\tau\right] e^{-i\omega t}\ dt,$$

and we can view this as an evaluation by means of repeated integration of the integral

$$= \int_R\!\!\int f(\tau)\ g(t-\tau)\ e^{-i\omega t}\ d\tau\ dt, \tag{9.32}$$

where R is the entire (t, τ) plane. We now make a change of variables in this double integral, defined by

$$\tau \to \tau \quad \text{and} \quad t - \tau \to z.$$

The modulus of the Jacobian of this transformation,

$$\left|\ \left|\frac{\partial(\tau,z)}{\partial(\tau,t)}\right|\ \right|$$

is 1, and it is easy to see from Fig. 9.15 that we can express this double integral as the sum of two repeated integrals, each taken first with respect to τ and then with respect to z. We thus obtain

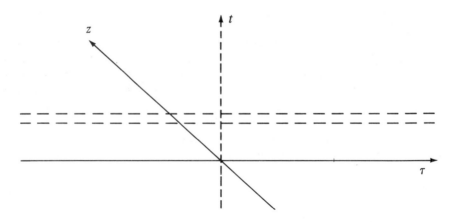

Fig. 9.15 — The coordinates for the repeated integral evaluation of (9.32) using (τ, z) coordinates.

$$\mathcal{F}\{f(t)*g(t)\} = \int_{-\infty}^{\infty} \int_{-\infty}^{z} e^{-i\omega(\tau+z)} f(\tau)\, g(z)\, d\tau\, dz$$

$$+ \int_{-\infty}^{\infty} \int_{z}^{\infty} e^{-i\omega(\tau+z)} f(\tau)\, g(z)\, d\tau\, dz.$$

These integrals can now be combined together, and since the integrand then consists of a product of functions of τ with functions of z, we can write finally

$$\mathcal{F}\{f(t)*g(t)\} = \int_{-\infty}^{\infty} f(\tau)\, e^{-i\omega\tau}\, d\tau \int_{-\infty}^{\infty} g(z)\, e^{-i\omega z}\, dz$$

$$= F(i\omega)G(i\omega). \tag{9.33}$$

The significance of this result is that we now have an explicit time domain representation of the product of two Fourier transforms. This result is sometimes known as the time domain convolution result, and the interested reader may wish to derive a proof based on that given above for the corresponding result for Laplace transforms.

In a similar manner, we can derive a result which relates products of signals in the time domain with a convolution operation, involving the transforms of the signals, in the frequency domain. To achieve this objective, we consider the time domain image of the convolution $F(i\omega)*G(i\omega)$ in the frequency domain. Now

$$\mathcal{F}^{-1}\{F(i\omega)*G(i\omega)\} = \frac{1}{2\pi} \int_{-\infty}^{\infty} \left[\int_{-\infty}^{\infty} F(ix)G(i\omega - ix)\, dx \right] e^{i\omega t}\, d\omega$$

and proceeding in the same way as for time domain convolution; after making the transformation $x \to x$, $\omega - x \to z$, we find that

$$\mathcal{F}^{-1}\{F(i\omega)*G(i\omega)\} = \frac{1}{2\pi} \int_{-\infty}^{\infty} F(ix)\ e^{ixt}\ dx \int_{-\infty}^{\infty} G(iz)\ e^{izt}\ dz$$

$$= 2\pi\ f(t)\ g(t).$$

Here, we have established the transform pair

$$f(t)g(t) \leftrightarrow 1/2\pi\ F(i\omega)*G(i\omega), \tag{9.34}$$

showing that a product of time domain signals has as its image a convolution integral in the frequency domain. These two results again illustrate the symmetry which exists between time and frequency domains, with a multiplication in one domain corresponding to a convolution operation in the other. The presence of the $1/2\pi$ factor is an unfortunate consequence of the choice of frequency measurement. However, we are becoming quite used to its appearance!

9.9 SAMPLING OF TIME SIGNALS AND ITS IMPLICATIONS

The later chapters of this book will be concerned with discrete-time systems which process signals obtained by sampling continuous-time signals. The sampling process produces signal sequences, representing signals defined only at discrete time intervals. In this section, we examine a representation of the sampling process and determine the Fourier spectrum of the signal sequences so obtained.

Suppose that a continuous-time signal $u(t)$ has been sampled at equal intervals T to produce the signal sequence

$$\{u(kT)\} = \{u(0),\ u(T),\ u(2T),...\ u(kT)...\}. \tag{9.35}$$

(The reader who is unfamiliar with sequence notation should note that this topic is discussed in Chapter 11.)

We now examine the effect of presenting each of these samples in turn, that is each term of the sequence (9.35), at the appropriate instant as the input to a continuous-time linear system with impulse response $h(t)$. The resulting output can be expressed in terms of the convolution operation (7.31). (Actually, we use the more general form of the convolution integral appropriate to non-causal functions, as discussed in the exercises following Chapter 7.)

Thus we obtain for the output signal

$$y(t) = \int_{-\infty}^{\infty} h(t-\tau)u(0)\delta(\tau)\ d\tau + \int_{-\infty}^{\infty} h(t-\tau)u(T)\delta(\tau-T)\ d\tau$$

$$+ \ldots + \int_{-\infty}^{\infty} h(t - \tau)u(kT)\delta(\tau - kT) \, d\tau + \ldots$$

$$= \int_{-\infty}^{\infty} h(t - \tau) \sum_{k=0}^{\infty} u(kT)\delta(\tau - kT) \, d\tau$$

$$= \int_{-\infty}^{\infty} h(t - \tau)u_s(\tau) \, d\tau,$$

where

$$u_s(\tau) = \sum_{k=0}^{\infty} u(kT) \, \delta(\tau - kT)$$

$$= u(\tau) \sum_{k=0}^{\infty} \delta(\tau - kT). \tag{9.36}$$

The relation (9.34) means that we can identify

$$u_s(t) = u(t) \sum_{k=0}^{\infty} \delta(t - kT) \tag{9.37}$$

as a 'continuous-time' representation of the (idealized) sampled version of $u(t)$. Notice that we have again made use of the idea discussed in Chapter 8 of using a measuring instrument to investigate signals involving generalized functions. In this case the measuring instrument is the continuous-time system with impulse response $h(t)$. We can generalize (9.37), to include the possibility of non-causal signals, by writing

$$u_s(t) = u(t) \sum_{k=-\infty}^{\infty} \delta(t - kT). \tag{9.38}$$

The relation (9.38) leads us to picture $u_s(t)$ as in Fig. 9.16. We now seek to determine the spectrum of such a representation of sampled time signals. We find that the investment of time in the study of generalized functions and convolution is now fully rewarded!

Let $U_s(i\omega)$ be the Fourier transform of $u_s(t)$; then

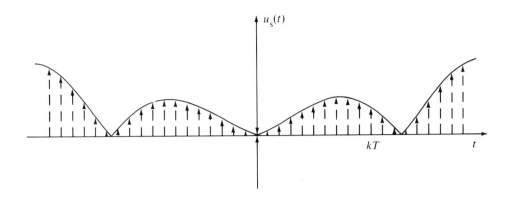

Fig. 9.16 — A pictorial representation of the sampled signal $u_s(t)$.

$$U_s(i\omega) = \mathcal{F}\{u_s(t)\} = \mathcal{F}\left\{u(t) \sum_{k=-\infty}^{\infty} \delta(t - kT)\right\}$$

$$= \frac{1}{2\pi} \mathcal{F}\{u(t)\} * \mathcal{F}\left\{\sum_{k=-\infty}^{\infty} \delta(t - kT)\right\},$$

using (9.34). Now,

$$\mathcal{F}\left\{\sum_{k=-\infty}^{\infty} \delta(t - kT)\right\} = \omega_0 \sum_{n=-\infty}^{\infty} \delta(\omega - n\omega_0),$$

from (9.31), where $\omega_0 = 2\pi/T$.
   Thus, if $U(i\omega)$ is the Fourier transform of $u(t)$,

$$U_s(i\omega) = \frac{1}{2\pi} U(i\omega) * \frac{2\pi}{T} \sum_{n=-\infty}^{\infty} \delta(\omega - n\omega_0) \tag{9.39}$$

$$= \frac{1}{T} \int_{-\infty}^{\infty} U(i\omega - i\omega') \sum_{n=-\infty}^{\infty} \delta(\omega' - n\omega_0) \, d\omega'$$

$$= \frac{1}{T} \sum_{n=-\infty}^{\infty} \int_{-\infty}^{\infty} U(i\omega - i\omega') \, \delta(\omega' - n\omega_0) \, d\omega'$$

$$= \frac{1}{T} \sum_{n=-\infty}^{\infty} U(i\omega - in\omega_0) = \frac{1}{T} \sum_{n=-\infty}^{\infty} U(i(\omega - 2\pi n/T)) \qquad (9.40)$$

From (9.40), we see that the spectrum of the sampled signal $u_s(t)$ consists of scaled periodic repeats of the spectrum of the unsampled version $u(t)$. These repeats are centred on the frequencies $n\omega_0 = 2\pi n/T$, $n = 0$, ± 1, $\pm 2,...$, and the resulting amplitude spectrum is shown in Fig. 9.17.

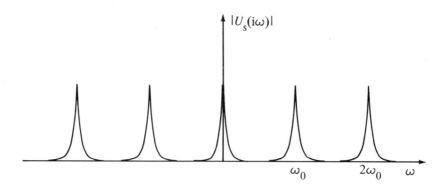

Fig. 9.17 — The amplitude spectrum of the sampled signal $u_s(t)$.

The separation in frequency between the centre of successive repeats of the spectrum of the unsampled signal is $\Delta\omega = 2\pi/T$, which depends on the sampling interval T. Suppose that the spectrum of an unsampled continuous-time signal $u(t)$ is bounded so that the amplitude spectrum $|U(i\omega)|$ satisfies

$$|U(i\omega)| = 0, \ |\omega| > \omega_m, \text{ say.}$$

Such a signal is said to be band-limited, and it follows that the successive scaled repeats of $|U(i\omega)|$ in the amplitude spectrum $|U_s(i\omega)|$ of the sampled version $u_s(t)$ will not overlap provided that

$$\Delta\omega > 2\omega_m,$$

that is,

$$2\pi/T > 2\omega_m.$$

This means that we must sample $u(t)$ at such a rate that

$$T < \pi/\omega_{\mathrm{m}}. \tag{9.41}$$

If we define $f_s = 1/T$, the sampling frequency measured in Hertz, and $f_m = \omega_m/2\pi$ as the band limit of $u(t)$, also now measured in Hertz, we can write (9.41) as

$$f_s > 2f_m.$$

This condition on the sampling frequency, known as the Nyquist condition, implies that we must take samples from $u(t)$ at a frequency greater than twice the band-limiting frequency, if 'overlaps' are to be avoided. We will see that if this condition is satisfied, then it will be possible to reconstruct $u(t)$ from its samples. The (theoretical) minimum sampling frequency $f_N = 2f_m$ for which this recovery is possible is sometimes called the Nyquist frequency or Nyquist rate. Fig. 9.17 has been drawn on the assumption that the sampling frequency exceeded the Nyquist rate. If the sampling rate had been less than the Nyquist rate, then the amplitude spectrum $|U_s(i\omega)|$ would be as illustrated in Fig. 9.18. In Fig. 9.18, we see that at each of the

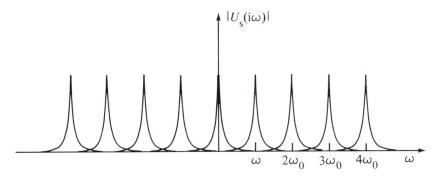

Fig. 9.18 — Amplitude spectrum exhibiting aliasing effects.

edges of the repeats of the spectrum of the unsampled signal, there is 'interference' from its neighbours. This 'interference' due to overlapping is known as aliasing, and we observe that erroneous values are generated for the spectrum at each end, when this takes place. Such a situation precludes the exact reconstruction of the unsampled signal from its samples. The recovery process is achieved by the use of a low-pass filter, of bandwidth ω_b, say. This is a device which passes exactly signals, or components of signals of frequency less than or equal to ω_b, and rejects all components of frequency above ω_b. In the frequency domain, the filtering process is achieved by the multiplication of the spectrum of the signal to be filtered by such a device, with frequency transfer function

$$|H(i\omega)| = \begin{bmatrix} 1, & |\omega| \le \omega_b \\ 0, & |\omega| > \omega_b \end{bmatrix}.$$

To illustrate the process, suppose that a signal $g(t)$ has been sampled at a frequency f above the Nyquist frequency f_N, so that

$$f = A f_N = 2 A f_m, \quad A > 1.$$

We will multiply the spectrum of the sampled sequence by $H(i\omega)$ and invert the result. The resulting time domain signal will be

$$(1/T)\breve{g}(t)$$

where $g(t)$ is the reconstructed version of $g(t)$. Notice that $T = 2\pi/\omega_0 = 1/f = 1/A f_N = 1/2 A f_m = \pi/A\omega_m$, and this means that the separation between the copies of $G(i\omega)$ is ω_0, where $\omega_0 = 2 A\omega_m$. Now,

$$G_s(i\omega) = \frac{1}{T} G(i\omega) * \sum_{-\infty}^{\infty} \delta(\omega - n\omega_0)$$

from (9.39), and thus the spectrum of the filtered signal is

$$G_s(i\omega)\, H(i\omega) = \left[\frac{1}{T} G(i\omega) * \sum_{-\infty}^{\infty} \delta(\omega - n\omega_0) \right] H(i\omega)$$

and inverting, we have

$$\mathcal{F}^{-1}\{G_s(i\omega)H(i\omega)\} = \mathcal{F}^{-1}\left[\frac{1}{T} G(i\omega) * \sum_{-\infty}^{\infty} \delta(\omega - n\omega_0) \right] * \mathcal{F}^{-1}\{H(i\omega)\}$$

$$= \left[g(t) \sum_{-\infty}^{\infty} \delta(t - nT) \right] * \frac{\omega_h}{\pi} \operatorname{sinc}(t\omega_b).$$

Here we have used the result that $\mathcal{F}^{-1}\{H(i\omega)\} = \omega_b/\pi \operatorname{sinc}(\omega_b t)$, which follows easily from the symmetry property and which the reader is invited to establish in the exercises. We select the bandwidth of the filter to be $\omega_b = \omega_0/2$, so that the filtered signal contains exactly one copy of the spectrum of $u(t)$, to obtain

$$(1/T)\tilde{g}(t) = \frac{1}{T} \int_{-\infty}^{\infty} \sum_{-\infty}^{\infty} g(nT)\,\delta(\tau - nT)\,\text{sinc}\,\omega_0(t - \tau)/2\;d\tau.$$

Thus

$$\tilde{g}(t) = \sum_{-\infty}^{\infty} g(nT)\,\text{sinc}\,\omega_0(t - nT)/2$$

and we see that the signal is reconstructed using a superposition of sinc functions, each one centred on a sample point. Since $T = 2\pi/\omega_0$, all the terms in the sum except one vanish at each sample point, and the remaining term takes the value $g(nT)$. This means that the reconstruction gives the exact value at each sample point, with the accuracy of the interpolation between sample points depending on the sampling rate. It is an illustrative exercise to construct a computer program to investigate the reconstruction process with different sampling rates. The exercise becomes even more relevant when signals which are not strictly band-limited are considered. In fact, all finite-duration signals will have amplitude spectra which do not vanish outside a finite interval defined by $|\omega| < \omega_m$. Usually, such signals have amplitude spectra which decay rapidly with increasing ω, and the value of ω at which a particular ampltidue spectrum has become negligible is a matter of judgement. This judgement is used to set a Nyquist-like rate, implying that above a certain value of ω, the signal contains no further significant components. The sampling rate is then chosen based on this Nyquist-like rate, and whilst if sampling is sufficiently fast, good reconstructions are obtained, the process can never be completely exact.

REFERENCE

(1) M. J. Lighthill, *Introduction to Fourier Analysis and Generalised Functions*, Cambridge University Press, Cambridge, 1964.

EXERCISES

1. Verify the orthogonality result

$$\frac{1}{T} \int_{t_0}^{t_0 + T} e^{in\omega_0 t}\,e^{-im\omega_0 t}\;dt = \delta_{mn}$$

$$= \begin{bmatrix} 0, & m \neq n \\ 1, & m = n. \end{bmatrix}$$

2. Determine the Fourier coefficients in the expansion of the periodic pulse shown

in Fig. 9.19. Sketch the amplitude spectrum for this signal and compare with Fig. 9.2. Apply the time-shifting result in section 9.2 to deduce the result in Example 9.1.
3. Verify the results for the Fourier transforms of

$$f(t) = t\,e^{-at}\,\xi(t),\ a>0\quad \text{and}$$
$$g(t) = e^{-a|t|},\ a>0,$$

given in Table 9.1.
4. Use the result that the Fourier transform of

$$h(t) = 1/(a^2 + t^2)$$

is $\pi/a\,e^{-a|\omega|}$, and the frequency-shifting property to deduce the transform of $\cos(at)/(1+t^2)$. Hence find the transform of $\sin(bt)/(a^2+t^2)$.
5. Show that the Fourier transform of the symmetric unit pulse of duration T, given by

$$f(t) = \begin{cases} 1, & |t| \leqslant T/2, \\ 0, & |t| > T/2, \end{cases}$$

is $T\,\text{sinc}\,(\omega T/2)$. Use the symmetry property to find the transform of $h(t) = \omega_b/\pi\,\text{sinc}\,(\omega_b t)$, where $\omega_b = T/2$. Sketch the amplitude spectrum of this signal. If this signal is the impulse response of a linear system, how would you describe the frequency response, and what could be its use?
6. Prove that if $f(t)$ is a real signal then $|F(i\omega)|$ is an even function of ω. {Hint: consider $F(i\omega).F^*(i\omega)$}.
7. Define the function sgn (t) as:

$$\text{sgn}\,(t) = \begin{bmatrix} -1, & t<0 \\ 1, & t\geqslant 0, \end{bmatrix}$$

and confirm that $\xi(t)$, the Heaviside step function, is given by

$$\xi(t) = 1/2(1 + \text{sgn}\,(t)).$$

Prove that $d/dt\{\text{sgn}\,(t)\} = 2\delta(t)$, and hence deduce that

(a) the Fourier transform of sgn (t) is $2/i\omega$, and
(b) the step function has transform $\pi\delta(\omega) + 1/i\omega$.

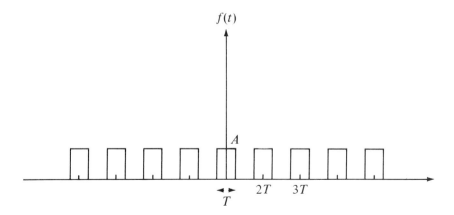

Fig. 9.19 — Figure for Exercise 2.

Finally, use the frequency convolution theorem to deduce the transforms of the causal functions,

$$f(t) = A \cos (\omega_0 t) \, \xi(t) \text{ and}$$
$$g(t) = A \sin (\omega_0 t) \, \xi(t).$$

8. Obtain the amplitude response of the time invariant linear system with Laplace transfer function

$$H(s) = \frac{1}{s^2 + \sqrt{2}s + 1},$$

and illustrate with a sketch. Follow the method of Example 9.9 to discuss the transmission of the signal consisting of a symmetric unit pulse of duration 1 sec., together with a copy of the pulse modulating a carrier signal at frequency $\omega_0 = 10$ rad/sec.

9. Establish Parseval's formula

$$\int_{-\infty}^{\infty} f(t)G(it)dt = \int_{-\infty}^{\infty} g(t)F(it)dt$$

where $f(t) \leftrightarrow F(i\omega)$ and $g(t) \leftrightarrow G(i\omega)$ are Fourier transform pairs. Show also that

$$\int_{-\infty}^{\infty} |f(t)|^2 \, dt = \frac{1}{2\pi} \int_{-\infty}^{\infty} |F(i\omega)|^2 \, d\omega.$$

10. Show that

(a)
$$\int_{-\infty}^{\infty} \text{sinc}^2(x)\, dx = \int_{-\infty}^{\infty} \text{sinc}(x)\, dx.$$

(b)
$$\int_0^{\infty} \int_0^{\infty} e^{-ax} \sin(x)\, dx\, da = \pi/2,$$

and by reversing the order, show that

$$\int_0^{\infty} \int_0^{\infty} e^{-ax} \sin(x)\, da\, dx = \int_{-\infty}^{\infty} \text{sinc}\,(x)\, dx.$$

Hence deduce that

$$\int_{-\infty}^{\infty} \text{sinc}\,(x)\, dx = \pi.$$

11. Show that

$$\int_{-\infty}^{\infty} \text{sinc}\,\omega_b(t - nT)\, \text{sinc}\,\omega_b(t - mT)\, dT = 0,$$

where n,m are integers or zero, and $n \neq m$, and where $\omega_b = \pi/T$. Use this result with that of Exercise 10 to show that the set $\{f_n(t)\} = \{1/\sqrt{T}\, \text{sinc}\,\omega_b(t - nT)\}$ is orthonormal on $-\infty < t < \infty$.

10

Analogue filters

10.1 INTRODUCTION

In this chapter we make use of our understanding of the representation of signals in the frequency domain and the concept of system frequency response. Bringing these ideas together allowed us to form a model of how systems operate on signals. This concept was discussed in Chapters 8 and 9. At this point, we turn our attention to the *design* or *synthesis* of systems which will process signals in a predetermined manner. This is in contrast to our discussion so far, where we have concentrated on the *analysis* of systems, assumed 'given' in the traditional mathematical sense. We will, however, draw on this experience!

We now consider the problem of how to design *filters*; that is, devices which are capable of processing input signals in such a way that the output signal depends, in a predetermined manner, on the frequency of the input signal. In this chapter we will examine the design of analogue filters, which operate on continuous-time signals to produce continuous-time signals as output. In Chapter 12, we discuss the design of digital filters which operate on discrete-time signals.

10.2 ANALOGUE FILTER TYPES

Analogue filters are classified according to their capability in either *passing* or *rejecting* signals of different frequencies. An ideal 'low-pass' filter passes all signals of frequencies less than a 'cut-off', or 'critical' frequency ω_c. From our work on the frequency domain decomposition of signals, using the methods of Fourier analysis, we can see that a low-pass filter would have the effect of filtering out the higher frequency components in a composite signal. The amplitude response of an ideal low-pass filter is illustrated in Fig. 10.1.

A filter with the opposite effect to that of an ideal low-pass filter is an ideal high-pass filter. Such a filter will reject all signals (or components of signals) of frequency less than the cut-off or critical frequency ω_c, and pass signals of frequency above ω_c.

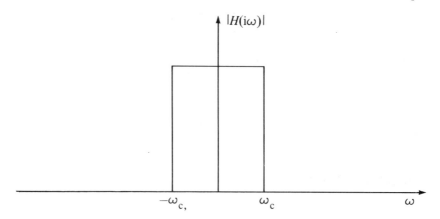

Fig. 10.1 — Ideal low-pass filter amplitude response.

The amplitude response of such an ideal high-pass filter is shown in Fig. 10.2. An ideal band-reject filter rejects signals of frequency ω, where

$$\omega_1 < \omega < \omega_u.$$

The ideal amplitude response of this filter is illustrated in Fig. 10.3. The final type we shall consider is the ideal band-pass filter. Such a filter rejects all signals except those with frequencies between the lower critical frequency ω_1 and the upper critical frequency ω_u. The amplitude response of such a filter is shown in Fig. 10.4. It is not necessary to study each of these filter types separately. We shall see in a later section that we can find *filter transformations*, that is transformations which can be used to map low-pass filter designs into any of the above types. For this reason, we restrict our attention to methods of designing satisfactory low-pass filters.

10.3   A CLASS OF LOW-PASS FILTERS

In this section we shall consider the design of an important class of filters known as Butterworth filters. Viewed from the frequency domain, the design problem is to determine a system whose amplitude response approximates the ideal amplitude response of Fig. 10.1 above. There is a second stage to the process, the so-called realization problem, the solution of which involves the specification of a circuit which will implement the filter design. First we examine the approximation stage, and we see that the ideal low-pass response is given by

$$|H(i\omega)| = \left[\begin{array}{l} 1, \; |\omega| < \omega_c \\ 0, \; |\omega| > \omega_c \end{array} \right.$$

The Butterworth approximation to this ideal response is to set

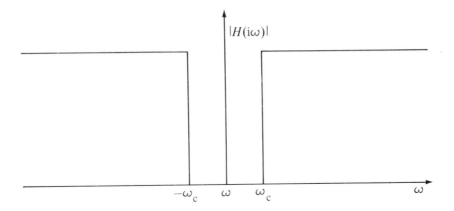

Fig. 10.2 — Ideal high-pass filter amplitude response.

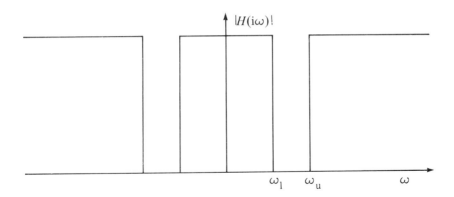

Fig. 10.3 — Amplitude reponse of an ideal band-reject filter, with lower cut-off frequency ω_l and upper cut-off frequency ω_u.

$$|H(i\omega)| = \frac{1}{\sqrt{(1 + (\omega/\omega_c)^{2n})}} \tag{10.1}$$

It is easy to see that if $|\omega| < \omega_c$ then as $n \to \infty$, $|H(i\omega)| \to 1$. However if $|\omega| > \omega_c$, $|H(i\omega)| \to 0$ as $n \to \infty$; thus for large values of n, we obtain a good approximation to the desired response. The amplitude response of some filters designed on this basis is depicted in Fig. 10.5.

Observe that we may write (10.1) in the form

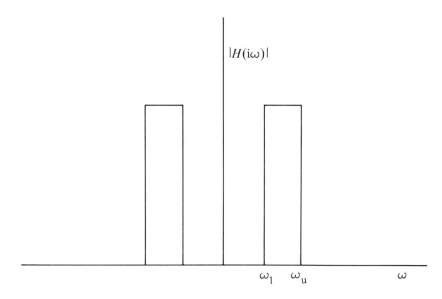

Fig. 10.4 — Amplitude response of an ideal band-pass filter, with critical frequencies ω_l and ω_u.

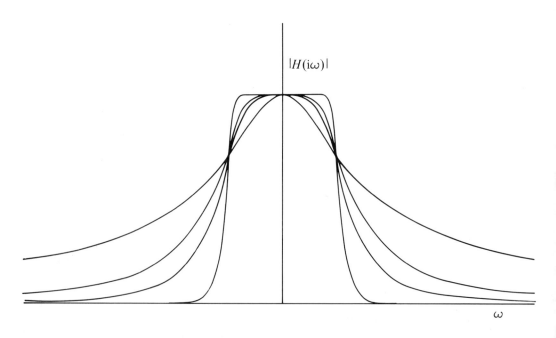

Fig. 10.5 — The amplitude response of the Butterworth filters of orders 1,2,3 and 9.

$$|H(i\omega)|^2 = \frac{1}{(1 + (\omega/\omega_c)^{2n})} \qquad (10.2)$$

We then argue that this is the square of the amplitude response of a system with Laplace transfer function $H(s)$, obtained by replacing s with $i\omega$. This assumes that the system will be a stable sytem, and the process is only valid if such a stable system can be found.

Note that in general,

$$|H(i\omega)|^2 = H(i\omega)H^*(i\omega)$$

and if $H(s)$ is to have real coefficients then

$$H^*(i\omega) = H(-i\omega). \qquad (10.3)$$

Then we see that we will obtain (10.2) on putting $s = i\omega$ if $H(s)$ is such that

$$H(s)H(-s) = \frac{1}{(1 + (s/i\omega_c)^{2n})} \qquad (10.4)$$

This process is called the process of analytic continuation and is a part of the theory of functions of a complex variable.

We now find the poles of this function by setting

$$1 + (s/i\omega_c)^{2n} = 0,$$

meaning that

$$(s/i\omega_c)^{2n} = \exp(i(2k + 1)\pi)$$

with k an integer or zero. Thus,

$$s/i\omega_c = \exp(i(2k + 1)\pi/2n),$$

and we obtain.

$$s = \omega_c \exp(i((2k + 1)\pi/2n + \pi/2)) \qquad (10.5)$$

where k is an integer or zero. We examine the locations of these poles for the cases $n = 1,2,3$ and 5. In Fig. 10.6. From Fig. 10.6, we see that in each case there are $2n$

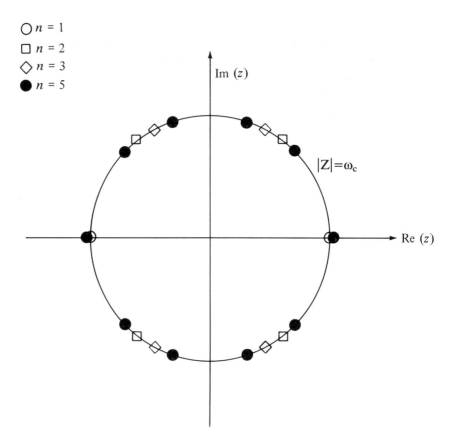

Fig. 10.6 — Pole locations given by (10.5).

poles equally spaced around the circle of radius ω_c in the complex plane. Also, we note that there are no poles on the imaginary axis and that this will be the case for all values of n. Clearly if $s = s_p$ is a pole of $H(s)H(-s)$, then so is $s = -s_p$. This means that we may select as the poles corresponding to $H(s)$ those which lie in the left-half plane, that is, in the stable region. The remaining poles, in the right half-plane, are then associated with $H(-s)$. Thus a design *is* possible satisfying the criterion that the proposed system should be a stable system.

We next obtain the transfer functions, $H(s)$, in a few cases. When $n = 1$, (10.4) becomes

$$H(s)H(-s) = \frac{1}{(1 + (s/(i\omega_c))^2)}$$

$$= \frac{\omega_c^2}{(\omega_c^2 - s^2)}$$

$$= \frac{\omega_c^2}{(\omega_c + s)(\omega_c - s)}$$

We select the pole at $s = -\omega_c$ to be the single pole of our system, thus generating the simple first-order system defined by the Laplace transfer function

$$H(s) = \frac{\omega_c}{(s + \omega_c)} \tag{10.6}$$

We turn our attention to the case $n = 2$, when (10.4) becomes

$$H(s)H(-s) = \frac{1}{(1 + (s/i\omega_c)^4)}$$

$$= \frac{\omega_c^4}{(\omega_c^4 + s^4)}$$

$$= \frac{\omega_4^4}{(s^4 + \omega_c^4)}.$$

Now factorise $(s^4 + \omega_c^4)$ as

$$s^4 + \omega_c^4 = (s^2 + i\omega_c^2)(s^2 - i\omega_c^2)$$
$$= (s + (1+i)\omega_c/\sqrt{2})(s + (1-i)\omega_c/\sqrt{2})(s + (-1+i)\omega_c/\sqrt{2})$$
$$(s + (-1-i)\omega_c/\sqrt{2})$$

Thus selecting the left-half plane poles for the transfer function, $H(s)$, we obtain,

$$H(s) = \frac{\omega_c^2}{(s + (1+i)\omega_c/\sqrt{2})(s + (1-i)\omega_c/\sqrt{2})}$$

$$= \frac{\omega_c^2}{(s^2 + \sqrt{2}\omega_c s + \omega_c^2)} \tag{10.7}$$

Proceeding in the same way it is easy to show that in the case $n = 3$, the transfer function obtained is,

$$H(s) = \frac{\omega_c^3}{(s + \omega_c)\,(s + (1 + \sqrt{3})\omega_c/2)\,(s + (1 - \sqrt{3})\omega_c/2)}$$

$$= \frac{\omega_c^3}{s^3 + 2s^2\omega_c + 2s\omega_c^2 + \omega_c^3} \tag{10.8}$$

Examining each of the transfer functions obtained, we see that in each case, the index n gives the order of the denominator or characteristic equation. This, in turn, is the order of the resulting linear system modelled by a differential equation with $H(s)$ as its transfer function. It is natural, therefore, to call n the order of the Butterworth filter design. It would be a tedious operation to continue to calculate the transfer functions of the higher-order filters in this manner. Fortunately, we can avoid this chore, as we shall see.

Having obtained the transfer functions of some filters, we will turn our attention to the second part of the design process, that is the realization stage. As we discussed earlier, this involves the specification of a circuit which will implement the filter design. In order to see how to do this for the designs we have already obtained, let us construct the time-domain representations of each filter in turn.

For the first-order Butterworth filter, when $n = 1$, we have,

$$H(s) = \frac{\omega_c}{s + \omega_c} \tag{10.9}$$

If $Y(s) = H(s)U(s)$, we see that this is equivalent to,

$$(s + \omega_c)Y(s) = \omega_c U(s),$$

the Laplace transform of a differential equation. This may now be inverted, with the assumption of a zero initial condition on $y(t)$, to give

$$\frac{dy(t)}{dt} + \omega_c y(t) = \omega_c u(t),$$

where

$$y(t) = L^{-1}\{Y(s)\}, \text{ and } u(t) = L^{-1}\{U(s)\}.$$

If we set $y(t) = v_c(t)$, $u(t) = e(t)$ and choose the values of R and C so that $1/RC = \omega_c$, then we obtain equation (7.10). This means that the first-order Butterworth filter can be realized by the simple C–R circuit of Example 7.2! In fact we could have anticipated that this would be the case from the transform domain. This is because equation (7.28) can be written as

$$Y(s) = \frac{1/RC}{(s + 1/RC)} \, U(s) = H(s)U(s)$$

and we see that putting $1/RC = \omega_c$ leads immediately to the transfer function $H(s)$ of (10.9). In a similar way we can investigate the second-order design corresponding to the case $n = 2$. Setting $Y(s) = H(s)U(s)$, with the transfer function $H(s)$ given by (10.7) as

$$H(s) = \frac{\omega_c^2}{(s^2 + \sqrt{2}\omega_c s + \omega_c^2)} \tag{10.10}$$

we obtain $(s^2 + \sqrt{2}s + \omega_c^2)Y(s) = \omega_c^2 U(s)$.

Again, inverting this Laplace transform, under the assumption of zero initial conditions on both y and dy/dt, leads to the time-domain representation of the system. Carrying out the inversion yields

$$\frac{d^2y(t)}{dt^2} + \sqrt{2}\omega_c \frac{dy(t)}{dt} + \omega_c^2 y(t) = \omega_c^2 u(t) \ . \tag{10.11}$$

Again our earlier examples are useful. Notice that (7.37) can be re-written as

$$\frac{d^2v_c(t)}{dt^2} + \frac{R}{L}\frac{dv_c(t)}{dt} + \frac{1}{LC}v_c(t) = \frac{1}{LC}e(t) \ .$$

Thus if we set $R/L = \sqrt{2}\omega_c$, and $1/LC = \omega_c^2$, we can use the L–C–R circuit of section 7.3 as our second-order Butterworth filter. Notice that the input to the system is the voltage $e(t)$, while the output is the voltage drop measured across the capacitor. The value of R may be chosen at will, and the values of L and C are then determined uniquely.

Finally for the case $n = 3$, the transfer function for the third-order filter is given by (10.8), and it is straightforward to show that the system generated in the time domain is

$$\frac{d^3y(t)}{dt^3} + 2\omega_c \frac{d^2y(t)}{dt^2} + 2\omega_c^2 \frac{dy(t)}{dt} + \omega_c^3 y(t) = \omega_c^3 u(t) \tag{10.11}$$

Observing that this is a third-order differential equation, we return to Chapter 7 and examine the system of Example 7.6. In equation (7.62), we obtained the time domain representation of the so-called ladder network of Fig. 7.17. This circuit is re-drawn here as Fig. 10.7.

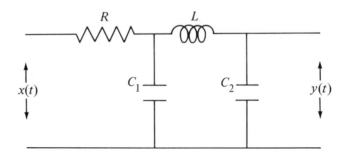

Fig. 10.7 — The ladder network of Fig. 7.17.

This circuit can be represented in the time domain by the equation

$$\frac{d^3y(t)}{dt^3} + \frac{1}{C_1R}\frac{d^2y(t)}{dt^2} + \frac{(C_1+C_2)}{LC_1C_2}\frac{dy(t)}{dt} + \frac{1}{LC_1C_2R}y(t) = \frac{1}{LC_1C_2R}x(t) \quad (7.62)$$

The only possibility open to us is to see if the component values in (7.62) can be chosen in such a way as to produce a form equivalent to (10.11). Clearly the input will be the voltage $x(t)$, and the output the voltage measured across the capacitor C_2.

Evidently, we must have

$$2\omega_c = 1/C_1R \ ,$$

$$2\omega_c^2 = \frac{C_1+C_2}{LC_1C_2} \ ,$$

$$\omega_c^3 = \frac{1}{LC_1C_2R} \ ,$$

from which it follows that,

$$C_1 = \frac{1}{2R\omega_c} \ , \quad C_2 = \frac{3}{2R\omega_c}$$

and

$$L = \frac{4R}{3\omega_c} \; .$$

We can see again that R can be chosen at will, with the other circuit parameters then determined uniquely.

It is clear that we cannot continue in this way. Valuable as our previous experience based on the analysis of elementary circuits has been, it is time to seek a more general approach. This is the purpose of the next section.

10.4 BUTTERWORTH FILTERS — THE GENERAL CASE

We will approach the generalization problem in two stages. First, we will show that the transfer functions themselves can be generated easily for arbitrary filter orders. This will be achieved by using a recurrence relation, or generating function, for the coefficients of the appropriate denominators, called the Butterworth polynomials. The approach used is similar to that given in Weinberg [3]. When we have completed this task, we will address the realization problem in the general case. At that point we will show that it is always possible to give a circuit construction which will operate as a Butterworth filter of any specified order.

In order to deal with the first stage, recall from (10.4) that if $H(s)$ is the tansfer function of the nth-order filter, then

$$H(s)H(-s) = \frac{1}{(1 + (s/i\omega_c)^{2n})}$$

Now, writing $x = s/\omega_c$, we have

$$1 + (s/i\omega_c)^{2n} = 1 + x^{2n}/(-1)^n = \prod_{k=0}^{2n-1} (x - \lambda_k) \tag{10.12}$$

where $\lambda_k = \exp(i(2k+1+n)\pi/2n)$, $k = 0,1,\ldots 2n-1$, are the zeros of $1 + x^{2n}/(-1)^n$. As we observed, none of these zeros lie on the imaginary axis and this means that $|H(i\omega)|^2$ is always finite for all values of ω.

Noting that

$$\lambda_{k+n} = \exp(i(2k+2n+1+n)\pi/2n)$$
$$= \exp(i\pi)\exp(i(2k+1+n)\pi/2n)$$
$$= -\lambda_k,$$

we see that we can write (10.12) as

$$1 + x^{2n}/(-1)^n = \prod_{k=0}^{n-1} (x - \lambda_k) \prod_{k=0}^{n-1} (x + \lambda_k)$$

$$= (-1)^n \prod_{k=0}^{n-1} (x - \lambda_k) \prod_{k=0}^{n-1} (-x - \lambda_k) \tag{10.13}$$

Now, defining $B_n(x)$ as

$$B_n(x) = \prod_{k=0}^{n-1} (x - \lambda_k) , \tag{10.14}$$

where now λ_k, $k = 0, 1, \ldots, n-1$, are the zeros in the left half plane, we may write (10.13) as

$$1 + x^{2n}/(-1)^n = (-1)^n B_n(x)B_n(-x) .$$

We are now able to write $H(s)H(-s)$ in the alternative form

$$H(s)H(-s) = \frac{(-1)^n}{B_n(x)B_n(-x)}$$

and we choose $H(s) = \dfrac{1}{B_n(x)}$, in order to generate a stable system. $H(-s)$ is then given by

$$H(-s) = \frac{(-1)^n}{B_n(-x)} .$$

The process continues with an examination of $B_n(x)$ itself; clearly $B_n(x)$ is a polynomial of degree n in x, the normalized variable. Thus we write

$$B_n(x) = \sum_{k=0}^{n} a_k x^k , \tag{10.15}$$

and our task is now to determine the values of the coefficients a_k, $k = 0, 1, \ldots, n$. First we rewrite the product formula for $B_n(x)$ in a more useful form.
    Writing $W = \exp(i\pi/2n)$, we have

$$B_n(x) = \prod_{k=0}^{n-1} (x - W^{2k+1+n})$$ (10.16)

Putting $x = 0$ in (10.15) and (10.16) shows that

$$a_0 = \prod_{k=0}^{n-1} (-W^{2k+1+n})$$

and recalling that $W = \exp(i\pi/2n)$, we have

$$a_0 = \prod_{k=0}^{n-1} \{-\exp((2k+1+n)i\pi/2n)\}$$

$$= \prod_{k=0}^{n-1} \{\exp(2k+1+3n)i\pi/2n\} .$$ (10.17)

This is just the product of n complex numbers each of unit modulus (or magnitude), and thus the product also has modulus 1. The argument of the product is given by the sum of the arguments of each term of the product as

$$\arg(a_0) = \sum_{k=0}^{n-1} (2k+1+3n)\pi/2n$$

$$= \sum_{k=0}^{n-1} (k\pi/n + n(1+3n)\pi/2n)$$

$$= n(n-1)\pi/2n + (1+3n)\pi/2$$

$$= 2n\pi$$

Thus we have established that for all filter orders n, the argument of a_0 is an integral multiple of 2π, and so $a_0 = 1$, for all integers n.

Returning to the product formula for $B_n(x)$, we write this as

$$B_n(x) = (x - W^{n+1}) \prod_{k=1}^{n-1} (x - W^{2k+1+n})$$

$$= \frac{(x - W^{n+1})}{(x - W^{3n+1})} \prod_{k=1}^{n} (x - W^{2k+1+n})$$

Now put $q = k - 1$, and

$$B_n(x) = \frac{(x - iW)}{(x + iW)} \prod_{q=0}^{n-1} W^2(x/W^2 - W^{2q+1+n})$$

$$= \frac{(x - iW)}{(x + iW)} W^{2n} \prod_{q=0}^{n-1} (x/W^2 - W^{2q+1+n})$$

$$= -\frac{(x - iW)}{(x + iW)} \prod_{k=0}^{n-1} (x/W^2 - W^{2k+1+n})$$

$$= -\frac{(x - iW)}{(x + iW)} B_n(x/W^2),$$

that is,

$$(x + iW) \, B_n(x) + (x - iW) \, B_n(x/W^2) = 0 \qquad\qquad (10.18)$$

We now substitute (10.15) into (10.18) and obtain

$$(x + iW) \sum_{k=0}^{n} a_k x^k + (x - iW) \sum_{k=0}^{n} a_k W^{-2k} x^k = 0.$$

Equating coefficients of like powers of x, we find that

$$a_k + iW a_{k+1} + W^{-2k} a_k - iW^{-2k-1} a_{k+1} = 0.$$

or

$$a_{k+1} = a_k \frac{(1 + W^{-2k})}{\mathrm{i}(W^{-2k-1} - W)}$$

$$= a_k \frac{(W^k + W^{-k})}{\mathrm{i}(W^{-k-1} - W^{k+1})}$$

$$= a_k \frac{\cos(k\alpha)}{\sin((k+1)\alpha)} \tag{10.19}$$

where $\alpha = \pi/2n$.

It is easy to see that using the recurrence relation (10.19), with $a_0 = 1$, we can generate the filter coefficients for any order n. It is also easy to see that the coefficients are given explicitly by the formula:

$$a_k = \prod_{r=1}^{k} \cos((r-1)\alpha)/\sin(r\alpha), \tag{10.20}$$

by repeated use of (10.19). (Here, k takes the values $1, 2, \ldots, n$, but if we adopt the usual convention that if the upper limit of the product is less than the lower, then the value of the product is one; the result holds for $n = 0$, also.)

It is also possible to establish that $a_k = a_{n-k}$, a result which can be used used to avoid a significant amount of calculation. This is achieved using (10.20), as follows.

At once, we have

$$a_k = \prod_{r=1}^{k} \frac{\cos(r-1)\alpha}{\sin(r\alpha)}$$

$$= \prod_{r=1}^{n-k} \frac{\cos(r-1)\alpha}{\sin(r\alpha)} \prod_{r=n-k+1}^{k} \frac{\cos(r-1)\alpha}{\sin(r\alpha)}$$

$$= a_{n-k} \frac{\displaystyle\prod_{r=n-k+1}^{k} \cos(r-1)\alpha}{\displaystyle\prod_{r=n-k+1}^{k} \sin(r\alpha)}$$

Now put $r - 1 = p$ in the upper product and $r = n - 1$ in the lower, and

$$a_k = a_{n-k} \frac{\displaystyle\prod_{p=n-k}^{k-1} \cos(p\alpha)}{\displaystyle\prod_{l=k-1}^{n-k} \sin(l-r)\alpha}$$

$$= a_{n-k} \prod_{p=n-k}^{k-1} \frac{\cos(p\alpha)}{\sin(n-p)\alpha}$$

and since $\sin(n-p)\alpha = \cos(p\alpha)$, we have shown that

$$a_k = a_{n-k}, \quad k = 0, 1, \ldots, n. \tag{10.21}$$

Example 10.1
Calculate the coefficients of the fourth-order Butterworth polynomial.
    Since $n = 4$, we have that $\alpha = \pi/2n = \pi/8$, meaning that the coefficients are given by (10.20) as

$$a_k = \prod_{r=1}^{k} \cos\{(r-1)\pi/8\}/\sin(r\pi/8), \quad k = 0, \ldots, n.$$

$a_0 = 1$, as discussed above, and when $k = 1$, we obtain

$$a_1 = \prod_{r=1}^{1} \cos\{(r-1)\pi/8\}/\sin(r\pi/8)$$

$$= 1/\sin(\pi/8)$$
$$= 2.6131.$$

Also,

$$a_2 = \prod_{r=1}^{2} \cos\{(r-1)\pi/8\}/\sin(r\pi/8)$$

$$= \frac{1}{\sin(\pi/8)} \frac{\cos(\pi/8)}{\sin(\pi/4)}$$

$$= 3.4140.$$

It would be possible to find a_3 and a_4 in this way; however, 10.21 allows us to write

$$a_3 = a_{4-3} = a_1 = 2.6131, \text{ and}$$

$$a_4 = a_{4-4} = a_0 = 1.$$

We may deduce that the transfer function of the fourth-order, low-pass Butterworth filter with cut-off frequency ω_c is

$$H(s) = \frac{\omega_c^4}{s^4 + 2.6131\omega_c s^3 + 3.4140\omega_c^2 s^2 + 2.6131\omega_c^3 s + \omega_c^4}$$

In order to avoid the tedium of repeating this type of calculation, the coefficients for the polynomials of orders $n = 1, 2, \ldots, 9$ are given in Table 10.1 below. The class of

Table 10.1 — Coefficients of the Butterworth polynomials, for the cases $n = 1$ to $n = 9$

n	a_0	a_1	a_2	a_3	a_4	a_5	a_6	a_7	a_8	a_9
1	1.00000	1.00000								
2	1.00000	1.41421	1.00000							
3	1.00000	2.00000	2.00000	1.00000						
4	1.00000	2.61313	3.41421	2.61313	1.00000					
5	1.00000	3.23607	5.23607	5.23607	3.23607	1.00000				
6	1.00000	3.86370	7.46410	9.14162	7.46410	3.86370	1.00000			
7	1.00000	4.49396	10.09783	14.59179	14.59179	10.09783	4.49396	1.00000		
8	1.00000	5.12583	13.13707	21.84615	25.68835	21.84615	13.13707	5.12583	1.00000	
9	1.00000	5.75877	16.58172	31.16344	41.98640	41.98640	31.16344	16.58172	5.75877	1.00000

Butterworth filters provide a practical solution to the low-pass filter design problem. We will show later that it is possible to give a procedure for the implementation of a Butterworth filter of arbitrary order.

One of the desirable properties of such filters is the particularly flat nature of the amplitude response in the pass-band. This effect is evident in Fig. 10.5, and can be explained as follows. Since

$$|H_n(i\omega)| = \frac{1}{\sqrt{(1 + (\omega/\omega_c)^{2n})}}$$

$$= [1 + (\omega/\omega_c)^{2n}]^{-1/2}$$

$$\sim 1 - \tfrac{1}{2}(\omega/\omega_c)^{2n} + \tfrac{3}{8}(\omega/\omega_c)^{4n} - \dots,$$

when $\omega/\omega_c \ll 1$, we see that the first $2n - 1$ derivatives of $|H(i\omega)|$ are zero at $\omega = 0$. This is the reason for the flat shape of the amplitude response near $\omega = 0$ and is known as the 'maximally flat' property.

The total filter design process is beyond the scope of this text, and forms a part of a study of electrical engineering. We may however consider how simple design criteria are used to determine a suitable order for a Butterworth filter. (The choice of a Butterworth filter is of course, a design decision in itself!)

Example 10.2
A low-pass Butterworth filter with cut-off frequency ω_c is to be designed to meet the following specifications.

The amplitude response magnitude at $\omega = 3\omega_c/4$ must be not less than 95% of the maximum value (the dc gain at $\omega = 0$).

Also at $\omega = 5\omega_c/4$, the amplitude response magnitude must be less than 20% of the maximum value.

For the Butterworth filter of order n, the amplitude response is given by

$$|H(i\omega)| = \frac{1}{\sqrt{(1 + (\omega/\omega_c)^{2n})}},$$

with a maximum value of 1 at $\omega = 0$.

Our first requirement is thus that

$$|H(i3\omega_c/4)| = \frac{1}{\sqrt{(1 + (3/4)^{2n})}} = > \frac{95}{100}$$

This means that

$$1 + (3/4)^{2n} \leq \frac{10000}{9025}$$

or

$$(3/4)^{2n} \leq 0.1080$$

and we seek the smallest integer n for which the inequality holds.
Taking logs, we have that

$$2n\log_e[3/4] \leqslant \log_e[0.1080]$$

or, $n \geqslant 3.8682$. Thus the smallest integer value for n is $n = 4$.

The second requirement means that we must have

$$|H(i5\omega_c/4)| = \frac{1}{\sqrt{(1 + (5/4)^{2n})}} < \tfrac{1}{5}.$$

Rearranging and taking logs leads to

$$n > \log_e(24)/2\log_e(5/4) = 7.1200,$$

and the smallest integer values of n is thus $n = 8$.

In order that both requirements may be simultaneously satisfied, we choose $n \geqslant \max[4,8] = 8$, leading us to propose an eighth-order filter design. The coefficients can now be read off from Table 10.1.

We are now ready to proceed to the second part of our generalization process. The task is now to show that any Butterworth filter, generated by the above procedure, can be implemented using analogue circuits of the type discussed earlier.

Consider the structure of the transfer function of the nth-order filter. We have

$$H_n(s) = 1/B_n(x) = 1/B_n(s/\omega_c) = \omega_c^n/B_n(s)$$
$$= B_n(0)/B_n(s).$$

Also, $B_n(s) = M_n(s) + N_n(s)$,

where $M_n(s)$ is an even polynomial, called the even part, and $N_n(s)$ is an odd polynomial, called the odd part. For example, When $n = 3$, we have

$$B_3(s) = s^3 + 3\omega_c s^2 + 3\omega_c^2 s + 1$$
$$= (s^3 + 3\omega_c^2 s) + (3\omega_c s^2 + \omega_c^3)$$

so that $M_3(s) = (3\omega_c s^2 + \omega_c^3)$, $N_3(s) = (s^3 + 3\omega_c^2 s)$.

Clearly $B_n(0) = M_n(0)$, and so we can write,

$$H_n(s) = M_n(0)/(M_n(s) + N_n(s))$$

$$= \frac{A\, M_n(0)/N_n(s)}{A + A\, M_n(s)/N_n(s)}, \tag{10.22}$$

where A is any constant. Notice that if n, the filter order, is even, then

$$\deg\{M_n(s)\} = \deg\{N_n(s)\} + 1, \tag{10.23}$$

whilst if n is odd, then

$$\deg\{N_n(s)\} = \deg\{M_n(s)\} + 1. \tag{10.24}$$

In Fig. 10.8 we show an L–C ladder network, which represents an extension of the type of circuit already seen to be suitable for the implementation of low-order filters.

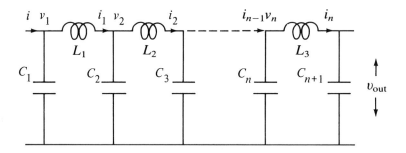

Fig. 10.8 — An L–C ladder network.

Using the techniques of Chapter 7, we analyse this circuit as follows. For the capacitor, C_1, we have from (7.4),

$$i(t) - i_1(t) = C_1 \frac{dv_1}{dt},$$

and on taking the Laplace transform we can express this relation as

$$I(s) = C_1 s V_1(s) + I_1(s).$$

For the first inductance, L_1, we use (7.2) and obtain

$$v_1(t) - v_2(t) = L \frac{di_1(t)}{dt}$$

which becomes in the transform domain,

$$V_1(s) = LsI_1(s) + V_2(s).$$

Proceeding in this manner for the other components, we eventually find the set of equations,

$$I(s) = C_1(s)V_1(s) + I_1(s)$$
$$V_1(s) = L_1sI_1(s) + V_2(s)$$
$$I_1(s) = C_2sV_2(s) + I_2(s)$$
$$\cdot$$
$$\cdot$$
$$\cdot$$
$$I_{n-1}(s) = C_n(s)V_n(s) + I_n(s)$$
$$V_r(s) = L_n(s)I_n(s) + V_{\text{out}}(s)$$
$$I_n(s) = C_{n+1}(s)sV_{\text{out}}(s).$$

Then, back-substituting, we see that

$$V_n(s) = [L_nC_ns^2 + 1]V_{\text{out}}(s)$$
$$I_{n-1}(s) = [C_nC_{n+1}L_ns^3 + (C_n + C_{n+1})s]V_{\text{out}}(s)$$

Continuing this process, we soon see that we obtain

$$V_1(s) = F(s)V_{\text{out}}(s) \qquad\qquad\qquad\qquad (10.25)$$
$$I(s) = G(s)V_{\text{out}}(s), \qquad\qquad\qquad\qquad (10.26)$$

where $F(s)$ is an even polynomial in s, with coefficients determined by the component values, and $F(0) = 1$.

Similarly, $G(s)$ is an odd polynomial and

$$\deg\{G(s)\} = \deg\{F(s)\} + 1. \qquad\qquad\qquad\qquad (10.27)$$

We can write (10.25) and (10.26) as

$$V_1(s)/I(s) = F(s)/G(s) \qquad\qquad\qquad\qquad (10.28)$$

and

$$V_{\text{out}}(s)/I(s) = 1/G(s) = F(0)/G(s), \tag{10.29}$$

which shows that we can determine $V_{\text{out}}(s)/I(s)$ from a knowledge of $V_1(s)/I(s)$.

In Fig. 10.9 we show such an L–C ladder network with input voltage v_{in} 'driving' the circuit through a resistance R. Using (7.1), we can write at once,

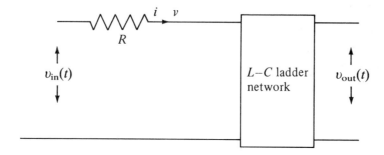

Fig. 10.9 — A 'type 1' L–C ladder network with input voltage $v_{\text{in}}(t)$ and output voltage $v_{\text{out}}(t)$.

$$v_{\text{in}}(t) - v_1(t) = i(t)R,$$

which becomes in the transform domain,

$$V_{\text{in}}(s) = V_1(s) + I(s)R.$$

Thus,

$$\frac{V_{\text{out}}(s)}{V_{\text{in}}(s)} = \frac{V_{\text{out}}(s)}{V_1(s) + RI(s)}$$

$$= \frac{V_{\text{out}}(s)/I(s)}{R + V_1(s)/I(s)}$$

$$= \frac{1/G(s)}{R + F(s)/G(s)}, \tag{10.30}$$

from (10.28) and (10.29).

We now compare (10.30) with (10.22) and deduce that in order to use this type of circuit to implement a Butterworth filter, we should set $A = R$ and choose

$$1/G(s) = R \, M_n(0)/N_n(s), \tag{10.31}$$

and

$$F(s)/G(s) = R \, M_n(s)/N_n(s). \tag{10.32}$$

However, we must have

$$\deg\{G(s)\} = \deg\{F(s)\} + 1$$

that is,

$$\deg\{N_n(s)\} = \deg\{M_n(s)\} + 1,$$

which, from (10.24), means that n, the filter order must be odd.

Recall that we start from a position of knowing the transfer function of our filter, that is, we know

$$H_n(s) = M_n(0)/(M_n(s) + N_n(s)).$$

Our design method will be to use (10.31) and (10.32) to obtain $G(s)$ and $F(s)$ for the implementation of our desired filter.

We have thus established that Butterworth filters of odd order, can be implemented using 'type 1' L–C ladder networks. We have not yet shown how to calculate the component values, but we will address this matter after we have considered the case when the filter order, n, is an even integer.

In Fig. 10.10 we illustrate a second, or type 2, L–C ladder network. Following the same procedure as for the type 1 network, it is easily shown that

$$V_{out}(s)/V_{in}(s) = \frac{V_{out}(s)}{V_1(s) + RI(s) + LsI(s)}$$

$$= \frac{V_{out}(s)/I(s)}{R + Ls + V_1(s)/I(s)}$$

$$= \frac{1/G(s)}{R + Ls + F(s)/G(s)}$$

Comparing with (10.22) shows that we must set $A = R$ and

$$1/G(s) = RM_n(0)/N_n(s)$$

with

$$Ls + F(s)/G(s) = RM_n(s)/N_n(s) \ . \tag{10.33}$$

It then follows that

$$\deg\{M_n(s)\} = \deg\{N_n(s)\} + 1,$$

meaning that $B_n(s)$ is an even polynomial.

The details of this case are left as an exercise. We have now established that the Butterworth filter can be realized in the general case, by use of an L–C ladder network. The network will be of type 1 or 2, depending upon whether the filter order is odd or even. To complete the design exercise, we must give a method by which the circuit parameters, or component values, may be obtained from a specification of the transfer function. An elegant way of achieving this objective is by use of a technique known as continued fraction expansion.

For both cases (n odd or n even), we have seen that the desired filter transfer function is given by

$$H_n(s) = \frac{B_n(0)}{B_n(s)} = \frac{V_{out}(s)}{V_{in}(s)} = \frac{1/G(s)}{R + F(s)/G(s)}$$

When n is odd, then $F(s)/G(s) = RM_n(s)/N_n(s)$, with $M_n(s)$ the even part of $B_n(s)$ and $N_n(s)$ the odd part.

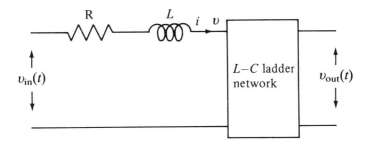

Fig. 10.10 — The 'type 2' L–C ladder network.

However, if we look again at (10.25) and (10.26) we see that if we use the L–C ladder of Fig. 10.8 then $F(s)/G(s)$ is also given by $V_1(s)/I(s)$. We now set up a continued fraction representation of this quotient by proceeding as follows. Write

$$F(s)/G(s) = V_1(s)/I(s)$$

$$= \frac{1}{I(s)/V_1(s)}$$

$$= \frac{1}{C_1 s + I_1(s)/V_1(s)}$$

$$= \frac{1}{C_1 s + \dfrac{1}{V_1(s)/I_1(s)}}$$

$$= \frac{1}{C_1 s + \dfrac{1}{L_1 s + V_2(s)/I_1(s)}}$$

$$= \frac{1}{C_1 s + \dfrac{1}{L_1 s + \dfrac{1}{I_1(s)/V_2(s)}}}$$

$$= \frac{1}{C_1 s + \dfrac{1}{L_1 s + \dfrac{1}{C_2 s + \ldots}}} \qquad (10.34)$$

and so on. In this continued fraction form, the parameter values emerge explicitly. Using the fact that $F(s)/G(s) = RM_n(s)/N_n(s)$, the design process is completed by carrying out the continued fraction development of $RM_n(s)/N_n(s)$ and reading off corresponding values.

We demonstrate the method by an example.

Example 10.3
Determine a realization for the third-order Butterworth filter.

From Table 10.1 above, we obtain the required transfer function as

$$H_3(s) = \frac{\omega_c^3}{s^3 + 2\omega_c s^2 + 2\omega_c^2 s + \omega_c^3}$$

Thus

$$M_3(s) = 2\omega_c s^2 + \omega_c^3$$

and

$$N_3(s) = s^3 + 2\omega_c^2 s.$$

Then $F(s)/G(s) = RM_3(s)/N_3(s)$, and using the substitution $x = s/\omega_c$,

$$F(s)/G(s) = RM_3(s)/N_3(s)$$

$$= R\frac{[2x^2 + 1]}{[x^3 + 2x]}$$

$$= \frac{1}{\dfrac{[x^3 + 2x]}{R[2x^2 + 1]}}$$

$$= \cfrac{1}{\cfrac{x[2x^2 + 1 + 3]}{2R\,[2x^2 + 1]}}$$

$$= \cfrac{1}{\cfrac{x}{2R} + \cfrac{3x}{2R[2x^2 + 1]}}$$

$$= \cfrac{1}{\cfrac{x}{2R} + \cfrac{1}{\cfrac{2R[2x^2 + 1]}{3x}}}$$

$$= \cfrac{1}{\cfrac{x}{2R} + \cfrac{1}{\cfrac{4Rx}{3} + \cfrac{2R}{3x}}}$$

$$= \cfrac{1}{\cfrac{x}{2R} + \cfrac{1}{\cfrac{4Rx}{3} + \cfrac{1}{\cfrac{3x}{2R}}}} \qquad (10.35)$$

With $x = s/\omega_c$, it is now easy to read off corresponding values between (10.34) and (10.35) to obtain

$$C_1 = 1/2R\omega_c$$
$$L_1 = 4R/3\omega_c$$
$$C_2 = 3/2R\omega_c \ ,$$

exactly in accord with the results of section 10.3. The circuit design is shown in Fig. 10.11.

To conclude this discussion, we examine the procedure when n is an even integer. From (10.33) and (10.34) we see that in this case,

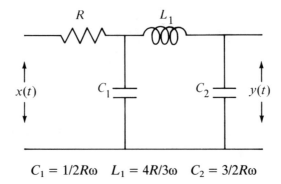

$$C_1 = 1/2R\omega \quad L_1 = 4R/3\omega \quad C_2 = 3/2R\omega$$

Fig. 10.11 — An implementation of the third-order Butterworth low-pass filter.

$$Ls + \cfrac{1}{C_1 + \cfrac{1}{L_1 s + \cfrac{1}{C_2 s + \ \ldots}}}$$

$$= RM_n(s)/N_n(s). \tag{10.36}$$

Again, the procedure reduces to a continued fraction development of $RM_n(s)/N_n(s)$.

Example 10.4
Find a realization of the second-order Butterworth filter, given by

$$H_2(s) = \frac{\omega_c^2}{s^2 + \sqrt{2}\omega_c s + \omega_c^2}$$

We have $M_s(s) = s^2 + \omega_c^2$, and

$$N_2(s) = \sqrt{2}\omega_c s \ ;$$

thus, writing $x = s/\omega_c$, we expand $\dfrac{R[x^2 + 1]}{\sqrt{2}x}$
as

$$\frac{R[x^2 + 1]}{\sqrt{2}x} = \frac{Rx}{\sqrt{2}} + \frac{R}{\sqrt{2}x} = \frac{Rx}{\sqrt{2}} + \cfrac{1}{\cfrac{\sqrt{2}x}{R}}$$

Then, from (10.36), and remembering that $s = x\omega_c$, we have

$$L_1 = \frac{R}{\sqrt{2}\omega_c}, \text{ and } C_1 = \frac{\sqrt{2}}{R\omega_c},$$

again in agreement with the result in section (10.3). The circuit design is shown in Fig. 10.12.

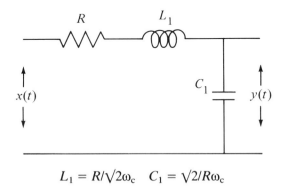

$$L_1 = R/\sqrt{2}\omega_c \quad C_1 = \sqrt{2}/R\omega_c$$

Fig. 10.12 — A realization of the second-order Butterworth low-pass filter.

10.5   FILTER TRANSFORMATIONS

So far, our discussion has concentrated on the design of low-pass filters. For many applications, a filter of another type will be required. For example, we may wish to design a filter to reject a band of frequencies which contains signals *interfering* with signals we wish to observe. In section 10.1, we illustrated the ideal frequency responses of the different filter types. We now wish to design filters of these types, again with frequency responses which are approximations to the ideal response.

It is not necessary to repeat the exercise carried out for the design of low-pass filters because we are able to define *filter transformations*. These transformations are applied to the transfer functions of low-pass filters to produce filters with high-pass, band-pass, or band-reject characteristics. In fact, it is also unnecessary to re-work the circuit synthesis calculations, since methods are known for the modification of low-pass designs to produce circuits which will operate as filters of the other types. This latter topic is beyond the scope of this book; however, the interested reader should consult Kuo [1].

The first transformation we study is that which produces a high-pass filter from a low-pass prototype. It is reasonable to suppose that such a transformation could be achieved by replacing s in the transfer function of the low-pass filter, by $1/s$. We will demonstrate that this is indeed a sensible procedure.

Define the prototype low-pass filter by its transfer function, $H_{LP}(s)$, and we again introduce the non-dimensional or normalized frequency variable, $x = s/\omega_c$. Now make the transformation $x \rightarrow 1/y$, where $y = s/\omega_\alpha$ is a second normalized frequency variable. This means that in the transfer function of the low-pass prototype, $H_{LP}(s)$, s/ω_c is replaced by ω_α/s. The critical, or cut-off, frequencies of the low-pass prototype filter were located at $\omega = \pm\omega_c$, corresponding to $x = \pm i$. Thus, the normalized critical frequencies of the high-pass design are given by

$$1/y = \pm i, \text{ or } y = \pm i.$$

Since $y = s/\omega_\alpha$, we see that setting $s = i\omega_c'$, where ω_c' is the critical frequency of the high-pass filter, yields

$$\omega_c' = \pm\omega_\alpha.$$

We can examine the effect of this transformation on the Butterworth filters. Since

$$H(s)H(-s) = \frac{1}{(1 + (s/i\omega_c)^{2n})},$$

or writing $x = s/\omega_c$,

$$H(s)H(-s) = \frac{1}{(1 + (x/i)^{2n})}.$$

Using the transformation $x \rightarrow 1/y$, we have, for the transfer function $H'(s)$ of the high-pass filter,

$$H'(s)H'(-s) = \frac{1}{(1 + (1/iy)^{2n})}$$

$$= \frac{1}{(1 + (\omega_\alpha/is)^{2n})}$$

leading to,

$$|H'(i\omega)| = \frac{1}{\sqrt{(1 + (\omega_\alpha/\omega)^{2n})}} \ .$$

Clearly, if $\omega > \omega_\alpha$, $|H'(i\omega)| \to 1$, whilst if $\omega < \omega_\alpha$, $|H'(i\omega)| \to 0$, and thus $H'(s)$ is indeed the transfer function of a high-pass filter.

Example 10.5
Using a fourth-order Butterworth low-pass filter as prototype, design a high-pass filter as prototype, design a high-pass filter with cut-off frequency 20 Hz.

With a cut-off frquency of 20 Hz, we have as cut-off frequency of the high-pass filter $\omega_c' = 2\pi.20 = 125.66$ radians/s. Selecting the fourth-order Butterworth low-pass filter, with cut-off frequency $\omega_c = 1$, we find from Table 10.1 that the prototype low-pass transfer function is given by

$$H_{\mathrm{LP}}(s) = \frac{1}{s^4 + 2.61313s^3 + 3.41421s^2 + 2.61313s + 1} \ .$$

We now replace s with $40\pi/s$, since for the prototype the cut-off frequency was $\omega_c = 1$, to obtain

$$H(s) = \frac{s^4}{s^4 + 2.61313(40\pi)s^3 + 3.41421(40\pi)^2s^2 + 2.61313(40\pi)^3s + (40\pi)^4}$$

This is the transfer function of the high-pass filter, and in Fig. 10.13, we illustrate the amplitude response. We now consider other filter transformations which will

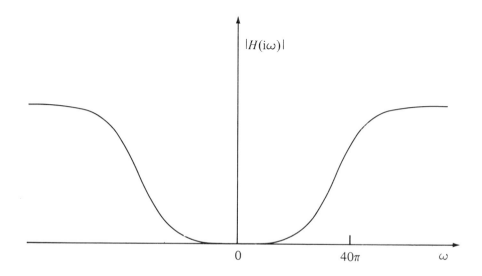

Fig. 10.13 — Amplitude response of the high-pass design.

produce the band-pass and band-reject filters of section 10.1. These transformations can be motivated from a deeper knowledge of circuit theory than we have developed in this book. Rather than pursue this here, we shall consider the transformations alone and content ourselves with a demonstration that each produces the desired filter type.

First we consider a transformation which will produce a band-pass filter, from a low-pass prototype. Again we work with the two non-dimensional frequency variables x and y, defined as above. The transformation we shall consider is defined by

$$x \rightarrow \frac{y^2 + 1}{y} \frac{\omega_\alpha}{\omega_\beta},$$

meaning that in the transfer function $H_{LP}(s)$ of the low-pass filter,

$$s/\omega_c \text{ is replaced by } \frac{s^2 + \omega_\alpha^2}{s\omega_\beta} \tag{10.37}$$

Recall that the critical frequencies of the low-pass filter were defined by $x = \pm i$, so that the critical frequencies of the new design are obtained by solving the equation

$$\frac{y^2 + 1}{y} \frac{\omega_\alpha}{\omega_\beta} = \pm i .$$

That is,

$$(y^2 + 1)\omega_\alpha/\omega_\beta = \pm iy .$$

We thus have two quadratic equations to solve,

$$\omega_\alpha y^2 - i\omega_\beta y + \omega_\alpha = 0 \tag{10.38}$$

and

$$\omega_\alpha y^2 + i\omega_\beta y + \omega_\alpha = 0 \tag{10.39}$$

Solving (10.38), we obtain for the critical values of y, y_c, say,

$$y_c = \frac{i\omega_\beta \pm i\sqrt{(\omega_\beta^2 + 4\omega_\alpha^2)}}{2\omega_\alpha}$$

and we note that these values are purely imaginary with one on each side of the origin.

Similarly, from (10.39) we obtain

$$y_c = \frac{-i\omega_\beta \pm i\sqrt{(\omega_\beta^2 + 4\omega_\alpha^2)}}{2\omega_\alpha}$$

again obtaining purely imaginary values with one on each side of the origin. Essentially, what has happened here is that each critical frequency of the low-pass prototype has mapped into two critical values for the new design, one on each side of the origin.

Replacing y_c with $i\omega_c/\omega_\alpha$, we see that the four critical values of the real frequency variable ω are given by

$$\omega_c' = \frac{-\omega_\beta \pm \sqrt{(\omega_\beta^2 + 4\omega_\alpha^2)}}{2}$$

and

$$\omega_c' = \frac{\omega_\beta \pm \sqrt{(\omega_\beta^2 + 4\omega_\alpha^2)}}{2}.$$

Now define

$$\omega_u = \frac{\omega_\beta + \sqrt{(\omega_\beta^2 + 4\omega_\alpha^2)}}{2}$$

and

$$\omega_l = \frac{-\omega_\beta + \sqrt{(\omega_\beta^2 + 4\omega_\alpha^2)}}{2},$$

so that the critical frequencies ω_c' can be written as

$$\omega_c' = -\omega_u, \ -\omega_l, \ \omega_l, \text{ and } \omega_u .$$

We must now show that we have indeed generated a band-pass filter. First we show that ω_α lies between ω_l and ω_u, and hence that $-\omega_\alpha$ lies between $-\omega_u$ and $-\omega_l$. Since

$$\omega_l = \frac{-\omega_\beta + \omega_\beta\sqrt{(1 + 4\omega_\alpha^2/\omega_\beta^2)}}{2}$$

$$< \frac{-\omega_\beta + \omega_\beta\sqrt{(1 + 4\omega_\alpha^2/\omega_\beta^2 + 4\omega_\alpha/\omega_\beta)}}{2}$$

$$= \frac{-\omega_\beta + \omega_\beta(1 + 2\omega_\alpha/\omega_\beta)}{2} = \omega_\alpha \ ,$$

then $\omega_\alpha > \omega_l$.

Also, since

$$\omega_u = \frac{\omega_\beta + 2\omega_\alpha\sqrt{(1 + \omega_\beta^2/4\omega_\alpha^2)}}{2} > \omega_\alpha \ ,$$

we have established that $\omega_l < \omega_\alpha < \omega_u$. In Fig. 10.14 we illustrate the distribution of these values.

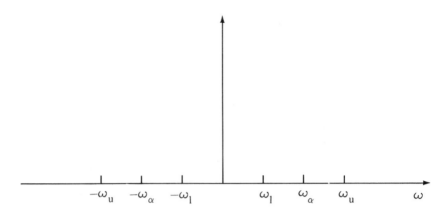

Fig. 10.14 — Location of critical frequencies.

This result enables us to locate the pass-band of the new filter, by investigating the effect of the transformation on the pass-band of the prototype low-pass filter. This was described, using the non-dimensional frequency variable x, by $|x| < 1$. Under the transformation, this becomes

$$|(y^2 + 1)/y|(\omega_\alpha/\omega_\beta) < 1 \ .$$

Since, when $s = i\omega$, $y = i\omega/\omega_\alpha$, we have

$$|(\omega_\alpha^2 - \omega^2)/\omega\omega_\beta| < 1 \ .$$

Restricting ourselves for the moment to the case $\omega > 0$ we have to examine the two cases

(1) $0 < \omega < \omega_\alpha$, and
(2) $\omega > \omega_\alpha$.

In case (1), we have

$$\omega_\alpha^2 - \omega^2 < \omega\omega_\beta,$$

or

$$\omega^2 + \omega\omega_\beta - \omega_\alpha^2 > 0.$$

Since $\omega > 0$, this means that

$$\omega > \frac{-\omega_\beta + \sqrt{(\omega_\beta^2 + 4\omega_\alpha^2)}}{2} = \omega_1 \ .$$

Thus if $\omega < \omega_\alpha$, then $\omega > \omega_1$.
   On the other hand, if $\omega > \omega_\alpha$, we must have

$$\omega^2 - \omega_\alpha^2 < \omega\omega_\beta \ ,$$

which leads to the requirement that

$$\omega < \omega_u \ .$$

So we may conclude that the pass-band of the low-pass filter has been mapped to the interval $\omega_1 < \omega < \omega_u$.
   In a similar way we can analyse the situation when $\omega < 0$, to establish that the total effect of the transformation is to produce two images of the pass-band of the low-pass filter located in the intervals

$$\omega_1 < \omega < \omega_u \text{ and } -\omega_u < \omega < -\omega_1 \ .$$

We can now be sure that the transformation defined by (10.37) does produce a band-pass filter when applied to a low-pass prototype.

Before leaving this discussion, notice that

$$\omega_u - \omega_l = \omega_\beta ,$$

and for this reason, ω_β is called the *bandwidth* of the filter. Also,

$$\omega_u \omega_l = \omega_\alpha^2, \text{ or } \omega_\alpha = \sqrt{(\omega_u \omega_l)},$$

and ω_α is thus called the geometric centre frequency of the band-pass filter. This means that the low-pass to band-pass transformation can be written as

$$s/\omega_c \rightarrow \frac{s^2 + \omega_u \omega_l}{s(\omega_u - \omega_l)} .$$

Finally, we see that if

$$\omega_b \ll \omega_\alpha, \text{ then}$$

$$\omega_u \sim \omega_\alpha + \omega_\beta/2$$

and

$$\omega_l \sim \omega_\alpha - \omega_\beta/2,$$

so that

$$\omega_\alpha \sim (\omega_u + \omega_l)/2.$$

The use of a design procedure based on this transformation is demonstrated in example 10.6.

Example 10.6

Using as prototype a second-order Butterworth low-pass filter, design a band-pass filter which has the following properties

(1) The geometric centre frequency is specified as $f_\alpha = 20$ Hz, and
(2) the bandwidth is to be $f_\beta = 1$ Hz.

Here, $\omega_\alpha = 2\pi f_\alpha = 40\pi$ radians/s, and $\omega_\beta = 2\pi f_\alpha = 2\pi$. The prototype low-pass filter is defined by its transfer function as

$$H_{LP}(s) = \frac{1}{(s/\omega_c)^2 + 1.4142(s/\omega_c) + 1} \ .$$

Making the transformation

$$s/\omega_c \rightarrow \frac{s^2 + \omega_\alpha^2}{s\omega_\beta} \ ,$$

we obtain the transfer function of the band-pass filter as

$$H(s) = \frac{1}{((s^2 + \omega_\alpha^2)/s\omega_\beta)^2 + 1.4142((s^2 + \omega_\alpha^2)/s\omega_\beta) + 1}$$

$$= \frac{s^2\omega_\beta^2}{s^4 + 1.4142\omega_\beta s^3 + (2\omega_\alpha^2 + \omega_\beta^2)s^2 + 1.4142\omega_\beta\omega_\alpha^2 s + \omega_\alpha^4}$$

To obtain the transfer function of the design corresponding to our specification, we substitute

$$\omega_\alpha = 40\pi, \text{ and } \omega_\beta = 2\pi \text{ to give}$$

$$\frac{(2\pi)^2 s^2}{s^4 + 1.4142(2\pi)s^3 + (2(40\pi)^2 + (2\pi)^2)s^2 + 1.4142(40\pi)^2 2\pi s + (4)\pi^4} \ .$$

In Fig. 10.15 we illustrate the amplitude response of this filter, and in Fig. 10.16, we illustrate the response of a similar design having a band-width of $\omega_\beta = 20\pi$. In view of our discussion of the two previous transformations, it will come as no surprise that the transformation from low-pass to band-reject filter is given by

$$s/\omega_c \rightarrow \frac{s(\omega_u - \omega_l)}{s^2 + \omega_u\omega_l} \ ,$$

which is simply the reciprocal of the transformation used to produce band-pass designs. Here ω_l and ω_u denote the lower and upper edges of the stop band of the filter.

The details of the analysis of this transformation are left as an exercise.

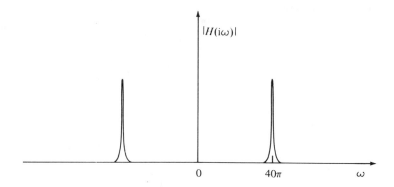

Fig. 10.15 — Amplitude response of band-pass filter of Example 10.6.

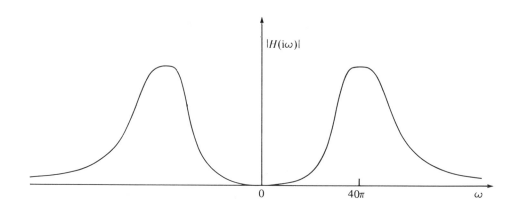

Fig. 10.16 — Amplitude response of band-pass filter with band-width $\omega_\beta = 20\pi$.

10.6 OTHER FILTER DESIGNS

In the discussion so far, we have used the Butterworth filter, both as a low-pass filter and as the prototype for other designs using the transformations of section 10.5. Whilst the Butterworth filters are widely used, other designs are possible, and indeed give superior performance in some applications. In all cases, the design of a low-pass filter reduces to the approximation of the ideal frequency response shape of Fig. 10.1. We have seen that the Butterworth filters have the 'maximally flat' property; however, other designs have sharper cut-off characteristics. The penalty for this increased sharpness is 'ripple', perhaps in the pass-band or in the stop-band, or possibly in both. In this section, we briefly consider another filter design which is in use, and we illustrate a typical frequency response.

The design we consider is the Chebyshev design, which is based on the properties of the Chebyshev polynomials. The amplitude response of an nth-order Chebyshev low-pass filter, with cut-off frequency ω_c, is given by

$$|H_n(i\omega)|^2 = \frac{K^2}{1 + \varepsilon^2 T_n^2(\omega/\omega_c)} \tag{10.40}$$

where

$$T_n(\omega) = \cos(n\cos^{-1}\omega) \tag{10.41}$$

and K is a constant.

The relation (10.41) defines the Chebyshev polynomials of the first kind, and we note that when $|\omega| > 1$, this becomes '

$$T_n(\omega) = \cosh\,(n\cosh^{-1}\omega)\;.$$

The motivation for choosing the form specified by (10.40) for the design of a low-pass filter follows from the well-known properties of the polynomials. These ensure that as n increases we will obtain an increasingly good approximation to the ideal low-pass frequency response of Fig. 10.1.

Table 10.2 lists the first few Chebyshev polynomials

Table 10.2 — The Chebyshev polynomials

n	$T_n(\omega)$
0	1
1	ω
2	$2\omega^2 - 1$
3	$4\omega^3 - 3\omega$
4	$8\omega^4 - 8\omega^2 + 1$
5	$16\omega^5 - 20\omega^3 + 5\omega$
6	$32\omega^6 - 48\omega^4 + 18\omega^2 - 1$
7	$64\omega^7 - 112\omega^5 + 56\omega^3 - 7\omega$

A more useful formula for generating the polynomials can be obtained from (10.40) as follows.

Write $\alpha = \cos^{-1}\omega$, so that $T_n(\omega) = \cos n\alpha$, and then use the identity,

$$\cos((n+1)\alpha) + \cos((n-1)\alpha) = 2\cos n\alpha \cos\alpha. \qquad (10.41)$$

But $\cos((n+1)\alpha) = T_{n+1}(\omega)$, and $\cos((n-1)\alpha) = T_{n-1}(\omega)$, and thus we have

$$T_{n+1}(\omega) + T_{n-1}(\omega) = 2\omega T_n(\omega) \ ,$$

or

$$T_{n+1}(\omega) = 2\omega T_n(\omega) - T_{n-1}(\omega) \ .$$

From (10.40) we note that

$$T_n(0) = \left| \begin{array}{ll} (-1)^{n/2} & n \text{ even,} \\ 0 & n \text{ odd,} \end{array} \right.$$

and that $T_n(1) = 1$ for all n.
   Furthermore, we can see that

$$T_n(-1) = \left| \begin{array}{ll} 1 & n \text{ even} \\ -1 & n \text{ odd.} \end{array} \right.$$

It is also clear from (10.40) that $T_n(\omega)$ oscillates between -1 and 1, when $|\omega| \leqslant 1$, whilst $T_n(\omega)$ increases monotonically when $|\omega| > 1$. These properties indicate that a generally satisfactory response shape can be obtained; however, there will be an element of ripple in the filter pass-band. ˙
   In order to proceed with the design process, we need to determine the filter transfer function. This is achieved by following the general method as derived for the Butterworth filters.
   As before, set

$$H(s)H(-s) = \frac{K^2}{1 + \varepsilon^2 T_n^2(s/i\omega_c)}$$

where $H(s)$ is the transfer function of the desired filter. Now $H(s)H(-s)$ has poles determined by

$$T_n^2(s/i\omega_c) = -1/\varepsilon^2$$

that is,

$$T_n(s/i\omega_c) = \pm i/\varepsilon,$$

or

$$\cos(n\cos^{-1}(s/i\omega_c)) = \pm i/\varepsilon .$$

Now, define $\cos^{-1}(s/i\omega_c) = a + ib$, to give

$$\cos(n(a + ib)) = \cos(na)\cosh(nb) - i\,\sin(na)\sinh(nb) = \pm i/\varepsilon . \qquad (10.42)$$

Equating real and imaginary parts means that we must have

$$\cos(na)\cosh(nb) = 0 \qquad\qquad (10.43)$$

and

$$\sin(na)\sinh(nb) = \pm 1/\varepsilon . \qquad\qquad (10.44)$$

Since $\cosh(nb) \neq 0$, (10.43) implies that

$$\cos(na) = 0,$$

or

$$a = (2k + 1)\pi/2n, \ k = 0,1,2,\ldots, 2n - 1.$$

This means that $\sin(na)$ takes the values ± 1, and so from (10.44) we have,

$$\sinh(nb) = \pm (1/\varepsilon).$$

We can now determine the poles from (10.42) as

$$\begin{aligned}
s_\kappa &= i\omega_c\cos(a + ib) \\
&= i\omega_c[\cos(a)\cosh(b) - i\,\sin(a)\sinh(b)] \\
&= \omega_c[\sin(a)\sinh(b) + i\,\cos(a)\cosh(b)]
\end{aligned}$$

$$= \omega_c[\sin((2k+1)\pi/2n)\sinh((1/n)\sinh^{-1}(\pm 1/\varepsilon))$$
$$+ i \cos((2k+1)\pi/2n)\cosh((1/n)\sinh^{-1}(\pm 1/\varepsilon))] \tag{10.45}$$

with $k = 0,1,2,\ldots, 2n-1$.

From (10.45) we see that the poles are placed symmetrically about the imaginary axis, because $\sinh^{-1}(-x) = \sinh^{-1}(x)$, and lie on the ellipse,

$$\frac{x_k^2}{\{\sinh((1/n)\sinh^{-1}(1/\varepsilon))\}^2} + \frac{y_k^2}{\{\cosh((1/n)\sinh^{-1}(1/\varepsilon))\}^2} = \omega_c^2 \ .$$

We choose as the poles of the transfer function $H(s)$ those poles which lie in the left half-plane, that is

$$\lambda_k = \omega_c[-x_k + iy_k], \tag{10.46}$$

where

$$x_k = \sin(2k+1)\pi/2n.\sinh((1/n)\sinh^{-1}(1/\varepsilon)),$$

and

$$y_k = \cos(2k+1)\pi/2n.\cosh((1/n)\sinh^{-1}(1/\varepsilon)),$$

with $k = 0.1,2,\ldots, n-1$. We can then write the transfer function in the compact form

$$H(s) = \frac{K'}{\displaystyle\prod_{k=0}^{n-1} (s - \lambda_k)} \ .$$

Notice that when $s = 0$, corresponding to $\omega = 0$,

$$H(0) = \frac{K'}{\displaystyle\prod_{k=0}^{n-1} (-\lambda_k)} \ ,$$

thus choosing

$$K' = K(-1)^n \prod_{k=0}^{n-1} \lambda_k$$

means that the zero-frequency gain of the filter design will be K or $K/\sqrt{(1+\varepsilon^2)}$, depending on the filter order.

Finally, we can write the transfer function in the form

$$H(s) = \frac{(-1)^n K \prod_{k=0}^{n-1} \lambda_k}{\prod_{k=0}^{n-1} (s - \lambda_k)}$$

$$= \frac{K}{(-1)^n \prod_{k=0}^{n-1} (s/\lambda_k - 1)}$$

with the λ_k defined by (10.46).

We will now look at an example which again highlights some of the features of the design process. When we wish to carry out a design using a Chebyshev filter we must specify the parameter ε, which controls the amplitude of the pass-band ripple. In view of the oscillatory properties of $T_n(\omega)$ when $|\omega| < 1$, we see that the minimum and maximum values of $H_n(i\omega)$ in the pass-band are K and $K/\sqrt{(1+\varepsilon^2)}$. A convenient definition of the ripple magnitude, r, is the ratio of these two quantities, that is

$$r = \sqrt{(1 + \varepsilon^2)} \; .$$

For reasons of greater clarity, particularly in graphical work, it is common to use a decibel (dB) scale in the measurement of such quantities. This is a logarithmic scale, defined by

$$A_{dB} = 20 \log_{10} A,$$

where A is a scalar quantity, usually related to amplitude response. The ripple magnitude in decibels is then

$$r_{dB} = 20 \log_{10} \sqrt{(1 + \varepsilon^2)} = 10 \log_{10}(1 + \varepsilon^2) \; . \tag{10.47}$$

This scale is also used in other ways to specify the desired performance of filters at the design stage. Specifically, the degree of attenuation to be achieved by the filter at multiples of the cut-off frequency is an important characteristic, often expressed using the decibel scale. We will see in the last example for this chapter that this latter requirement effectively specifies the lowest filter order suitable for the task in hand.

Example 10.7
In view of the superior performance near the cut-off frequency $f_c = 5$ Hz, a Chebyshev filter is to be designed to meet the following specifications.

1. The amplitude of the ripple in the pass-band must be no more than 1 dB and,
2. At twice the cut-off frequency, the attenuation must be at least 15 dB relative to the gain at the cut-off frequency.

We will derive the minimum filter order which will meet this specification, and calculate the transfer function for the resulting design.

From the requirement of a maximum of 1 dB ripple in the pass-band, we have from (10.47)

$$1 = 10 \log_{10} (1 + \varepsilon^2)$$

so that

$$\varepsilon = \sqrt{(10^{0.1} - 1)}$$
$$= 0.5088.$$

We chose to use the maximum permitted value of the ripple amplitude because this parameter also influences the filter-order calculation, as we now see.

The ratio of the amplitude response at 10 Hz $= 2f_c$ to that at f_c is A, where

$$A = \frac{\sqrt{(1 + \varepsilon^2 T_n^2(1))}}{\sqrt{(1 + \varepsilon^2 T_n^2(2))}} .$$

Thus $A_{dB} = 20 \log_{10} A$
$$= 10 [\log_{10}(1 + \varepsilon^2 T_n^2(1)) - \log_{10}(1 + \varepsilon^2 T_n^2(2))]$$
$$\leq -15,$$
or, using the calculated value for ε,

$$\log_{10}[1 + 0.5088^2 T_n^2(2)] - \log_{10}[1 + 0.5088^2 T_n^2(1)] \geq 1.5.$$

We now use Table 10.2 to evaluate the expression on the left, stopping as soon as the inequality is satisfied. The corresponding value of n is then the minimum filter order which we may adopt.

With $n = 0$ we obtain the value 0 for the left-hand side, whereas $n = 1$ yields 0.2087 and $n = 2$ gives 0.3491. When $n = 3$, we obtain 2.1455, and the inequality is satisfied. Thus a third-order Chebyshev filter is the design we should implement, and in order to determine the transfer function, we must first find the pole locations. Recall that these were given by (10.46) so that with $\omega_c = 2\pi f_c$

$$\lambda_k = 2\pi.5[-x_k + iy_k]$$

where, since $n = 3$ and $\varepsilon = 0.5088$,

$$x_k = \sin\left((2k+1)\pi/6\right).\sinh(1/3)\sinh^{-1}(1.9654))$$
$$= 0.4942 \sin\left((2k+1)\pi/6\right), \quad k = 0,1,2,$$

and

$$y_k = \cos\left(2k+1)\pi/6\right).\cosh\left(1/3)\sinh^{-1}(1.9654\right)$$
$$= 1.1155 \cos\left((2k+1)\pi/6\right), \quad k = 0,1,2.$$

Thus,

$$x_0 = 0.2471, \qquad y_0 = 0.9661$$
$$x_1 = 0.4942, \qquad y_1 = 0.0$$
$$x_2 = 0.2471, \qquad y_2 = 0.9661.$$

Having obtained the pole locations, the transfer function follows at once as

$$H(s) = \frac{(-1)^3 K\lambda_0\lambda_1\lambda_2}{(s-\lambda_0)\,(s-\lambda_1)\,(s-\lambda_s)}$$

$$= \frac{K(15237.6082)}{(s+15.5258)\,(s^2+15.5258s+981.4410)}.$$

A plot of the amplitude response of this filter is shown in Fig. 10.17.

This example concludes our discussion of analogue filters and their design. In Chapter 12, we shall make use of the designs we have obtained here when we wish to construct discrete-time structures which will perform similar tasks. The interested

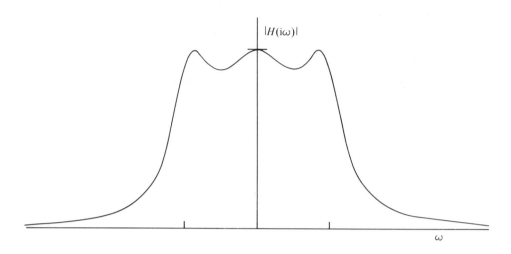

Fig. 10.17 — Amplitude response of the Chebyshev filter of Example 10.7

reader may wish to consult specialist texts in the area of filter design and synthesis. The material of section 10.4 is based on the treatments of Weinberg [3] and Kuo [1], whereas Oppenheim [2] is a valuable reference work.

REFERENCES

[1] F. F. Kuo, *Network Analysis and Synthesis*, Wiley, New York, 1966.
[2] A. V. Oppenheim, A. S. Willsky and I. T. Young, *Signals and Systems*, Prentice-Hall, Englewood Cliffs, New Jersey, 1983.
[3] L. Weinberg, *Network Analysis and Synthesis*, McGraw-Hill, New York, 1962.

EXERCISES

1. Determine the pole locations for the Butterworth filter of order 5. Hence find the transfer function.

2. Determine the transfer function of a Butterworth filter such that the cut-off frequency is at $f_c = 2$ kHz and that the attenuation is at least 15 dB at twice the cut-off frequency. What order of filter would be required if the 15 dB target were to be achieved at one-and-a-half times the cut-off frequency?

3. Using a first-order low-pass Butterworth filter as prototype, design a band-pass filter with geometric centre frequency at $f = 500$ Hz and bandwidth 25 Hz. Sketch the amplitude response.

4. Repeat Exercise 3, this time using a second-order prototype.

5. Using the methods of section 10.4, determine a realization of the fourth-order Butterworth filter.

6. Design a second-order high-pass filter with cut-off frequency 100 Hz, based on a Butterworth prototype.

7. Use the low-pass to band-reject transformation to design a fourth-order filter, based on a second-order Butterworth prototype, such that the geometric centre frequency, $\sqrt{\omega_u \omega_1}$, is located at 100 rad/sec. and the bandwidth, $\omega_u - \omega_1 = 10$ rad/sec.

8. Determine a low-pass Chebyshev filter which satisfies the following specifications.

   (i) The pass-band ripple level is 1 dB.
  (ii) The cut-off frequency is 20 kHz.
 (iii) The gain at zero frequency is unity.
 (iv) The attenuation at 100 kHz is 100 dB.

9. Use as prototype, a second-order Chebyshev filter, with 1 dB ripple in the pass-band, to design a band-pass filter, with geometric centre frequency 150 Hz and bandwidth 20 Hz. Adjust your design so that the gain at 150 Hz is 1 and plot the amplitude response. Calculate the attenuation in dB at 100, 120 and 140 Hz.

11

Discrete-time signals and systems

11.1 INTRODUCTION

In the last four chapters, we have developed a theory of continuous-time linear systems, adequate for the purposes of analysing analogue filter behaviour. The problem of filter design has also been approached at least in outline. For many years this was effectively the end of the story so far as relevant mathematical background is concerned. More recently, however, fast, robust, digital computing equipment has become readily available, and, in line with other areas of engineering, this has changed the technology of signal processing out of all recognition. The implications extend naturally into the field of mathematics, and it is the purpose of the remaining chapters of this book to describe the basic concepts and techniques necessary to understand and apply this developing technology. First, though, we introduce some new concepts with which to describe discrete-time signals and systems.

11.2 SEQUENCES

We define the sequence $\{x\}$ as an ordered list of real or complex numbers, with $\{x\}$ being specified in one of two distinct methods. The most elementary way, only appropriate to sequences with a finite number of terms, is to list all the members of the sequence. As an example, consider the sequence $\{x\}$ where $\{x\}$ is defined by

$$\{x\} = \{1, 1, 0, 1, 0, 1\} \ . \tag{11.1}$$
$$\uparrow$$

Position in the sequence is important, and an index of position, usually denoted by k or n (when appropriate), is employed. As we shall see, sequences will arise in our work from the sampling of continuous-time signals, and the positional index will relate to an underlying time measurement. This means that we must be able to locate the position 'zero' in the sequence. Usually this will be at the left-hand end, but if this is not the case, the ' ↑ ' symbol will be used as in (11.1).

Thus, we could write, to specify the sequence $\{x\}$ of (11.1),

$$\{x\} = \{x_{-2}, x_{-1}, x_0, x_1, x_2, x_3\} \ ,$$

where $x_{-2} = 0, x_{-1} = 1, x_0 = 0, x_1 = 1, x_2 = 0, x_3 = 1$.

Notice that the sequence

$$\{y\} = \{0, 1, 0, 1, 0, 1\} \tag{11.2}$$

is *not* the same sequence as (11.1). [In this case, since no ' ↑ ' is present, y_0 is the left-hand member of the sequence and $y_0 = 0, y_1 = 1, y_2 = 0$, etc.]

The second way of specifying the sequence, appropriate for finite or infinite sequences, is to define the general term of the sequence as a function of position. Thus if we write

$$\{x\} = \{x_k\}$$

and

$$x_k = \begin{cases} 0 & k < 0 \\ (\tfrac{1}{3})^k & k \geq 0 \end{cases}, \tag{11.3}$$

we generate the sequence

$$\{x\} = \{\ldots 0, 0, 1, \tfrac{1}{3}, \tfrac{1}{9}, \tfrac{1}{27}, \ldots\} \ ,$$
$$\uparrow$$

Example 11.1
What sequence $\{y\}$ is generated when

$$y_k = \begin{cases} 0 & k < 0 \\ \sin \dfrac{k\theta}{2} & k \geq 0 \ , \end{cases} \tag{11.4}$$

where θ is a constant?

At once, $\{y\} = \{y_k\}$

$$= \{\ldots 0, 0, 0, \sin \frac{\theta}{2}, \sin \theta, \sin \frac{3\theta}{2}, \ldots\} \ .$$

$\uparrow$

By analogy with the continuous-time situation, we define *causal sequences* as sequences which are zero for $k < 0$. The sequences (11.3) and (11.4) are thus causal sequences. We shall see later that it is convenient to consider finite sequences to be of infinite length, with additional zeros appended to each end. With this convention we conclude that (11.1) is not causal $(x_{-1} \neq 0)$ but (11.2) is a causal sequence.

In section 9.9, we examined the process of sampling a time signal $u(t)$ at intervals T. This operation generated the sequence $\{u_k\}$ with

$$u_k = u(kT) \qquad k = 0, 1, \ldots \quad .$$

It is natural to write such sequences using the notation $\{u(kT)\}$, since the kth term of the sequence is generated by evaluating $u(t)$ at time $t = kT$. We will make use of this notation extensively in Chapter 12.

We define two basic operations on sequences — addition and scaling — and these are summarized in the defining relationship

$$a\{x\} + b\{y\}$$
$$\equiv a\{x_k\} + b\{y_k\}$$
$$= \{ax_k + by_k\} \qquad \text{with } a, b \text{ (complex) constants} \ . \tag{11.5}$$

Example 11.2
If

$$\{x\} = \{x_k\} \ , \qquad x_k = \left(\frac{1}{2}\right)^k$$

$$\{y\} = \{y_k\} \qquad \text{where } y_k = \begin{cases} 0 & k < 0 \\ 1 & k \geq 0 \end{cases}$$

and

$$\{z\} = \{\alpha, \beta, \gamma\} \ ,$$

write down the sequences $a\{x\} + b\{y\}$, $\frac{1}{2}\{x\}$, $\frac{1}{4}\{y\}$ and $\{y\} + \{z\}$.

Now $a\{x\} + b\{y\} = \{ax_k + by_k\} = \{p_k\}$ say, where

$$p_k = \begin{cases} a(\frac{1}{2})^k & k < 0 \\ a(\frac{1}{2})^k + b & k \geq 0 \end{cases} .$$

Also

$$\frac{1}{2}\{x\} = \{\frac{1}{2}x_k\} = \left\{ \frac{1}{2} \cdot \frac{1}{2^k} \right\} = \left\{ \frac{1}{2^{k+1}} \right\} .$$

Similarly $\frac{1}{4}\{y\} = \{\frac{1}{4}y_k\} = \{q_k\}$ say, where

$$q_k = \begin{cases} 0 & k < 0 \\ \frac{1}{4} & k \geq 0 \end{cases} .$$

Finally, $\{y\} + \{z\} = \{y_k + z_k\}$

$$= \{\ldots 0, 0, 1 + \alpha, 1 + \beta, 1 + \gamma, 1, 1, \ldots\} .$$
$$\uparrow$$

It is not necessary to define the product of two sequences, although the convolution of two sequences $\{x\}*\{y\}$ will emerge as a vital concept. This will be explored when required.

11.3   THE Z-TRANSFORM

By now the reader will be familiar with the concept of a transform, and perhaps persuaded of their value. Without for the moment discussing the purpose of so doing we will define a transform for sequences. Given a sequence $\{x\} = \{x_k\}$ we define $\mathscr{X}(z)$, the Z-transform of $\{x\}$, as

$$Z\{x\} = \mathscr{X}(z) = \sum_{k=-\infty}^{\infty} \frac{x_k}{z^k} , \tag{11.6}$$

whenever the sum exists, with z a complex number, as yet undefined.

Recall that the operation of taking the Laplace transform involved the generation of a function $F(s)$ of the complex variable s from a time signal $f(t)$. Here, we are producing a function $\mathscr{X}(z)$ of another complex variable z, with the starting point the sequence $\{x\} = \{x_k\}$.

Example 11.3
Calculate the Z-transform of the sequence

$$\{x\} = \{\dots 0, 1, 1, 1, 0, 0, 1, 0, 0, 1, 1, 1, 0, 0, \dots\} .$$
$$\uparrow$$

Here we see that

$$x_k = \begin{cases} 0 & |k| > 5 \\ 1 & 3 \leqslant |k| \leqslant 5 \\ 0 & 0 < |k| < 3 \\ 1 & k = 0 , \end{cases}$$

and so $Z\{x\} = \displaystyle\sum_{k=-\infty}^{\infty} \frac{x_k}{z^k} = z^5 + z^4 + z^3 + 1 + \frac{1}{z^3} + \frac{1}{z^4} + \frac{1}{z^5}.$

$$= \mathcal{X}(z) .$$

This sum exists for all z, and we write

$$\mathcal{X}(z) = \frac{z^{10} + z^9 + z^8 + z^5 + z^2 + z + 1}{z^5}$$

as the Z-transform of the sequence $\{x\}$.

Notice that, for causal sequences, that is sequences $\{x_k\}$ for which $x_k = 0$, $k < 0$, then (11.6) reduces to

$$Z\{x\} = \mathcal{X}(z) = \sum_{k=0}^{\infty} \frac{x_k}{z^k} . \qquad (11.7)$$

Our concern will be mainly with causal sequences, and (11.7) will be the appropriate definition for most purposes. Non-causal sequences are, however, of importance in the field of image processing etc.

Example 11.4
Calculate the Z-transform of the causal sequence

$$\{x\} = \{(\tfrac{1}{2})^k\} , \qquad k \geqslant 0 .$$

(Here, causality is implied by writing $k \geqslant 0$; $x_k = 0$, $k < 0$ is understood.)
    From the definition,

$$Z\{x\} = \sum_{k=0}^{\infty} \frac{x_k}{z^k} = \sum_{k=0}^{\infty} \frac{1}{2^k z^k} \ .$$

This is a geometric series with common ratio $1/(2z)$ and first term 1. The sum to infinity is thus

$$\frac{1}{1 - \dfrac{1}{2z}}$$

provided that $|1/(2z)| < 1$, i.e. $|z| > \frac{1}{2}$.
    We then write

$$\mathscr{X}(z) = \frac{z}{z - \frac{1}{2}}, \qquad |z| > \tfrac{1}{2} ,$$

$$= \frac{2z}{2z - 1}$$

as the Z-transform of the sequence $\{x\} = \{(\frac{1}{2})^k\}$, and we observe that the transform exists only outside the circle $|z| = \frac{1}{2}$ in the complex plane.

    We can generalize this example to discover the Z-transform of the sequence $\{x\} = \{a^k\}$, $k \geqslant 0$, when a is a real or complex constant. From the definition, we have

$$Z\{x\} = \sum_{k=0}^{\infty} \frac{a^k}{z^k} = \frac{1}{1 - \dfrac{a}{z}} \qquad \text{whenever } |z| > |a| \ .$$

Thus

$$\mathscr{X}(z) = \frac{z}{z - a}, \qquad |z| > |a| , \tag{11.8}$$

which exists outside the circle $|z| = |a|$ in the complex plane. The reader may spot a similarity between (11.8) and $e^{at}\xi(t)$ and its Laplace transform, $1/(s - a)$.

Example 11.5
Write down the Z-transform of the sequence $\{x\} = \{(-\frac{1}{3})^k\}$.
    At once, since $Z\{a^k\} = z/(z - a)$, $|z| > |a|$, we see that

$$Z\{(-\tfrac{1}{3})^k\} = \frac{z}{z+\tfrac{1}{3}} = \frac{3z}{3z+1} , \qquad |z| > \tfrac{1}{3} .$$

A useful notation carries over from our work in Fourier transforms — the ↔ notation. We write

$$\{a^k\} \leftrightarrow \frac{z}{z-a} , \qquad |z| > |a| , \tag{11.9}$$

meaning that $z/(z-a)$ is the Z-transform of the sequence $\{a^k\}$. We now establish two more transforms based on the pair (11.9). First note that if

$$\{x_k\} \leftrightarrow \mathscr{X}(z) \qquad \text{is a transform pair,}$$

then

$$\{kx_k\} \leftrightarrow \sum_{k=0}^{\infty} \frac{kx_k}{z^k} ,$$

but

$$\sum_{k=0}^{\infty} \frac{k\,x_k}{z^k} = z \sum_{k=0}^{\infty} \frac{kx_k}{z^{k+1}} = z \sum_{k=0}^{\infty} x_k \frac{d}{dz}\left(-\frac{1}{z^k}\right)$$

$$= -z \frac{d}{dz} \sum_{k=0}^{\infty} \frac{x_k}{z^k} = -z \frac{d}{dz} \mathscr{X}(z) .$$

That is

$$\{kx_k\} \leftrightarrow -z \frac{d}{dz} \mathscr{X}(z) , \tag{11.10}$$

with convergence region (or region of existence) as for $\mathscr{X}(z)$.   At once, from (11.9) and (11.10) we see that

$$\{ka^k\} \leftrightarrow -z\frac{d}{dz}\left(\frac{z}{z-a}\right) = -z\left[\frac{(z-a)-z}{(z-a)^2}\right]$$

$$= \frac{az}{(z-a)^2} \qquad |z| > |a| \ .$$

Then on putting $a = 1$, we find that

$$\{k\} \leftrightarrow \frac{z}{(z-a)^2} \ . \tag{11.11}$$

We summarize our results so far obtained in Table 11.1. Somewhat surprisingly we will find that with one addition, the table will be adequate for most of our work. The one addition is the transform of the unit pulse sequence $\{x\} = \{1, 0, 0, \ldots\} = \{\delta_k\}$ where

Table 11.1 — Elementary Z-transforms.

Causal sequence $\{x\}$ generated by x_k, with $k \geq 0$, where		Z-transform $\mathcal{X}(x)$	Convergence region
$x_k = \begin{cases} 1 & k=0 \\ 0 & k \neq 0 \end{cases}$	Unit pulse	1	all z
$x_k = 1$	Unit step	$\dfrac{z}{z-1}$	$|z| > 1$
$x_k = a^k$		$\dfrac{z}{z-a}$	$|z| > |a|$
$x_k = ka^k$		$\dfrac{az}{(z-a)^2}$	$|z| > |a|$
$x_k = k$		$\dfrac{z}{(z-1)^2}$	$|z| > 1$
$x_k = \begin{cases} 0 & k=0 \\ a^{k-1} & k \geq 1 \end{cases}$		$\dfrac{1}{z-a}$	$|z| > |a|$

$$\delta_k = \begin{cases} 1 & k=0 \\ 0 & k \neq 0 \end{cases} .$$

From the definition, we see that

$$Z\{\delta_k\} = \sum_{k=0}^{\infty} \frac{\delta_k}{z^k} = 1 .$$

Readers will note that rather less effort is required to determine a sequence with unit Z-transform than was required in the case of the Laplace transform!

11.4   PROPERTIES OF THE Z-TRANSFORM

In order to apply Z-transform techniques to the analysis of discrete-time systems, we must establish a few basic properties. Our treatment will be formal in the sense that infinite series in the complex variable z will be manipulated without a full discussion of convergence implications. Readers wishing to pursue this topic more thoroughly should consult specialist texts on the theory of functions of a complex variable, for example Page [3].

The linearity property

In section 11.2 we defined addition and scalar multiplication (scaling) of sequences. Suppose that in some region R of the z-plane, the Z-transforms of two causal sequences $\{x\}$ and $\{y\}$ are known to exist. If the two sequences are combined to produce a new causal sequence $\{w\}$, where $w_k = ax_k + by_k$, and if

$$Z\{x\} = \mathcal{X}(x)$$

and

$$Z\{y\} = \mathcal{Y}(x) \quad \text{in } R ,$$

then also in R,

$$Z\{w\} = \mathcal{W}(z) = a\mathcal{X}(x) + b\mathcal{Y}(z) . \tag{11.12}$$

To establish this result, consider

$$\mathcal{W}(z) = \sum_{k=0}^{\infty} \frac{w_k}{z^k} = \sum_{k=0}^{\infty} \frac{(ax_k + by_k)}{z^k}$$

$$= \sum_{k=0}^{\infty} \frac{ax_k}{z^k} + \sum_{k=0}^{\infty} \frac{by_k}{z^k}$$

$$= a \sum_{k=0}^{\infty} \frac{x_k}{z^k} + b \sum_{k=0}^{\infty} \frac{y_k}{z^k}$$

$$= a\mathscr{X}(z) + b\mathscr{Y}(z), \text{ as required.}$$

Note that with $b = 0$ we have also established that

$$Z\{ax_k\} = aZ\{x_k\} = a\mathscr{X}(x) \ . \tag{11.13}$$

Example 11.6
Calculate the z-transform of the sequence

$$\{x\} = \left\{ 2 \cdot \left(\frac{1}{3^k} \right) \right\} \ .$$

At once, from (11.13),

$$\mathscr{X}(z) = 2Z \left\{ \frac{1}{3^k} \right\}$$

$$= 2 \frac{z}{z - \frac{1}{3}} = \frac{6z}{3z - 1} \qquad |z| > \tfrac{1}{3} \ .$$

Example 11.7
Find the Z-transform of the sequence $\{w\} = \{\sin k\theta\}$.
    Here, write $\sin k\theta = (e^{ik\theta} - e^{-ik\theta})/(2i)$, and we see that

$$Z\{\sin k\theta\} = Z \left\{ \frac{1}{2i} (e^{ki\theta} - e^{-ki\theta}) \right\}$$

$$= \frac{1}{2i} Z\{(e^{i\theta})^k\} - \frac{1}{2i} Z\{(e^{-i\theta})^k\} \ , \qquad \text{using (11.12)}$$

$$= \frac{1}{2i} \frac{z}{z - e^{i\theta}} - \frac{1}{2i} \frac{z}{z - e^{-i\theta}}$$

$$= \frac{1}{2i} \left[\frac{z(e^{i\theta} - e^{-i\theta})}{z^2 - z(e^{i\theta} + e^{-i\theta}) + 1} \right]$$

$$= \frac{z \sin \theta}{z^2 - 2z \cos \theta + 1} . \tag{11.14}$$

The first shifting property (delaying)

Suppose two causal sequences $\{x\}$ and $\{y\}$ have Z-transforms $\mathscr{X}(z)$ and $\mathscr{Y}(z)$ in a region R of the z-plane. Suppose also that the general terms of each sequence are related by

$$y_k = x_{k - k_0} .$$

Clearly the sequence $\{y\}$ is just the sequence $\{x\}$ *delayed* by k_0 'steps'. For example, if $y_k = x_{k-2}$, and

$$\{x\} = \{0, \sin\theta, \sin 2\theta, \sin 3\theta, \sin 4\theta, \ldots\} ,$$

then

$$\{y\} = \{y_0, y_1, y_2, \ldots\} = \{x_{-2}, x_{-1}, x_0, x_1, \ldots\}$$
$$= \{0, 0, 0, \sin \theta, \sin 2\theta, \sin 3\theta, \ldots\}, \text{ because } \{x\} \text{ is causal.}$$

We now calculate the Z-transform of the sequence $\{y\}$ in the general case. At once we have that

$$\mathscr{Y}(z) = Z\{y\} = \sum_{k=0}^{\infty} \frac{y_k}{z^k} = \sum_{k=0}^{\infty} \frac{x_{k-k_0}}{z^k} = \frac{1}{z^{k_0}} \sum_{k=0}^{\infty} \frac{x_{k-k_0}}{z^{k-k_0}}$$

$$= \frac{1}{z^{k_0}} \sum_{j=-k_0}^{\infty} \frac{x_j}{z^j} = \frac{1}{z^{k_0}} \sum_{j=0}^{\infty} \frac{x_j}{z^j}$$

because $\{x\}$ is causal. Thus

$$\mathcal{Y}(z) = \frac{1}{z^{k_0}} \mathcal{X}(z) , \qquad \text{also in } R \ . \tag{11.15}$$

Example 11.8
Calculate the transform of the sequence

$$\{y\} = \{0, 0, 0, \sin \theta, \sin 2\theta, \sin 3\theta \ldots\} \ .$$

We know that the sequence $\{y\}$ is just the sequence

$$\{x\} = \{0, \sin \theta, \sin 2\theta, \sin 3\theta, \ldots\}$$

delayed by two steps. Thus, using (11.15), with $k_0 = 2$, and (11.14), we see that

$$\mathcal{Y}(z) = \frac{1}{z^2} Z\{\sin k\theta\}$$

$$= \frac{1}{z^2} \frac{z \sin \theta}{z^2 - 2z \cos \theta + 1}$$

$$= \frac{\sin \theta}{z(z^2 - 2z \cos \theta + 1)} \ .$$

The second shifting property (advancing)
Now the shift is to be in the opposite direction. With the same notation as for
equation (11.13), the sequence $\{y\}$ is now generated by

$$y_k = x_{k+k_0} \ .$$

By definition

$$\mathcal{Y}(z) = Z\{y_k\} = \sum_{k=0}^{\infty} \frac{x_{k+k_0}}{z^k}$$

$$= z^{k_0} \sum_{k=0}^{\infty} \frac{x_{k+k_0}}{z^{k+k_0}}$$

$$= z^{k_0} \sum_{j=k_0}^{\infty} \frac{x_j}{z^j}$$

$$= z^{k_0} \left[\sum_{j=0}^{\infty} \frac{x_j}{x^j} - \sum_{j=0}^{k_0-1} \frac{x_j}{z^j} \right]$$

$$= z^{k_0} \mathcal{X}(z) - z^{k_0} \sum_{j=0}^{k_0-1} \frac{x_j}{z^j}, \qquad \text{in } R . \tag{11.16}$$

In particular, if $k_0 = 1$

$$\mathcal{Y}(z) = Z\{x_{k+1}\} = z\mathcal{X}(z) - zx_0 \tag{11.17}$$

and if $k_0 = 2$

$$\mathcal{Y}(z) = Z\{x_{k+2}\} = z^2\mathcal{X}(z) - z^2 \left[x_0 + \frac{x_1}{z} \right]$$

$$= z^2\mathcal{X}(z) - z^2 x_0 - zx_1 . \tag{11.18}$$

The reader may be struck by the structural similarity of (11.17) and (11.18) to the results for the transforms of first and second derivatives in the Laplace transform domain. Notice, however, that the similarity is not total in view of the powers of z beyond the first term of the right-hand side in each case.

Finally in this section, we note that we established one additional transform property in section 11.3. This was the 'multiplication by k' property, (11.10). The properties discussed above are collected in Table 11.2.

11.5 DISCRETE-TIME SYSTEMS AND DIFFERENCE EQUATIONS

We can understand the motivation for studying the Z-transform by discussing the idea of a linear, time invariant, causal discrete-time system. We shall see that such systems are naturally described by linear, constant coefficient difference equations, which can be viewed as the discrete-time 'analogue' of differential equations. The Z-transform will emerge as a major technique in the analysis and synthesis of such

Table 11.2 — Z-transform properties.

Property

Linearity: (1) $Z\{a\{x_k\}\} = Z\{ax_k\} = a\mathcal{X}(z)$

: (2) $Z\{a\{x_k\} + b\{y_k\}\} = a\mathcal{X}(z) + b\mathcal{Y}(z)$

First shift: $Z\{x_{k-k_0}\} = \dfrac{1}{z^{k_0}} \mathcal{X}(z)$

Second shift: $Z\{x_{k+k_0}\} = z^{k_0}\mathcal{X}(z) - z^{k_0} \displaystyle\sum_{k=0}^{k_0-1} \dfrac{x_k}{z^k}$

Multiplication by k: $Z\{kx_k\} = -z \dfrac{d}{dz} \mathcal{X}(z)$

---

systems, complementing exactly the role of the Laplace transform for continuous-time systems.

To harden our ideas, consider the discrete-time system of Fig. 11.1. The

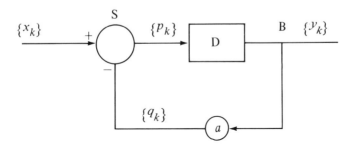

Fig. 11.1 — A discrete-time system.

'dynamics' of this system are contained in the block labelled D, a unit delay block. It is supposed that the system is regulated by a clock issuing pulses at (equal) intervals. At the instant of the kth pulse, the following events occur.

At the left-hand (or input) side, the kth member of the input signal sequence $\{x_k\}$ arrives at S, a summing point. Instantaneously it is combined with the kth member of the feedback signal sequence $\{q_k\}$ to form the kth term of the signal sequence $\{p_k\}$. This signal makes no further progress at this time. The function of the delay block D is to hold the incoming signal p_k on its left-hand (input) side unaltered and un-corrupted by the next arrival until the next clock pulse, that is, pulse $k + 1$. At this instant, perfect transmission takes place and the signal p_k emerges on the right as y_{k+1}, the $(k+1)$th term of the output sequence. At the branch point B, simultaneous splitting occurs and an exact copy of y_{k+1} is fed back and scaled to become the $(k+1)$th term of the feedback sequence $\{q_k\}$. This feedback signal is then combined at S with x_{k+1} to generate p_{k+1}, as before. The essence of this somewhat complicated description can be reduced to a simple rule for the operation of delay blocks, as follows:

'The output of a delay block at step (or pulse) $k+1$ is the signal on the input side at step (or pulse) k'.

All other signal flows are instantaneous.

To examine the system of Fig. 11.1, write, using the rule above,

$$y_{k+1} = p_k \ . \tag{11.19}$$

Then from the summing point at step k

$$p_k = x_k - q_k \tag{11.20}$$

but

$$q_k = a y_k \ . \tag{11.21}$$

Our aim is to obtain an input–output relationship, meaning that we must eliminate the internal signal sequences $\{p_k\}$ and $\{q_k\}$.

Using (11.19) and (11.20), we have

$$y_{k+1} = x_k - q_k$$

and using (11.53), we obtain

$$y_{k+1} = x_k - a y_k \ .$$

In other words,

$$y_{k+1} + a y_k = x_k \ . \tag{11.22}$$

Equation (11.22) relates the kth term of the output sequence $\{y_k\}$, together with the $(k+1)$st term, to the kth term of the input sequence $\{x_k\}$, as required. This type of equation is known as a difference equation, largely for historical reasons, and its solution is the sequence $\{y_k\}$.

Structurally, we can observe the similarity with a first-order differential equation, with shifting in place of differentiation.

Example 11.9
Obtain a difference equation which represents the system shown in Fig. 11.2.

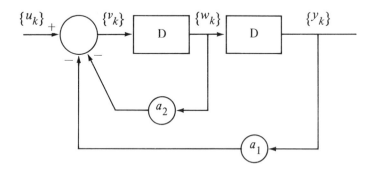

Fig. 11.2 — Discrete-time system for Example 11.9.

Working from the right, introducing internal signal sequences

$\{v_k\}$ and $\{w_k\}$

as shown, we have (using the rule for delay blocks)

$$y_{k+1} = w_k \tag{11.23}$$

$$w_{k+1} = v_k \ . \tag{11.24}$$

For the summing point we see that

$$v_k = u_k - a_1 y_k - a_2 w_k \ . \tag{11.25}$$

To obtain an input–output relationship, notice that (11.23) implies that

$$y_{k+2} = w_{k+1}$$

$$= v_k \qquad\qquad \text{from (11.24)}$$

$$= u_k - a_1 y_k - a_2 w_k \qquad\qquad \text{from (11.25)}$$

$$= u_k - a_1 \, y_k - a_2 \, y_{k+1} \qquad\qquad \text{using (11.23)}$$

That is

$$y_{k+2} + a_2 \, y_{k+1} + a_1 \, y_k = u_k \; . \qquad\qquad (11.26)$$

The final result for Example 11.9, equation (11.26) is a second-order difference equation. The order of difference equation in the form (11.26) is measured by the highest degree of shift of the solution sequence $\{y_k\}$ appearing in the equation. In this case, the highest degree of shift is 2 in view of the presence in the term in y_{k+2}. Thus the order is 2, whereas the order (11.22) is 1. We note that there is a relationship between the number of delay blocks needed to 'realize' the system, that is, to obtain a physically implementable block diagram. However, it is possible to realize the system using more than the minimum number of blocks. The reader is invited to show that the system of Fig. 11.3 has the same difference equation representation

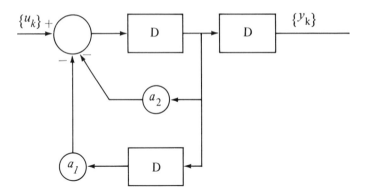

Fig. 11.3 — Non-minimal realization of the system of Example 11.9.

(11.26) as that of Fig. 11.2. The system of Fig. 11.3 is thus a second-order system, despite the use of three delay blocks in this realization.

The analysis of discrete-time systems in the time domain requires the solution of difference equations of the type discussed above. The Z-transform provides a simple, easy-to-apply method, which also serves as a tool for system design. To illustrate the technique we will apply the method to a specific case of (11.26), with $a_1 = 1/8$ and $a_2 = 3/4$, and when the input $\{u_k\}$ is the step sequence $\{1, 1, 1, \ldots\}$. Thus we have to solve

$$y_{k+2} + \tfrac{3}{4} \, y_{k+1} + \tfrac{1}{8} \, y_k = u_k \, , \qquad k \geqslant 0 \, , \qquad\qquad (11.27)$$

for the generating formula y_k of the output sequence $\{y_k\}$.

Now (11.27) defines a relationship between each corresponding term of two sequences. On the left we have

$$\{y_{k+2} + \tfrac{3}{4} y_{k+1} + \tfrac{1}{8} y_k\} \ ,$$

which is a sequence $\{p_k\}$, say with general term

$$p_k = y_{k+2} + \tfrac{3}{4} y_{k+1} + \tfrac{1}{8} y_k \ .$$

On the right, we have a sequence $\{u_k\}$, and (11.27) is simply a statement that these two sequences are equivalent, that is

$$\{y_{k+2} + \tfrac{3}{4} y_{k+1} + \tfrac{1}{8} y_k\} = \{u_k\} \ . \tag{11.28}$$

Taking the Z-transform for both sides of (11.28) we obtain

$$Z\{y_{k+2} + \tfrac{3}{4} y_{k+1} + \tfrac{1}{8} y_k\} = Z\{u_k\} \ . \tag{11.29}$$

Using the linearity property section 11.4, we can write (11.29) as

$$Z\{y_{k+2}\} + \tfrac{3}{4} Z\{y_{k+1}\} + \tfrac{1}{8} Z\{y_k = Z\{u_k\} \ . \tag{11.30}$$

Now define $Z\{y_k\} = \mathcal{Y}(z)$, the Z-transform of the output sequence, and use of the second shifting of section 11.4 shows that

$$Z\{y_{k+1}\} = z\mathcal{Y}(z) - zy_0 \tag{11.31}$$

and

$$Z\{y_{k+2}\} = z^2 \, \mathcal{Y}(z) - z^2 y_0 - zy_1 \ . \tag{11.32}$$

We see that, in order to write down these two terms in their entirety, a knowledge of the first two terms of the output sequence is required. This is obviously the analogue of the 'initial condition' requirement when transforming differential equations used to model continuous-time systems. The analogy goes further because it is easy to see from Fig. 11.2 that the value of y_0 must be stored on the second delay element prior to its emergence at the output at $k = 0$. Similarly the value of y_1 must have been stored on the first delay element, proceeding to the second delay at $k = 0$, and then onward at $k = 1$ to become y_1 in the output sequence. The input, which commences at $k = 0$, cannot influence these values, and so they are a true analogue of the continuous-time initial condition, conveying information on the initialization of the system prior to the application of the input.

If the system is quiescent initially, meaning that the value zero is stored in each element, then we have

$$y_0 = y_1 = 0$$

and (11.31) and (11.32) become

$$Z\{y_{k+1}\} = z\mathcal{Y}(z)$$

and

$$Z\{y_{k+2}\} = z^2\mathcal{Y}(z) \text{ respectively.}$$

Then (11.30) becomes

$$z^2\mathcal{Y}(z) + \tfrac{3}{4} z \; \mathcal{Y}(z) + \tfrac{1}{8} \; \mathcal{Y}(z) = Z\{u_k\}$$
$$= \mathcal{U}(z) \text{ say,}$$

where $\mathcal{U}(z)$ is the transform of the input sequences $\{u_k\}$. Thus

$$(z^2 + \tfrac{3}{4} z + \tfrac{1}{8}) \; \mathcal{Y}(z) = \mathcal{U}(z)$$

or

$$\mathcal{Y}(z) = \frac{1}{z^2 + \tfrac{3}{4} z + \tfrac{1}{8}} \; \mathcal{U}(z) \; . \tag{11.33}$$

With

$$\{u_k\} = \{1, \, 1, \, 1, \, \ldots\} \, ,$$

$$\mathcal{U}(z) = \frac{z}{z - 1} \, ,$$

and so

$$\mathcal{Y}(z) = \frac{1}{z^2 + \frac{3}{4}z + \frac{1}{8}}\frac{z}{z - 1}$$

$$= \frac{z}{(z + \frac{1}{2})(z + \frac{1}{4})(z - 1)} \ . \tag{11.34}$$

Determination of the sequence $\{y_k\}$ means the inversion of (11.34). The techniques for the inversion of the Laplace transform carry over to the inversion problem for Z-transforms, with one significant modification. This is in view of the factor z in the numerator of (most) transforms in Table 11.1. For this reason we write (11.34) as

$$\frac{\mathcal{Y}(z)}{z} = \frac{1}{(z + \frac{1}{2})(z + \frac{1}{4})(z - 1)}$$

$$= \frac{\frac{8}{3}}{z + \frac{1}{2}} - \frac{\frac{16}{5}}{z + \frac{1}{4}} + \frac{\frac{8}{15}}{z - 1} \ .$$

Thus

$$\mathcal{Y}(z) = \frac{8}{3}\frac{z}{z + \frac{1}{2}} - \frac{16}{5}\frac{z}{z + \frac{1}{4}} + \frac{8}{15}\frac{z}{z - 1}$$

and from Table 11.1 we obtain

$$\{y_k\} = \left\{\frac{8}{3}\left(-\frac{1}{2}\right)^k - \frac{16}{5}\left(-\frac{1}{4}\right)^k + \frac{8}{15}\right\} \ .$$

This response is depicted in Fig. 11.4. This calculation demonstrates the main steps in the analysis of discrete-time systems by transform methods. We demonstrate the technique by considering a further example.

Example 11.10
Find the response of the system

$$y_{k+2} + 2y_{k+1} + 2y_k = u_k + u_{k+1}$$

to the input $\{u_k\} = \{(\frac{1}{2})^k\}$ $k \geqslant 0$. The system is quiescent initially. Finally draw a block diagram representing the system in the z-domain.

Taking transforms, with $Z\{y_k\} = \mathcal{Y}(z)$ and $Z\{u_k\} = \mathcal{U}(z)$, we find that

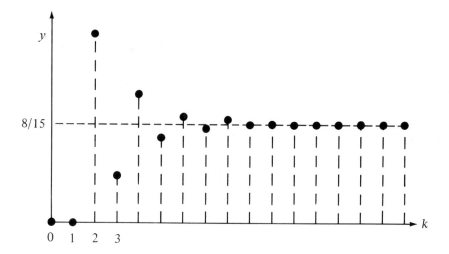

Fig. 11.4 — Step response the system (11.27).

$$\mathcal{Y}(z) = \frac{1+z}{z^2 + 2z + 2}\,\mathcal{U}(z) \ .$$

Since

$$\mathcal{U}(z) = Z\left\{\left(\frac{1}{2}\right)^k\right\} = \frac{z}{z - \frac{1}{2}}$$

$$\mathcal{Y}(z) = \frac{z(1+z)}{(z^2 + 2z + 2)(z - \frac{1}{2})}\ ,$$

that is

$$\frac{\mathcal{Y}(z)}{z} = \frac{z+1}{(z^2 + 2z + 2)(z - \frac{1}{2})} = \frac{z+1}{(z + 1 - i)(z + 1 + i)(z - \frac{1}{2})}\ .$$

We now express $\mathcal{Y}(z)/z$ in partial fraction form, so that

$$\frac{\mathcal{Y}(z)}{z} = \frac{1}{13}\left[\frac{-3 - 2i}{z + 1 - i} + \frac{(-3 + 2i)}{z + 1 + i} + \frac{6}{z - \frac{1}{2}}\right]\ ,$$

and so

$$\mathcal{Y}(z) = \frac{1}{13}\left[(-3-2i)\,\frac{z}{z+1-i} + (-3+2i)\,\frac{z}{z+1-i} + 6\,\frac{z}{z-\frac{1}{2}}\right].$$

Now

$$z+1-i = z + \sqrt{2}e^{-i\pi/4} = z - \sqrt{2}e^{3i\pi/4}$$
$$z+1+i = z + \sqrt{2}e^{i\pi/4} = z - \sqrt{2}e^{-3i\pi/4}$$

thus

$$\mathcal{Y}(z) = \frac{1}{13}\left[(-3-2i)\,\frac{z}{z+\sqrt{2}e^{3i\pi/4}} + (-3+2i)\,\frac{z}{z+\sqrt{2}e^{-3i\pi/4}} + \frac{6z}{z-\frac{1}{2}}\right].$$
$$(11.35)$$

It is now possible to invert (11.35) using Table 11.1, to obtain

$$y_k = \frac{1}{13}\left[(-3-2i)\,(\sqrt{2}\,e^{3i\pi/4})^k + (-3+2i)(\sqrt{2}\,e^{-3i\pi/4})^k + 6(\tfrac{1}{2})^k\right]$$

$$= \frac{1}{13}\left[(-3-2i)\,(\sqrt{2})^k e^{3ik\pi/4} + (-3+2i)(\sqrt{2})^k e^{-3ik\pi/4} + 6(\tfrac{1}{2})^k\right]$$

$$= \frac{1}{13}\,(\sqrt{2})^k\,2\,\mathcal{R}(-3-2i)\,e^{3ki\pi/4} + \frac{6}{13}\left(\frac{1}{2}\right)^k.$$

Here, $\mathcal{R}\,(-3-2i)\,e^{3ki\pi/4}$ 'denotes the real part of' $(-3-2i)\,e^{3ki\pi/4} = \mathcal{R}(-3-2i)$ $(\cos 3k\pi/4 + i \sin 3k\pi/4)$, from which we see that

$$\mathcal{R}(-3-2i)\,e^{3ki\pi/4} = -3\cos k\pi/4 + 2\sin 3k\pi/4 .$$

Hence

$$\{y_k\} = \left\{\frac{2}{13}\,(\sqrt{2})^k\,(-3\,\cos 3k\pi/4 + 2\,\sin 3k\pi/4) + \frac{6}{13}\left(\frac{1}{2}\right)^k\right\}. \qquad (11.36)$$

To draw a block diagram, noting that

$$\mathcal{Y}(z) = \frac{z+1}{z^2 + 2z + 2}\, \mathcal{U}(z)\ ,\qquad (11.37)$$

we adopt the following device. Write (11.37) as

$$(z^2 + 2z + 2)\, \mathcal{Y}(Z) = (z+1)\, \mathcal{U}(z)$$

and suppose that the signal sequence $\{p_k\}$, with Z-transform $\mathcal{P}(z)$, is such that

$$(z^2 + 2z + 2)\, \mathcal{P}(z) = \mathcal{U}(z)\ . \qquad (11.38)$$

It is easy to represent the system in the z-domain described by (11.38) as in Fig. 11.5.

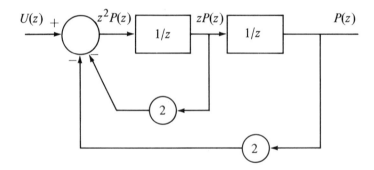

Fig. 11.5 — z-domain block diagram for (11.38).

Notice that in the transform domain, $D \leftrightarrow 1/z$. (This is as discussed in section 7.8 for continuous-time systems.) Suppose we now multiply (11.38) by $z + 1$, then

$$(z+1)(z^2 + 2z + 2)\, \mathcal{P}(z) = (z+1)\, \mathcal{U}(z)$$

or

$$(z^2 + 2z + 2)\, [(z+1)\, \mathcal{P}(z)] = (z+1)\, \mathcal{U}(z)\ . \qquad (11.39)$$

From (11.39), we see that setting

$$\mathcal{Y}(z) = (z+1)\, \mathcal{P}(z) = z\mathcal{P}(z) + \mathcal{P}(z) \qquad (11.40)$$

will produce the output $\mathcal{Y}(z)$ we require. Thus the system of Fig. 11.6, in which the signal transform $\mathcal{Y}(z)$ is constructed from Fig. 11.5 using the prescription (11.40), is our required block diagram.

At this point, our readership will divide into two groups: those who check the result for system output in the example above, and those who don't! We are compelled to point out that from (11.36), with $k=0$, we find that $y_0 = 0$, but with $k = 1$, $y_1 = 1$. There is an apparent contradiction here with the assumptions made in transforming from time domain to z-domain, that is in transforming from

$$y_{k+2} + 2y_{k+1} + 2y_k = u_k + u_{k+1} \tag{11.41}$$

to

$$z^2 \mathcal{Y}(z) + 2z \mathcal{Y}(z) + 2\mathcal{Y}(z) = \mathcal{U}(z) + z \mathcal{U}(z) \ . \tag{11.42}$$

Examination of the block diagram of Fig. 11.7, the time domain version of Fig. 11.6, with input sequence $\{u_k\} = \{\frac{1}{2}^k\}$, confirms that $y_0 = 0$ and $y_1 = 1$ and we must resolve this conflict.

Readers may also worry about the second discrepancy associated with the input transform, the apparent assumption of a zero initial value for the input sequence in the determination of $Z\{u_{k+1}\}$. However, both problems may be removed by further investigation along the following lines. The representation (11.41) is somewhat unsatisfactory in that the right-hand side contains terms in the current input (u_k) and the future input (u_{k+1}). If we set $j = k + 1$ in (11.41) we obtain

$$y_{j+1} + 2y_j + 2y_{j-1} = u_j + u_{j-1} \ . \tag{11.43}$$

By re-indexing time (or position in the sequence) in this way we have a more satisfactory form, with the right-hand side now consisting of current input (u_j) and a past input (u_{j-1}). Using (11.43) to chart the evolution of the system in the time domain we see that to obtain y_0 we must set $j = -1$, and

$$y_0 = -2y_{-1} - 2y_{-2} + u_{-1} + u_{-2} \ .$$

Similarly with $j = 0$,

$$y_1 = -2y_0 - 2y_{-1} + u_0 + u_{-1} \tag{11.44}$$

and with $j = 1$

$$y_2 = -2y_1 - 2y_0 + u_1 + u_0 \ .$$

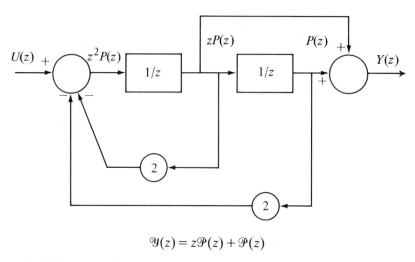

$$\mathcal{Y}(z) = z\mathcal{P}(z) + \mathcal{P}(z)$$

Fig. 11.6 — z-transform domain block diagram for the system of Example 11.10.

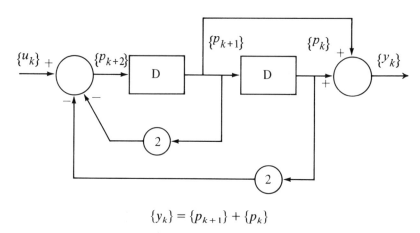

$$\{y_k\} = \{p_{k+1}\} + \{p_k\}$$

Fig. 11.7 — Time domain version of Fig. 11.6.

From the casuality of $\{u_k\}$, meaning that $u_k = 0$, $k < 0$, we see that

$$y_0 = -2y_{-1} - 2y_{-2}$$
$$y_1 = -2y_0 - 2y_{-1} + u_0 \qquad\qquad (11.45)$$
$$y_2 = -2y_1 - 2y_0 + u_1 + u_0 \ .$$

Inspection of (11.45) shows that whilst we are free to specify y_0 as zero as a consequence of the assumed initial quiescence of the system, we cannot infer that y_1

is also zero. This is because the value of y_1 depends on the first input u_0 and so it is not under our control through the initialization process. In fact the latest two conditions we may specify are y_{-1} and y_0, and we must use these two conditions to convey information on the initial quiescence of our second-order system. For a higher-order system, we would have to progress further to the left of $k = 0$.

In order to incorporate the quiescent conditions we return to the basic definition (11.6) of the Z-transform. At that point we argued that for causal sequences

$$Z\{x\} = \sum_{-\infty}^{\infty} \frac{x_k}{z^k} = \sum_{0}^{\infty} \frac{x_k}{z^k}$$

to produce the 'unilateral form' (11.7). In view of our need for the transform to be 'aware' of conditions at $k = -1$, let us define the 'sufficiently aware' transform

$$Z'\{y\} = \sum_{-1}^{\infty} \frac{y_k}{z^k} \tag{11.46}$$

for this problem. It is easy to check that for causal sequences $\{z\}$, $Z'\{x\} = Z\{x\}$, but notice that

$$Z'\{y_{k+1}\} = \sum_{k=-1}^{\infty} \frac{y_{k+1}}{z^k}$$

$$= z \sum_{k=-1}^{\infty} \frac{y_{k+1}}{z^{k+1}} = z \sum_{0}^{\infty} \frac{y_j}{z^j}$$

$$= z \left\{ \sum_{j=-1}^{\infty} \frac{y_j}{z^j} - \frac{y_{-1}}{z^{-1}} \right\}$$

$$= z\, Z'\{y_k\} - z^2\, y_{-1} \tag{11.47}$$

whilst

$$Z'\{y_{k+2}\} = z^2\, Z'\{y_k\} - z^3\, y_{-1} - z^2\, y_0 . \tag{11.48}$$

Use of the transform (11.46) with (11.47) and (11.48) on (11.41) then produces (11.42) under the assumptions of a quiescent initial state (that is $y_{-1} = y_0 = 0$) and of a causal input sequence $\{u_k\}$, so that $u_{-1} = 0$. The rest of the analysis, including inversion, is unchanged, and the point of the discussion is that, provided quiescent initial conditions are properly understood, a 'sufficiently aware transform' may be assumed when transforming *without formality*. If this view is taken, then no real thought is required, and the reader may be assured that there is no problem with initial quiescent conditions.

11.6 THE Z-TRANSFER FUNCTION

In section 7.9 we introduced the concept of a system Laplace transfer function for continuous-time systems. This idea led us to an understanding of system stability, and hence to a frequency domain characterization of systems using the frequency response. Drawing on this experience we wish to develop the corresponding theory for discrete-time systems.

The examples we have considered so far indicated that linear, time invariant systems are modelled by constant coefficient difference equations of the form

$$y_{k+n} + a_1 y_{k+n-1} + a_2 y_{k+n-2} \cdots a_n y_k$$
$$= b_0 u_{k+m} + b_1 u_{k+m-1} \ldots + b_m u_k , \tag{11.49}$$

where $k \geq 0$ and n, m are positive integers with $n \geq m$.

The order of the difference equation is n, and we note that difference equations of the form

$$y_{k+n} + a_1 y_{k+n-1} + a_2 y_{k+n-2} \cdots + a_n y_k$$
$$= c_m u_{k-m} + c_{m-1} u_{k-m+1} \cdots + c_0 u_k , \tag{11.50}$$

n, m positive integers with $n \geq m$ can be written in the form (11.49) by the substitution

$$k - m = j .$$

The order of (11.50) is then $n + m$ if $c_m \neq 0$.

Difference equations of the form (11.49) are linear with constant coefficients and can be used to model linear, time invariant systems. We may write (11.49) as

$$L_1\{y_k\} = L_2\{u_k\}$$

where now L_1 and L_2 are linear shift operations, with

$$L_1 \equiv [S_n + a_1 S_{n-1} + \ldots a_n]$$
$$L_2 \equiv [b_0 S_m + b_1 S_{m-1} + \ldots b_m] .$$

Here S is the shift operator, such that

$$S_n\{y_k\} = \{y_{k+n}\} \text{ etc.}$$

We do not wish to explore this further here, save to remark that the arguments of section 7.4 translate easily to the discrete-time domain. In particular, it is easily shown that the principle of linear superposition of zero-state responses applies also to discrete-time systems.

Taking the Z-transform throughout (11.49), with an initially quiescent system, leads to

$$(z^n + a_1 z^{n-1} + a_2 z^{n-2} \ldots a_n) \, \mathcal{Y}(z) = (b_0 z^m + b_1 z^{m-1} + \ldots b_m) \, \mathcal{U}(z)$$

or

$$\frac{\mathcal{Y}(z)}{\mathcal{U}(z)} = \mathcal{D}(z) = \frac{b_0 z^m + b_1 z^{m-1} \ldots + b_m}{z^n + a_1 z^{n-1} + \ldots + a_n} \; . \tag{11.51}$$

$\mathcal{D}(z)$ is then the Z-transfer function of the system (11.49).

Example 11.11
Find the Z-transfer functions of the systems

(1) $y_{k+3} + 2y_{k+2} + y_{k+1} = u_k + u_{k+1}$

(2) $y_{k+1} - y_k = u_{k-2} + u_{k-1} - 2u_k \; .$

(1) At once, with a quiescent system, we have

$$(z^3 + 2z^2 + z) \, \mathcal{Y}(z) = (1 + z) \, \mathcal{U}(z)$$

so $\mathcal{D}(z) = (1 + z)/(z^3 + 2z^2 + z)$.
(2) Putting $k - 2 = j$, we see that

$$y_{j+3} - y_{j+2} = u_j + u_{j+1} - 2u_{j+2} \; .$$

Then taking the Z-transform we have

$$(z^3 - z^2) \, \mathcal{Y}(z) = (1 - z - 2z^2) \, \mathcal{U}(z) \; ;$$

thus

$$\mathcal{U}(z) = \frac{1 + z - 2z^2}{z^3 - z^2} = \frac{1 + z - 2z^2}{z^2(z - 1)} \quad .$$

The same result is obtained by transforming without obtaining the standard from (11.49). Transforming

$$y_{k+1} - y_k = u_{k-2} + u_{k-1} - 2u_k$$

we obtain

$$(z - 1)\mathcal{Y}(z) = \left(\frac{1}{z^2} + \frac{1}{z} - 2\right) \mathcal{U}(z) \quad .$$

This means that

$$\mathcal{D}(z) = \frac{\dfrac{1}{z^2} + \dfrac{1}{z} - 2}{z - 1}$$

$$= \frac{1 + z - 2z^2}{z^2(z - 1)} \quad , \qquad \text{as before.}$$

From Table 11.1 we know that the unit pulse sequence

$$\{\delta_k\} = \{1, 0, 0, \ldots\}$$

has Z-transform

$$Z\{\delta_k\} = 1 \quad .$$

It follows at once from (11.51) and $\mathcal{Y}_\delta(z)$, the Z-transform of the pulse response, is given by

$$\mathcal{Y}_\delta(z) = \mathcal{D}(z) \ Z\{\delta_k\} = \mathcal{D}(z) \quad . \tag{11.52}$$

Often this response is called the impulse response, in line with the terminology of

continuous-time systems. We will sometimes write (im)pulse response, in recognition of this convention. In the time domain this response is $\{y_{\delta_k}\}$, and

$$\{y_{\delta_k}\} = Z^{-1}\{\mathcal{D}(z)\} \ ,$$

the inverse Z-transform of the transfer function.

Example 11.12
Find the impulse response of the system with transfer function

$$\mathcal{D}(z) = \frac{z+1}{z^2 + 0.75z + 0.125} \ .$$

We see that

$$\mathcal{D}(z) = \frac{z+1}{(z+0.5)(z+0.25)}$$

$$= \frac{-2}{z+0.5} + \frac{3}{z+0.25}$$

$$= \mathcal{Y}_\delta(z) \ .$$

Thus

$$\{y_{\delta_k}\} = Z^{-1}\left\{\frac{3}{z+0.25} - \frac{2}{z+0.5}\right\} \ ,$$

so

$$y_{\delta_k} = \begin{bmatrix} 0 & k=0 \\ 3(-0.25)^{k-1} - 2(-0.5)^{k-1} & k \geq 1 \end{bmatrix}$$

from Table 11.1.

Arguing as in the continuous-time case, we characterize discrete-time system
stability in terms of the long-term behaviour of the impulse response of the system.
The development is exactly parallel to that of section 8.2, with attention now on the
Z-transfer function $\mathcal{D}(z)$.
    Define $g(z) = z^n + a_1 z^{n-1} + \ldots + a_n$, the denominator of $\mathcal{D}(z)$, as the character-
istic polynomial of the system. Then

$$g(z) = \prod_{i=1}^{n} (z - \lambda_i)$$

where λ_i, $i = 1, 2, \ldots n$, are the roots of

$$g(z) = 0 \ ,$$

and are again called the poles of the system. Note that the λ_i will be real or will occur in complex conjugate pairs. This means that, provided $n > m$ and $\lambda_i \neq \lambda_j$, $i \neq j$, that is, if the degree of the denominator of $\mathcal{D}(z)$ is greater than that of the numerator, and the roots of $g(z)$ are distinct, then

$$\mathcal{D}(z) = \sum_{j=1}^{n} \frac{\alpha_j}{z - \lambda_j} \ . \tag{11.53}$$

This is the partial fraction form of $\mathcal{D}(z)$, where $\mathcal{D}(z)$ is a strictly proper transfer function. Inverting (11.53) yields the impulse response and Table 11.1 shows that the general term of the sequence $\{y_{\delta_k}\}$ is

$$y_{\delta_k} = \begin{cases} 0 & k = 0 \\ \displaystyle\sum_{j=1}^{n} \alpha_j \, (\lambda_j)^{k-1} & k \geq 1 \end{cases} \ . \tag{11.54}$$

Now, in general, $\lambda_j = r_j \, e^{i\theta_j}$, $j = 1, \ldots, n$, where $r_j \geq 0$ is the amplitude of λ_j and $-\pi < \theta_j \leq \pi$, the argument, and it is easy to see that

$$y_{\delta_k} \rightarrow 0 \qquad \text{as } k \rightarrow \infty \text{ if } |\lambda_j| = r_j < 1 \ , \qquad j = 1, \ldots, n$$

whilst y_{δ_k} becomes unbounded as $k \rightarrow \infty$ if $|\lambda_j| = r_j > 1$ for any $j \in [1, \ n]$.

Thus, based on the behaviour of the impulse response, we define a discrete-time system to be *stable* if all the poles of the transfer function lie in the unit disc $|z| < 1$. It is unstable if any pole lies outside the unit circle $|z| = 1$. The system is said to be marginally stable if the transfer function has simple poles on the unit circle $|z| = 1$; however, repeated poles on $|z| = 1$ generate unstable systems.

It is easy to extend the analysis to include transfer functions when $\mathcal{D}(z)$ is proper, rather than strictly proper. In this case the degrees of numerator and denominator are equal, and polynomial division leads to

$$\mathcal{D}(z) = \alpha' + \sum_{j=1}^{n} \frac{\alpha_j}{z - \lambda_j} \ .$$ (11.55)

Inversion of (11.55) leads to an impulse response containing an impulse at $k = 0$, which does not alter the long-term behaviour. Similarly, since it is true that if a is a complex number such that $|a| < 1$

$$\lim_{k \to \infty} k^n a^k = 0$$

where n is a positive integer, repeated poles inside the unit disc imply that the impulse response will decay in the long term. We thus conclude that discrete-time systems of the type modelled by difference equations of the form (11.49) are stable if an only if all the poles, real or complex, simple or repeated, lie in the unit disc $|z| < 1$. Fig. 11.8 illustrates these concepts.

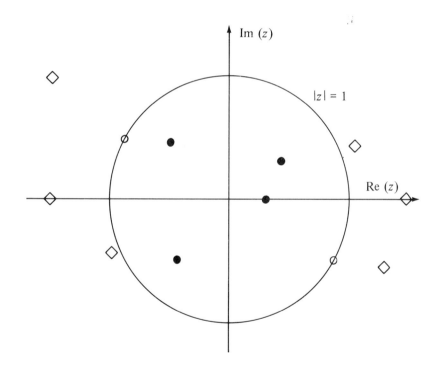

Fig. 11.8a — Stability region $|z| < 1$ for discrete-time systems.

● — Some possible pole locations for stable systems
○ — Simple pole leading to marginal stability for otherwise stable systems
◇ — Some possible pole locations for unstable systems

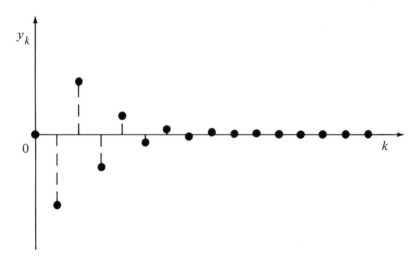

Fig. 11.8b — Impulse response of a stable system.

Example 11.13
Classify the stability of the following systems.

(1) $$\frac{\mathcal{Y}(z)}{\mathcal{U}(z)} = \mathcal{D}_1(z) = \frac{1}{z^2 + \frac{3}{2} z + \frac{1}{2}}$$

(2) $$\frac{\mathcal{Y}(z)}{\mathcal{U}(z)} = \mathcal{D}_2(z) = \frac{z^2}{z^2 + 2z + 2} \ .$$

(1) Here $g_1(z) = z^2 + \frac{3}{2} z + \frac{1}{2} = (z + \frac{1}{2})(z + 1)$ with roots at $\lambda_i = -\frac{1}{2}$, $\lambda_2 = -1$. The system is thus marginally stable.

(2) In this case, $g_2(z) = z^2 + z + 1 = (z + \frac{1}{2} - \frac{1}{2}i)(z + \frac{1}{2} + \frac{1}{2}i)$ with roots at

$$z = -\frac{1}{2} + \frac{i}{2} = \frac{1}{\sqrt{2}} \, e^{3i\,\pi/4} \quad \text{and} \quad \lambda_2 = -\frac{1}{2} - \frac{i}{2} = \frac{1}{\sqrt{2}} \, e^{-3i\pi/4}.$$

Since $|\lambda_1| = |\lambda_2| = \dfrac{1}{\sqrt{2}} < 1$, this system is stable.

11.7 TIME DOMAIN SIGNAL DECOMPOSITION AND CONVOLUTION

In analysing continuous-time systems, we went to considerable trouble to find a decomposed form of a signal in the time domain. The purpose of this decomposition was to interpret general system responses in the form of superimposed impulse responses. We first met this idea in section 7.9, in seeking an interpretation of the transform domain input–output relationship:

$$Y(s) = H(s)\ U(s)\ .$$

This was achieved by using the convolution result for the inversion of the product of two Laplace transforms. Later, in section 8.6, we transferred our attention to the time domain to gain some understanding of the convolution process. In this section, we will attempt to achieve the same degree of insight into the behaviour of discrete-time systems. First we will seek a signal decomposition for discrete-time signals, and we will see that this is a considerably simpler task than for the continuous-time case.

Consider a discrete-time signal sequence

$$\{u_k\} = \{u_o, u_1, u_2, \ \ldots\ u_n, \ \ldots\}\ . \tag{11.56}$$

Now define the shifted pulse sequence $\{\delta_{k-j}\}$ generated by

$$\delta_{k-j} = \begin{cases} 0 & k \neq j \\ 1 & k = j \end{cases},$$

and illustrated in Fig. 11.9.

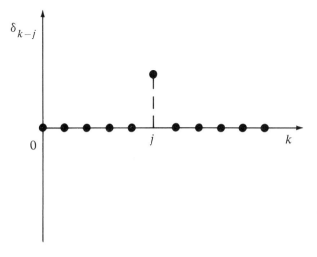

Fig. 11.9 — The shifted pulse sequence $\{\delta_{k-j}\}$.

We can write (11.56) in the equivalent form

$$\{u_k\} = u_0\{\delta_k\} + u_1\{\delta_{k-1}\} + \ldots + u_n\{\delta_{k-n}\} + \ldots$$

$$= \sum_{j=0}^{\infty} u_j\{\delta_{k-j}\} \; . \tag{11.57}$$

(11.57) is the desired time domain decomposition of the signal (11.56) and is the analogue (perhaps 'discretealogue' is a better word!) of equation (8.23).

Let us now supply the signal sequence (11.56) as the input to a causal linear time invariant system, with impulse response sequence $\{y_{\delta_k}\}$. Notice that time invariance means that the zero-state response to the shifted pulse sequence will be just $\{y_{\delta_{k-j}}\}$, a shifted version of the impulse response sequence $\{y_{\delta_k}\}$. Then linearity allows us to superimpose the individual zero-state responses to obtain the output sequence as

$$\{y_k\} = u_0\{y_{\delta_k}\} - u_1 \{y_{\delta_{k-1}}\} + \ldots + u_n\{y_{\delta_{k-n}}\} + \ldots$$

$$= \sum_{j=0}^{\infty} u_j\{y_{\delta_{k-j}}\} \; . \tag{11.58}$$

(11.58) represents the response of the system to an input signal sequence $\{u_k\}$, and writing this out we have

$$
\begin{array}{llllllll}
\{y_k\} = & u_0 & \{y_{\delta_0}, & y_{\delta_1}, & y_{\delta_2} & \cdots & y_{\delta_k}, & \cdots & \cdots\} \\
& + u_1 & \{0, & y_{\delta_0}, & y_{\delta_1}, & \cdots & y_{\delta_{k-1}}, & \cdots & \cdots\} \\
& + u_2 & \{0, & 0, & y_{\delta_0} & \cdots & y_{\delta_{k-2}}, & \cdots & \cdots\} \\
& + & \cdots & \cdots & \cdots & \cdots & \cdots & \cdots \\
& + u_k & \{0, & 0, & 0, & & y_{\delta_0}, & \cdots & \cdots\} \\
& \vdots \\
& + u_p & \{0, & 0, & 0, & & 0, & \cdots & y_{\delta_0}, \cdots\} \\
& + \ldots
\end{array}
$$

$$\text{kth position} \quad \text{pth position .}$$

Writing out the kth (or general) term of this sequence we have

$$y_k = \sum_{j=0}^{k} u_j \, y_{\delta_{k-j}} \tag{11.59}$$

and so

$$\{y_k\} = \left\{ \sum_{j=0}^{k} u_j \, y_{\delta_{k-j}} \right\} . \tag{11.60}$$

Writing (11.60) stresses that each term of the sequence $\{y_k\}$ is itself a sum over k terms. This sum, as in (11.59), is a convolution sum and its structure is perhaps more obvious than the corresponding convolution integral discussed for continuous-time systems. Here it is easily seen to represent a sum of appropriately weighted and delayed impulse responses which combine to produce each output term. Notice that writing $k - j = p$ in (11.59) yields

$$y_k = \sum_{p=k}^{0} u_{k-p} \, y_{\delta_p} = \sum_{p=0}^{k} u_{k-p} \, y_{\delta_p} , \tag{11.61}$$

showing that convolution is a commutative operation in discrete time also.
When each sequence is causal, so that

$$u_k = 0 , \qquad k < 0 , \quad \text{and} \quad y_{\delta_k} = 0 , \qquad k < 0 ,$$

(11.59) can be written

$$y_k = \sum_{j=-\infty}^{\infty} u_j y_{\delta_{k-j}} . \tag{11.62}$$

We in fact regard (11.62) as the fundamental convolution operation and interpret (11.59) as the special case arising when only causal sequences are involved.

Example 11.14
Calculate the impulse response for the system with Z-transfer function

$$\mathcal{D}(z) = \frac{z}{(z+1)(z+\tfrac{1}{2})} .$$

Hence find the step response and check the result by direct calculation.
The impulse response is

$$\{y_{\delta_k}\} = Z^{-1}(\mathcal{D}(z)) = Z^{-1}\left[\frac{2z}{z+\tfrac{1}{2}} - \frac{2z}{z+1} \right]$$

$$= \{2(-\tfrac{1}{2})^k - 2(-1)^k\} \ .$$

Using (11.61) with input $\{u_k\} = \{1, 1, 1, \ldots\}$ to calculate the step response, we see that this response sequence is generated by

$$y_k = \sum_{p=0}^{k} u_{k-p} \, y_{\delta_p}$$

$$= \sum_{p=0}^{k} y_{\delta_p}$$

$$= \sum_{p=0}^{k} [2 - (\tfrac{1}{2})^p - 2(-1)^p]$$

$$= 2 \sum_{p=0}^{k} (-\tfrac{1}{2})^p - 2 \sum_{p=0}^{k} (-1)^p$$

$$= 2 \left[\frac{1 - (-\tfrac{1}{2})^{k+1}}{1 + \tfrac{1}{2}} \right] - 2 \left[\frac{1 - (-1)^{k+1}}{1 + 1} \right]$$

$$= \frac{4}{3} [1 - (-\tfrac{1}{2})^{k+1}] - [1 - (-1)^{k+1}]$$

$$= \frac{1}{3} - \frac{4}{3} \left(-\frac{1}{2} \right)^{k+1} + (-1)^{k+1}$$

$$= \frac{1}{3} + \frac{1}{3} \left(-\frac{1}{2} \right)^{k} - (-1)^{k}, \qquad k \geqslant 0 \ . \tag{11.63}$$

Calculating the step response directly, with $Z\{u_k\} = z/(z-1)$, we see that

$$\mathcal{Y}(z) = \frac{z^2}{(z+1)(z+\tfrac{1}{2})(z-1)} \ .$$

Thus

$$\frac{\mathcal{Y}(z)}{z} = \frac{z}{(z+1)(z+\tfrac{1}{2})(z-1)}$$

$$= \frac{1}{3}\frac{1}{z-1} + \frac{1}{3}\frac{1}{z+\frac{1}{2}} - \frac{1}{z+1} \; ,$$

and so

$$\mathcal{Y}(z) = \frac{1}{3}\frac{z}{z-1} + \frac{1}{3}\frac{z}{z+\frac{1}{2}} - \frac{z}{z+1} \; .$$

Inverting, we see that $\{y_k\} = \{\frac{1}{3} + \frac{1}{3}(-\frac{1}{2})^k - (-1)^k\}$, in aggreement with (11.63).

The experience gained in analysing continuous-time systems, which showed that if a particular response is required, then a direct calculation is more efficient than the use of convolution integrals, is clearly relevant here also. Nevertheless, convolution again provides a solution *formula* for the output in the general case, and this is its major value.

Our last task in this section is to link time domain convolution with its image in the Z-transform domain. Proceeding as for continuous time, we focus attention on the transform domain input-output relationship

$$\mathcal{Y}(z) = \mathcal{D}(z)\mathcal{U}(z)$$
$$= \mathcal{Y}_\delta(z)\mathcal{U}(z)$$

where $\mathcal{Y}_\delta(z)$ is the Z-transform of the impulse response. Now for the causal systems and sequences,

$$\mathcal{Y}_\delta(z) = \sum_{k=0}^{\infty} \frac{y_{\delta_k}}{z^k} = y_{\delta_0} + \frac{y_{\delta_1}}{z} + \frac{y_{\delta_2}}{z^2} + \ldots \frac{y_{\delta_k}}{z^k} + \ldots$$

$$\mathcal{U}(z) = \sum_{k=0}^{\infty} \frac{u_k}{z^k} = u_0 + \frac{u_1}{z} + \frac{u_2}{z^2} + \ldots + \frac{u_k}{z^k} + \ldots$$

and so

$$\mathcal{Y}_\delta(z)\mathcal{U}(z) = y_{\delta_0} u_0 + (y_{\delta_0}u_1 + y_{\delta_1}u_0)\frac{1}{z} + (y_{\delta_0}u_2 + y_{\delta_1}u_1 + y_{\delta_2}u_0)\frac{1}{z^2} + \ldots$$

$$(11.64)$$

We infer that the term in $1/z^k$ in (11.64) will have coefficient

$$\sum_{j=0}^{k} y_{\delta_j} u_{k-j} \ . \tag{11.65}$$

Thus the kth term in the output sequence $\{y_k\} = Z^{-1}(\mathcal{Y}(z)) = Z^{-1}(\mathcal{Y}_\delta(z)\mathcal{U}(z))$ is

$$y_k = \sum_{j=0}^{k} y_{\delta_j} u_{k-j} \ ;$$

in other words

$$Z\left\{\sum_{j=0}^{k} y_{\delta_j} u_{k-j}\right\} = \mathcal{Y}_\delta(z)\mathcal{U}(z) \ . \tag{11.66}$$

As perhaps anticipated, (11.66) shows that products in the transform domain have, as image, a convolution operation in the time domain, and for discrete-time systems the operation is a convolution sum. The '*' notation is often used for convolution, and we write for causal sequences

$$\{u_k\} * \{v_k\} = \left\{\sum_{j=0}^{k} u_j\, v_{k-j}\right\}$$

$$= \left\{\sum_{j=0}^{k} u_{k-j}\, v_j\right\}$$

$$= \{v_k\} * \{u_k\} \ ,$$

again showing that convolution is commutative
    The extension to non-causal sequences has been discussed earlier.

11.8 THE FREQUENCY RESPONSE OF A DISCRETE-TIME SYSTEM

The next phase of our development moves to the frequency domain. First we will examine the response of a discrete-time system to a 'pure' complex exponential input. This corresponds to a real input $\cos \omega t$, an oscillatory signal at frequency ω, and when this has been explored we will turn our attention to a wider class of inputs. This will generate the need for a frequency domain decomposition of signal sequences, requiring an extension of our work on Fourier analysis.
    To discuss the frequency response of a discrete-time system we again make use of the Z-transform input–output relationship (11.51):

$$\mathcal{Y}(z) = \mathcal{D}(z)\,\mathcal{U}(z) \tag{11.67}$$

where

$$\mathcal{D}(z) = \frac{b_0\,z^m + b_1 z^{m-1} + \ldots + b_m}{z^n + a_1\,z^{n-1} + \ldots + a_n}.$$

We are now interested only in the case when the input sequence $\{u_k\}$ consists of samples from the continuous-time signal

$$u(t) = e^{i\omega t}\ ,$$

that is, when $\{u_k\} = \{u(kT)\} = \{e^{ik\omega T}\} = \{e^{ik\theta}\}$, where $\theta = \omega T$ is a normalized frequency variable, and T, the inter-sample (or sampling) time, is assumed constant. Now the Z-transform of $\{u_k\}$ is

$$\mathcal{U}(z) = Z\{e^{ik\theta}\}$$

$$= \frac{z}{z - e^{i\theta}} \tag{11.68}$$

and thus the transform of the system response is from (11.67),

$$\mathcal{Y}(z) = \mathcal{D}(z)\,\frac{z}{z - e^{i\theta}}\ . \tag{11.69}$$

Arguing as in section 11.6, we see that

$$\frac{\mathcal{Y}(z)}{z} = \mathcal{D}(z)\,\frac{1}{z - e^{i\theta}}$$

has a partial fraction development

$$\frac{\mathcal{Y}(z)}{z} = \mathcal{D}(z) \cdot \frac{1}{z - e^{i\theta}} = \sum_{j=1}^{n} \frac{\beta_j}{z - \lambda_j} + \frac{\beta'}{z - e^{i\theta}} \ . \tag{11.70}$$

Here we assume that all the poles λ_j of the transfer function are distinct and $\lambda_j \neq e^{i\theta}$, $j = 1, 2, \ldots, n$, As usual, the extension to multiple poles follows easily, with the final conclusion unchanged.

Inversion of (11.70) for $\{y_k\}$ then yields

$$\{y_k\} = Z^{-1}\{\mathcal{Y}(z)\} = Z^{-1}\left(\sum_{j=1}^{n} \beta_j \frac{z}{z - \lambda_j} + \frac{\beta' z}{z - e^{i\theta}}\right)$$

$$= \left\{\sum_{j=1}^{n} \beta_j(\lambda_j)^k + \beta' \, e^{ik\theta}\right\} \ . \tag{11.71}$$

If our system is stable, then $|\lambda_j| < 1, j = 1, 2, \ldots, n$, and all terms in the summation decay to zero as $k \to \infty$. Moreover, we are assured that $\lambda_j \neq e^{i\theta}, j = 1, 2, \ldots, n$. Thus in the long term, the sequence $\{y_k\} \to \{\beta' e^{ik\theta}\}$. This means that the long-term or steady-state response of a stable system with input sequence $\{u_k\} = \{e^{ik\theta}\}$ is simply $\{\beta' e^{ik\theta}\} = \beta'\{e^{ik\theta}\} = \beta'\{u_k\}$, the input sequence by the factor β'. The factor β' is easy to determine using the cover-up rule, or otherwise, from (11.70) as

$$\beta' = \mathcal{D}(e^{i\theta}) \ . \tag{11.72}$$

Thus β' is just the transfer function $\mathcal{D}(z)$ evaluated on the unit circle $z = e^{i\theta}$, the stability boundary for discrete-time systems. Notice that such an evaluation is possible for stable systems since $\mathcal{D}(z)$ exists outside any circle containing all the poles of $\mathcal{D}(z)$. In the case of a stable system, all the poles lie inside the unit circle $|z| = 1$ and thus $\mathcal{D}(z)$ exists on $|z| = 1$.

Example 11.15
Calculate the frequency response of the system of Fig. 11.10.
      The Z-transfer function is calculated following the methods of section 11.5 as

$$\mathcal{D}(z) = \frac{z+1}{z^2 + 0.5z + 0.06} = \frac{z+1}{(z+0.3)(z+0.2)} \ .$$

We see that since the poles are at $\lambda_1 = -0.3, \lambda_2 = -0.2$, so that $|\lambda_j| < 1, j = 1, 2$, the system is stable. The frequency response is then

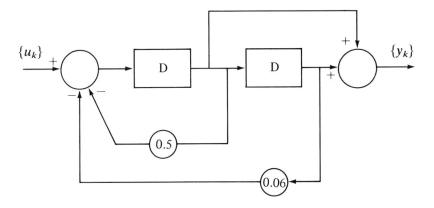

Fig. 11.10 — Discrete-time system of Example 11.15.

$$\mathcal{D}(e^{i\theta}) = \frac{e^{i\theta} + 1}{(e^{i\theta} + 0.3)(e^{i\theta} + 0.2)} \quad.$$

Example 11.15 shows us that, as we expect, the scaling factor β' of (11.72) is a complex quantity, We thus write

$$\beta' = \mathcal{D}(e^{i\theta})$$
$$= |\mathcal{D}(e^{i\theta})|e^{i\phi_0}$$

where $\phi_0 = \arg [\mathcal{D}(e^{i\theta})]$. We see that both $|\mathcal{D}(e^{i\theta})|$ and $\arg [\mathcal{D}(e^{i\theta})]$ will depend on θ, the normalized input frequency, and in line with continuous-time terminology, $|\mathcal{D}(e^{i\theta})|$ is called the amplitude response and $\arg [\mathcal{D}(e^{i\theta})]$ is known as the phase response. In the long term, the effect of the system on the input signal sequence $\{e^{ik\theta}\}$ is the production of an output signal at the same frequency θ, subject to

(1) a frequency-dependent amplitude scaling of amount $|\mathcal{D}(e^{i\theta})|$ and
(2) a frequency-dependent phase shift of amount $\arg [\mathcal{D}(e^{i\theta})]$.

The dependence of the amplitude scaling on the input frequency θ is the key to the use of such systems for frequency domain operations on signals.

Example 11.16
Calculate the amplitude and phase responses for the system of Example 11.15.
    In example 11.15 we established the frequency response as

$$\mathcal{D}(e^{i\theta}) = \frac{e^{i\theta} + 1}{(e^{i\theta} + 0.3)(e^{i\theta} + 0.2)}$$

Now

$$|\mathscr{D}(e^{i\theta})| = \frac{|e^{i\theta}+1|}{|e^{i\theta}+0.3||e^{i\theta}+0.2|}$$

$$= \frac{\sqrt{((1+\cos\theta)^2+\sin^2\theta)}}{\sqrt{((0.3+\cos\theta)^2+\sin^2\theta)}\ \sqrt{((0.2+\cos\theta)^2+\sin^2\theta)}}$$

$$= \frac{\sqrt{(2+2\cos\theta)}}{\sqrt{(1.09+0.6\cos\theta)}\ \sqrt{(1.04+0.4\cos\theta)}}\ .$$

A sketch of this response is shown in Fig. 11.11. The phase response ϕ_θ is given by

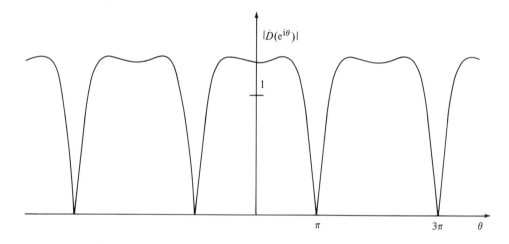

Fig. 11.11 — Amplitude response for the system of Example 11.16.

$$\phi_\theta = \arg(e^{i\theta}+1) - \arg(e^{i\theta}+0.3) - \arg(e^{i\theta}+0.2)\ , \qquad \phi_\theta \in (-\pi, \pi]\ .$$

We now have a picture of the steady-state operation of causal, linear, time invariant stable systems in the frequency domain. To make use of this concept we must seek a decomposition of general signal sequences in the frequency domain. This is the task of the next section. However, before doing this, we observe an important difference between the frequency response functions for continuous-time systems and those for discrete-time systems. This difference is apparent in Fig. 11.11, where we see that $|\mathscr{D}(e^{i\theta})|$ is a periodic function of θ, of period

$$\theta_p = \omega_p T = 2\pi\ , \tag{11.73}$$

in contrast to the non-periodic responses obtained for continuous-time systems. It is clear that this periodicity is inevitable for discrete-time systems, and, using the physical frequency variable ω, the period is

$$\omega_p = \frac{2\pi}{T} \ . \tag{11.74}$$

If we assume that we have control over T, the inter-sample time, then it appears that we may be able to arrange that the effects of periodicity are not impossible to manage. We return to this point later.

11.9   A FREQUENCY DOMAIN REPRESENTATION OF DISCRETE-TIME SIGNALS

In order to make use of our frequency domain characterization of a discrete-time system, that is, the system frequency response, we must obtain a frequency domain portrait of discrete-time signals. In effect, this means that we seek a frequency domain decomposition of such signals similar to that obtained in Chapter 9 for continuous-time signals. To see how to do this, we use our intuition based on experience gained in the continuous-time domain. There we saw that the continuous Fourier transform was the appropriate representation of signals in the frequency domain, essentially because the Fourier transform of the impulse response was the system frequency response. This meant that when the Fourier transform of the input signals was

$$\mathcal{F}\{u(t)\} = U(i\omega) \ ,$$

then the input–output relationship in the frequency domain became

$$Y(i\omega) = \mathcal{F}\{h(t)\} \ U(i\omega) \ , \tag{11.75}$$

where $h(t) = \mathcal{L}^{-1}\{H(s)\}$ is the impulse response.

Let us try a similar approach in discrete time, and attempt to infer a suitable transform from time to frequency domain. Using the usual notation, we may write a Z-transform input–output relationship for a causal system as

$$\mathcal{Y}(z) = \mathcal{D}(z) \ \mathcal{U}(z) \ . \tag{11.76}$$

If $\mathcal{D}(z)$ is the Z-transfer function, $\mathcal{D}(e^{i\theta})$ is the frequency response. Moreover, if $\mathcal{U}(z) = 1$, $\mathcal{Y}_\delta(z) = \mathcal{D}(z)$ is the Z-transform of the impulse response of the system and $Z^{-1}(\mathcal{Y}_\delta(z)) = Z^{-1}(\mathcal{D}(z)) = \{y_{\delta_0}, y_{\delta_1}, \ldots, y_{\delta_n}, \ldots\}$, say, where $\{y_{\delta_0}, y_{\delta_1}, \ldots, y_{\delta_n}, \ldots\}$ is the impulse response sequence. This means that, by definition of the Z-transform (11.7),

$$\mathcal{D}(z) = \sum_{k=0}^{\infty} y_{\delta_k} z^{-k}$$

so that

$$\mathcal{D}(e^{i\theta}) = \sum_{k=0}^{\infty} y_{\delta_k} e^{-ik\theta} , \qquad (11.77)$$

Now (11.77) defines a transform of the impulse response sequence $\{y_{\delta_k}\}$, in the time domain, to $\mathcal{D}(e^{i\theta})$, in the frequency domain. We see, then, that if $z = e^{i\theta}$ in (11.76), we obtain the frequency domain representation of our system as

$$\mathcal{Y}(e^{i\theta}) = \mathcal{D}(e^{i\theta})\mathcal{U}(e^{i\theta}) . \qquad (11.78)$$

Here

$$\mathcal{Y}(e^{i\theta}) = \sum_{k=0}^{\infty} y_k e^{-ik\theta} \qquad (11.79)$$

$$\mathcal{U}(e^{i\theta}) = \sum_{k=0}^{\infty} e^{-ik\theta} \qquad (11.80)$$

are the transforms of the sequences $\{y_k\}$ and $\{u_k\}$ respectively. We have not given these transforms a name as yet, but examination of (11.77), (11.79) and (11.80) leads us to recall (9.1) with $\theta = -\omega_0 t$. That is, (11.77) resembles the Fourier series representation of the *periodic* function $\mathcal{D}(e^{i\theta})$, using complex exponential functions as basis! The resemblance is closer when we recall that our sequences are causal, so that $y_{\delta_k} = y_k = u_k = 0$, $k < 0$. Then we can rewrite (11.77), (11.79) and (11.80) as

$$\mathcal{D}(e^{i\theta}) = \sum_{k=-\infty}^{\infty} y_{\delta_k} e^{-ik\theta} , \qquad (11.81)$$

$$\mathcal{Y}(e^{i\theta}) = \sum_{k=-\infty}^{\infty} y_k e^{-ik\theta} , \qquad (11.82)$$

$$\mathcal{U}(e^{i\theta}) = \sum_{k=-\infty}^{\infty} u_k\, e^{-ik\theta} \ . \tag{11.83}$$

The resemblance is now complete except that the set of basis functions

$$\{e^{ik\theta}\} \qquad k \text{ an integer} \qquad \text{and} \qquad -\infty < k < \infty$$

has been used in a different order. That is, $e^{ik'\theta}$ is now assigned to $y_{-k'}$, instead of $y_{k'}$. This re-ordering is of no significance and it is natural to call the transform defined by

$$\{x_k\} \to \sum_{k=-\infty}^{\infty} x_k\, e^{-ik\theta} = \mathcal{X}(e^{i\theta}) \tag{11.84}$$

a discrete-time Fourier transform. It is not yet the discrete Fourier transform, because $\mathcal{X}(e^{i\theta})$ is a continuous function of the frequency variable θ. Nevertheless, denoting the discrete-time Fourier transform of the impulse response sequence $\{y_{\delta_k}\}$ as $\overline{\mathcal{F}}[y_{\delta_k}]$ we see that we can write (11.78) as

$$\mathcal{Y}(e^{i\theta}) = \overline{\mathcal{F}}[y_{\delta_k}]\mathcal{U}(e^{i\theta}) \tag{11.85}$$

which is the discrete-time analogue of (11.75). Thus (11.84) defines the appropriate frequency domain decomposition of discrete-time signal sequences for linear system analysis.

Example 11.17
Calculate the discrete-time transform of the sequence

$$\{x\} = \{1,\, 2,\, 2,\, 1\} \ .$$

Using the defining relation (11.84), we have

$$\overline{\mathcal{F}}[\{x_k\}] = \mathcal{X}(e^{i\theta}) = \sum_{k=-\infty}^{\infty} x_k\, e^{-ik\theta}$$

$$= \sum_{k=0}^{3} x_k\, e^{-ik\theta}$$

$$= 1 + 2e^{-i\theta} + 2e^{-i\theta} + e^{-3i\theta}$$

$$= e^{-3i\theta/2} \left[e^{3i\theta/2} + e^{-3i\theta/2} \right] + 2e^{-3i\theta/2} \left[e^{i\theta/2} + e^{-i\theta/2} \right]$$

$$= e^{-3i\theta/2} \left[2 \cos 3\theta/2 + 4 \cos \theta/2 \right] . \qquad (11.86)$$

We see that $\mathcal{X}(e^{i\theta})$ is a complex-valued function of θ, periodic with period $\theta_p = 2\pi$. A sketch of $|\mathcal{X}(e^{i\theta})| = |2 \cos 3\theta/2 + 4 \cos \theta/2|$ is given in Fig. 11.12. $|\mathcal{X}(e^{i\theta})|$ is called the

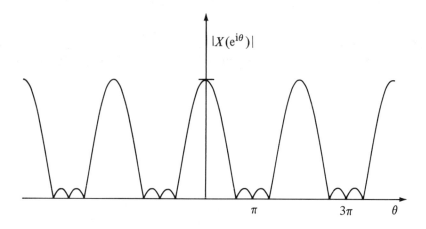

Fig. 11.12 — Amplitude spectrum $|\mathcal{X}(e^{i\theta})|$ for Example 11.17.

amplitude spectrum of the sequence $\{x\}$. Fig. 11.12 clearly shows the periodicity of $|\mathcal{X}(e^{i\theta})|$, which by now is not surprising

In on sense, we have achieved the objective of this chapter, since we have now developed a theory of discrete-time, linear, time invariant systems, in both the time and the frequency domains.

There is, however, a problem. This becomes evident when we consider the task of finding the discrete-time Fourier transform of a sequence of (say) 200 terms. Unless the sequence has a general term of a very restricted type, attempting to calculate the sum (11.84), let alone interpret the result, would be a task of awful magnitude. Clearly some form of computer assistance would be needed, meaning that we could no longer expect to be able to calculate the continuous function $\mathcal{X}(e^{i\theta})$. Rather we must calculate a set, or sequence, of values of $\mathcal{X}(e^{i\theta_j})$ at distinct points θ_j, in such a way that we obtain an accurate estimate of $\mathcal{X}(e^{i\theta})$. This development is examined in the next section.

11.10   THE DISCRETE FOURIER TRANSFORM

Let us now consider the problem mentioned at the end of section 11.9, and, in particular, how to make use of a computer to aid in the Fourier analysis of discrete-time signals and systems. We concern ourselves here with a signal sequence $\{x\}$ consisting of N values, that is

$$\{x\} = \{x_k\} \qquad k = 0, N-1 \ .$$

For the purpose of Fourier transformation we imagine that the sequence $\{x\}$ is padded with zeros, so that in fact

$$\{x\} = \begin{cases} x_k & k \in [0, N-1] \\ 0 & \text{otherwise} \end{cases}$$

which can be compactly represented as

$$\{x\} = \{x_k\}_{k=0}^{N-1} \ .$$

In the last section, we saw how to generate a continuous function of a (frequency) variable θ from this sequence, by taking the discrete-time Fourier transform. We now generate a sequence of values, or samples, of *that* transform to produce the discrete Fourier transform itself. Suppose we do this in such a way that we produce the same number N of values as were in the original sequence. Then since we wish to encompass one full period of the discrete-time transform, given by $\theta_p = 2\pi$, we should choose $\Delta\theta$, the distance between sample values, to satisfy

$$N\Delta\theta = 2\pi \ . \tag{11.87}$$

Recall that θ is a normalized frequency variable and

$$\theta = \omega T$$

where T is the constant inter-sample time in the time domain. This means that $\Delta\theta = T\Delta\omega$, so that we may write (11.87) as

$$\Delta\omega = \frac{2\pi}{NT} \ . \tag{11.88}$$

We generate our sequence of N samples from the discrete-time Fourier transform of the sequence $\{x\}$, that is, from

$$\mathscr{X}(e^{i\theta}) = \sum_{k=-\infty}^{\infty} x_k \, e^{-ik\theta}$$

$$= \sum_{k=0}^{N-1} x_k \, e^{-ik\theta}$$

to produce the sequence $\{X_k\}$, with

$$X_n = \sum_{k=0}^{N-1} x_k \, e^{ik(n\Delta\theta)} \ . \tag{11.89}$$

From (11.89) we see that with $n = 0, \ldots, N-1$ we generate the sequence of N terms

$$\{X_0, X_1, \ldots, X_{N-1}\} = \left\{ \sum_{k=0}^{N-1} x_k, \ \sum_{k=0}^{N-1} x_k \, e^{-ik\Delta\theta}, \ldots, \ \sum_{k=0}^{N-1} x_k \, e^{-i(N-1)\Delta\theta} \right\}$$

$$= \left\{ \sum_{k=0}^{N-1} x_k, \ \sum_{k=0}^{N-1} x_k \, e^{-ik2\pi/N}, \ \ldots, \ \sum_{k=0}^{N-1} x_k \, e^{-ik(N-1)2\pi/N} \right\} \ . \tag{11.90}$$

The sequence $\{X_n\}$ is then the discrete Fourier transform sequence of the sequence $\{x_k\}_{k=0}^{N-1}$. Notice that each term of the transformed sequence involves a sum over the N terms of the original sequence. Each term involves N complex multiplications (trivial in the case of the first term), meaning that a total of N^2 complex multiplications must be performed. Working out each of the N sums requires $N-1$ complex additions, imnplying a total of $N(N-1)$ complex additions. Measured in terms of the number of complex multiplications, a direct calculation of the sequence (11.90) would be a computation of complexity of order N^2. The time requirements of such computations rapidly become unacceptable as N increases, meaning that an alternative approach has to be adopted. This is discussed in section 11.11.

Example 11.18
Calculate the discrete Fourier transform of the sequence of example (11.17), $\{x\} = \{x_0, x_1, x_2, x_3\} = \{1, 2, 2, 1\}$.
    In this case, $N = 4$, and so using the form (11.90) we have that.

$$\{X\} = \{X_0, X_1, X_2, X_3\}$$

$$= \left\{ \sum_{k=0}^{3} x_k, \ \sum_{k=0}^{3} x_k \, e^{-ik\pi/2}, \ \sum_{k=0}^{3} x_k \, e^{-ik\pi}, \ \sum_{k=0}^{3} x_k \, e^{-ik3\pi/2} \right\} \ .$$

Thus

$$X_0 = x_0 + x_1 + x_2 + x_3 = 6$$

$$X_1 = x_0 + x_1 e^{-i\pi/2} + x_2 e^{-i\pi} + x_3 e^{-3i\pi/2}$$

$$= 1 + 2(-i) + 2(-1) + 1(i) = -1 - i$$

$$X_2 = x_0 + x_1 e^{-i\pi} + x_2 e^{-i2\pi} + x_3 e^{-i3\pi}$$

$$= 1 + 2(-1) + 2(1) + 1(-1) = 0$$

$$X_3 = x_0 + x_1 e^{-i3\pi/2} + x_2 e^{-i3\pi} + x_3 e^{-i9\pi/2}$$

$$= 1 + 2(i) + 2(-1) + 1(-i) = -1 + i \ .$$

And so

$$\{X\} = \{6, \ -1-i, \ 0, \ -1+i\} \ .$$

These results are in agreement with (11.86) with $\theta = 0$, $\pi/2$, π, $3\pi/2$ respectively.

We now turn our attention to the recovery of a sequence from its discrete Fourier transform. Suppose the sequence

$$\{x\} = \{x_n\}_{n=0}^{N-1}$$

has discrete Fourier transform sequence

$$\{X\} = \{X_k\} \ ,$$

with

$$X_k = \sum_{m=0}^{N} x_k e^{-ikm2\pi/N} \qquad n = 0, 1, \ldots, N-1 \ . \qquad (11.91)$$

Let us investigate the sequence $\{y\} = \{y_r\}$, where

$$y_r = \sum_{k=0}^{N-1} x_k e^{-ikr\Delta\theta} \qquad r = 0, 1, \ldots, N-1 \qquad (11.92)$$

$$= \sum_{k=0}^{N-1} x_k \, e^{-ikr\,2\pi/N} \qquad r = 0, 1, \ldots, N-1 \; .$$

Substitute for X_k, using (11.91) and

$$y_r = \sum_{k=0}^{N-1} \left(\sum_{m=0}^{N-1} x_m \, e^{-ikm\,2\pi/N} \right) e^{-ikr\,2\pi/N}$$

$$= \sum_{m=0}^{N-1} x_m \sum_{k=0}^{N-1} e^{-ik(m+r)\,2\pi/N} \; , \qquad r = 0, 1, \ldots, N-1 \; . \tag{11.93}$$

Now, the inner sum in (11.93),

$$\sum_{k=0}^{N-1} e^{-ik(m+r)\,2\pi/N}$$

is a geometric progression and

$$\sum_{k=0}^{N-1} e^{-ik(m+r)\,2\pi/N} = \frac{1 - e^{-i(m+r)2\pi}}{1 - e^{-i(m+r)2\pi/N}}$$

$$= 0, \quad m \neq -r \; . \tag{11.94}$$

However, when $m = -r$

$$\sum_{k=0}^{N-1} e^{-ik(m+r)\,2\pi/N} = N\,\delta_{m,\,-r} \tag{11.95}$$

where $\delta_{p,q} = \begin{cases} 0 & p \neq q \\ 1 & p = q \end{cases}$ is the Kronecker delta.

With this notation, we can write (11.93) as

$$y_r = \sum_{m=0}^{N-1} x_m \, N\delta_{m,-r}$$

$$= Nx_{-r} \, . \tag{11.96}$$

Writing $r = -p$ in (11.96) we obtain

$$x_p = \frac{1}{N} y_{-p} \qquad p = 0, 1, \ldots, N-1$$

$$= \frac{1}{N} \sum_{k=0}^{N-1} x_k \, e^{ikp\Delta\theta}$$

$$= \frac{1}{N} \sum_{k=0}^{N-1} x_k \, e^{ikp2\pi/N} \qquad p = 0, 1, \ldots, N-1$$

using (11.92).

We have now shown how to invert the discrete Fourier transform and we notice that the inversion is exact. We may now define the discrete Fourier transform sequence pair

$$\{x\} \leftrightarrow \{X\}$$

defined by $\{X\} = \{X_n\}$, $n = 0, \ldots, N-1$, with

$$X_n = \sum_{k=0}^{N-1} x_k \, e^{-ikn2\pi/N} \qquad n = 0, 1, \ldots, N-1 \tag{11.97}$$

and

$$\{x\} = \{x_n\} \qquad n = 0, \ldots, N-1$$

with

$$x_n = \frac{1}{N} \sum_{k=0}^{N-1} X_k \, e^{ikn2\pi/N} \qquad n = 0, 1, \ldots, N-1 \, . \tag{11.98}$$

We recall that θ is a normalized frequency variable, with $\theta = \omega T$, where T is the inter-sample time. Writing $\Delta\theta = T\Delta\omega$ we can obtain the transform pair (11.97) and (11.98) as

$$X_n = \sum_{k=0}^{N-1} x_k\, e^{-ikn\,\Delta\omega T} \qquad (11.99)$$

and

$$x_n = \frac{1}{N} \sum_{k=0}^{N-1} X_n\, e^{ikn\Delta\omega T}, \qquad (11.100)$$

with

$$\Delta\omega = \frac{2\pi}{NT}.$$

Example 11.19
Calculate the inverse discrete Fourier transform of the sequence

$$\{X\} = \{X_0,\ X_1,\ X_2,\ X_3\} = \{6,\ -(1+i),\ 0,\ -(1-i)\}$$

of Example 11.17.
    Using (11.98) with $N = 4$ we obtain, in turn,

$$x_0 = \frac{1}{4} \sum_{k=0}^{3} X_k = \frac{1}{4}\,[6 - (1+i) - (1-i)] = 1$$

$$x_1 = \frac{1}{4} \sum_{k=0}^{3} X_k\, e^{ik\pi/2} = \frac{1}{4}\,(X_0 + X_1\, e^{i\pi/2} + X_2\, e^{i\pi} + X_3\, e^{i3\pi/2})$$

$$= \tfrac{1}{4}\,[6 - (1+i)i + 0(-1) - (1-i)\,(-i)]$$

$$= \tfrac{1}{4}\,(6 - i + 1 + i + 1) = 2$$

$$x_2 = \frac{1}{4} \sum_{k=0}^{3} X_k\, e^{ik\pi} = \frac{1}{4}\,(X_0 + X_1\, e^{i\pi} + X_2\, e^{2i\pi} + x_3 e^{3i\pi})$$

$$= \tfrac{1}{4} \left[6 - (1+\mathrm{i})\,(-1) + 0(1) - (1-\mathrm{i})\,(-1) \right]$$

$$= \tfrac{1}{4}\,(6 + 1 + \mathrm{i} + 1 - \mathrm{i}) = 2$$

$$x_3 = \frac{1}{4} \sum_{k=0}^{3} X_k \, \mathrm{e}^{\mathrm{i}k3\pi/2} = \frac{1}{4}\,(X_0 + X_1\,\mathrm{e}^{3\mathrm{i}\pi/2} + X_2\,\mathrm{e}^{3\mathrm{i}\pi} + X_3\,\mathrm{e}^{9\mathrm{i}\pi/2})$$

$$= \tfrac{1}{4} \left[6 - (1+\mathrm{i})(-\mathrm{i}) + 0(-1) - (1-\mathrm{i})(\mathrm{i}) \right] = \tfrac{1}{4}\,(6 + \mathrm{i} - 1 - \mathrm{i} - 1) = 1 \ .$$

Thus $\{x\} = \{x_0, x_1, x_2, x_3\} = \{1, 2, 2, 1\}$, which was the starting sequence of Example 11.17. We have obtained an exact inversion, as predicted.

We expect that the discrete Fourier transform will yield a periodic sequence because this behaviour is inherent in the process leading to the calculation of the discrete-time Fourier transform. We remember that the discrete Fourier transform is just a sequence of samples derived from the discrete-time Fourier transform chosen to cover one period. Hence, if we compute further samples outside this 'fundamental' interval, we simply obtain copies of values within that interval. Consideration of the inversion formula (11.98) immediately shows that

$$x_{n+N} = \sum_{k=0}^{N-1} X_k \, \mathrm{e}^{\mathrm{i}k(n+N)\,2\pi/N}$$

$$= \sum_{k=0}^{N-1} X_k \, \mathrm{e}^{\mathrm{i}kn\,2\pi/N} \cdot \mathrm{e}^{\mathrm{i}kN2\pi/N}$$

$$= \sum_{k=0}^{N-1} X_k \, \mathrm{e}^{\mathrm{i}kn\,2\pi/N} = x_n \ .$$

This means that the inverted sequence $\{x\} = \{x_n\}$, $-\infty < n < \infty$, is periodic of period N, and this is unavoidable. In fact before transforming the sequence $\{x\}$ we insisted that

$$\{x\} = \begin{cases} x_k & k\in[0,\,N-1] \\ 0 & \text{otherwise} \end{cases} = \{x_k\}_{k=0}^{N-1} \ ,$$

so that outside the fundamental interval $k\in[0,\,N-1]$, the terms of the sequence are all zero. Our results have shown that within the fundamental interval $[0,\,N-1]$, the inversion procedure is exact; however, outside that period the zeros are replaced by repetitions of the values contained in the fundamental interval. These ideas can be

clarified in the context of Examples (11.17), (11.18) and (11.19). For these examples
we set

$$\{x\} = \{x_k\}_{k=0}^3 = \{1, 2, 2, 1\} = \{\ldots 0, 0, 0, \overline{1, 2, 2, 1}, 0, 0, 0, \ldots\} .$$
$$\uparrow$$

Transformation generated the sequence $\{X\}$ where

$$\{X\} = \{\ldots, -1+i, \overline{6, -1-i, 0, -1+i}, 6, -1-i, 0 \ldots\} .$$
$$\uparrow$$

Inversion of this sequence then produces the periodic sequence

$$\{x'\} = \{\ldots 2, 1, \overline{1, 2, 2, 1}, 1, 2, \ldots\} .$$
$$\uparrow$$

In each case, the fundamental interval is indicated with a bar, and we see that on the
fundamental interval

$$\{x\} = \{x'\} .$$

In this sense, the inverse transformation recovers the starting sequences, but only on
the fundamental interval. On that interval, (11.97) and (11.98) define the discrete
Fourier transform and its inverse, and since the length of the interval is

$$\theta_p = \omega_p T = 2\pi , \qquad \text{so that } \omega_p = \frac{2\pi}{T} ,$$

we see that by choice of T we may exercise control over its length along the physical
(unnormalized) frequency axis ω. In concluding this section, we draw attention to the
effort involved in the working of Examples 11.18 and 11.19, for just $N = 4$. Since the
calculations increase in number with N^2, our remarks earlier on the non-feasibility of
using this approach for even modest N are endorsed.

Section 11.11 introduces a technique called the fast Fourier transform, for the
efficient evaluation of discrete Fourier transforms.

11.11   THE FAST FOURIER TRANSFORM

In this section we present a brief introduction to a highly efficient algorithm for the
calculation of discrete Fourier transforms. The algorithm is capable of generalization, but we restrict ourselves to the case when N, the number of points in the

sequence to be transformed, is a power of 2. That is, $N = 2^\gamma$ for some positive integer γ. This restriction is in fact not always troublesome because, in many applications, sequence lengths are selected rather than imposed, and the selection is then made of the smallest number of terms of the form $N = 2^\gamma$ consistent with sampling constraints. This point is further examined in the next chapter.

The algorithm we discuss was given by Cooley and Tukey [2] in 1965. The reader who wishes to see a fuller discussion should consult Brigham [1] where a similar approach to that used in this section is adopted.

To explore the algorithm we consider the special case $\gamma = 2$, so that $N = 4$. In this way, the key steps in the algorithm are exposed, and the generalization to other values of γ should be apparent. We divide the description of the algorithm into three stages:

(1) matrix formulation of the calculation,
(2) factorization of the resulting matrices,
(3) re-ordering of the calculation.

Let us proceed with the matrix formulation stage. From (11.97) we know that the discrete Fourier transform sequence $\{X_n\}$, $n = 0, 1, \ldots, N-1$, of the sequence

$$\{x_n\}, \; n = 0, 1, \ldots, N-1 \;,$$

is generated by

$$X_n = \sum_{k=0}^{N-1} x_k \, e^{-ikn\,2\pi/N} \tag{11.101}$$

$$= \sum_{k=0}^{N-1} x_k \, W^{nk} \;,$$

where

$$W = e^{-i2\pi/N} \;. \tag{11.102}$$

In this case, $N = 2^2 = 4$, and we see that

$$\{X_n\} = \{X_0, X_1, X_2, X_3\}$$

and

$$X_n = \sum_{k=0}^{3} x_k \, W^{nk} \quad n = 0, 1, 2, 3 \tag{11.103}$$

where $W = e^{-i\pi/2}$

Expanding (11.103) we obtain

$$X_0 = \sum_{k=0}^{3} x_k \, W^{0k} = x_0 \, W^0 + x_1 \, W^0 + x_2 \, W^0 + x_3 \, W^0$$

$$X_1 = \sum_{k=0}^{3} x_k \, W^{1k} = x_0 \, W^0 + x_1 \, W^1 + x_2 \, W^2 + x_3 \, W^3$$

$$X_2 = \sum_{k=0}^{3} x_k W^{2k} = x_0 \, W^0 + x_1 \, W^2 + x_2 \, W^4 + x_3 \, W^6$$

$$X_3 = \sum_{k=0}^{3} x_k \, W^{3k} = x_0 \, W^0 + x_1 \, W^3 + x_2 \, W^6 + x_3 \, W^9 \; .$$

In matrix form we have

$$\begin{bmatrix} X_0 \\ X_1 \\ X_2 \\ X_3 \end{bmatrix} = \begin{bmatrix} W^0 & W^0 & W^0 & W^0 \\ W^0 & W^1 & W^2 & W^3 \\ W^0 & W^2 & W^4 & W^6 \\ W^0 & W^3 & W^6 & W^9 \end{bmatrix} \begin{bmatrix} x_0 \\ x_1 \\ x_2 \\ x_3 \end{bmatrix} \tag{1.104}$$

Or,

$$\mathbf{X}_n = \mathbf{W}^{nk} \mathbf{x}_k \; .$$

We now exploit the special properties of the entries W^{nk} of the matrix $\mathbf{W}^{nk}$. We see that since

$$W^{nk} = \left(e^{-i2\pi/N} \right)^{nk} \, ,$$

then

$$W^{nk+pN} = (e^{-i2\pi/N})^{nk} \cdot (e^{-i2\pi/N})^{pN}$$

$$= (e^{-i2\pi/N})^{nk} \cdot (e^{-i2\pi p})$$

$$= (e^{-i2\pi/N})^{nk} \quad \text{when } p \text{ is an integer}$$

$$= W^{nk} \quad . \tag{11.105}$$

This result is true for all values of N, and allows us to eliminate powers of W greater than N Thus we see that when $N = 4$

$$W^4 = W^0$$

$$W^6 = W^2$$

$$W^9 = W^5 = W^1 \quad .$$

Then (11.104) becomes

$$\begin{bmatrix} X_0 \\ X_1 \\ X_2 \\ X_3 \end{bmatrix} = \begin{bmatrix} W^0 & W^0 & W^0 & W^0 \\ W^0 & W^1 & W^2 & W^3 \\ W^0 & W^2 & W^0 & W^2 \\ W^0 & W^3 & W^2 & W^1 \end{bmatrix} \begin{bmatrix} x_0 \\ x_1 \\ x_2 \\ x_3 \end{bmatrix}$$

$$= \begin{bmatrix} 1 & 1 & 1 & 1 \\ 1 & W^1 & W^2 & W^3 \\ 1 & W^2 & W^0 & W^2 \\ 1 & W^3 & W^2 & W^1 \end{bmatrix} \begin{bmatrix} x_0 \\ x_1 \\ x_2 \\ x_3 \end{bmatrix} \quad . \tag{11.106}$$

In (11.106) we have used $W^0 = 1$ in the first row and first column of the matrix, but not in the interior. The reason for this is that whilst the terms in the first row and first column will always take the value $W^0 = 1$, that at position (3,3) in the interior is generated by the particular value $N = 4$. Thus, to aid generalization, we do not make the substitution at position (3,3).

This completes the matrix formulation stage of the development, and the reader is invited to confirm in the exercises that in the case $\gamma = 3$, so that $N = 8$, the matrix $\mathbf{W}^{nk}$ is given by

$$
\begin{bmatrix}
W^0 & W^0 & W^0 & W^0 & W^0 & W^0 & W^0 & W^0 \\
W^0 & W^1 & W^2 & W^3 & W^4 & W^5 & W^6 & W^7 \\
W^0 & W^2 & W^4 & W^6 & W^8 & W^{10} & W^{12} & W^{14} \\
W^0 & W^3 & W^6 & W^9 & W^{12} & W^{15} & W^{18} & W^{21} \\
W^0 & W^4 & W^8 & W^{12} & W^{16} & W^{20} & W^{24} & W^{28} \\
W^0 & W^5 & W^{10} & W^{15} & W^{20} & W^{25} & W^{30} & W^{35} \\
W^0 & W^6 & W^{12} & W^{18} & W^{24} & W^{30} & W^{36} & W^{42} \\
W^0 & W^7 & W^{14} & W^{21} & W^{28} & W^{35} & W^{42} & W^{49}
\end{bmatrix}
$$

Using (11.105) we see that

$$
\mathbf{W}^{nk} =
\begin{bmatrix}
1 & 1 & 1 & 1 & 1 & 1 & 1 & 1 \\
1 & W^1 & W^2 & W^3 & W^4 & W^5 & W^6 & W^7 \\
1 & W^2 & W^4 & W^6 & W^0 & W^2 & W^4 & W^6 \\
1 & W^3 & W^6 & W^1 & W^4 & W^7 & W^2 & W^5 \\
1 & W^4 & W^0 & W^4 & W^0 & W^4 & W^0 & W^4 \\
1 & W^5 & W^2 & W^7 & W^4 & W^1 & W^6 & W^3 \\
1 & W^6 & W^4 & W^2 & W^0 & W^6 & W^4 & W^2 \\
1 & W^7 & W^6 & W^5 & W^4 & W^3 & W^2 & W^1
\end{bmatrix}
$$

using the same convention concerning the replacement of W^0.

The second stage of development involves the factorization of the matrix $\mathbf{W}^{nk}$. We will return to the case $N = 2^2 = 4$ to illustrate the process. When $N = 4$, the indices n and k can only take the values 0, 1, 2, or 3, and these numbers can be represented in two-digit binary form. (Generally when $N = 2^\gamma$, it is easy to see that γ binary digits (bits) will be required.)

Thus with $N = 4$ we write k as $k_0 k_1$ and n as $n_0 n_1$ where k_0, k_1 and n_0, n_1 may only take the values 0 or 1; then, for example, $k = 3$ becomes $k = 11$ and so on.

Decimal form is easily recovered, because

$$
\left.
\begin{aligned}
k &= 2k_0 + k_1 \\
n &= 2n_0 + n_1
\end{aligned}
\right\} .
\tag{11.107}
$$

Example 11.20

Obtain the corresponding binary indexing for the case $N = 2^3 = 8$.

Here the numbers k and n may only take the values 0, 1, ..., 7 and we may represent each of these using 3 binary digits. Thus

$$\left. \begin{array}{l} k \rightarrow k_0\, k_1\, k_2 \\ n \rightarrow n_0\, n_1\, n_2 \end{array} \right\} \tag{11.108}$$

so that $k = 6$ becomes 110 and $n = 5$ becomes 101.

Decimal recovery follows from

$$\left. \begin{array}{l} k = 2^2 k_0 + 2k_1 + k_0 \\ n = 2^2 n_0 + 2n_1 + n_0 \end{array} \right\} \tag{11.109}$$

Notice that when $N = 2\gamma$, for γ an integer, (11.108) becomes

$$k \rightarrow k_0\, k_1\, k_2 \ldots k_{\gamma-1}$$

$$n \rightarrow n_0\, n_1\, n_2 \ldots n_{\gamma-1}$$

with (11.109) taking the form

$$k = 2^{\gamma-1} k_0 + 2^{\gamma-2} k_1 \ldots + k_{\gamma-1}$$

$$n = 2^{\gamma-1} n_0 + 2^{\gamma-2}\, n_1 \ldots + n_{\gamma-1} \; .$$

Returning to the case $N = 2^2 = 4$, we rewrite the sum (11.103) using the binary representation for n and k. Thus X_n becomes $X_{n_0 n_1}$, x_k becomes $x_{k_0 k_1}$ and the single sum over k becomes two sums, one over k_0 and one over k_1. (11.103) then becomes

$$X_{n_0 n_1} = \sum_{k_1=0}^{1} \sum_{k_0=0}^{1} x_{k_0 k_1}\, W^{(2n_0+n_1)(2k_0+k_1)} \tag{11.110}$$

and we see that in general γ sums would be required.

Consider the factor $W^{(2n_0+n_1)(2k_0+k_1)}$ in (11.110); now

$$W^{(2n_0+n_1)(2k_0+k_1)} = W^{(2n_0+n_1)2k_0}\, W^{(2n_0+n_1)k_1}$$

$$= W^{4n_0 k_0}\, W^{2n_1 k_0}\, W^{(2n_0+n_1)k_1} \; . \tag{11.111}$$

In our case, $W = e^{-2\pi i/4}$ and so

$$W^{4n_0k_0} = e^{-n_0k_02\pi i} = 1$$

and it is clear that such a factor will occur in the general case.
    We can now write (11.110) as

$$X_{n_0n_1} = \sum_{k_1=0}^{1} \sum_{k_0=0}^{1} x_{k_0k_1} \, W^{2n_1k_0} \, W^{(2n_0+n_1)k_1}$$

$$= \sum_{k_1=0}^{1} \left[\sum_{k_0=0}^{1} x_{k_0k_1} \, W^{2n_1k_0} \right] W^{(2n_0+n_1)k_1} \, . \tag{11.112}$$

Now define

$$x'_{n_1k_1} = \sum_{k_0=0}^{1} x_{k_0k_1} \, W^{2n_1k_0} \tag{11.113}$$

allowing us to write (11.112) as

$$X_{n_0n_1} = X'_{n_1n_0} = \sum_{k_1=0}^{1} x'_{n_1k_1} \, W^{(2n_0+n_1)k_1} \, , \tag{11.114}$$

where $X'_{n_1n_0} = X_{n_0n_1}$ is called the bit-reversed form of $X_{n_0n_1}$.
    If we write out the equations in (11.113) we obtain

$$x'_{00} = x_{00} \, W^0 + x_{10} \, W^0 = x_{00} + x_{10} \, W^0$$
$$x'_{01} = x_{01} \, W^0 + x_{11} \, W^0 = x_{01} + x_{11} \, W^0$$
$$x'_{10} = x_{00} \, W^0 + x_{10} \, W^2 = x_{00} + x_{10} \, W^2$$
$$x'_{11} = x_{01} \, W^0 + x_{11} \, W^2 = x_{01} + x_{11} \, W^2 \, .$$

In matrix form we have

$$
\begin{bmatrix} x'_{00} \\ x'_{01} \\ x'_{10} \\ x'_{11} \end{bmatrix} = \begin{bmatrix} 1 & 0 & W^0 & 0 \\ 0 & 1 & 0 & W^0 \\ 1 & 0 & W^2 & 0 \\ 0 & 1 & 0 & W^2 \end{bmatrix} \begin{bmatrix} x_{00} \\ x_{01} \\ x_{10} \\ x_{11} \end{bmatrix} \tag{11.115}
$$

or $x'_{n_1 k_1} = W^{2n_1 k_0} x_{k_0 k_1}$.

In obtaining the matrix $W^{2n_1 k_0}$, we have differentiated between terms in W^0. Where the zero index has arisen by the value of the summation index k_0 (that is, in the first term of each sum in (11.113)), we have set $W^0 = 1$. On the other hand, when the zero occurs in view of the value of n_1 only, we preserve the form W^0. Again, this distinction is made as an aid to generalization.

Turning our attention to (11.114), writing out the equation in full we see that

$$
\begin{aligned}
X'_{00} &= x'_{00} W^0 + x'_{01} W^0 = x'_{00} + x'_{01} W^0 \\
X'_{01} &= x'_{00} W^0 + x'_{01} W^2 = x'_{00} + x'_{01} W^2 \\
X'_{10} &= x'_{10} W^0 + x'_{11} W^1 = x'_{10} + x'_{11} W^1 \\
X'_{11} &= x'_{10} W^0 + x'_{11} W^3 = x'_{10} + x'_{11} W^3 \;.
\end{aligned}
$$

In matrix form, using $X'_{n_0 n_1}$, we obtain

$$
X'_{n_0 n_1} = \begin{bmatrix} X'_{00} \\ X'_{01} \\ X'_{10} \\ X'_{11} \end{bmatrix} = \begin{bmatrix} 1 & W^0 & 0 & 0 \\ 1 & W^2 & 0 & 0 \\ 0 & 0 & 1 & W^1 \\ 0 & 0 & 1 & W^3 \end{bmatrix} \begin{bmatrix} x'_{00} \\ x'_{01} \\ x'_{10} \\ x'_{11} \end{bmatrix}
$$

or $X'_{n_0 n_1} = W^{(2n_0 + n_1)k_1} x'_{n_1 k_1}$.

It is easy to see that

$$
X_{n_1 n_0} = X'_{n_0 n_1} = W^{(2n_0 + n_1)} W^{2n_1 k_0} x_{k_0 k_1} \;,
$$

that is

$$\begin{bmatrix} X'_{00} \\ X'_{01} \\ X'_{10} \\ X'_{11} \end{bmatrix} = \begin{bmatrix} 1 & W^0 & 0 & 0 \\ 1 & W^2 & 0 & 0 \\ 0 & 0 & 1 & W^1 \\ 0 & 0 & 1 & W^3 \end{bmatrix} \times$$

$$\begin{bmatrix} 1 & 0 & W^0 & 0 \\ 0 & 1 & 0 & W^0 \\ 1 & 0 & W^2 & 0 \\ 0 & 1 & 0 & W^2 \end{bmatrix} \begin{bmatrix} x_{00} \\ x_{01} \\ x_{10} \\ x_{11} \end{bmatrix} = \begin{bmatrix} 1 & W^0 & W^0 & W^0 \\ 1 & W^2 & W^0 & W^2 \\ 1 & W^1 & W^2 & W^3 \\ 1 & W^3 & W^2 & W^5 \end{bmatrix} x_{k_0 k_1}$$

$$= \begin{bmatrix} 1 & W^0 & W^0 & W^0 \\ 1 & W^2 & W^0 & W^2 \\ 1 & W^1 & W^2 & W^3 \\ 1 & W^3 & W^2 & W^1 \end{bmatrix} x_{k_0 k_1} = \begin{bmatrix} X_{00} \\ X_{10} \\ X_{01} \\ X_{11} \end{bmatrix} = \begin{bmatrix} X_0 \\ X_2 \\ X_1 \\ X_3 \end{bmatrix}.$$

So we see that the matrix factorization is correct, provided we accept the re-ordering of the vector of transforms as $[X_0 \ X_2 \ X_1 \ X_3]$.

To appreciate the savings inherent in a coding based on this formulation, we trace the computation step by step.

From (11.115) we have

$$x'_{00} = x_{00} + W^0 x_{10}$$
$$x'_{10} = x_{00} + W^2 x_{10}$$

but because $W^{nk+N/2} = W^{nk} W^{N/2} = W^{nk} e^{i\pi} = -W^{nk}$, we can write

$$\left. \begin{array}{l} x'_{00} = x_{00} + W^0 x_{10} \\ x'_{10} = x_{00} - W^0 x_{10} \end{array} \right\}.$$

Thus we can compute x'_{00} by using one complex multiplication (trivial in this case, because $W^0 = 1$) followed by one addition. Then using the complex multiplication already performed, x'_{10} follows with one further addition. This is the so-called 'dual node' effect, which allows computation to be performed 'in place' with overwriting of x_{00} and x_{10} by the values of x'_{00} and x'_{10}. Also

$$x'_{01} = x_{01} + W^0 x_{11}$$

and

$$x'_{11} = x_{01} + W^2 x_{11}$$
$$= x_{01} - W^0 x_{11}$$

showing that x'_{01} is obtained by a further multiplication and addition with x'_{11} following with one further addition. This means that the transformation

$$\mathbf{x}_{k_0 k_1} \to \mathbf{x}'_{n_1 k_1}$$

has been performed using 2 complex multiplications and 4 additions. Examining the second phase, we see from (11.116)

$$X'_{00} = x'_{00} + W^0 x'_{01}$$
$$X'_{01} = x'_{00} + W^2 x'_{01}$$
$$= x'_{00} - W^0 x'_{01}$$

and

$$X'_{10} = x'_{10} + W^1 x'_{11}$$
$$X'_{10} = x'_{10} + W^3 x'_{11}$$
$$= x'_{10} - W^1 x'_{11}$$

Thus, the transformation

$$\mathbf{x}'_{n_1 k_1} \to \mathbf{X}'_{n_0 n_1}$$

is achieved with 2 further complex multiplications and 4 further additions. The total number of computations involved is thus 4 complex multiplications and 8 complex additions. The saving is significant when we recall that direct calculation would involve $N^2 = 4^2 = 16$ multiplications and $N(N-1) = 12$ additions. It is possible to show that for general γ, the algorithm will require $n\gamma/2 = \frac{1}{2} N \log_2 N$ complex multiplications and $N\gamma$ complex additions. For example, when $N = 256$, direct evaluation of the discrete Fourier transform would require

$$N^2 = 256^2 = 65{,}536 \text{ complex multiplications and}$$

$N(N-1) = 256 \times 255 = 65{,}280$ complex additions.

The fast Fourier transform algorithm needs only

$\frac{1}{2}N\log_2 N = \frac{1}{2} \times 256 \times 8 = 1024$ multiplications and
$N\gamma = 256 \times 8 = 2048$ additions.

The third and final stage of the algorithm is the recovery of the natural order of the output or transform sequence. The re-ordering or scrambling process occurred at the stage (11.114) when we defined

$$X'_{n_1 n_0} = \sum_{k_1=0}^{1} x'_{n_1 k_1} W^{(2n_0+n_1)k_1} = X_{n_0 n_1} \,.$$

Such a scrambling process, which amounts to a re-ordering of the calculation sequence, is not necessary for a successful formulation, but structural symmetry is lost, meaning that storage requirements increase. The unscrambling process is obvious. Since $X_{n_0 n_1} = X'_{n_1 n_0}$ we simply have to reverse the digits in the binary labelling of $X'_{n_1 n_0}$ to obtain natural order for the transform vector $X_{n_1 n_0}$.

In summary, we can present the FFT (fast Fourier transform) algorithm for the case $N = 2^2 = 4$ by restating the relationships (11.113) and (11.114):

$$x'_{n_1 k_1} = \sum_{k=0}^{1} x_{k_0 k_1} W^{2n_1 k_0} \qquad n_1 = 0, 1; \qquad k_1 = 0, 1 \qquad\qquad (11.113)$$

$$X'_{n_1 n_0} = \sum_{k_1=0}^{1} x'_{n_1 k_1} W^{(2n_0+n_1)k_1} \qquad n_1 = 0, 1; \qquad n_0 = 0, 1. \qquad (11.114)$$

with $X_{n_0 n_1} = X'_{n_1 n_0} \qquad n_0 = 0, 1; \qquad n_1 = 0, 1 \,.$ \qquad\qquad\qquad (11.115)

As we have seen, the order in which the terms of the vectors $\mathbf{x}'$ and $\mathbf{X}'$ are generated is important, if in-place computation is to be performed. The diagram, or signal flow graph, in Fig. 11.13 illustrates this point. We see from Fig. 11.13 that each 'node' of each of the computed vectors or computational arrays involves data from just two nodes of the previous array.

Moreover, at each stage there are precisely two nodes which involve data from the same pair of nodes in the previous array. For example, the computation of x'_{00} involves the values of x_{00} and x_{10}, and these values only are required to compute x'_{10}.

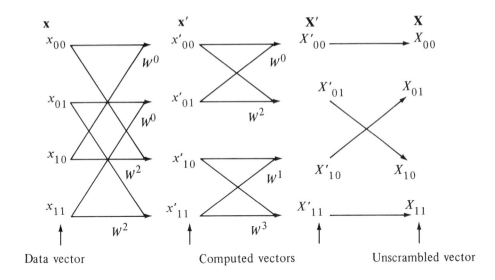

x   x'   X'   X

x_{00} —————→ x'_{00} —————→ X'_{00} —————→ X_{00}
       w^0 w^0

                                               X'_{01} X_{01}

x_{01} —————→ x'_{01} —————→
       w^0 w^2

x_{10} —————→ x'_{10} —————→ X'_{10} X_{10}
       w^2 w^1

x_{11} —————→ x'_{11} —————→ X'_{11} —————→ X_{11}
       w^2 w^3

   ↑   ↑   ↑   ↑
Data vector   Computed vectors   Unscrambled vector

Fig. 11.13 — Signal flow graph for FFT algorithm with $N = 4$ data points.

Such nodes are called 'dual nodes', and provided that dual-node computations are performed simultaneously, then the results may be returned to the original locations, overwriting data which will not be required further. In the example above, the value of x'_{00} overwrites that of x_{00} in the same location; similarly the value of x'_{10} is placed in the location which previously held the value of x_{10}.

Signal flow graphs for $N = 2^3 = 8$ and $N = 2^4 = 16$ may be developed in a similar manner and exhibit the same key features.

Example 11.21
Compute the DFT for the sequence $\{x\} = \{1,2,2,1\}$ of Example 11.17, using the stages of the FFT algorithm.

Here $N = 4 = 2^2$, so $\gamma = 2$, and our first step is to index $\{x\}$ using 2-bit binary notation, and to write the result as a vector (or array). Thus

$$\{x\} = \{x_{00}, x_{01}, x_{10}, x_{11}\} \ ,$$
$$= \{1, 2, 2, 1\} \ .$$

Define $\mathbf{x} = [x_{00}, x_{01}, x_{10}, x_{11}]^T = [1, 2, 2, 1]^T$ and note that since $N = 4$, $W = e^{-2\pi i/n} = e^{-i\pi/2} = -i$. Using the signal flow graph, Fig. 11.13, we compute the array or vector $\mathbf{x}'$ as

$$
\begin{bmatrix} x'_{00} \\ x'_{01} \\ x'_{10} \\ x'_{11} \end{bmatrix} = \begin{bmatrix} x_{00} + x_{10} \\ x_{01} + x_{11} \\ x_{00} - x_{10} \\ x_{01} - x_{11} \end{bmatrix} \begin{bmatrix} 3 \\ 3 \\ -1 \\ 1 \end{bmatrix}
$$

(since $W^2 = -W^0 = -1$). Then

$$
\mathbf{X} = \begin{bmatrix} X'_{00} \\ X'_{01} \\ X'_{10} \\ X'_{11} \end{bmatrix} = \begin{bmatrix} x'_{00} + W^0 x'_{01} \\ x'_{00} + W^2 x'_{01} \\ x'_{10} + W^1 x'_{11} \\ x'_{10} + W^3 x'_{11} \end{bmatrix} = \begin{bmatrix} 6 \\ 0 \\ -1-i \\ -1+i \end{bmatrix}
$$

(note that $W^3 = -W^1$).

Finally, 'unscrambling' to obtain the transform vector $\mathbf{X}$

$$
\mathbf{X} = \begin{bmatrix} X_{00} \\ X_{01} \\ X_{10} \\ X_{11} \end{bmatrix} = \begin{bmatrix} X'_{00} \\ X'_{10} \\ X'_{01} \\ X'_{11} \end{bmatrix} = \begin{bmatrix} 6 \\ -1-i \\ 0 \\ -1+i \end{bmatrix}.
$$

The DFT sequence is then

$$
\{X\} = \{6, \; -1-i, \; 0, \; -1+i\},
$$

in agreement with Example 11.17.

In view of the structural similarity between the DFT and its inverse, the IDFT, it is a simple matter to modify the coding of the algorithm in order to compute inverse transforms also. Many codes in fact incorporate this feature. A BASIC code for the FFT algorithm (including this and other features) is listed in the Appendix to this chapter.

11.12 ESTIMATING FOURIER TRANSFORMS

The latter part of this chapter has been devoted to the efficient computation of Fourier transforms in discrete time. The purpose of this study is two-fold. In the first place we wish to obtain a frequency domain representation of discrete-time signals and also a representation of the frequency response of a discrete-time system. These tasks can only be undertaken in a reasonable time if the FFT algorithm is invoked for the computation of the required discrete Fourier transforms. The second purpose of our study is to determine a method by which we may obtain numerical estimates of continuous-time Fourier transforms. This latter operation concludes this chapter.

From Chapter 9 we recall that the Fourier transform $F(i\omega)$ of a continuous-time function $f(t)$ is given by

$$F(i\omega) = \int_{-\infty}^{\infty} f(t)e^{-i\omega t}\, dt \; , \tag{11.116}$$

whenever the integral exists.

The calculation of the complex-valued function $F(i\omega)$ in (11.116) involves the evaluation of two real integrals I_1 and I_2, say, where if $f(t)$ is real,

$$F(i\omega) = I_1 + iI_2$$

with

$$I_1 = \int_{-\infty}^{\infty} f(t) \cos \omega t\, dt \; , \tag{11.117}$$

and

$$I_2 = -\int_{-\infty}^{\infty} f(t) \sin \omega t\, dt \; . \tag{11.118}$$

Suppose we now wish to approximate $F(i\omega)$, by estimating the values of I_1 and I_2, using a piecewise constant approximation to the integrand in each case. We then write

$$f(t) \cos \omega t \sim f(kT) \cos \omega kT \qquad kT \leqslant t < (k+1)T$$
$$f(t) \sin \omega t \sim f(kT) \sin \omega kt \qquad kT \leqslant t < (k+1)T \; .$$

The approximation scheme is illustrated in Fig. 11.14 for I_1.

With the piecewise constant approximation to the integrand

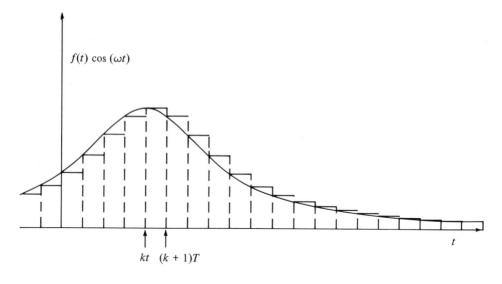

$f(t) \cos (\omega t)$

$kt \quad (k + 1)T$

Fig. 11.14 — Piecewise constant approximation to $f(t) \cos \omega t$.

$f(t) \cos \omega t$

for I_1, we see that I_1 can be estimated by the total area of all the rectangles of base length T and height

$$f(kT) \cos \omega kT \qquad kT \leqslant t < (k + 1)T \ .$$

That is,

$$I_1 \sim \sum_{k = -\infty}^{\infty} Tf(kT) \cos (\omega kT) \ .$$

In a similar manner we see that

$$I_2 \sim - \sum_{k = -\infty}^{\infty} Tf(kT) \sin (\omega kT)$$

whence $F(i\omega) = I_1 + iI_2$

$$\sim \sum_{k=-\infty}^{\infty} Tf(kT) \left(\cos\left(\omega kT\right) - i \sin\left(\omega kT\right)\right)$$

$$= \sum_{k=-\infty}^{\infty} Tf(kT) e^{-i\omega kT} \qquad (11.119)$$

The estimate (11.119), with $\theta = \omega T$, becomes

$$F(i\omega) \sim \sum_{k=-\infty}^{\infty} Tf(kT) \, e^{-ik\theta} = T \sum_{k=-\infty}^{\infty} f(kT) \, e^{ik\theta} \, ,$$

which is recognized as the discrete-time Fourier transform of the sequence $\{f_k\} = \{f(kT)\}$, multiplied by T. We discussed this transform in section 11.9, and in section 11.10 we recognized the fact that computation for the continuum of values of ω (or θ) was impossible numerically. Provided that the signal (or function) $f(t)$ is zero outside a finite interval, so that the number of non-zero terms in the sum (11.119) is finite, we may proceed in a similar manner now. Suppose we use N sample values $f(kT)$, $k = 0$, $1, \ldots, N-1$, from $f(t)$ (implying $N-1$ rectangles in the approximation!) and we seek also N values of the transform. We know that our estimate will be periodic of period $\theta_p = \omega_p T = 2\pi$, and so we choose

$$\Delta\theta = \frac{2\pi}{N}$$

or

$$\Delta\omega = \frac{2\pi}{NT} \, ,$$

so that our estimated values cover just one period. The sequence of N estimates is then periodic of period N.
   Now (11.119) becomes

$$F(in\Delta\omega) \sim \sum_{k=-k_1}^{(N-1)-k_1} Tf(kT) e^{-in\Delta\omega kT},$$

$$n = -n_1, \ldots, 0, \ldots, ([N-1] - n_1) \, . \qquad (11.120)$$

We see that (11.120) generates N estimates of $F(i\omega)$ at frequency spacing $\Delta\omega =$

$2\pi/(NT)$. It is usual, although not necessary (or indeed consistent with earlier work!), to choose $n_1 = 0$ so that n takes the values 0, 1, ..., $(N-1)$. The value of k_1, of course, depends on the time signal being transformed, but we may set $k_1 = 0$ by choosing a suitable time origin. Writing $F_n = F(in\Delta\omega)$ and using (11.99) we see that

$$F_n \sim \sum_{k=0}^{N-1} Tf(kT)\, e^{-nik\Delta\omega T}$$

or

$$\{F_n\} \sim T\{\mathrm{DFT}\{f(kT)\}\} \ . \tag{11.121}$$

That is, the sequence $\{F_n\}$ which approximates the Fourier transform of the (finite duration) continuous-time signal $f(t)$ is a scaled version of the discrete Fourier transform of the sequence of samples, $\{f(kT)\}$. We illustrate the approximation method by use of an example.

Example 11.22
Suppose $f(t)$ is as illustrated in Fig. 11.15. Estimate the Fourier transform and compare with the exact values.

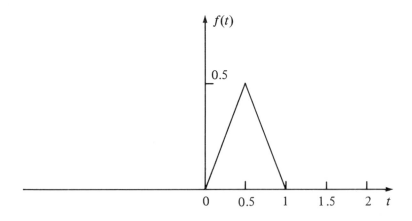

Fig. 11.15 — Signal for Example 11.22 — the delayed triangular pulse.

We will use $N = 8$ samples at intervals $T = 0.25$ sec. Thus we generate the sequence $\{f(kT)\}_{k=0}^{7} = \{f(0), f(0.25), f(0.5), f(0.75), f(1.0), f(1.25), f(1.5), f(1.75)\}$.

$$\text{Now } f(t) = \begin{cases} t & 0 \leqslant t < 0.5 \\ 1-t & 0.5 \leqslant t < 1 \\ 0 & t \geqslant 1 \end{cases}$$

and so $\{f(kT)\}_{k=0}^{7} = \{0, 0.25, 0.5, 0.25, 0, 0, 0, 0,\}$. The DFT of this sequence is the sequence $\{F_n\}_{n=0}^{7}$, generated by

$$F_n = \sum_{k=0}^{7} f(kT)\, e^{-ikn\Delta\omega T}\ ,$$

where $\Delta\omega = 2\pi/(NT) = 2\pi/(8 \times 0.25) = \pi$. Thus

$$F_n = \sum_{k=0}^{7} f(kT)\, e^{-ikn\pi/4}$$

$$= \sum_{k=0}^{3} f(kT)\, e^{-ikn\pi/4}\ ,$$

because $f(1) = f(1.25) = f(1.5) = f(1.75) = 0$.

The DFT sequence is quickly computed by hand, although a less artificial example would require the use of an FFT algorithm.

By whichever method chosen, our estimate of the Fourier transform is the sequence

$$\{TF_n\}_{n=0}^{7}\ ,$$

yielding 8 valuesd approximating the transform at

$$\omega = n\Delta\omega\ ,\qquad n = 0, \ldots, 7\ ,$$

that is, $\omega = 0, \pi, 2\pi, \ldots, 7\pi$. At $\omega = 0$, our estimate is

$$TF_0 = T \sum_{k=0}^{3} f(kT)\, e^{-ik0\pi/4}$$

$$= T\ (f(0) + f(0.25) + f(0.5) + f(0.75))$$

$$= 0.25 \times 1 = 1.25\ .$$

At $\omega = \pi$, we obtain the estimate

$$TF_1 = T \sum_{k=0}^{3} f(kT)\, e^{-ik1\pi/4}$$

$$= T(f(0) + f(0.25)\, e^{-i\pi/4} + f(0.5)e^{-i\pi/2} + f(0.75)\, e^{-3i\pi/4})$$

$$= 0.25 \left(0 + 0.25\left(\frac{\sqrt{2}}{2}\right)(1-i) + 0.5(-i) + 0.25\left(\frac{\sqrt{2}}{2}\right)(-1-i) \right)$$

$$= 0.25\left(\frac{\sqrt{2}}{8}\right)\left(-2i - \frac{i}{2}\right)$$

$$= 0.25\left(\frac{\sqrt{2}+2}{4}\right)(-i)$$

$$= -0.21339i \ .$$

Continuing in a similar manner, we obtain the sequence

$$\{TF_0,\ TF_1,\ \ldots,\ TF_7\}$$

$$= \{0.25,\ -0.21339i,\ -0.125, 0.03661i, 0,\ -0.03661i,\ -0.125, 0.21339i\}.$$
The exact transform is easily computed as

$$F(i\omega) = \mathcal{F}\{f(t)\}$$

$$= \frac{e^{-i\omega/2}}{4}\ \text{sinc}^2\frac{\omega}{4}$$

and using this result, we can examine our estimate for the modulus of the transform. We will compare not only with the hand calculation of the DFT alone, but also with more accurate values obtained using the FFT algorithm.

Table 11.3 summarizes the results, (a) using 8-point DFT and (b) 64-point DFT calculated via the FFT algorithm.

In Table 11.3 we see that the estimate using 8 points provides values at intervals $\Delta\omega = \pi$, up to $\omega = 7\pi$. We note that beyond $\omega = 4\pi$, the values obtained are copies of those values obtained at $\omega = 3\pi, 2\pi$ and π respectively. This is not surprising, because the DFT is periodic of period $N = 8$, and so $F_5 = F_{-3}$, $F_6 = F_{-2}$ and $F_7 = F_{-1}$. For a real signal, the amplitude spectrum $|F(i\omega)|$ will be symmetric and thus for real signals, the second half of the estimated spectrum will always be a copy of the first.

In order to obtain estimates of the amplitude spectrum at higher frequencies, and improve those already obtained, we can reduce the value of T, and increase the value of N. Setting $NT = 2$, with $N = 64$, gives $T = 0.03125$ and the corresponding estimates are quickly calculated using the FFT algorithm. Table 11.3 shows that good estimates

Table 11.3 — Exact values of $|F(i\omega)|$ and estimates.

ω	$|F(i\omega)|$	Est $|F(i\omega)|$(a)	Est $|F(i\omega)|$(b)
0	0.25000	0.25000	0.25000
π	0.20264	0.21339	0.20281
2π	0.10133	0.1250	0.10165
3π	0.02516	0.03361	0.02679
4π	0	0	0
5π	0.00811	0.03661	0.00827
6π	0.01258	0.1250	0.01159
7π	0.00414	0.21339	0.00430
8π	0	X	0
9π	0.00251	X	0.00267
10π	0.00405	X	0.00439

are obtained over the range $\omega = 0$ to $\omega = 10\pi$, and also in fact well beyond. The sequence obtained is again periodic, but now the period is $N = 64$, corresponding to a frequency period

$$\omega_p = \frac{2\pi}{T} = \frac{2\pi}{0.03125} = 201.062.$$

Again, symmetry in the spectrum of a real signal means that the second half of the amplitude spectrum is a copy of the first half. It is interesting to observe that whereas decreasing T and increasing N has improved the estimated values, the frequency spacing is unchanged. That is, estimates are still obtained at separation $\Delta\omega = \pi$. To decrease this spacing, in other words to improve the frequency resolution, we must examine the factors which determine $\Delta\omega$. Now

$$\Delta\omega = \frac{2\pi}{NT},$$

and we see that to decrease $\Delta\omega$ we must increase the product NT. This means that we must observe the time signal $f(t)$ over a larger time period, from $t = 0$ until $t = NT$. Table 11.4 shows the results of two sets of calculations with NT increased from 2 to 4. In case (a), N was set to 64, meaning that $T = 0.0625$ whereas in case (b), N was set at $N = 128$ so that $T = 0.03125$, as before.

The information in Tables 11.3 and 11.4 is shown graphically in Fig. 11.16.

We may derive this method of approximating the continuous-time Fourier transform from an alternative point of view. From section 8.6 we know that we may write a continuous function $f(t)$ as

Table 11.4 — Improved resolution in the frequency domain: (a) DFT with $N = 64$, (b) DFT with $N = 128$, both calculated via the EFT algorithm.

ω	Exact $|F(i\omega)|$	Est $|F(i\omega)|$(a)	Est $|F(i\omega)|$(b)
0	0.25000	0.25000	0.25000
$\pi/2$	0.23741	0.23760	0.23746
π	0.20264	0.20329	0.20281
$3\pi/2$	0.15375	0.15487	0.15403
2π	0.10132	0.10263	0.10165
$5\pi/2$	0.05535	0.05647	0.05563
3π	0.02252	0.02318	0.02268
$7/\pi2$	0.00485	0.00504	0.00489
4π	0.0	0.0	0.0
$9/\pi2$	0.00293	0.00313	0.00298
5π	0.00811	0.00879	0.00827

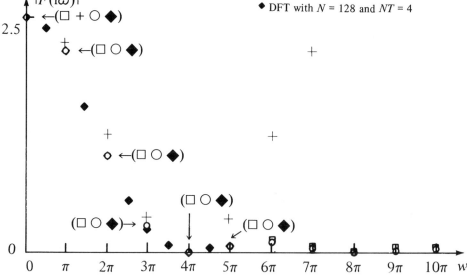

Fig. 11.16 — DFT estimate for $|F(i\omega)|$.

$$f(t) = \int_{-\infty}^{\infty} f(t)\, \delta(t - \tau)\mathrm{d}\tau \ .$$

If $f(t)$ is of finite support (that is zero outside finite time interval) we may approximate this integral as follows.

$$f(t) = \int_{-\infty}^{\infty} f(t)\,\delta(t-\tau)\,d\tau$$

$$\sim \sum_{k} Tf(kT)\,\delta(t-kT)$$

$$= \sum_{k} Tf(t)\,\delta(t-kT)$$

$$= Tf(t) \sum_{k=-\infty}^{\infty} \delta(t-kT) \tag{11.122}$$

$$= Tf_s(t) \tag{11.123}$$

where

$$f_s(t) = f(t) \sum_{k=-\infty}^{\infty} \delta(t-kT) \ , \tag{11.124}$$

and we have used the equivalence $f(kT)\,\delta(t-kT) = f(t)\,\delta(t-kT)$.
    We may now compute the Fourier transform on the basis of the estimate (11.122) as

$$F(i\omega) \sim \int_{-\infty}^{\infty} Tf(t) \sum_{k=-\infty}^{\infty} \delta(t-kT)\,e^{-i\omega t}\,dt$$

$$= T \sum_{k=-\infty}^{\infty} \int_{-\infty}^{\infty} f(t)\,\delta(t-kT)\,e^{-i\omega t}\,dt$$

$$= T \sum_{k=-\infty}^{\infty} f(kT)\,e^{-i\omega kT} \ ,$$

which is precisely (11.119) again, showing that this is an alternative way of viewing the approximation process.
    Thus, from (11.123) we see that

$$F(i\omega) \sim T\mathscr{F}\{f_s(t)\}$$

$$= T\mathscr{F}\{f(t) \sum_{k=-\infty}^{\infty} \delta(t - kT)\}$$

$$= \frac{T\mathscr{F}(i\omega) * \omega_0 \sum_{n=-\infty}^{\infty} \delta(\omega - n\omega_0)}{2\pi} , \quad \text{where } \omega_0 = \frac{2\pi}{T}$$

$$= \mathscr{F}(i\omega) * \sum_{n=-\infty}^{\infty} \delta(\omega - n\omega_0)$$

$$= \sum_{n=-\infty}^{\infty} \mathscr{F}(i\omega) * \delta(\omega - n\omega_0)$$

$$= T\mathscr{F}_s(i\omega)$$

$$= \sum_{n=-\infty}^{\infty} \mathscr{F}(i\omega - in\omega_0) , \quad \text{from (9.40) .} \tag{11.125}$$

The relation (11.125) explains the problem of DFT-based approximation to continuous-time Fourier transforms.

It is clear that if T is too large then reference to Fig. 9.18 shows that successive repetitions of $|F(i\omega)|$ will interfere with one another. As discussed in section 9.9, it is necessary to choose

$$T < \pi/\omega_m \tag{11.126}$$

where ω_m is the maximum frequency which occurs in the signal $f(t)$, to avoid aliasing error.

It should be remarked that band-limited signals must be of infinite duration, and so for finite duration signals, error due to aliasing can never be totally eliminated. For finite duration signals, ω_m is taken as the highest significant frequency and a healthy 'safety-factor' inserted in (11.126). Quality of estimate is not only a matter of choosing T correctly. Recall that, for high resolution in the frequency domain, we must observe the signal $f(T)$ for an adequate time ($t = NT$). Thus for accuracy (small T) and high resolution (large NT) we must choose large values of N. This is why the FFT algorithm is of such vital importance.

APPENDIX

```
10 REM THIS PROGRAMME IS BASED ON THAT GIVEN IN E.O BRIGHAM
20 REM THE FAST FOURIER TRANSFORM, REWRITTEN IN BASIC
30 REM IT HAS BEEN  RUN USING GWBASIC AND TURBO BASIC
40 REM SET, OR READ XREAL AND XIMAG FOR YOUR OWN APPLICATION
50 REM SET NU AND FFT,FFT=1 FOR DFT,-1 FOR IDFT
51 REM NU SHOULD BE SET TO 2 AS THE PROGRAMME STANDS
60 DEFINT I-N
65 PRINT"NU MUST BE SET TO 2 WITH THE CURRENT DATA"
80 PRINT"SET NU, WHERE N=2^NU                                        "
90 INPUT NU:N=2^NU:PRINT"NOW SET FFT = 1 FOR FFT, -1 FOR IFFT"
95 DIM XREAL(N),XIMAG(N)
100 INPUT FFT
120 REM DATA FOR EXAMPLE 11.19
130 XREAL(1)=6
140 XREAL(2)=-1
150 XREAL(3)=0
160 XREAL(4)=-1
170 FOR IH=1 TO 4
180 XIMAG(IH)=0
190 NEXT IH
200 XIMAG(2)=-1
210 XIMAG(4)=1
220 IF FFT=1 GOTO 260
230 FOR IK=1 TO N
240 XIMAG(IK)=FFT*XIMAG(IK)
250 NEXT IK
260 N2=N\2
270 NU1=NU-1
280 K=0
290 FOR L= 1 TO NU
300 FOR I= 1 TO N2
310 J=K\2^NU1
320 GOSUB 750
330 P=IBITR
340 ARG=6.283185*P/N
350 C=COS(ARG)
360 S=SIN(ARG)
370 K1=K+1
380 K1N2=K1+N2
390 TREAL=XREAL(K1N2)*C+XIMAG(K1N2)*S
400 TIMAG=XIMAG(K1N2)*C-XREAL(K1N2)*S
410 XREAL(K1N2)=XREAL(K1)-TREAL
420 XIMAG(K1N2)=XIMAG(K1)-TIMAG
430 XREAL(K1)=XREAL(K1)+TREAL
440 XIMAG(K1)=XIMAG(K1)+TIMAG
450 K=K+1
460 NEXT I
470 K=K+N2
480 IF K<N GOTO 300
490 K=0
500 NU1=NU1-1
510 N2=N2\2
520 NEXT L
530 FOR K =1 TO N
540 J=K-1
550 GOSUB 750
560 I=IBITR+1
570 IF I<K GOTO 640
580 TREAL=XREAL(K)
```

```
590 TIMAG= XIMAG(K)
600 XREAL(K)=XREAL(I)
610 XIMAG(K)=XIMAG(I)
620 XREAL(I)=TREAL
630 XIMAG(I)=TIMAG
640 NEXT K
650 IF FFT=1 GOTO 690
660 FOR JK =1 TO N
670 XREAL(JK)=XREAL(JK)/N:XIMAG(JK)=FFT*XIMAG(JK)/N
680 NEXT JK
690 PRINT "           FFT      "
700 PRINT "XREAL            XIMAG"
710 FOR IH=1 TO N
720 PRINT   XREAL(IH),XIMAG(IH)
730 NEXT IH
740 END
750 J1=J
760 IBITR=0
770 FOR M=1 TO NU
780 J2=J1\2
790 IBITR=IBITR*2+(J1-2*J2)
800 J1=J2
810 NEXT M
820 RETURN


10   REM THIS VERSION CALCULATE ESTIMATES OF THE CONTINUOUS FT
20   REM AND IS SET UP FOR EXAMPLE 11.22
30   REM THE CODE IS BASED ON THAT GIVEN IN E O BRIGHAM
40   REM AND HAS BEEN TESTED USING GWBASIC AND TURBO BASIC
50   REM SET  NU
60   DEFINT I-N
70   PRINT "WHAT IS NU WHERE N=2^NU?"
80   INPUT NU
90 REM THIS PROGRAM USES THE TRIANGULAR  PULSE
100 N=2^NU:T=2/N
110 DELW=6.283185/(T*N)
120 DIM XREAL(N),XIMAG(N)
130 FOR JM =1 TO N
140 XIMAG(JM)=0
150 IF (JM-1)*T >.5 GOTO 180
160 XREAL(JM)=(JM-1)*T
170 GOTO 220
180 IF (JM-1)*T > 1 GOTO 210
190 XREAL(JM)=1-(JM-1)*T
200 GOTO 220
210 XREAL(JM)=0
220 NEXT JM
230 PRINT "STARTING DATA"
240 PRINT " N            XREAL               XIMAG"
250 FOR NL=1 TO N
260 PRINT   (NL-1),XREAL(NL),XIMAG(NL)
270 NEXT NL
280 N2=N\2
290 NU1=NU-1
300 K=0
310 FOR L= 1 TO NU
320 FOR I= 1 TO N2
330 J=K\2^NU1
340 GOSUB 770
```

```
350 P=IBITR
360 ARG=6.283185*P/N
370 C=COS(ARG)
380 S=SIN(ARG)
390 K1=K+1
400 K1N2=K1+N2
410 TREAL=XREAL(K1N2)*C+XIMAG(K1N2)*S
420 TIMAG=XIMAG(K1N2)*C-XREAL(K1N2)*S
430 XREAL(K1N2)=XREAL(K1)-TREAL
440 XIMAG(K1N2)=XIMAG(K1)-TIMAG
450 XREAL(K1)=XREAL(K1)+TREAL
460 XIMAG(K1)=XIMAG(K1)+TIMAG
470 K=K+1
480 NEXT I
490 K=K+N2
500 IF K<N GOTO 320
510 K=0
520 NU1=NU1-1
530 N2=N2\2
540 NEXT L
550 FOR K =1 TO N
560 J=K-1
570 GOSUB 770
580 I=IBITR+1
590 IF I<K GOTO 660
600 TREAL=XREAL(K)

610 TIMAG= XIMAG(K)
620 XREAL(K)=XREAL(I)
630 XIMAG(K)=XIMAG(I)
640 XREAL(I)=TREAL
650 XIMAG(I)=TIMAG
660 NEXT K
670 PRINT "        FFT            "
680 PRINT " N               XREAL            XIMAG"
690 FOR IH=1 TO N
700 PRINT IH-1,  XREAL(IH),XIMAG(IH)
710 NEXT IH
720 PRINT "FT ESTIMATES"
730 FOR IH=1 TO N
740 PRINT (IH-1)*DELW,XREAL(IH)*T,XIMAG(IH)*T
750 NEXT IH
760 END
770 J1=J
780 IBITR=0
790 FOR M=1 TO NU
800 J2=J1\2
810 IBITR=IBITR*2+(J1-2*J2)
820 J1=J2
830 NEXT M
840 RETURN
```

REFERENCES

[1] E. O. Brigham, *The Fast Fourier Transform*, Prentice-Hall, Englewood Cliffs, New Jersey, 1974.

[2] J. W. Cooley and J. W. Tukey, An Algorithm for Machine Calculation of Complex Fourier Series, *Math. Computation*, **19**, 297–301 (1965).

[3] A. Page, *Mathematical Analysis and Techniques*, Oxford University press, London, 1976.

EXERCISES

1. Calculate the Z-transform of the following causal sequences.

   (a) $\{0,0,1,2, -2, -1,2,0\}$
   (b) $\{x_k\}$, with $x_k = 1, 0 < k \leqslant 5; x_k = 0, k > 5$
   (c) $\{5^k\}$
   (d) $\{(-1/4)^k\}$
   (e) $\{5k\}$
   (f) $\{\sin(2k\theta)\}$: hint express $\sin(2k\theta)$ in terms of the exponential function.

2. Invert the following Z-transforms of causal sequences:

   (a) $$\frac{2z^2 - 3z}{z^2 - 3z + 2}$$

   (b) $$\frac{z^2 - z}{(z-4)(z-2)^2}$$

   (c) $$\frac{z - 3}{z^2 - 3z + 2}.$$

3. Solve the following difference equations:

   (a) $2y_{k+2} - 5y_{k+1} + 2y_k = 0,$ $y_0 = 1, \ y_1 = 0$
   (b) $6y_{k+2} + 5y_{k+1} - y_k = 10,$ $y_0 = 0, \ y_1 = 1$
   (c) $12y_{k+2} - 7y_{k+1} + y_k = 18,$ $y_0 = 0, \ y_1 = 3$
   (d) $y(k+2) + 2y(k) = 0,$ $y(0) = 1, \ y(1) = 2.$

4. Find the impulse response of the system

   $$8y_{k+2} - 6y_{k+1} + y_k = u_k.$$

   Is the system stable? Illustrate the response with a sketch.

5. The system

   $$10y(k+2) - 7y(k+1) + 1.2y(k) = 5(u(k+1) + u(k))$$

is initially quiescent. Find the impulse response, and the response to the step input, $u(k) = 1, k \geqslant 0$.

6. Calculate the frequency response function for the stable system

$$2y_{k+1} + y_k = u_k \ .$$

Plot the amplitude response over the range $-2\pi \leqslant 0 \leqslant 2\pi$.

7. Find the Z-transfer function for the system

$$8y(k+2) + 2y(k+1) - y(k) = u(k) + 2u(k+1)$$

and verify that it is a stable system. Plot the amplitude response function over the range $-2\pi \leqslant 0 \leqslant 2\pi$.

8. Draw block diagrams to represent the systems of Exercises 3(b), 4, 5 and 7.

9. Calculate the discrete-time transform of the sequence

$$\{1,0,2,1,2,0,1\} \ .$$

Sketch the amplitude spectrum of the transform.

10. Find the DFT of the sequence $\{x_k\}$, where

$$x_k = \begin{cases} e^{-0.3k} & 0 \leqslant k \leqslant 9 \\ 0 & 10 \leqslant k \leqslant 31 \end{cases} .$$

11. Show that if the discrete-time system has a repeated pole on the unit circle, $|z| = 1$, then it is unstable irrespective of the other pole locations.

12. Verify the structure of the 8-point FFT matrix of section 11.11.

12

The design of digital filters

12.1 INTRODUCTION

In this final chapter, we bring together many of the ideas of the earlier chapters to discuss the process of design of digital filters. We regard digital filters as discrete-time systems which will perform similar tasks to the analogue filter designs of Chapter 10. In essence, we are laying the foundations for the software replacement of such analogue devices, although a discussion of the effects of signal quantization, would be required for a full treatment. Obviously such software will process samples drawn from continuous-time signals, and we are well aware from Chapters 9 and 11 of the implications of the sampling process on signal spectra, particularly in terms of the appearance of periodic effects.

This book is designed to illustrate the mathematical aspects of communication theory. For this reason, this chapter sets out only to explain some underlying ideas in the theory, and does not attempt to give an exhaustive treatment of current engineering practice. It is hoped that the reader will find the material in this chapter a sufficient introduction to the more advanced modern engineering texts. A secondary aim of the book is to highlight the place of applied mathematics as an aid in the design or synthesis task. Thus, in this chapter our object is to produce digital filter designs, and readers are encouraged to extend the work to produce and experiment with their own designs. Access to a PC is valuable in this respect, although not essential; however those who do have such access will quickly appreciate the ease of production of the necessary code to test designs.

12.2 AN 'INDIRECT' DESIGN METHOD — THE IMPULSE INVARIANT APPROACH

In this section we explore a method of obtaining a discrete-time system which emulates, in a particular sense, the behaviour of a continuous time prototype system.

First we will describe the way in which the discrete-time system is to emulate the prototype, and, having determined the design, we will go on to analyse its behaviour.

At an intuitive level, we know that the impulse response of a linear system serves to characterize that system. We mean by this that the output response $y(t)$ arising from any input signal $u(t)$ can be expressed as a convolution integral:

$$y(t) = \int_{-\infty}^{\infty} u(\tau)h(t-\tau)\,d\tau \ ,$$

with $h(t)$ the system impulse response, as the 'kernel'.

Thus, we could postulate as a design strategy a method which would produce a discrete-time system such that its response to the unit (im)pulse sequence $\{u(kT)\}$, where

$$u(kT) = \begin{bmatrix} 1 & k=0 \\ 0 & k\neq 0 \ , \end{bmatrix}$$

would produce exactly the same values as samples drawn from the impulse response $h(t)$ of the prototype at the same instants. Notice that we have again adopted the form of sequence notation $\{u(kT)\}$, which emphasizes the fact that the kth term in the sequence is generated from $u(t)$ by a sample taken at time $t = kT$. This approach to discrete-time system design can be demonstrated as follows.

Suppose that we have a prototype analogue system, specified in the Laplace transform domain by its transfer function $H(s)$. Then for input signals $u(t)$ and output signals $y(t)$, with Laplace transforms $U(s)$ and $Y(s)$ respectively, we have

$$Y(s) = H(s)U(s) \ .$$

In particular, if $u(t) = \delta(t)$, so that $U(s) = 1$, we generate the impulse response $y_\delta(t)$. Writing $Y_\delta(s)$ as the Laplace transform of $y_\delta(t)$, we have

$$y_\delta(t) = \mathcal{L}^{-1}\{Y_\delta(s)\} = \mathcal{L}^{-1}\{H(s)\} = h(t) \ .$$

If we now sample this response at intervals T, we generate the sequence $\{h(kT)\}$, and taking the Z-transform, we obtain

$$\mathcal{H}(z) = Z\{h(kT)\} \ .$$

We then construct the discrete-time system so that its transfer function $\mathcal{D}(z)$ is given by

$$\mathcal{D}(z) = K.\mathcal{H}(z) \ ,$$

where K is a constant, which will initially be set to unity.

Clearly when $\mathcal{U}(z) = 1$, so that the input sequence is the unit (im)pulse sequence, the output will be

$$\{y(kT)\} = Z^{-1}\{K\mathcal{H}(z)\} = \{Kh(kT)\} \ ,$$

showing that the impulse responses of continuous- and discrete-time systems are matched at the sampling instants if K is set to unity. For this reason the design method is known as the impulse invariant technique. Later, we will see that there are persuasive arguments for selecting an alternative value for K.

We examine the method in detail in the following example.

Example 12.1
Use the impulse invariant method to design a discrete-time replacement for the first-order Butterworth filter with cut-off frequency ω_c.

From Chapter 10 the transfer function of the first-order Butterworth filter is

$$H(s) = \frac{\omega_c}{s + \omega_c} \ .$$

At once we obtain the impulse response as $h(t) = \omega_c e^{-k\omega_c t}$, $t \leqslant 0$, and so $\{h(kT)\} = \{\omega_c e^{-k\omega_c T}\}$, $k \geqslant 0$. Now,

$$\mathcal{H}(z) = Z\{\omega_c e^{-k\omega_c T}\} = \omega_c \frac{z}{z - e^{-\omega_c T}}$$

and we set

$$\frac{\mathcal{Y}(z)}{\mathcal{U}(z)} = K\mathcal{H}(z) = K\omega_c \frac{z}{z - e^{-\omega_c T}} \ , \tag{12.1}$$

as the transfer function of the discrete-time system.

From the transform domain representation, we can derive the time domain difference equation which will represent the system. From (12.1) we obtain

$$(z - e^{-\omega_c T})\mathcal{Y}(z) = K\omega_c z\mathcal{U}(z)$$

and inverting, we obtain the difference equation

$$y[(k+1)T] - e^{-\omega_c T} y(kT) = K\omega_c u[(k+1)T] \ ,$$

or,

$$y(kT) - e^{-\omega_c T} y[(k-1)T] = K\omega_c u(kT) \ , \qquad k \geqslant 1 \ .$$

This design can be implemented by the system of Fig. 12.1.

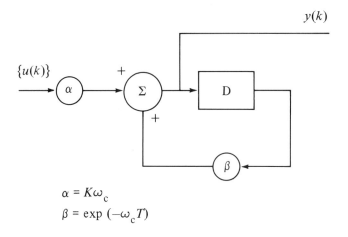

$$\alpha = K\omega_c$$
$$\beta = \exp(-\omega_c T)$$

Fig. 12.1 — Time domain block diagram for the system of Example 12.1.

The impulse invariant technique can be derived from a more rigorous basis by examining the response of a continuous-time system to the sampled version of $u(t)$. The discrete-time system is then obtained by matching repsonses at the sampling instants. In section 9.9, we saw that continuous-time 'representation' of the (causal) sampled signal was

$$u_s(t) = \sum_{k=0}^{\infty} u(t)\delta(t - kT) \ .$$

If this signal is applied to our prototype continuous-time system, with impulse response $h(t)$, the output will be

$$y(t) = \int_{-\infty}^{\infty} h(t-\tau) \sum_{k=0}^{\infty} u(\tau)\delta(t-\tau) \, d\tau$$

$$= \sum_{k=0}^{\infty} h(t - kT)u(kT) \ .$$

If we examine the response at the sampling times given by $t = nT$ we see that

$$y(nT) = \sum_{k=0}^{\infty} h([n-k]T)u(kT)$$

$$= \sum_{k=0}^{n} h([n-k]T)u(kT) \tag{12.2}$$

if $h(t)$ is causal.

The result (12.2) is in the form of a convolution sum, and from equation (11.59) we identify (12.2) as the response of a discrete-time system with (im)pulse response sequence $\{h(kT)\}$. That is, an (im)pulse response sequence identical with the sequence obtained by sampling the impulse response of the prototype continuous time system. Thus we have re-established the impulse invariant technique.

We now turn to the frequency response of a discrete-time filter designed using the impulse invariant technique. The impulse response sequence of the discrete-time system is

$$\{h(kT)\}$$

and representing this in the 'continuous-time' form (see section 9.9), we have

$$h_s(t) = \sum_{k=-\infty}^{\infty} h(t)\delta(t-kT) \ ,$$

where $h(t)$ is the impulse response of the prototype analogue system. The frequency response of the discrete-time system is then, from (9.40),

$$H_s(i\omega) = \frac{1}{T} \sum_{n=-\infty}^{\infty} H(i(\omega - 2n\pi/T)) \tag{12.3}$$

where $H(i\omega)$ is the frequency response of the prototype. We see that the frequency response of our design consists of a series of scaled repeats of the frequency response of the prototype system. In passing, we note that the scaling can be removed if we set $K = T$ in the specification of the design procedure, and this option is frequently selected. We do of course have some control over the spacing of the repeats, and this control is exercised by a suitable choice of T. This control has to be used in order to reduce the effects of 'aliasing' error. To be precise about the nature of this error we have to consider two types of filter amplitude response. First, we consider the ideal case when the amplitude response is of bounded support, that is, it is zero outside some finite range of the frequency variable ω. We should point out that this is never precisely the case, although good analogue filter designs approximate this ideal. Under this assumption, if components of a signal were located at a frequency so far above cut-off frequency that they were actually located in one of the pass-band repetitions then such components would be passed by the filter, contrary to the design intent. It is easy to deduce from Fig. 12.2 that to avoid this situation, we must

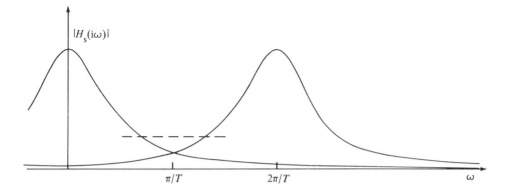

Fig. 12.2 — Amplitude spectrum of a digital design obtained using the impulse invariant technique.

set the sampling frequency $\omega_s = 2\pi/T \geqslant 2\omega_m$, that is, $T \leqslant \pi/\omega_m$ at least, where ω_m is the largest frequency expected to occur in the input signal.

The second case we consider is that which is depicted in Fig. 12.2, where the 'tail' of the amplitude response overlaps with the 'leading tail' of the adjacent repeat. In this case, unwanted transmission can occur for signals or components of signals with frequencies located close to half the sampling frequency, $\omega_s/2$, owing to the doubling-up effect on the amplitude response at the overlap. This problem can be reduced to an acceptable level by further increasing ω_m, that is decreasing T, although, at least theoretically, it can never be eliminated for a filter whose amplitude response is not of bounded support.

Obviously, if frequency components *do* exist above ω_m in the input signal, then as we have said, they may be 'passed' through one of the repetitions of the designed pass band. For this reason, in most real applications an analogue pre-filter is employed to enforce band limitation on input signals to a digital process. The interested reader should consult Jackson [1] for further information.

In conclusion, we note that designs produced using the impulse invariant techniques and based upon stable prototypes will also be stable. This follows because 's-plane' poles of the continuous-time system are mapped into 'z-plane' poles of the discrete-time design by the mapping.

$$z = e^{sT} .$$

The reader is invited to verify the stability result as an exercise.

12.3 THE STEP INVARIANT METHOD

A second indirect method of filter design, based on emulating a specific response of an analogue prototype, is the so-called step invariant method. As the name implies, in this method we generate a discrete-time design which produces, as its step response sequence, a sequence identical with a sequence of samples drawn from the step response of the analogue prototype at the appropriate instants.

The motivation for this approach becomes clear when we examine the response of the prototype system to a piecewise constant approximation to an input signal $u(t)$. In discussing the impulse invariant technique, we examined the response of the prototype to the sampled version of $u(t)$. Now we imagine the sampling operation to be followed by a zero-order hold device. Such a device, on receiving a sample value $u(kT)$ from $u(t)$, 'holds' this value as its output until the next sample, $u([k+1]T)$, arrives, when the process repeats. Fig. 12.3 illustrates the piecewise constant signal

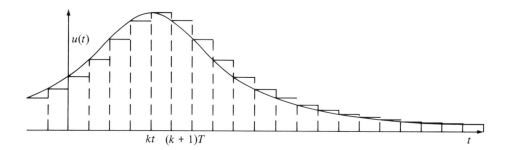

Fig. 12.3 — The piecewise constant signal obtained from the sample and zero-order hold processes applied to $u(t)$.

obtained by following the sampling operation on the signal $u(t)$ by a zero-order hold device.

The zero-order hold device clearly provides a method for analogue signal reconstruction following some digital signal processing operation.

To continue our development, we now consider the effect of supplying the (causal) piecewise constant input signal

$$u(t) = u(kT) \qquad kT \leqslant t < (k+1)T \tag{12.4}$$

to a continuous-time system with step response $y_s(t)$. To do this, write (12.4) as

$$u(t) = u(0)\xi(t) + [u(T) - u(0)]\xi(t - T) +$$
$$[u(2T) - u(T)]\xi(t - 2T) + \dots$$

$$= u(0)\xi(t) + \sum_{n=1}^{\infty} \{u(nT) - u([n-1]T)\}\xi(t - nT) \ .$$

Using the properties of linear, time invariant systems, we can see that the output will be a series of appropriately timed scaled step responses, that is,

$$y(t) = u(0)y_s(t) + \sum_{n=1}^{\infty} \{u(nT) - u\{[n-1]T\}\}y_s(t - nT) \ . \tag{12.5}$$

Our design strategy will then be to produce a discrete-time system with step response sequence identical to the sequence of samples $\{y(kT)\}$, obtained from (12.5). Now

$$y(kT) = u(0)y_s(kT) + \sum_{n-1}^{\infty} [u(nT) - u(\{n-1\}T)]y_s(\{k-n\}T)$$

$$= \sum_{n=1}^{\infty} [u(nT)y_s(\{k-n\}T) - \sum_{n=1}^{\infty} u\{(n-1)T\}y_s\{(k-n)T\} \ .$$

We recognize these sums as convolution sums; thus on taking the z-transform, we find that

$$Z\{y(kT)\} = \mathcal{U}(z)\mathcal{Y}_s(z) - 1/z\mathcal{U}(z)\mathcal{Y}_s(z)$$

$$= \frac{z-1}{z}\mathcal{Y}_s(z)\mathcal{U}(z) \ ,$$

where $\mathcal{Y}_s(z) = Z\{y_s(kT)\}$.

This suggests that we should calculate the step response of our prototype design, sample it and take the Z-transform of the sequence so obtained, to obtain $\mathcal{Y}_s(z)$. We should then use as our transfer function of the digital design,

$$D(z) = (z-1)\mathcal{Y}_s(z)/z \ .$$

We demonstrate the design procedure in Example 12.2.

Example 12.2
Determine the step invariant design based on the first-order Butterworth filter of Example 12.1.

The transfer function of the prototype analogue design is again

$$H(s) = \frac{\omega_c}{s + \omega_c}$$

and thus the transform of the step response is $Y_s(s)$, where

$$Y_s(s) = \frac{1}{s}\frac{\omega_c}{s + \omega_c} \; .$$

We can invert this to obtain,

$$y_s(t) = (1 - e^{-\omega_c t})\xi(t) \; ,$$

and sampling this response at intervals T produces the sequence $\{y_s(kT)\}$, where $y_s(kT) = (1 - e^{-\omega_c kT})$, $k \geqslant 0$. Now take the Z-transform of this sequence to obtain

$$Z\{y_s(kT)\} = \frac{z}{z - 1} - \frac{z}{z - e^{-\omega_c T}}$$

$$= \mathcal{Y}_s(z).$$

The transfer function $\mathcal{D}(z)$ is now selected as

$$\mathcal{D}(z) = \frac{z - 1}{z} \mathcal{Y}_s(z) = 1 - \frac{z - 1}{z - e^{-\omega_c T}}$$

$$= \frac{1 - e^{-\omega_c T}}{z - e^{-\omega_c T}} \; . \qquad (12.6)$$

Working from this transfer function, we can obtain a difference equation which represents our design. Writing $\mathcal{Y}(z) = \mathcal{D}(z)\,\mathcal{U}(z)$, then from (12.6), we have

$$(z - e^{-\omega_c T})\mathcal{Y}(z) = (1 - e^{\omega_c T})\mathcal{U}(z) \; ,$$

and inverting we see that this produces the difference equation

$$y[(k+1)T] - e^{-\omega_c T}y(kT) = (1 - e^{-\omega_c T})u(kT) , \qquad k \geqslant 0 .$$

12.4 THE BILINEAR TRANSFORM METHOD

Also known as Tustin's method or the trapezoidal integration technique, this is the final indirect method of design based on an analogue prototype which we shall consider. The approach used is somewhat different from the two previous methods, in that we do not attempt to match specified responses of the analogue prototype. Rather, we note that in the Laplace transform domain, multiplication by $1/s$ represents integration in the time domain. This operation is then emulated in the z-domain, using a representation of the trapezoidal approximation to integration. Fig. 12.4 shows a schematic representation of the integration operation in the Laplace

Fig. 12.4 — Integration in the transform domain.

transform domain.

In Fig. 12.4, we see that $Q(s) = (1/s)P(s)$, or $sQ(s) = P(s)$. In the time domain, this corresponds to the relationship

$$\frac{dq(t)}{dt} = p(t) \tag{12.7}$$

and integrating (12.7) between $\tau = (k-1)T$ and $\tau = t \geqslant (k-1)T$, we obtain

$$q(t) - q([k-1]T) = \int_{(k-1)T}^{t} p(\tau)\,d\tau .$$

The integral on the right-hand side is now approximated using the trapezoidal scheme, as shown in Fig. 12.5. The procedure leads to the estimate

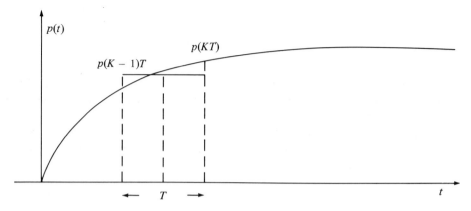

Fig. 12.5 — The trapezoidal integration scheme.

$$\int_{(k-1)T}^{kT} p(\tau)\, d\tau = \frac{T}{2}[p(kT) + p([k-1]T)] \ ,$$

and thus we deduce that

$$q(kT) - q([k-1]T) \sim T/2[p(kT) + p([k-1]T)] \qquad k > 0 \ . \tag{12.8}$$

Defining $Z\{q(kT)\} = Q'(z)$, and $Z\{p(kT)\} = P'(z)$ we can take the Z-transform in (12.8) to obtain

$$\left(1 - \frac{1}{z}\right) Q'(z) \sim \frac{T}{2}\left(1 + \frac{1}{z}\right) P'(z)$$

or

$$\frac{P'(z)}{Q'(z)} \sim \frac{2}{T}\frac{z-1}{z+1} \ .$$

Recall that in the Laplace transform domain, for the continuous-time integration process we found that

$$\frac{P(s)}{Q(s)} = s \ ,$$

and we are thus led to propose a discretization scheme based on replacing s in the transfer function of the continuous-time prototype by

$$\frac{2}{T}\frac{z-1}{z-1} \, .$$

This operation will yield the Z-transfer function of a discrete-time system, and the relationship between the performance of this design and that of a continuous-time prototype must now be examined.

First of all, it is easy to establish that designs produced by this procedure, based on stable analogue prototypes, will themselves be stable. This result follows from an analysis of the mapping

$$s \rightarrow \frac{2}{T}\frac{z-1}{z+1} \, ,$$

and the proof is left as an exercise.

The issue of frequency response is somewhat more complicated, and before examining this point, we demonstrate the design procedure by means of an example.

Example 12.3
Use the trapezoidal integration technique to construct a discrete-time filter based on the second-order Butterworth low-pass filter with cut-off frequency ω_c.

From Chapter 10, we recall that the transfer function of the prototype is

$$H(s) = \frac{\omega_c^2}{s^2 + \sqrt{2}\omega_c s + \omega_c^2} \, ,$$

and making the transformation

$$s \rightarrow \frac{2}{T}\frac{(z-1)}{(z+1)}$$

we obtain

$$\mathcal{D}(z) = H\left(\frac{2}{T}\frac{(z-1)}{(z+1)}\right) = \frac{\omega_c^2}{\dfrac{4(z-1)^2}{T^2(z+1)^2} + \dfrac{2\sqrt{2}\omega_c(z-1)}{T(z+1)} + \omega_c^2}$$

$$= \frac{T^2\omega_c^2(z^2 + 2z + 1)}{z^2(4 + 2\sqrt{2}T\omega_c + T^2\omega_c^2) + z(2T^2\omega_c^2 - 8) + (4 - 2\sqrt{2}T\omega_c + T^2\omega_c^2)} \, .$$

If the cut-off frequency is $\omega_c = 100$ rad/sec., with sampling interval $T = 0.01$ sec, say, then the product $\omega_c T = 1$, and the transfer function of the digital design becomes

$$\mathscr{D}(z) = \frac{z^2 + 2z + 1}{7.8284z^2 - 6z + 2.1716} \ .$$

A plot of the amplitude response of this system is shown in Fig. 12.6.

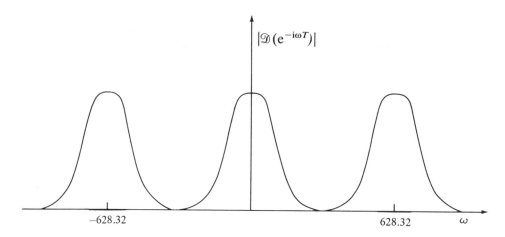

Fig. 12.6 — The amplitude response of the system of Example 12.3.

From Fig. 12.6, we see that the amplitude response of our design is periodic, with the centres of the repetitions separated by a 'distance' $2\pi/T = 628.32$ rad/sec. on the horizontal axis. In the designs we have considered earlier, this periodicity has led to the possibility of serious error due to 'aliasing'. We now show that for this design, in one sense, such problems do not occur. To demonstrate this, we must examine in more depth the frequency response of filters designed by the trapezoidal integration process.

The key point is that the bilinear transformation

$$s \to \frac{2(z-1)}{T(z+1)}$$

introduces a distortion or warping of the frequency axis. To aid clarity, we consider the slightly more general form of transformation

$$s \to K\frac{2(z-1)}{T(z+1)}$$

where K is some constant. Also we denote the frequency variable for the resulting discrete-time system by $\phi(\omega)$, where ω is the frequency variable for the prototype system. We now have to determine the nature of $\phi(\omega)$. If the frequency responses of a prototype continuous-time system and the resulting discrete-time system were to take the same values at all frequencies ω and ϕ, we must have

$$H(s)|_{s=i\omega} = \mathscr{D}(\exp(i\phi T)) = H(s)|_{s=K2(z-1)/T(z+1)|_{z=\exp(i\phi T)}} \ .$$

This (perhaps idiosyncratic) notation charts the steps taken in reaching the frequency response of the discrete-time system from the transfer function of the prototype via the bilinear transform. We can, however, see that for equality, the values of the argument of $H(x)$ must be the same. That is

$$i\omega = K\frac{2}{T}\frac{(e^{i\phi T}-1)}{(e^{i\phi T}+1)} = iK\frac{2}{T}\tan\left(\frac{\phi T}{2}\right) \ ,$$

and so

$$\omega = \frac{2K}{T}\tan\left(\frac{\phi T}{2}\right) \qquad \text{or} \qquad \phi(\omega) = \frac{2}{T}\tan^{-i}\left(\frac{\omega T}{2K}\right) \ . \tag{12.9}$$

Equation (12.9) shows that, as expected, the relationship between frequency variables ω and ϕ is non-linear. Also $\omega = 0$ corresponds to $\phi = 0$, and as $\omega \to \infty$, $\phi \to \pi T$, showing that the positive frequency axis for continuous-time systems is mapped into the interval $[0, \pi/T]$ on the ϕ-axis. Recall that the sampling frequency $\omega_s = 2\pi/T$, so that the entire ω-axis is mapped into the interval $[-\omega_s/2, \omega_s/2]$. This means that since the entire ω-axis is mapped into just *one* period, then the form of aliasing error due to overlapping of 'tails', applicable to filters whose amplitude response is not of bounded support, cannot occur. It must be remembered, however, that the discrete-time system does have a periodic frequency response, meaning that it can be dangerously imprecise to consider this design as free from aliasing error. We can, however, be sure that for all signals or components of signals at frequencies less than $\phi = \omega_s/2$, then processing by a digital filter designed by this technique will introduce no aliasing errors whatsoever. For this reason, among others, the bilinear transform method is one of the most often used methods of digital filter design based on 'classical' prototypes.

The purpose of introducing the constant K into the transformation is to allow the matching of the two frequency scales at certain critical frequencies, for example, the cut-off frequency of a low-pass filter. Suppose that a prototype design has cut-off frequency ω_c; then if the digital filter is to have its cut-off frequency at the same value, so that $\phi_c = \omega_c$, we must have

$$\omega_c = \frac{2K}{T} \tan\left(\frac{\phi_c T}{2}\right) = \frac{2k}{T} \tan\left(\frac{\omega_c T}{2}\right)$$

or

$$K = \frac{T}{2}\omega_c \cot\left(\frac{\omega_c T}{2}\right) = \frac{T}{2}\omega_c \cot\left(\frac{\omega_c \pi}{\omega_s}\right) \ ,$$

where $\omega_s = 2\pi/T$ is the sampling frequency.

Using this value for K, we can specify the s- to z-plane transformation in the helpful form

$$s \to \alpha\omega_c(z-1)/(z+1) \ ,$$

with $\alpha = \cot(\omega_c\pi/\omega_s)$. Use of the constant K in this fashion can be thought of as having the effect of altering the cut-off frequency of the prototype analogue filter. Use of the bilinear mapping then restores tha cut-off frequency to its correct value for the digital filter. This process, notional rather than actual, is known as *prewarping* because the frequency axis for the analogue filter is suitably warped prior to the application of the transformation.

We demonstrate the use of the transformation in this form in the following example.

Example 12.4
Using as prototype the second-order Butterworth filter of Example 12.3, design a low-pass digital filter with cut-off frequency $\omega_c = \omega_s/4$, where $\omega_s = 2\pi/T$ is the sampling frequency.

Using the bilinear transformation in the form

$$s \to \alpha\omega_c\frac{(z-1)}{(z+1)} \ ,$$

it is easy to show, following the method of Example 12.3, that the transfer function $D(z)$ of the digital design will be

$$D(z) = \frac{z^2 + 2z + 1}{z^2(\alpha^2 + \sqrt{2}\alpha + 1) + z(2 - 2\alpha^2) + (1 - \sqrt{2}\alpha + \alpha^2)} \ .$$

When $\omega_c = \omega_s/4$, $\alpha = \cot(\pi/4) = 1$, and so

$$\mathcal{D}(z) = \frac{z^2 + 2z + 1}{3.41421z^2 + 0.585786} \quad .$$

Finally, the frequency domain performance of our digital filter is determined by the choice of sampling time T:

T	ω_s	ω_c
1	2π	$\pi/2$
0.5	4π	π
0.1	20π	5π
0.01	200π	50π

Other formulations of this technique are available; for example, see Poularikas and Seely [3].

12.5   A DIRECT DESIGN METHOD — THE FOURIER SERIES APPROACH

The methods we have studied so far have all been based on emulating the response of a prototype continuous-time filter. We now examine an entirely different approach to the design problem. Suppose that $\mathcal{D}(z)$ is the transfer function of a stable discrete-time system; then we can write as usual,

$$\mathcal{Y}(z) = \mathcal{D}(z)\mathcal{U}(z) \quad .$$

If the input sequence is $\{u_k\} = \{\delta_k\} = \{1, 0, 0, 0, \ldots\}$, the unit (im)pulse sequence, with Z-transform $\mathcal{U}(z) = 1$, then the transform of the output sequence, the (im)pulse response will be

$$\mathcal{Y}_\delta(z) = \mathcal{D}(z) = \sum_{n = -\infty}^{\infty} h_d(n)z^{-n} \quad .$$

Since the system is stable, by assumption, there is a frequency response, obtained by taking the DFT of the impulse response sequence. This is achieved by replacing z by $e^{i\omega t}$ in $\mathcal{D}(z)$ to obtain

$$\mathcal{D}(e^{i\omega T}) = \mathcal{D}(e^{i\theta}) = \sum_{-\infty}^{\infty} h_d(n)e^{-in\theta} \tag{12.10}$$

where $\theta = \omega T$.

Now (12.10) can be interpreted as the Fourier expansion of $\mathcal{D}(e^{i\theta})$, using as basis functions the orthogonal set $\{e^{-in\theta}\}$. It is then easy to show that the Fourier coefficients relative to this base, $\{h_d(n)\}$, are given by

$$h_d(n) = \frac{1}{2\pi} \int_{-\pi}^{\pi} \mathcal{D}(e^{i\theta})e^{in\theta}\,d\theta = \frac{T}{2\pi} \int_{-\pi/T}^{\pi/T} \mathcal{D}(e^{i\omega T})e^{in\omega T}\,d\omega \ .$$

We now set $\mathcal{D}(e^{i\theta})$ to the desired frequency response function and calculate the resulting Fourier coefficients. If the filter is to be realized using a finite number of delay elements, some form of truncation must take place. It is helpful to think of this truncation being performed by the application of a 'window', defined by a window weighting function $w(n)$. The simplest window is the rectangular window with weighting function $w(n)$ defined by

$$w(n) = \begin{vmatrix} 1, & -n_1 \leqslant n \leqslant n_2 \\ 0, & \text{otherwise} \ . \end{vmatrix}$$

Using this window, we actually form

$$\sum_{-\infty}^{\infty} w(n)h_d(n)e^{-in\theta} = \sum_{-n_1}^{n_2} h_d(n)e^{-in\theta} = \mathcal{D}'(e^{i\theta}) \ ,$$

where, if n_1 and n_2 are sufficiently large, $\mathcal{D}'(e^{i\theta})$ will be an adequate approximation to $\mathcal{D}(e^{i\theta})$, the desired frequency response. It is important to note that the filter 'length', that is, the number of delay elements, or terms in the difference equation depends on the choice of n_1 and n_2. This means that some accuracy will always have to be sacrificed in order to produce an acceptable design.

We will explore the technique by designing a low-pass filter in the following example.

Example 12.5
Use the Fourier series, or direct design method, to produce a low-pass digital filter with cut-off frequency $f_c = 1000\,\text{Hz}$, when the sampling frequency is $f_s = 5000\,\text{Hz}$.

We wish to make use of the non-dimensional frequency variable θ, and since

$$T = \frac{1}{f_s} = \frac{1}{5000} \ .$$

$$\theta = \omega T = 2\pi f T = \frac{2\pi f}{5000} \ .$$

The cut-off frequency is then $\theta_c = 2\pi f_c/5000 = 2\pi/5$, and the ideal frequency response $\mathcal{D}(e^{i\theta})$ is now defined by

$$\mathcal{D}(e^{i\theta}) = \begin{vmatrix} 1, & |\theta| \leqslant 2\pi/5 \\ 0, & |\theta| > 2\pi/s \end{vmatrix}.$$

We now calculate the coefficients $h_d(n)$ as

$$h_d = \frac{1}{2\pi} \int_{-\pi}^{\pi} \mathcal{D}(e^{i\theta}) e^{in\theta} \, d\theta$$

$$= \frac{1}{2\pi} \int_{-2\pi/5}^{2\pi/5} e^{in\theta} \, d\theta$$

$$= \frac{1}{n\pi} \sin \frac{2n\pi}{5}$$

$$= \frac{2}{5} \text{sinc} \frac{2n\pi}{5}.$$

At this stage, we have to choose the length of the filter. By now, we know that a 'long' filter is likely to produce superior results in terms of frequency domain performance. However, experience again tells us that there will be penalties in some form or other! Let us choose a filter of length 9, with the coefficients selected for simplicity as symmetric about $n = 0$. The astute reader may anticipate that this choice will lead to a non-causal system, but we will deal with this problem when it arises.

This scheme is equivalent to specifying the use of a rectangular window defined by

$$w(n) = \begin{vmatrix} 1, & -4 \leqslant n \leqslant 4 \\ 0, & \text{otherwise} \end{vmatrix}.$$

We can now calculate the coefficients $h_d(-4), h_d(-3), \ldots h_d(0), \ldots, h_d(4)$ as

$h_d(\pm 4)$	$h_d(\pm 3)$	$h_d(\pm 2)$	$h_d(\pm 1)$	$h_d(0)$
-0.07568	-0.06237	0.09355	0.30273	0.40000

The transfer function of the digital filter is then $\mathcal{D}'(z)$, where

$$\mathcal{D}'(z) = \sum_{-4}^{4} h_{\mathrm{d}}(n)z^{-n}$$

$$= -0.07568z^{-4} - 0.06237z^{-3} + 0.09355z^{-2} + 0.30273z^{-1} + 0.40000$$
$$+ 0.30273z + 0.09355z^{2} - 0.06237z^{3} - 0.07568z^{4}.$$

Although this system is indeed non-causal, since its impulse response sequence contains terms in positive powers of z, we can calculate the frequency response as

$$\mathcal{D}'(e^{i\theta}) = -0.15156\cos(4\theta) - 0.12474\cos(3\theta) + 0.18710\cos(2\theta)$$
$$+ 0.6054\cos(\theta) + 0.40000 \ .$$

Fig. 12.7 illustrates the corresponding amplitude response.

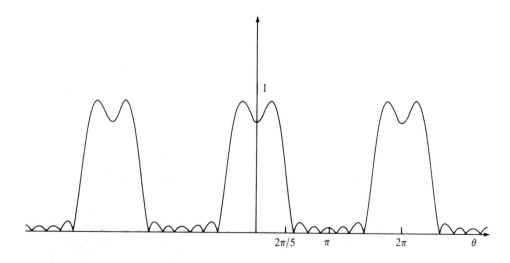

Fig. 12.7 — Amplitude response of the non-causal filter of Example 12.5.

Fig. 12.7 shows us that the amplitude response of our filter is a reasonable approximation to the design specification. We do, however, notice that there are some oscillations in both pass- and stop-bands. These are due to the abrupt cut-off of the rectangular window function, and the effect is known as Gibb's phenomenon. A way of improving the performance in this respect is discussed in section 12.6. The immediate problem is the realization of this non-causal design. To see how we can circumvent the difficulty, we proceed as follows.

The transfer function we have derived is of the general form

$$\mathcal{D}'(z) = \sum_{k=-n}^{n} h_d(k) z^{-k} \ ,$$

$$= z^n [h_d(-n) + h_d(-n+1) z^{-1} + \ldots$$
$$+ h_d(0) z^{-n} + \ldots \qquad + h_d(n) z^{-2n}] \ .$$

Suppose that we implement the system with transfer function

$$\mathcal{D}''(z) = z^{-n} \mathcal{D}'(z) \ ,$$

which is a causal system. First we notice that on setting $z = \mathrm{e}^{\mathrm{i}\omega T}$, the amplitude response $|\mathcal{D}(\mathrm{e}^{\mathrm{i}\omega T})|$ is given by

$$|\mathcal{D}''(\mathrm{e}^{\mathrm{i}\omega T})| = |\mathrm{e}^{-\mathrm{i}\omega n T}| . |\mathcal{D}'(\mathrm{e}^{\mathrm{i}\omega T})|$$
$$= |\mathcal{D}'(\mathrm{e}^{\mathrm{i}\omega T})| \ ,$$

that is, it is identical with that of the desired design. Furthermore, $\arg\{\mathcal{D}''(\mathrm{e}^{\mathrm{i}\omega T})\} = \arg\{\mathcal{D}'(\mathrm{e}^{\mathrm{i}\omega T})\} - n\omega T$, indicating a pure delay of amount nT in the response of the second system. This means that provided that we are prepared to accept this delay, then our design objective can be met by the system with transfer function $\mathcal{D}''(z)$, given by

$$\mathcal{D}''(z) = [-0.07568 - 0.06237 z^{-1} + 0.09355 z^{-2} + 0.30273 z^{-3}$$
$$+ 0.40000 z^{-4} + 0.30273 z^{-5} + 0.09355 z^{-6} - 0.06237 z^{-7} - 0.07568 z^{-8}] \ .$$

It is evident from Fig. 12.8 that the filter designed in Example 12.5 differs from the previous designs. The nature of this difference is the absence of feedback paths in the block diagram realization of Fig. 12.8. One effect of this is that the (im)pulse response sequence is finite, a fact which we already know, since the design method involved truncating the impulse response sequence! Filters of this type are known as finite impulse response designs (FIR designs), and may always be implemented using structures not involving feedback loops. Another name used for such structures is 'non-recursive', but it is not correct to assume that the only possible realization of an FIR filter is by use of a non-recursive structure; for details, see Jong [2].

12.6 WINDOWS

In this concluding section we consider the problem identified in Example 12.5 above in connection with the sharp cut-off of the rectangular window function. A considerable amount of research has been carried out, aimed at determining suitable alternative window functions which will smooth the transition, and thus reduce the

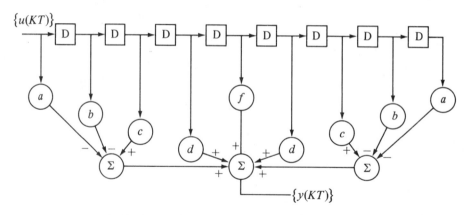

$a = 0.07568; \quad b = 0.06237; \quad c = 0.09355; \quad d = 0.30273; \quad f = 0.400000$

Fig. 12.8 — A realization of the final system of Example 12.5.

Gibb's phenomena effects observed in the amplitude response of Fig. 12.7. We do not discuss the derivation of the various window functions; rather we tabulate some of the more popular examples in a form suitable for symmetric filters of length $2N + 1$. Formulations for other configurations can easily be deduced, or may be found in, for example, Jackson [1] or Ziemer *et al.* [4]. The section closes with an example of the application to the design of Example 12.5 above

Window name	$w(n)$
Triangular or Bartlett	$w(n) = \begin{vmatrix} (k+N)/N, & -N \leqslant k < 0 \\ (N-k/N, & 0 \leqslant k \leqslant N \end{vmatrix}$
Von Hann or Hanning	$w(n) = 0.5 + 0.5 \cos(\pi k/N), \quad -N \leqslant k \leqslant N$
Hamming	$w(n) = 0.54 + 0.46 \cos(\pi k/N), \quad -N \leqslant k \leqslant n$
Blackman	$w(n) = 0.42 + 0.5 \cos(\pi k/N) + 0.08 \cos(2\pi k/N), \quad -N \leqslant k \leqslant N.$

In each case, $w(n) = 0$ for k outside the range $[-N, N]$.

Example 12.6
Plot the amplitude response for the filter design of Example 12.5, using (a) the Hamming window, and (b) the Blackman window.

(a) The transfer function coefficients are now given by $h_d(k)w_H(k)$, where $w_H(k)$ are the Hamming window coefficients, calculated with $N = 4$ and $-4 \leqslant k \leqslant 4$. These coefficients are

N	± 4	± 3	± 2	± 1	0
	0.08000	0.21473	0.54000	0.86527	1.00000

The transfer function then becomes

$$\mathscr{D}''_H(z) = [-0.00605 - 0.01339z^{-1} + 0.05052z^{-2} + 0.26194z^{-3}$$
$$+ 0.40000z^{-4} + 0.26194z^{-5} + 0.0502z^{-6} - 0.01339z^{-7} -$$
$$0.00605z^{-8}].$$

The frequency reponse is then obtained by writing $z = e^{i\theta}$, as

$$\mathscr{D}''_H(e^{i\theta}) = -0.01211\cos(4\theta) - 0.02678\cos(3\theta) + 0.10104\cos(2\theta)$$
$$+ 0.52388\cos(\theta) + 0.40000 \ .$$

Fig. 12.9 illustrates the magnitude of this response, and the reduction of oscillations

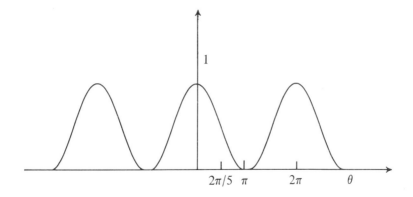

Fig. 12.9 — Amplitude response of filter of Example 12.5, with Hamming window.

in both the pass- and the stop-bands is striking. The penalty is the lack of sharpness near the cut-off frequency, although the stop-band characteristics close to $\theta = \pi$ are quite good.

(b) Proceeding as in case (a), we calculate the Blackman window coefficients as

N	± 4	± 3	± 2	± 1	0
	0.00000	0.06645	0.34000	0.77355	1.00000

The Blackman window transfer function is thus

$$\mathscr{D}''_B(z) = -0.00415z^{-1} + 0.03181z^{-2} + 0.23418z^{-3} + 0.40000z^{-4}$$
$$+ 0.23418z^{-5} + 0.03181z^{-6} - 0.00415z^{-7} \ ,$$

and the frequency response is found as

$$\mathscr{D}''(e^{i\theta}) = -0.00830\cos(3\theta) + 0.06362\cos(2\theta) + 0.46836\cos(\theta)$$
$$+ 40000 .$$

The amplitude response is shown in Fig. 12.10, and this design again suffers from a

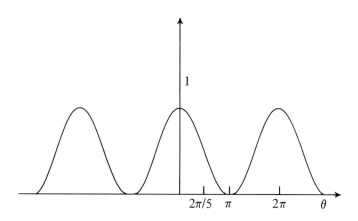

Fig. 12.10 — Amplitude response of filter of Example 12.5 with Blackman window.

relatively poor performance in terms of sharpness of cut-off. The ripples observed in the pass- and stop-bands with the rectangular window have been removed as before. However, the good characteristic of the Hamming design in the stop-band is not evident when using the Blackman window for this particular filter.

This chapter has given a very brief introduction to some methods of digital filter design. Space does not permit a longer discussion, and a number of important ideas have been ommitted; for example, we have not considered the possibility of direct filtering in the frequency domain, using the FFT. However, our aim has been to give a flavour of the role of mathematics in communication theory, and perhaps to encourage further study.

REFERENCES

[1] L. B. Jackson, *Digital Filters and Signal Processing*, Kluwer Academic Publishers, Boston, 1986.
[2] M. T. Jong, *Methods of Discrete Signal and System Analysis*, McGraw-Hill, New York, 1982.
[3] A. D. Poularikas and S. Seely, *Elements of Signals and Systems*, PWS-Kent Publishing Company, Boston, 1988.

[4] R. E. Ziemer, W. H. Tranter and D. R. Fannin, *Signals and Systems*, Macmillan, New York, 1983.

EXERCISES

1. Draw a block diagram representing an implementation of the digital filter designed in Example 12.4.
2. Show that under the mapping $z = e^{sT}$, points in the left half of the complex s-plane are mapped into the unit circle in the z-plane. Hence deduce that the impulse invariant design method produces stable filter designs provided that the continuous-time prototype is a stable design.
3. Use the impulse invariant method to design a digital replacement for the second-order Butterworth filter, with cut-off frequency $\omega_c = 10$ rad/sec. The sampling frequency is to be five times the cut-off frequency. Determine the sampling interval T and plot the amplitude of the frequency response.
4. Repeat the above exercise, this time using the step invariant technique.
5. By examining the bilinear mapping which defines the trapezoidal integration method of digital filter design, show that filters designed by this method will be stable provided that the continuous-time prototype is stable.
6. Use the bi-linear transform method to construct a digital filter with cut-off frequency ω_c, based upon the third-order Butterworth filter. If the sampling frequency ω_s is to be ten times the cut-off frequency, draw up a table showing the values of ω_c and ω_s obtained when the sampling interval T takes the values 1 s, 0.1 s and 0.0001 s.
7. Develop a digital filter design method based upon Simpson's rule for numerical integration, and design a digital replacement for the first-order Butterworth filter with cut-off frequency ω_c. Can you say anything about the stability of designs so produced?
8. Use the direct (Fourier) design method with the rectangular window to produce a causal filter of length 11 with non-dimensional cut-off frequency $\pi/2$. If T, the sampling interval, is 0.001 s, what frequency does this correspond to? Plot the amplitude of the frequency response.
9. Repeat the above exercise, this time using the Hamming window.
10. Follow the method of Example 12.4 to obtain a difference equation which represents a digital filter with cut-off frequency $\omega = \omega/10$. Sketch the amplitude response.

Index

*(Convolution) 151, 192, 340

ADD algorithm, 59
Adjacency,
  List, 26
  matrix, 26
Adjacent nodes, 21, 23
Algorithm,
  definition, 26
  efficiency, 26
  exponential time, 27
  polynomial time, 27
Aliasing, 249, 388, 397
Amplitude response, 203
Amplitude response,
  continuous time, 203
  discrete time system, 343
  discrete, 216
Amplitude spectrum,
  non-periodic signal, 223
  periodic signal, 216
Analogue filter, 255
Arc,
  definition, 23
  saturated, 90
Attenuation, 146
Average message delay,
  for a network, 112
  time, 109

Band pass filter, 256
Band-limited signal, 248
Bandwidth, 290
Bartlett window, 404
Best Bottleneck algorithm, 70
Bilateral Laplace transform, 147
Bilinear transform method, 393
Blackman window, 404
Block diagrams, 144, 152, 315
  discrete time, 315
Bottleneck of a path, 70
Butterworth filter,
  definition, 256
  general case, 265

  realisation, 273
Butterworth polynomial, 265
  table of coefficients, 271

C–R Circuit, 136
Capacity assignment strategy,
  equal, 112
  optimal, 113
  proportional, 112
Capacity,
  of a cut, 89
  of a node, 95
  of an arc, 88
Causal function, 147
Causal sequences, 304
Central processing unit (CPU), 51
Chain,
  defintion, 23
  flow-augmenting, 90
Chandy-Russell algorithm, 53
Characteristic polynomial, 158, 331
Chebyshev filter, 293
Chebyshev polynomial, 293
Circuit,
  C–R, 136
  L–R, 135
  L–C–R, 153
Components of a graph, 21
Concentrator, 51
Connectivity algorithm, 36
Constitutive equations, 133
Convolution,
  continuous-time, 150, 189, 243
  discrete time, 334
  Fourier transform, 243
  Laplace transform, 150
Cut,
  capacity of, 89
  definition, 89
Cut set of arcs, 89
Cycle, 21, 23

dB scale, 297
Degree of a node, 20
Delay block, 315

Delta function Dirac, 173
DFT, 349
Difference equations, 314
Digital filter design,
  direct methods, 399
  impulse invariant method, 384
  indirect methods, 384
  step invariant method, 390
  Tustin's method, 393
Digital filters, 384
Dijkstra's algorithm, 67
Dirac delta function, 173
Direct design methods digital filters, 399
Dirichlet conditions,
  non-periodic function, 221
  periodic function, 211
Discrete Fourier transform, 349
Discrete time,
  block diagrams, 315
  convolution, 334
  Fourier transform, 347
  impulse response, 330
  initial conditions, 319, 325
  signal, 132
  system, 314
Discrete time system,
  amplitude response, 343
  frequency response, 340
  phase response, 343
  stability, 332
DROP algorithm, 61
DTFT, 347

Edge,
  connectivity, 29
  definition, 20
  set, 20, 22
Energy signal, 134

Fast Fourier transform, 356
Father array, 44
Feedback, 146
FFT, 356
FFT algorithm listing, 379
Filter,
  analogue, 255
  band-reject, 256
  bandwidth, 290
  Butterworth, 256
  Chebyshev, 293
  digital, 384
  finite impulse response, 403
  high-pass, 255
  ideal band pass, 256
  ideal high pass, 256
  ideal low pass, 255
  low pass, 249
Filter transformation, 256, 283
FIR filters, 403
Flow,
  definition, 88
  value of, 88

Flow-equivalent, 97
Floyd's algorithm, 75
Ford's algorithm, 74
Ford-Fulkerson algorithm, 92
Fourier series, 210
Fourier series orthogonality relationship, 212
Fourier transform,
  definition, 217
  convolution theorems, 243
  discrete time, 347
  estimating, 369
  fast, 356
  frequency shifting property, 227
  generalised, 237
  linearity property, 226
  periodic signal, 240
  symmetry property, 228
  table, 223
  time differentiation property, 226
  time shifting property, 227
Frequency response,
  continuous time, 201
  discrete time systems, 340
Function,
  generalised, 172
  periodic, 210
  sinc, 214
  testing, 174

Gabow's algorithm, 54
Generalised function,
  definition, 172
  equivalence property, 175
Geometric centre frequency, 290
Gibb's phenomenon, 402
Graph,
  connected, 21
  directed, 22
  partial, 21, 24
  strongly connected, 24
  sub, 21, 24
  undirected, 20
  weighted, 32
Greedy algorithm, 33

Hamming window, 404
Hanning window, 404
Heaviside step function, 147, 186
High pass filter, 256

IFI network,
  algorithm, 39
  definition, 37
  minimal, 39
ILFI network,
  algorithm, 45
  definition, 41
  minimal, 43
Impulse invariant method, 384
Impulse response,
  continuous time, 178
  discrete time, 330

Indegree, 23
Independence of queues, 115
Indirect design methods digital filters, 384
Induced subnetwork, 38
Initial conditions,
    continuous time, 181
    discrete time, 319, 325
Inner product, 215

Kirchhoff's laws, 134
Kruskal's algorithm, 32
Kruskal's heuristic algorithm, 56

$L–C–R$ Circuit, 153
$L–R$ Circuit, 135
Label,
    pair, 92
    permanent, 66
    temporary, 67
Lagrange multiplier, 120
Laplace transfer function, 152
Laplace transform,
    bilateral, 147
    definition, 146
    properties, 148
    table, 148
Line failure, 37
Linear systems, 139
Low pass filter, 249, 255
LTI systems, 157

M/M/1 queue, 110
Marginal stability, 172, 180
Matrix,
    adjacency, 26
    reachability, 29, 79
Maximally flat property, 272
Minimum connector problem, 31
Modulation, 231
Multicommodity flow, 102

Network,
    abc, 43
    centralized, 111
    communication, 11
    definition, 31
    distributed, 117
    neighbourly, 38
    star, 11
    triangled, 43
    two-recursive, 42
Node,
    connectivity, 29
    definition, 20
    end, 23
    even, 20
    odd, 20
    set, 20, 22
    start, 23
Nyquist condition, 249
Nyquist rate, 249

Optimum communication spanning tree,
    algorithm, 101
    definition, 101
Out-of-kilter algorithm, 100
Outdegree, 23

Parseval's formula, 253
Path,
    best bottleneck, 70
    definition, 21, 23
    elementary, 21, 23
    least cost, 73
    most reliable, 70
    of minimum weight, 66
    second shortest, 72
    shortest, 66
    simple, 21, 23
Periodic signal Fourier transform, 240
Phase response,
    continuous time system, 203
    discrete time system, 343
Phase spectrum,
    discrete time signal, 216
    non-periodic signal, 223
    periodic signal, 216
Poles, 170
Pollack's algorithm, 72
Polynomial,
    Butterworth, 265
    Butterworth–table of coefficients, 271
    characteristic, 158
    Chebyshev, 293
    Chebyshev–table of coefficients, 293
Power signal, 234
Prewarping, 398
Prim's matrix algorithm, 34
Pulse response discrete time, 330

Rectangular window, 402
Response,
    amplitude, 203
    definition, 142
    frequency, 201
    impulse, 178
    phase, 203
    step, 186
    zero-state, 143
Ripple, 292, 297
Root, 44

Sampling, 241, 245
Sequence,
    causal, 304
    definition, 302
Shifting property Z transform, 312
Signal,
    band limited, 248
    continuous-time, 132
    decomposition, 189
    decomposition discrete-time, 334
    definition, 131
    deterministic, 131

discrete-time, 133
energy, 234
non-periodic, 217
periodic, 210
power, 234
stochastic, 131
Sinc(x), 214
Sink, 88
Site failure, 37
Source, 88
Stability,
    continuous-time systems, 168
    definition for LTI systems, 171
    discrete time system, 332
    marginal, 172, 180
State variable, 137
State-space form, 139
Step function, 147, 186
Step invariant method, 390
Step response, 186
Strictly proper transfer functions, 170
Strong connectivity algorithm (Warshall), 79
Sufficiently aware Z transform, 327
Superposition linear, 141
System,
    definition, 131
    poles, 170
Systems,
    discrete-time, 314
    linear, 135, 139
    LTI, 157
    time invariant, 140

Testing function, 174
Time invariant systems, 140
Traffic intensity parameter, 122
Transfer function,
    Laplace, 152
    proper, 157
    strictly proper, 170
    Z, 328
Transform,
    Fourier, 217, 226

Laplace, 146
Z, 305
Transformation filter, 256, 283
Tree,
    definition, 30
    directed (shortest path, or skim), 85
    maximum spanning, 35
    minimum spanning, 32
    search, 82
    spanning, 30
    two, 38
Triangular window, 404
Tustin's method, 393

Von Hann window, 404

Warshall's algorithm, 79
Weight,
    function, 32
    of a path, 66
    of a spanning tree, 32
Window,
    Bartlett, 404
    Blackman, 404
    Hamming, 404
    Hanning, 404
    rectangular, 402
    triangular, 404
    Von Hann, 404

Z transfer function, 328
Z transform,
    characteristic polynomial, 331
    definition, 305
    linearity property, 310
    shifting property, 312
    'sufficiently aware', 327
    table, 309
    table of properties, 315
Zero-state response, 143

~(is represented by), 212, 220

Mathematics and its Applications

Series Editor: G. M. BELL, Professor of Mathematics, King's College London, University of London

Gardiner, C.F.	**Algebraic Structures**
Gasson, P.C.	**Geometry of Spatial Forms**
Goodbody, A.M.	**Cartesian Tensors**
Goult, R.J.	**Applied Linear Algebra**
Graham, A.	**Kronecker Products and Matrix Calculus: with Applications**
Graham, A.	**Matrix Theory and Applications for Engineers and Mathematicians**
Graham, A.	**Nonnegative Matrices and Applicable Topics in Linear Algebra**
Griffel, D.H.	**Applied Functional Analysis**
Griffel, D.H.	**Linear Algebra and its Applications: Vol. 1, A First Course; Vol. 2, More Advanced**
Guest, P. B.	**The Laplace Transform and Applications**
Hanyga, A.	**Mathematical Theory of Non-linear Elasticity**
Harris, D.J.	**Mathematics for Business, Management and Economics**
Hart, D. & Croft, A.	**Modelling with Projectiles**
Hoskins, R.F.	**Generalised Functions**
Hoskins, R.F.	**Standard and Non-standard Analysis**
Hunter, S.C.	**Mechanics of Continuous Media, 2nd (Revised) Edition**
Huntley, I. & Johnson, R.M.	**Linear and Nonlinear Differential Equations**
Irons, B. M. & Shrive, N. G.	**Numerical Methods in Engineering and Applied Science**
Ivanov, L. L.	**Algebraic Recursion Theory**
Johnson, R.M.	**Theory and Applications of Linear Differential and Difference Equations**
Johnson, R.M.	**Calculus: Theory and Applications in Technology and the Physical and Life Sciences**
Jones, R.H. & Steele, N.C.	**Mathematics in Communication Theory**
Jordan, D.	**Geometric Topology**
Kelly, J.C.	**Abstract Algebra**
Kim, K.H. & Roush, F.W.	**Applied Abstract Algebra**
Kim, K.H. & Roush, F.W.	**Team Theory**
Kosinski, W.	**Field Singularities and Wave Analysis in Continuum Mechanics**
Krishnamurthy, V.	**Combinatorics: Theory and Applications**
Lindfield, G. & Penny, J.E.T.	**Microcomputers in Numerical Analysis**
Livesley, K.	**Mathematical Methods for Engineers**
Lord, E.A. & Wilson, C.B.	**The Mathematical Description of Shape and Form**
Malik, M., Riznichenko, G.Y. & Rubin, A.B.	**Biological Electron Transport Processes and their Computer Simulation**
Massey, B.S.	**Measures in Science and Engineering**
Meek, B.L. & Fairthorne, S.	**Using Computers**
Menell, A. & Bazin, M.	**Mathematics for the Biosciences**
Mikolas, M.	**Real Functions and Orthogonal Series**
Moore, R.	**Computational Functional Analysis**
Moshier, S.L.B.	**Methods and Programs for Mathematical Functions**
Murphy, J.A., Ridout, D. & McShane, B.	**Numerical Analysis, Algorithms and Computation**
Nonweiler, T.R.F.	**Computational Mathematics: An Introduction to Numerical Approximation**
Norcliffe, A. & Slater, G.	**Mathematics of Software Construction**
Ogden, R.W.	**Non-linear Elastic Deformations**
Oldknow, A.	**Microcomputers in Geometry**
Oldknow, A. & Smith, D.	**Learning Mathematics with Micros**
O'Neill, M.E. & Chorlton, F.	**Ideal and Incompressible Fluid Dynamics**
O'Neill, M.E. & Chorlton, F.	**Viscous and Compressible Fluid Dynamics**
Page, S. G.	**Mathematics: A Second Start**
Prior, D. & Moscardini, A.O.	**Model Formulation Analysis**
Rankin, R.A.	**Modular Forms**
Scorer, R.S.	**Environmental Aerodynamics**
Shivamoggi, B.K.	**Stability of Parallel Gas Flows**
Smith, D.K.	**Network Optimisation Practice: A Computational Guide**
Srivastava, H.M. & Manocha, L.	**A Treatise on Generating Functions**
Stirling, D.S.G.	**Mathematical Analysis**
Sweet, M.V.	**Algebra, Geometry and Trigonometry in Science, Engineering and Mathematics**
Temperley, H.N.V.	**Graph Theory and Applications**
Temperley, H.N.V.	**Liquids and Their Properties**
Thom, R.	**Mathematical Models of Morphogenesis**
Toth, G.	**Harmonic and Minimal Maps and Applications in Geometry and Physics**
Townend, M. S.	**Mathematics in Sport**
Townend, M.S. & Pountney, D.C.	**Computer-aided Engineering Mathematics**
Trinajstic, N.	**Mathematical and Computational Concepts in Chemistry**
Twizell, E.H.	**Computational Methods for Partial Differential Equations**
Twizell, E.H.	**Numerical Methods, with Applications in the Biomedical Sciences**
Vince, A. and Morris, C.	**Mathematics for Computing and Information Technology**
Walton, K., Marshall, J., Gorecki, H. & Korytowski, A.	**Control Theory for Time Delay Systems**
Warren, M.D.	**Flow Modelling in Industrial Processes**
Wheeler, R.F.	**Rethinking Mathematical Concepts**
Willmore, T.J.	**Total Curvature in Riemannian Geometry**
Willmore, T.J. & Hitchin, N.	**Global Riemannian Geometry**

Statistics, Operational Research and Computational Mathematics
Editor: B. W. CONOLLY, Emeritus Professor of Mathematics (Operational Research), Queen Mary College, University of London

Abaffy, J. & Spedicato, E.	**ABS Projection Algorithms: Mathematical Techniques for Linear and Nonlinear Equations**
Beaumont, G.P.	**Introductory Applied Probability**
Beaumont, G.P.	**Probability and Random Variables**
Conolly, B.W.	**Techniques in Operational Research: Vol. 1, Queueing Systems**
Conolly, B.W.	**Techniques in Operational Research: Vol. 2, Models, Search, Randomization**
Conolly, B.W.	**Lecture Notes in Queueing Systems**
Conolly, B.W. & Pierce, J.G.	**Information Mechanics: Transformation of Information in Management, Command, Control and Communication**
French, S.	**Sequencing and Scheduling: Mathematics of the Job Shop**
French, S.	**Decision Theory: An Introduction to the Mathematics of Rationality**
Griffiths, P. & Hill, I.D.	**Applied Statistics Algorithms**
Hartley, R.	**Linear and Non-linear Programming**
Jolliffe, F.R.	**Survey Design and Analysis**
Jones, A.J.	**Game Theory**
Kapadia, R. & Andersson, G.	**Statistics Explained: Basic Concepts and Methods**
Lootsma, F.	**Operational Research in Long Term Planning**
Moscardini, A.O. & Robson, E.H.	**Mathematical Modelling for Information Technology**
Moshier, S.L.B.	**Mathematical Functions for Computers**
Oliveira-Pinto, F.	**Simulation Concepts in Mathematical Modelling**
Ratschek, J. & Rokne, J.	**New Computer Methods for Global Optimization**
Schendel, U.	**Introduction to Numerical Methods for Parallel Computers**
Schendel, U.	**Sparse Matrices**
Sehmi, N.S.	**Large Order Structural Eigenanalysis Techniques: Algorithms for Finite Element Systems**
Späth, H.	**Mathematical Software for Linear Regression**
Stoodley, K.D.C.	**Applied and Computational Statistics: A First Course**
Stoodley, K.D.C., Lewis, T. & Stainton, C.L.S.	**Applied Statistical Techniques**
Thomas, L.C.	**Games, Theory and Applications**
Whitehead, J.R.	**The Design and Analysis of Sequential Clinical Trials**